Perspectives on Lexicography in Italy and Europe

Perspectives on Lexicography in Italy and Europe

Edited by

Silvia Bruti, Roberta Cella and Marina Foschi Albert

Perspectives on Lexicography in Italy and Europe,
Edited by Silvia Bruti, Roberta Cella and Marina Foschi Albert

This book first published 2009

Cambridge Scholars Publishing

12 Back Chapman Street, Newcastle upon Tyne, NE6 2XX, UK

British Library Cataloguing in Publication Data
A catalogue record for this book is available from the British Library

ISBN (10): 1-4438-1263-3, ISBN (13): 978-1-4438-1263-4

TABLE OF CONTENTS

FOREWORD

On October 19th and 20th 2007, the University of Pisa hosted the meeting *Lexicography in Italy and Europe*, devoted to the discussion of theoretical aspects concerning both historical and synchronic lexicography. Two of the main focuses of the discussion were the pragmatic perspective, i.e. the practical function of dictionaries and lexicographic resources in the field of translation, and the application of new technologies in lexicography.

The present volume, created from the aforementioned meeting, is organised into four sections, as specified below:

Section 1 deals with the different stages of elaboration of four important historical dictionaries of European languages:

- *Nuevo diccionario histórico de la lengua española* (NDHLE) for Spanish, in its first stage (J.A. Pascual);
- *Tesoro della lingua italiana delle Origini* (*TLIO*) for Italian, for which about a third of the entries have presently been completed (19,000 out of 50,000) (P.G. Beltrami);
- *Oxford English Dictionary* for English, in its third edition (J. Simpson);
- *Trésor de la Langue Française* (*TLF*) for French, concerning at the moment only the first edition in its electronic version (J.-M. Pierrel, É. Buchi).

Section 2 concerns monolingual and bilingual dictionaries of European languages as synchronically described in a specific stage of their development:

- Portuguese of the seventeenth, eighteenth and nineteenth centuries (T. Verdelho);
- Italian of the nineteenth century (M. Bricchi);
- German of the twentieth and twenty-first centuries (A. Klosa).

Section 3 deals with the impact of information technology on lexicography, exemplified by:

- a monolingual corpus of Anglo-Saxon texts (P. Stokes, E. Pierazzo);
- the digital corpus made up of the five editions of *Vocabolario degli Accademici della Crusca* (M. Biffi);
- a plurilingual specialised on-line dictionary of metalinguistic terminology (A. De Meo, F. Lorenzi).

An Appendix to the volume contains some contributions to the roundtable discussion held at the meeting, concerning the compilation and usage of dictionaries for translating purposes.

As a foreword to this book, we have included a short text, summarising the content of the introductory speech delivered by Edoardo Sanguineti, one of the most famous contemporary Italian authors of poetry, literary criticism, narratives, dramatic texts, and opera librettos, an esteemed translator from ancient Greek, Latin, and German, and an emeritus university professor. Quite recently, Edoardo Sanguineti became involved in lexicographical research, by collaborating on the project and scientific board of the *Grande Dizionario italiano dell'uso,* edited by Tullio De Mauro (published in six volumes in 2000, publishing house UTET). He was later appointed chief editor of the *Supplemento* 2004, which consists of two updated volumes to the *Grande Dizionario della Lingua italiana,* edited by Salvatore Battaglia.

Only a few contributions to this volume were originally written in English. Ilide Carmignani's contribution has been translated from Italian by Simon Turner. Some texts have been translated by students of the *Laurea Specialistica in Traduzione dei testi letterari e saggistici* (Master Study Programme in Translation) of the University of Pisa, under the supervision of Silvia Bruti and Roberta Cella. Nicola Spera translated J.A. Pascual's *Discontinuity of Linguistic Change and Historical Lexicography* from Spanish; Ilaria Tarasconi and Nicola Spera *Developments and New Results in the Lexicography of Old Italian* by P.G. Beltrami from Italian; the translation of T. Verdelho's *On the Origins of Modern Bilingual Lexicography: Comparing Portuguese with other European Languages* from Portuguese is due to Aurora Simoni; finally, Simone Dossi and Andrea Sumberaz translated M. Biffi's *Accademia della Crusca's Online Dictionaries* from Italian. E. Sanguineti's text has been translated from Italian by Nicola Spera. The majority of these texts have also been edited by mother tongue scholars: David Beneteau (Beltrami; Bricchi; Klosa); Aliette Françoise Boshier (Beltrami; Pascual; Verdelho), Sofia Pimentel Biscaia (Verdelho); John Simpson (Beltrami). We would like to sincerely thank all of them, as well as Marina Pascual (who reviewed the English version of Pascual's text), for their invaluable help.

We would also like to thank the Cambridge Scholar Press Publishing House – and in particular Ms. Carol Koulikourdi and Ms. Amanda Millar – for their interest in our project and for accepting our volume in their catalogue. We are grateful to Agnese Balducci, who contributed to the formal revision of the manuscript. Our warmest thanks to our colleague

Marcella Bertuccelli, Director of the Master Programme at the time of the meeting, and promoter of this cultural event.

Silvia Bruti, Roberta Cella, Marina Foschi Albert

PREFAZIONE / PREFACE

EDOARDO SANGUINETI

Il tradurre trova il suo più evidente e pratico emblema nella forma del dizionario bilingue (ed eventualmente multilingue). È lo strumento ovvio che permette il controllo di una versione interlinguistica.

Ma esiste la versione intralinguistica, che si rispecchia nel dizionario monolingue. I lemmi (vocaboli e locuzioni) sono tradotti all'interno di quello che viene considerato un medesimo codice verbale: sinonimi (più propriamente pseudosinonimi), definizioni, parafrasi, descrizioni (non di rado rafforzati da immagini illustrative), permettono di chiudere in cerchio, davvero enciclopedicamente (in senso linguistico) il tesoro, più o meno estensivamente articolato, di un tale codice.

È da rilevare che noi tutti comunichiamo traducendo, in ogni nostra relazione verbale, poiché diamo senso, anche intralinguisticamente, a quanto leggiamo o ascoltiamo, traducendo in un nostro codice personale i messaggi ricevuti. Il che può condurre alla sentenza, soltanto in apparenza paradossale, che, a questo mondo, non c'è che traduzione.

Colui che traduce (cioè tutti noi, infine) si assume la responsabilità dei significati che elabora, e risponde a ogni situazione in stretta relazione a quanto traduce, istante per istante, cioè a quanto intende, e cioè infine a quanto crede di intendere.

Ora, se non c'è che traduzione, è perché non c'è che interpretazione, a questo mondo. La storia umana si risolve in un perpetuo dibattito, pratico-concreto, socialmente esplicabile, intorno alla prassi interpretativa che si ha da tenere di fronte a ogni elemento della realtà.

Translation is most evidently and practically epitomised by bilingual dictionaries (and, if necessary, by multilingual dictionaries), the obvious instrument which makes it possible to transfer items interlinguistically.

There is, however, also intralinguistic translation, which is mirrored in monolingual dictionaries. Headwords (terms and locutions) find equivalent counterparts within the same code: synonyms (or, more appropriately, pseudosynonyms), definitions, paraphrases, descriptions (often reinforced by explanatory illustrations) make it possible to enclose in a true encyclopaedic way (linguistically speaking), the treasure, more or less broadly structured, of such code.

It is worth noting that we all communicate by means of translation, in all our verbal interactions, since we give sense, also intralinguistically, to what we are reading or listening to, by way of translating in a personal verbal code the messages we receive. This could bring to the conclusion, only seemingly paradoxical, that, in this world, there is nothing but translation.

The translator (i.e. all of us, after all) undertakes responsibility for the meanings he translates, and reacts to every situation in strict relation to what he translates, instant by instant, i.e. to what he understands, that is, in fact, to what he believes he understands.

Now, if there is nothing but translation, it is because in this world there is nothing but interpretation. Human history turns out to be a perpetual practical/concrete debate – a socially explicable activity – about the interpretative procedure that needs to be followed to come to terms with any element of reality.

PART I

HISTORICAL PERSPECTIVE ON LEXICOGRAPHY

THE PREPARATORY STAGE OF THE *NDHE*: "DIVIDE AND RULE"

JOSÉ ANTONIO PASCUAL

1 Introduction

The realisation of the *Nuevo diccionario histórico de la lengua española* de la Real Academia Española (*NDHE*), considered as a state project, is to be divided into three stages: after a three year introductory phase, from 2006 to the end of 2008, there will follow – all being well – the first stage of this work, which is to start in 2009 and will end in 2018; at the end of this period a draft of the dictionary with about 60,000 entries will be available. It will present a number of philological issues, even though they may be unresolved, the provisional definitions should enable the readers to find the meaning of most of the words listed. The second stage will start in 2019 and will last until 2029: it will deliver us a dictionary in which, unlike the version completed at the end of 2018, the number of words examined will be considerably increased, most of the pending problems solved, and the word definitions realised by using standardised patterns of definition. Although this stage could be considered as final, from that moment on the dictionary will be updated and refined according to a pre-established programme. Nevertheless, at the end of this second stage, the Spanish language will have a historical dictionary of average quality, but structured in such a way that it will be possible to add new entries and to improve the philological and lexicographic treatment of the material.

During these three "introductory" years, we (i.e. a group of philologists) have prepared the launch of the dictionary, which we have been promoting with publications,[1] congresses, conferences and discussions. This publication about historical dictionaries is a great opportunity for

[1] In the bibliographical references, preceded by one or two stars, publications on different aspects of the *NDHE* are reported. We will describe (see below) the dictionary development on a web site which makes it easier for us to show how the dictionary develops.

which I have to thank the three editors, since by agreeing to include this paper in they enable me to give a progress report on the project (its introductory stage is nearly completed) by reporting on some of the most significant preparatory tasks, which concern methodology and technical aspects, and on some other operational tasks we plan to develop in the remaining time, before embarking on the first stage of the dictionary.

2 Facing the Project

The making of a historical dictionary was one of the goals which the school of Menéndez Pidal set for itself before the Spanish Civil War, as part of a series of projects that served as foundations on which to erect the Hispanic philological building. The *Orígenes* by Menéndez Pidal (1956), the *ALPI* by Navarro (1962), the *Tesoro* by Gili Gaya (1947-1960), all belong to this body of work along with texts and documents critically edited by Menéndez Pidal himself and his disciples (by way of example I will mention Menéndez Pidal 1919, Navarro 1957, and Onís 1908), and with the *DCEC* and the *DECH* by Corominas (1955-1957 and 1980-1991), compiled after the war. The *Diccionario histórico de la lengua española* edited by the Real Academia Española (1933-1936 and 1960-1994 [from now on the last edition will be referred to as *DHLE*]) was one of these projects and, for reasons of little interest here, was never completed, either on the first or second occasion the attempt was made.

Now, for the third time, the Academia is undertaking this project; late, compared with other European languages, which have such works. Clearly, this time we have technology on our side: the information technology (IT) at our disposal allows us to present all materials at several stages, even if they are still under development and revision, and at the same time it enables users to contribute to improve the dictionary, thanks to the cooperation between its authors and the scholars who consult it. Consequently, we can expect the *NDHE* to be used even while it is under construction, without having to wait for it to be completed. Even from the very first provisional stages, where problems considered still outnumber solutions, this tool will make it possible for the researcher who accesses it to carry out his task in better conditions than before. Furthermore, technical possibilities offered by IT will allow us to compile the dictionary parting sections, and to assign the sections to different experts who will not need to work side by side in the same place. During this long journey, which began almost three years ago, we started dividing up tasks to gain time and to avoid discouragement. We did so in two ways: on the one hand, getting several researchers and research centers to cooperate with us and, on the other, subdividing the work into different tasks, each one tackled independently but integrated afterwards into a single whole.

Such a project requires complex management to develop hundreds of different tasks – lexicographic and computer tasks – all inter-related and undertaken inside or outside the coordination centre, so that there be no bottlenecks preventing their integration in the future. This means distinguishing between what is provisional, what is experimental, and what has to do with checking what has already been done. In this way, some elements will become definitive and will remain for the future, although this does not exclude the possibility of periodically revising – and also remaking if necessary – what has been previously developed.

There are many ways to accomplish a task which involves so many people and which seeks to achieve interesting results within a reasonable period of time. The one we chose involves gradually building up a team of specialists in different branchs of philology, linguistics, IT in the "Fundación Rafael Lapesa" of the *Real Academia Española*, established mainly to run the work of the *NDHE.* This team will apply its linguistic and philological expertise while avoiding intuitive solutions as well as too avantgardist hypotheses. Our means, our scope and our objectives mean we cannot rely on excellent specialists in only one particular branch of lexicography, but rather we need researchers who are competent in several fields of philology and linguistics – competent enough to act with initiative and to make decisions based on their expertise. Our centre is unpretentious and yet it develops innovative work which does not turn its back on the latest developments in philology and linguistics, and it avoids the previously mentioned bottlenecks which occur when one person ends up having to make all the decisions rather than individual assignments being undertaken and completed.

A basic team, like the one I have just mentioned, may occasionally need to be expanded to include external researchers who, although working in other centres, collaborate in our project. The fact that our project has been widely accepted has enabled us to start a fruitful cooperation with other centres and, at the same time, to create synergies in philological research. This brought about the possibility of developing individual works, at the same time breaking the customary isolation of the philologist. Little by little, independent teams of researchers are coming into contact to build together the *NDHE*, which is essential when studying old texts. Similarly, our centre supports research projects intended to merge with ours and we have also started cooperating with an important group of Hispanists willing to orient their work in such a way as to take advantage from ours and vice versa.

Clearly, our investigation is not based on philology only, but also on IT, which is crucial for the development of the work of the *NDHE* team members, as well as to making the data we are creating available in the future.

I mentioned above our efforts to ensure appropriate management for the project: however, I must admit that the actual conditions did not always allow us to proceed as planned, since we were affected by the way in which our project developed. In this way, since our project began without any preliminary, several tasks which were supposed to be carried out sequentially had to coincide in time. First, materials should have been prepared and processed, subsequently, with IT tools; then, a whole series of actions involving the use of linguistics to find solutions to the issues we were facing should have been carried out and tested; and finally, having completed these stages, it should have been possible to construct models which would have enabled the realisation of our dictionary with clear criteria. However, we were forced to combine different tasks together before they were finished, without the benefit of having complete materials at our disposal and without having established interpretative methods. This explains the adjustements we hsd to make during this experimental phase of the creation of our corpus, which is still in a process of disambiguation, and also when taking our first steps towards the compilation of our dictionary.

At the end of these three preparatory years, we will have at our disposal a portal which allows for the connection (Intranet) between all internal and external collaborators and which will give them all access to all the existing materials relevant for our work. We are also planning to grant scholars more complete access to the dictionary materials (Internet), which will open up the opportunity of interactively suggesting corrections to the materials they consult and answering questions posted on the portal. Finally, we aim to grant access to the dictionary and parts of its complementary materials to a no specialist public (Internet).

To conclude these reflections, which seek present a realistic picture of our plans, and also the difficulty of realising them in practice, I make just one more general remark: this dictionary, like any other, is one hypothesis formulated on many others, which cannot be disproved before the dictionary is ready. For this reason, during the realisation of the project we will be obliged to change our mind on times, for instance on graphics decisions, fixing the entries, dividing acceptations, establishing groups of words in order to define them, and so on.

But let's now describe in two general sections some of the tasks that have already been accomplished – or are still ongoing – relating to the preparation of the *NDHE*. Firstly, I will refer to completed materials or those under preparation (section 3); secondly, I will show how these will fit into the dictionary plans, which will be the basis for the compiling of the dictionary by the lexicographers (section 4). I will briefly refer to the myriad prior reports which we used as a basis for a series of activities which require prior examination, such as text selection, entries to be included, classifying parts of speech, setting definition templates and criteria to divide entries into acceptations, and so on.

3 The Basic Materials for the *NDHE*

An important part of the work consisted in preparing materials on which the *NDHE* will be based and which, in the future, can be used for other purposes too.

3.1 The Corpus of the *Nuevo Diccionario Histórico del Español*

Among these materials a very important source is the *Corpus del Nuevo Diccionario Histórico del Español* (*CNDH*),[2] which contains 52 million occurrences, deriving mainly from literary texts.[3] Had there been more time to prepare the first stage of the dictionary, it would have been wise to include data from a broader collection of documents, including scientific and technical texts, as well as American texts, as will be the case in future stages. We will shortly have to begin the first stage of our work without these materials, relying only on this literary corpus (easier and faster to build). Even so, as a precaution, we have subdivided it into different subcorpora which are being manually disambiguated. They will be useful during the difficult first stages of the compilation of the dictionary, when we will need to work with a manageable quantity of material. We started off with a narrower corpus by labelling the texts from different points of views (dialect and style, as well as philological status of

---

[2] The selection of texts for the *CNDH* was done by consulting several specialists in the history of the Spanish literature. For criteria, chronological partition, estimate of number of occurrences to be contained in each text and graphic choices, cf. Pascual / Domínguez in print.

[3] They have been annotated with textual markers, fixed according to the international XML standard, which guarantees plenty of possibilities of information retrieval and revising. A morphosyntactic mark-up of each occurrence is also being done, using specific tools: they include a lexical category and a grammatical (sometimes lexical) set of features, in order to link each word form requiring analysis to an entry.

the text: quality of the edition, and so on) so that the lexicographer can, in due course, use this information to evaluate data in a given text.

From this corpus of 52 million occurrences, we will build the draft of the dictionary model, which will be available on the web at the end of 2018. In the meantime, we will gradually enlarge the corpus by adding 90 million further occurrences, derived partly from scientific and technical lexicons and partly from American texts. With a view to enlarging this corpus, we have already started collecting additional texts during the preparatory stage, relying on the same selecting criteria developed for literary texts making up the current *CNDH*. Later, while the corpus is being expanded, the current one will continue to be refined, since this process will never be entirely completed.

To make the best possible use of the corpus, we are creating a set of "smart", non-aleatory filters, which will allow the lexicographer, in this first stage beginning in 2009, to organise the examples for each word, as a preliminary step before establishing acceptations and their definitions. We intend to enhance those data with other data, external to the corpus, only when the material provided is deemed inadequate, for the analysis of a word. During this first stage, which is more lexicographical than philological, we expect to spend as little time as possible choosing materials, although we know that, in this way, there will be unresolved problems.

3.2 Complementary Lexical Materials of the Corpus

Our dictionary does not set out to be a corpus dictionary, even though we wish to exploit the interpretative advantages offered by a corpus. The impossibility for the dictionary to be representative of the whole vocabulary – unfeasible even after ten years, when it will have tripled in size – suggested that it would be advisable to reinforce it with complementary materials, selected from texts read by philologists, as it used to be in the past, when dictionaries were compiled on the basis of index card files. Our intention is not to give up these index card files, but to extend them with some "modular corpora" and several lexicographic collections.

Apart from the assistance of María Jesús Mancho, Lourdes García Macho, Pilar Díaz de Revenga and Cecilio Garriga have supported our project by granting access to their lexical data bases.

3.2.1 Modular Corpora

We started creating some modular corpora to enhance data from those specialised fields which are underrepresented in the *CNDH*, such as private and public documents – Spanish and American – (in collaboration with Pedro Sánchez-Prieto Borja, of the University of Alcalá and José Ramón Morala of the University of León) as well as periodicals and newspapers from the end of the nineteenth century to the present day. These materials, halfway between the basic corpus and our files, will become an integral part of these, as specialised subcorpora in which it will be possible to undertake fairly complex searches.

The first subcorpus contains public and private documents from Spain and America. We want it to be varied, well-balanced and manageable, in order to provide a large number of words not strictly related to literature, science or technology, but referring to different domains of everyday life, including regional differences – an essential requirement in order to distinguish between American and Spanish varieties. We estimate that in this first phase it will contain about twenty million occurrences. The work plan has already been drawn up: it specifies philological and mark-up criteria and the possibility of introducing images of the transcribed documents as a trial with a view to extending this possibility to the rest of the corpora.

Texts collected in this second subcorpus, taken from periodicals and newspapers, will allow us to access the vocabulary of sport, fashion, and so on. In the case of the language of sport, for example, these texts enable us to move in a "semantic space" (deliberately using a non-technical term), guided by words in italics, in inverted commas or by journalists' comments. From these words it is possible to reach related terms: derivatives, synonyms, antonyms, and frequent word combinations. In this way, it is possible to integrate the words into a kind of conceptual map: all these data – organised on a template – will also enable accurate search into the diachronic evolution of some words connected to each other, located in the aforementioned semantic spaces (on this kind of corpus, cf. Pascual in print and Díaz de Atauri 2008). So far, several tests have already been done with a pilot corpus consisting of selected pages from periodicals and newspapers, in digital form, still in Word format but about to be converted into XML, like the rest of the material.

3.2.2 Glossary of Hispanic-Latin Words from the Early Middle Ages

We wish to extend data prior to the thirteenth century through a large file which will include medieval Latin-Romance vocabulary starting with the *Léxico hispánico primitivo* (Menéndez Pidal *et al.* 2003) and then enhancing and correcting it with data taken from other well-edited and easily accessible collections of medieval documents, like those of the Sahagún monastery or León cathedral, which have extremely useful indexes.[4]

3.2.3 Index Card File of the Real Academia Española

Among the materials which we intend to use to complete the corpora, a key tool will be what is known as the "Fichero de papel" [index card file] of the Real Academia Española – the basis for the old historical dictionary –, which has been scanned and will be available online. We will apply the same process to the so-called "Fichero de hilo" [older index card file] of the Academia, which contains about 200,000 index cards, among the oldest that the Academia has, and which are fundamental to an understanding of the revised version of the *Diccionario de autoridades*.

3.2.4 Bibliography

In our project we have taken up the ideas that Joan Corominas followed when compiling his dictionary, as well as those on which the *DHLE* was based, thus, we planned to study thousands of books and journals in which philologists, lexicographers, and experts give interesting information about words (etymological, historical, concerning usage, tagging, distribution, and so on). This task – which we are tackling together with Gloria Clavería, of the Universidad Autónoma de Barcelona and Abraham Madroñal of the Consejo Superior de Investigaciones Científicas –, although demanding and time-consuming, is extremely useful since, unlike other linguistic elements, each word is a unit that can be observed from different points of view. This requires an extremely large amount of data, most of which is unknown to lexicographers. We already have 120,000 bibliographical records, thanks to thorough prior source-tracing work and fact we have developed a database to manage the

---

[4] Published in the series "Fuentes y Estudios de Historia Leonesa", edited by the *Centro de Estudios e Investigación "San Isidoro"* of León, directed by José María Fernández Catón.

compiling process. This was developed from the database implemented by the Universidad Autónoma of Barcelona for the same purpose.

3.2.5 List of Entries

Starting basically from the different editions of the dictionary of the Academia, a provisional list of entries has been drafted, in which a grammatical category (noun, verb, adjective, preposition, etc.) is assigned to each headword. For the time being, this list of entries has been used to lemmatise the *CNDH*; in the future it will help us establish the final list of entries of the *NDHE*. The list of word forms, extracted from the twelve million index cards of the aforementioned *Index card file* of the Real Academia Española, is also being added. It will aid not only to the difficult task of disambiguating words in the *CNDH*, but also to future consultation of the *Index card file*.

3.3 Lexicographic Works Complementary to the Corpus

We did not wish to overlook other lexicographic references: not only because they may complete the materials referred to so far, but also because in some cases a word change in fact appears for the first time in a dictionary, from where it is taken up in common or formal use.

3.3.1 Map of Dictionaries

We are building a "map of dictionaries" in which, by comparing several editions of the dictionary of the Academia (*DRAE*), the evolution of words and meanings in these dictionaries over a period of more than two centuries can be traced (cf. Bomant / Noguerol in print). It will certainly not be possible to obtain a rigorous picture of the real language at that time, but even if this picture is fuzzy, it will provide some guidance as to the evolution of the vocabulary at a time when the number of words and meanings increased considerably, mainly because of the development of specialised languages.

In order to perform this task, we have selected some representative dictionaries: the 1780 edition (fundamental, since it was the first abridged edition of the academic dictionary), the 1817 edition (in which many definitions were improved and much attention was paid to correcting scientific and technical terms), the 1884 edition (easier to digitise than the 1843 edition, chosen initially), the 1925 edition (in which many provincialisms and Americanisms were introduced), the 1992 edition (very convenient, since it was already in digital form) and the 2001 edition (no special justification required for this choice). We also have at our disposal the common list of entries – without modifying the original spelling – to all these editions, an essential tool for organising and consulting them.

On the IT front, a database was created to store all the entries (subdivided by meanings) in the different editions of the academic *Diccionario*. Software to compare this material is already available; it enables automatic pre-assigning of equivalence when the textual content is identical or very similar and, depending on the degree of difference, will leave it for a careful revision when it does not coincide.

Incidentally, besides serving the needs of the historical dictionary, the map of dictionaries will also enable us to clean up many of our dictionaries – including the *DRAE* – removing straneus material that has accumulated in the course of successive revisions (where the inherited definitions were sometimes interpreted more from the lexicographer's personal perspective of a word than from its actual use). We will try to enhance this possibility with the digital facsimile of the so-called *Fichero de enmiendas y adiciones* [File of corrections and additions] of the *Real Academia Española* – essential to understand changes in definitions in the successive editions of the academic *Diccionario*.

3.3.2 A *Thesaurus* of Dictionaries

Thanks to the recently published *Nuevo tesoro lexicográfico* by Lidio Nieto and Manuel Alvar (2007), we do not need to consider dictionaries prior to the *Diccionario de Autoridades*, even though we are compiling a bibliography of specialised lexicographic works with the aim of extending the *Nuevo tesoro* to include dictionaries of technical terms from different historical periods, the eighteenth century in particular.

3.3.3 Dialectal Dictionaries

The *Nuevo tesoro* is an excellent support to our future work. It needs however to be complemented by a "dialectal thesaurus", which would facilitate access not only to some similar existing works – i.e. the dialectal dictionaries of Canarias (Zumbado Corbella / Álvarez 1992), Andalucía (Alvar 2000) and León (Le Men 2002-2007) – but also to future ones, yet to be compiled. For this purpose, selection criteria are being established for the *Tesoros de España y América*, while the database to store these data is being designed. Since this is an extremely demanding project, it has to be planned and started as soon as possible in order to have it ready for the second stage of our *Diccionario*.

3.3.4 Digitising the Previous *Diccionario histórico*

The paper volumes of the *Diccionario histórico* (1960-1996) have been digitised with a structural markup which allows for database storage and subsequent electronic data searching. When the time comes, it will also serve, on the one hand, to confirm, verify, correct or add data from the *Diccionario histórico* (most of the *A* and a short portion of the *B* list of entries) to the *NDHE*, and, on the other, as a benchmark for many decisions which will have to be made in the process of editing the new dictionary.

4 Tasks Related to the *NDHE* Plan

Not surprisingly, the plan of the *NDHE* emulates some of the best historical dictionaries, such as the Oxford English Dictionary, *Trésor de la langue française*, *Tesoro della lingua italiana delle Origini* or *Woordenboek der Nederlandsche Taal*. But it adds to them some lexicographic tasks fundamental to what we consider to be a relational historical dictionary, in which IT is not just a tool but a key element. That is why the plan we are drafting now for the future *NDHE*, although not yet finalised, is already being used as a guide for developing software tools. I will briefly describe below some of these tasks, included in the plan, related to the macro- and microstructure of the dictionary. I will leave all matters of a purely technical nature relating to our future lexicographic work, as well as most aspects of the software being developed for both editing and consultation purposes.

4.1 The Macrostructure

I will refer firstly to the macrostructure and related tasks which in my view are the most relevant.

4.1.1 Relationships between Words

When possible, we gather lemmas in superior units (hyperlemmas), to group those headwords which, even if they share the same etymology, have been re-categorised: for instance, *bajo* (adjective, noun and preposition), *jorobado* or *roto* (participle, adjective and noun).[5] The hyperlemmas also link together those words which are morphologically close to some extent, such as for instance *surger* and *surgir*, *ahorcar* and *enforcar* or *aburrición* and *aburrimiento*. The hyperlemma gives us the opportunity of establishing a first type of bond, reinforced by placing a brief description of the word history at the beginning (of course, when a lemma is isolated and it does not belong to a hyperlemma, the summary of its history will be part of its heading).

This is the first step – there will be more to follow – to establish relationships, not only between lemmas, but also between meanings, sub-meanings and also between combinations of words (García Pérez in print g). A model for a provisional interface has been developed, in which all the links which are to appear in the entries are organised and displayed (cf. Varela in print). I will refer to two of these relationships in particular: genetic and semantic relations.

By establishing genetic relationships, it is possible to show the intricate pattern of morphological connections which bind together the words of our language through history (for theoretical and methodological principles which support this derivative network, cf. Pena 2008; Campos 2007, 2008, 2009; Pascual / García Pérez 2007: 43-61); it makes it possible to understand not only the parallel evolution of related elements, but also discordant evolution, and even the insertion of a word into a family to which it did not originally belong. Furthermore, it is an important starting point for establishing some of the definition models.

In order to establish the derivative network, a morphological database is being developed; this will provide precise information on the way in which words are organised within a certain lexical family (in the broadest sense of the term), and at the same time it will enable future access to these data. Therefore, starting from the root-word of a family (in many cases the root-word will be Romance, but many others will be Latin), we will try to group the words which belong to the same family while meticulously analysing each of them from a morphological point of view. This task, which started more than twenty years ago though quite unconnected with our project,[6] is still ongoing, since not all the families

---

[5] There could have been other possibilities, such as that adopted in the *Diccionari descriptiu de la llengua catalana* edited by the *Institut d'Estudis Catalans*, in which these words are treated under the same entry, thus showing how the re-categorisation has been done).

[6] This work gave rise to *Base de datos de morfología del español. Versión 1 (BDME)* by Jesús Pena. In its current state it has more than 55,000 occurrences. Since this database starts off from Latin and builds families, it is easy to convert it

with verbal roots, (richer and more complex), which account for the most of the Spanish vocabulary, have been completed yet. This is another example in which the *NDHE* is benefiting from the support of philologists working outside our centre. In the final configuration, some tables will be added (e.g. about the situational use of words, facts concerning dating, etc.) to reinforce information relevant to the historical study of word families. The net result will be better and finer use of data provided by the database.

A framework for the second set of relationships which link together words in the dictionary, i.e. semantic relationships (synonymy, antonymy, hyperonymy/hyponymy, holonymy/meronymy, etc.) is being developed. We started from different reports, produced by project team members,[7] about how to outline the relationships of identity, opposition and inclusion in the history of Spanish vocabulary. We planned how we would consistently deal with different cases of synonymy. In this way, we will give an account of links between different words which during their history could be considered as absolute synonyms, partial (or propositional) synonyms and approximate synonyms (or quasi-synonyms), while even establishing different levels within partial synonyms. It will enable us to detect, for instance, that in some groups of words linked by synonymic relationships, there could be some internal tensions leading to the replacement of a word by another, or which have triggered the specialisation of a synonym in a specific field. These word replacements and rivalries prompted us to include in the *NDHE* a brief summary of the word history, as referred to before, explaining how synonymic relationships have to emerge. Although the most important relationships are those which affect meaning, we will always take into account combinations of existing words at lower levels, as long as they have semantic repercussions.

In order to understand the semantic evolution of a word, relationships of opposition are also crucial (cf. García Pérez 2007), as well as regularities and irregularities existing in the current vocabulary. All these relationships have led to parallel processes of change in the words they

into a historical database: the table designed for Latin may serve as a model for any stage of Spanish, and in turn, the table used for Spanish could be duplicated for each period analysed in the *NDHE*.

[7] These reports, drawn up by Mar Campos, Rafael García Pérez, Belén Villar and Juan Carlos Hoyos, deserve to become full essays, instead of remaining just internal papers for those working on the *NDHE*. For the lexicographical treatment given to instrumental substantives cf. González (2009). It goes without saying how indebted we are to Cruse 1986 and 2000.

affect. We will distinguish between opposite words (defined as those words which are in a binary relationship of opposition of an inherent nature), complementary words (recognised by a formal test: "X implies Y and it is implied by not Y") and antonyms proper (divided into polar antonyms, equipollent antonyms, partial antonyms, reverse and converse terms) and we will try to show the variable nature of these relationships over time, as they have not remained stable, nor have they always evolved in the same way.

As for the relationships of inclusion, we have provisionally outlined the characteristics that should be part of hypernymic, meronymic and holonymic definitions in the *NDHE*. We have established a provisional model for hypernymic definitions. As for meronymic definitions, we have started with four schemes: the first two, related to the traditional meronymic definition, will be the models of preference in drafting the *NDHE* (*N_1 generic or gradational meronym + of + SN_2 (whole)*; *Each one of + N_1 generic or gradational meronym*), while the third, concerning meronymic definition by context (*Context [of + SN_2], N_1 generic or gradational meronym*) and the fourth, corresponding to the adjectival meronymic definition (*N_1 generic or gradational meronym + relational adjective*) will be less used. Finally, the holonymic definition will follow the scheme "the totality – or any semantically equivalent element – of X", where X equals the number of parts which make up the referent of the defined entry.

As I mentioned with regard to derivative relationships, the structure shown in the semantic framework is extremely helpful when building models of definition. In this way, the definition will also serve indirectly as a yardstick for evaluating our prior organisation and analysis of entries.

4.1.2 Selecting Units to Establish List of Entries

4.1.2.1 There are possible connections between lexical units, not only in the macrostructure but also within each entry, starting from groups of interesting spelling and phonetic variants.[8] On many occasions, they are not justified as independent words, like *abisedo*, *abesedo*, *abisero*, *abijedo*, etc., since they are graphic and phonetic variants of the same word (cf. *DHLE* s.vv.); but they also need to be connected to other word forms with the same double outcome for the Latin sibilant which is in the etymological basis of *abesedo* and *abijedo*.

[8] It is unnecessary to specify that all spelling variants, meaningful or not, will appear in a complete list of word forms, linking each of them to its own etymon.

The treatment of graphic and phonetic variants poses a problem which we have had to address in preparing the dictionary plan. To show the difficulties we ran into, I will illustrate an example from the *DHLE* involving some verbs developed from *beldar*. These verbs are presented as distinct words, while most of them are phonetic variants of the same word:[9]

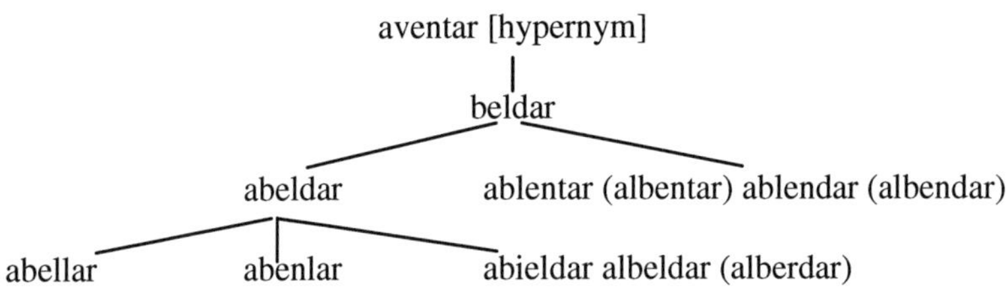

If we consider the internal relationships shown by the *DHLE*, it seems difficult to treat these forms as independent words. If we take *ablentar* as the thread running through their history, a table like the following, in which the historical axis is represented vertically, will lead us through the history of one word, which in different centuries and places has been pronounced (and written) differently:

			abellar	abenlar	ablentar	
					ablentar	
	albeldar	abieldar			ablentar	
abeldar	albeldar				ablentar	
abeldar	albeldar				ablentar	ablendar
abeldar	albeldar				ablentar	ablendar

This common history will be perceived more clearly if we group *ablentar*[10] and *ablendar* (marking the second as a dialectal variant –

[9] We put in brackets the words which do not head entries but are developed under other headwords. It is not possible to access *arvelar*, *aulentar* (nothing more than a spelling variant of *ablentar*) nor *beldar*, since the *DHLE* did not reach the alphabetical location in which these forms should appear.

[10] It is worth mentioning, as a matter of interest, that *ablentar* does not require more than two acceptations (the second current one is superfluous and the third move to second place, although since it is marginal it will need to be given special treatment, cf. Pascual / García Pérez 2007: 123 and ff.). It is understandable, however, that the editors did not refer in *abellar* and *abenlar* – unlike with other

typical of Rioja, Navarra and Aragón – of the first one), and if we do the same with *abieldar* (*albeldar*), *abellar* and *abenlar*, following the *DECH* (s.v. *beldar*). We have left out information about the conversion of these words into rural words or the comparison with *beldar*, since the *DHLE* never reached those terms. The point is that it is not a contrivance to organise all these forms under two words which would have variants – as the graphic representation of their evolutions in the dialectal space shows – as presented in the two columns of the following table:

abellar, abenlar	ablentar
	ablentar
abieldar, albeldar	ablentar
albeldar	ablentar
abeldar, albeldar	ablentar, ablendar
abeldar, albeldar	ablentar, ablendar

Information coming from a file should be organised according to different philological criteria – in this case spelling and phonetics, dialectology and semantics. This will allow us to "clothe" one word with all these variants, as explained in the *DECH* (s.v. *beldar*), where the somewhat provisional starting point is the entry *beldar* (which quotes a *bieldar* – until the 1914 edition of the *DRAE,* it was the headword of the entry for all these word forms) as etymological basis on which the others depend. From these data we can present the headword *abeldar*, under which the following variants are grouped:

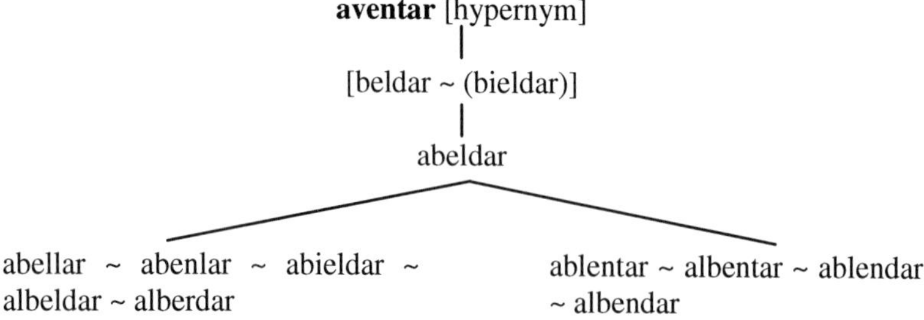

In this representation I base myself on the existence of an obvious link between *beldar* and *abeldar*, which will be resolved once we have studied

verbs – to *abeldar*, since, in fact they are two variants of *abeldar* (otherwise *abieldar* should have been treated in the same way).

data referring to the entry *beldar* and we have taken a decision on other similar cases in the dictionary (such as *juntar* and *ajuntar*, *rascar* and *arrascar*, etc.). For a language historian, the relationship between *abeldar*, *albeldar*, *abieldar*, as well as that between *abellar*, *abenlar* and between *ablentar*, *albentar*, *albendar*, *ablendar*, is clear. Therefore, we can carefully organise the data presented in the *DHLE*, showing the continuous use of the form *ablentar* through history (in the right-hand column) and presenting the forms in the left-hand column as its variants.

Middle Ages	*abellar* 1295 *FSepúlv.*: "trielle o abelle"; 1422 Mose Arragel: "ha de abelharla". *abenlar c*1272 *FBéjar*: "trile, abienle".	*ablentar c*1196 *FSoria* (ms. s. XIV): "siegue e abliente"; *c*1250 *FZorita*; *a*1253 *FNovenera*; 1284-95 *FCuenca*; 1343 JRuiz *Buen Amor*.
16th c.		*ablentar* 1540 Venegas: "la horca de ablentar"; Guadix, see *pala*.
17th c.	*abieldar*: "aventar con el bieldo las miesses", Palet's, Vittori's and Oudin's dictionary.	*ablentar* 1611 Covarrubias: "Vale auentar la parua; es palabra rústica"; 1616 Cáceres Sotomayor: "Vn pan [...] de trigo ablentado".
18th c.	*abieldar*: Stevens' and Terreros' dictionaries.	*ablentar* 1706 Stevens' *Dict.* 1726; *Ac.*: "~. Es voz antigua".
19th c.	*abeldar* 1808 A. Costa: "Abentar o abeldar es ...".	*ablentar* 1859 Borao *Dicc. Voces Arag.*; 1903 Baráibar *VÁlava*.
20th c.	*abeldar (abieldar)*: Dialectal Castilian data.	*ablentar* N. de Soria, villages of Cantabria neighbouring Palencia (Santander prefers *abieldar*), Treviño, Rioja, Ribera de Navarra (*ablientar* in Amescoa), Albacete, Murcia. In XIX and XX *ablendar* in the dialect of Rioja, Navarra and Aragón.

Among these variants, the *DRAE* chooses *beldar*, without marking it as rural (unlike some dictionaries in the past, which favoured *bieldar*), and *abeldar* and *ablentar* as cross-reference entries (the first to *beldar*, the second to *beldar* and *aventar*). Although *aventar* is still the hypernym used in the definitions, if we look carefully at the two cross-references of *ablentar*, the differences which used to separate *aventar* and *ablentar* have been eliminated.

4.1.2.2 We will also take into account so-called "multiword lexical units", which have a syntactically fixed structure and a unitary meaning. The identification of these units is undoubtedly problematic, especially when studing the history of our language, since not only do we not have the competence as speakers, but also the corpus does not provide us with spelling criteria to identify them, since most of these multiword lexical units have the same syntactic form as free phrases or sentences. Clearly, an additional difficulty is how to set the boundaries of a certain phrase. We also differentiate idioms from bound collocations (Cruse 1986: 41), which do not always have the same value from a lexicographic perspective. Finally, we must remember that collocations, in the strict sense of the word, even though less interesting for a dictionary than the previous cases, could allow us to discover unusual developments in the history of words which we should include. All this involves structuring entries in meanings and submeanings, but also with a section devoted to lexical combinations.

4.2 The Microstructure

As for the microstructure, we have already devised a final proposal for the display of entries in the *Diccionario*. Just listing the series of actions involved does not give an understanding of their complexity: a brief history of the word (see paragraph 4.1.1); subheadwords, where all significant spelling variants are organised, so that variants deriving from the same phonetic phenomenon can be linked together, as, for example, the aforementioned *abejedo* 'abesedo' with *colesial* 'colegial' and *ligión* 'lesión', or *labrantín* with ancient arag. *alvendín*, *amolanchín*, *calanchín*, *correntín*, *hablanchín*, *hablantín* or *parlanchín*); etymology; lexical and grammatical morphology; models for defining different kinds of words; criteria to establish meanings; ways of presenting examples (Pascual / García Pérez 2007: 183-210) – fundamental to understand discontinuities (Pascual 2008), dialectal interference and variational use of words in different registers, and so on.

From all of these, I would like to single out some specific aspects for particular attention. I will begin with two of them (§§ 4.2.1, 4.2.2), in which certain processes (devised to solve problems in a consistent manner – by working on lexical groups – which lexicographers use to solve the problems of individual words) are used in conjunction with linguistic solutions to problems. I will then discuss two (§§ 4.2.3, 4.2.4) of the many examples which of how we have subdivided the work, in application of the well-known principle mentioned earlier of "divide and rule".

4.2.1 The Path to Establishing Models for Definitions

The first task I have just mentioned involves fixing definition models for parallel words which, even if not synonyms, have significant connections or a similar history, by applying a series of preliminary classification; these will also show if there is interference or contamination between words belonging to the same semantic class and if some words suggest the evolution of others. What is more, all this will make future consultation of the dictionary easier, since users will be able to access the list of words, more specifically the list of verbs, starting with all those with the same syntactic-semantic classification.[11]

For verbs, we started separating auxiliary verbs from full verbs, with a view to establishing later new subgroups for the latter (González-Zapatero 2008; García Pérez 2006). In the case of nouns, we classified them by distinguishing between predicative and non-predicative ones, a distinction that has implications for their definitions as well as for those verbs with which they co-occur. We group together non-predicative nouns – i.e. those which do not have an argument structure but which are part of it – taking into account a small number of opposition features (we mostly relied on Bosque 1999; Flaux / Van de Velde 2000; García Meseguer 2007, 2008). These features allow for the establishment of a typology which combines together syntactic, semantic and referential elements.

The classification process is just one of the pillars on which the building of the central and peripheral elements in the definition must be based. The other pillar would be shifting through lexicographic or meta-lexicographic reference works, in an attempt to answer some of the questions we lexicographers constantly ask, such as when is it essential to consider the instrumental function of a substantive? Or when is it necessary to include time or space factors, etc.?

4.2.2 Segmentation into Meanings

In preparing the basis for the *NDHE* we are not trying to come up with any avant-gardist ideas in lexicography, semantics, syntax and philology. This does not mean, however, that we are not prepared to take risks, such as not contenting ourselves with intuitively breaking up the meaning of a word into different acceptations, in the knowledge that in this field, as with many other aspects of the dictionary, mistakes, to quote Joyce, could be the portals of discovery. Lexicographers tend to become discouraged with

[11] For the word classification, we have found of great assistance the very accurate reports of Gaston Gross, Xavier Blanco, Yuko Morimoto and Natalia Català.

having to establish the meanings of words intuitively,[12] and so we are attempting to make use of the classes of words that we have grouped together. This at least provides us with a systematic working technique for breaking up the polysemic *continuum* of words belonging to the same group into isolated sections – which we would like to use as the basis for acceptations and subacceptations. Our ambition is also to take this further, relying on semantics and also on syntax (cf. Pascual / García Pérez 2007: 117-146; García Pérez 2003-2004, 2008b, in print b; Sánchez 2008b; and, mostly, Cruse 1986, 2000).

There is no definitive solution to these, but this is no excuse for not facing up to them, to some extent at least. Even a minor breakthrough will make it easy to establish connections between a certain type of acceptation within the digital *NDHE*, and it will also help lexicographers if they do not have to solve, word by word, the problems posed by fragmenting the meanings of words.

4.2.3 A Specific Issue: A Database for Grammar Elements

We are currently trying to study the evolution of grammatical words, a task which gives rise to specific problems, in collaboration with Rosa Espinosa from the University of Valladolid. We already have the software needed to organise the materials. The drafting of a monograph explaining all the steps – and the reasons for them – in the completion of this task is at a very advanced stage (Espinosa in print).

4.3.4 Text Markup

We have not overlooked lexicographic text markup or labelling of words, an extremely important task for an electronic dictionary, since it provides privileged access to the onomasiological consultation and interpretation of data. For drafting this part of the plan, the *Diccionario académico de americanismos* of the Real Academia Española, directed by Humberto López Morales, and the *Centro de Investigación de la Lengua Española* of San Millán de la Cogolla (La Rioja) are of great assistance. A textual markup system for technical terms and their definitions has been developed (including the vocabulary of science, technology, professional activities and even certain aspects of everyday life). Besides the work on specialised languages, we have started to study other textual markup systems (diatopic, diachronic, pragmatic, etc.) with input from scholars

[12] This discouragement can also turn into defeat when tackling the meaning issue, as it happens, for instance, in the work of Hanks (2008).

from different universities and research centres. A monograph study, which we can use as a basis for different markup proposals is available (Carriazo / Gómez, eds, in print).

5 Conclusions

Far be it from me in these few pages a series of documents drafted by the RAE on the *Nuevo diccionario histórico*. Rather, I have endeavoured to provide an overall picture of the project, though without mentioning all the important aspects, such as those concerning management. Some other key issues, such as IT, I have only been able to mention in passing. I shall be satisfied if I have succeeded in demonstrating the *Real Academia Española*'s commitment – with the strong support of Spanish authorities – to ensuring that there will at last be a historical dictionary for the Spanish language.

References

Bibliographical references with an asterisk are works by project team members. In order to give a full record of all the scientific publications written by our team, works by team members which are not referred to in the body of the text are also included, with a double asterisk.

Alvar, Manuel (2000). *Tesoro léxico de las hablas andaluzas*. Madrid, Arco Libros.

Autoridades = *Diccionario de Autoridades*. Madrid (1726-1739) [repr. Madrid, Gredos, 1963].

Bernal, Elisenda / DeCesaris, Janet (eds) (2000). *Proceedings of the XIII Euralex International Congress*. Barcelona, IULA.

Bomant, Emilio / Noguerol, Eugenia (2008)*. "El mapa de diccionarios: historia de la lexicografía académica a través de las acepciones", in Garcés, Pilar (ed.). (2008): 113-121.

Bosque, Ignacio (1999). "El nombre común", in Bosque, Ignacio / Demonte, Violeta (eds). *Gramática descriptiva de la lengua española*. Madrid, Espasa-Calpe: 3-75.

Campos, Mar (2007)*. "Hacia la ordenación morfológica del *NDHE*: primer esbozo", in *Verba*, 34: 125-155.

—. (2008)*. "Morfología genética y etimología: los cruces léxicos", in Garcés García, Pilar (ed.) (2008): 41-63.

—. (2009)*. "Sobre algunos derivados corradicales del verbo *andar*", in de Miguel, Elena *et al.* (eds) (2009): 149-193.

Carriazo, José Ramón / Gómez, Marta (eds) (in print)*. *La marcación en lexicografía histórica*. San Millán de la Cogolla, Cilengua.

Corominas, Joan (1955-1957). *Diccionario crítico etimológico de la lengua castellana* [*DCEC*], 4 vols. Madrid, Gredos.

Corominas, Joan / Pascual, José Antonio (1980-1991). *Diccionario crítico etimológico castellano e hispánico* [*DECH*], 6 vols. Madrid, Gredos.

Corrales, Cristóbal / Corbella, Dolores / Álvarez, María Ángeles (1992). *Tesoro lexicográfico del español de Canarias*, 3 vols. Santa Cruz de Tenerife.

Cruse, Alan (1986). *Lexical Semantics*. Cambridge, Cambridge University Press.

—. (2000). *Meaning in Language: An Introduction to Semantics and Pragmatics*. Oxford, Oxford University Press.

Díaz de Atauri, Juan (2008)*. "La incorporación al léxico de las voces *bicicleta* y *ciclismo*. (Ensayo de un corpus modular)", in *Cuadernos del Instituto Historia de la Lengua* 1: 45-64.

Institut d'Estudis Catalans (ed.) (1985-). *Diccionari descriptiu de la llengua catalana*. [http://dlc.iec.cat.].

Espinosa, Rosa (in print)*. *Procesos de formación y cambio en las llamadas «palabras gramaticales»*.

Espinosa, Rosa (2008)**. "La semántica en los procesos de cambio categorial: las palabras gramaticales en un diccionario histórico", in Garcés, Pilar (ed.). (2008): 115-147.

Flaux, Nelly / Van de Velde, Danièle (2000). *Les noms en français: esquisse de classement*. Paris, Ophrys.

Garcés, Pilar (ed.) (2008)*. *Diccionario histórico: nuevas perspectivas lingüísticas*. Madrid / Frankfurt am Main, Iberoamericana / Vervuert.

García Meseguer, Álvaro (2007). "Nombres individuales y colectivos: una propuesta de clasificación", in *Revista de lexicografía* 13: 17-44.

—. (2008). *Clases y categorías de nombres comunes: un nuevo enfoque*. Madrid, Arco/Libros.

García Pérez, Rafael (2003-2004)*. "La ordenación de las acepciones en un diccionario histórico", in *Revista de lexicografía* 10: 103-131.

—. (2005)**. "¿Desde cuándo se cometen delitos? Relaciones entre léxico y sintaxis en la evolución histórica de la lengua del Derecho penal", in Santos Río, Luis / Borrego Nieto, Julio / García Santos, Juan Felipe / Gómez Asencio, Josè J./ Emilio Prieto de los Mozos (eds). *Palabras, norma, discurso. En memoria de Fernando Lázaro Carreter*, Salamanca, Universidad de Salamanca: 509-519.

—. (2006)*. "El proceso de formación de las clases léxicas y su importancia para un diccionario histórico: el ejemplo de la clase <odio>", in *Boletín de la Real Academia Española* 86: 317-332.

—. (2006b)**. "¿Desde cuándo se impone una pena por un delito?", in *Revista Iberoamericana de Lingüística* 1: 137-150.

—. (2007)*. "Tres modelos de oposición por conversión en un diccionario histórico", in *Revista de Filología Española* 87: 305-323.

—. (2008)*. *Qué hacemos, qué hacíamos. El verbo* hacer *en la historia del español*. San Millán de la Cogolla, Cilengua.

—. (2008b)*. "La organización de los materiales de un corpus y el establecimiento de las acepciones troncales en un diccionario histórico", in *Verba. Anuario galego de Filoloxía* 35: 257-274.

—. (2008c)**. "Etimología de acepción en un diccionario histórico: el ejemplo de la influencia de los modelos literarios europeos", in Garcés, Pilar (ed.) (2008): 277-294.

—. (in print a)**. "Dos ejemplos de relación entre las lenguas especializadas y la lengua general en un diccionario histórico: el caso del Derecho penal".

—. (in print b)*. "El tratamiento de las subacepciones en un diccionario histórico".

—. (in print c)**. "Hacia una teoría de la organización del artículo lexicográfico: el caso de los ejemplos en un diccionario histórico", in *Actas del Seminario Diccionario histórico II: nuevas perspectivas lingüísticas*, Madrid: Universidad Carlos III de Madrid.

—. (in print e)**. "Los marcadores rectificativos en un diccionario histórico". [accepted article for the proceedings of the *XXV Congreso Internacional de Lingüística y Filología Románica* (*CILPR* 2007), Innsbruck].

—. (in print f)**. "Neologismos jurídico-penales en los Siglos de Oro: procedimientos por derivación sobre bases cultas", in *Foro Hispánico, Revista hispánica de Flandes y Holanda, devoted to the processes of the lexical neology Turing the Siglo de Oro.*

—. (in print g)*. "Synonymie et restrictions lexicales dans un dictionnaire historique", in *Cahiers de Linguistique. Lexique, dictionnaire et connaissance dans une société multilangue.*

García Pérez, Rafael / Pascual, José Antonio (in print)**. "Aproximación a una teoría de la acepción", in *El diccionario como puente entre lenguas y culturas del mundo. Actas del II Congreso Internacional de Lexicografía Hispánica*. Alicante, Biblioteca Virtual Miguel de Cervantes: 7-21.

Gili, Samuel (1947-60). *Tesoro Lexicográfico* (1492/1726) [*A-C*]. Madrid, CSIC.

González, Jacinto (2009)*. "Los instrumentos de medida en el *DRAE*. Una propuesta de modelo de definición", in de Miguel *et al.* (eds) (2009): 121-147.

González-Zapatero, Blanca (2008)*. "La relación entre las formas verbales simples y analíticas en un diccionario histórico", in Garcés, Pilar (ed.) (2008): 95-111.

Hanks, Patrick (2008). "¿Do Words Meaning Exist?", in Fontenelle, Thierry (ed.). *Practical Lexicography. A Reader*. Oxford, Oxford University Press:125-134.

Le Men, Janick (2002-2007). *Léxico del leonés actual*. León, Centro de Estudios e Investigación San Isidoro. [Four volumes appeared gathering words from *A* to *M*].

Menéndez Pidal, Ramón (1919). *Documentos lingüísticos de España, I: Reino de Castilla*. Madrid, Anejos de la RFE.

—. (1956). *Orígenes del español*. Madrid: Espasa-Calpe [fourth edition].

Menéndez Pidal, Ramón / Lapesa, Rafael / García, Constantino / Seco, Manuel (2003). *Léxico hispánico primitivo (siglos* VIII *al* XII*)*. Madrid, Fundación Menéndez Pidal / Real Academia Española.

Miguel, Elena de *et al.* (eds) (2009)*. *Fronteras de un diccionario: las palabras en movimiento*. San Millán de la Cogolla, Cilengua.

Navarro, Tomás (1957). *Documentos lingüísticos del Alto Aragón*. New York, Syracuse University Press.

—. (1962). *Atlas lingüístico de la Península Ibérica*, 1, Madrid, CSIC.

Nieto, Lidio / Alvar, Manuel (2007). *Nuevo tesoro lexicográfico español (s. XIV-1726)*. Madrid, Arco / Libros.

Onís, Federico de (1908). *Contribución al estudio del dialecto leonés. Examen filológico de algunos documentos de la Catedral de Salamanca*. Salamanca, n.e.

Oxford English Dictionary (1989). Oxford, Clarendon Press. [http://www.oed.com].

Pascual, José Antonio (2008)*. "Sobre la discontinuidad en un diccionario histórico", in Bernal, Elisenda / De Cesaris, Janet (eds). *Proceedings of the XIII Euralex International Congress*. Barcelona, IULA: 69-88.

—. (ed.) (2008b)**. *Nomen exempli et exemplum vitae: studia in honorem sapientissimi Iohannis Didaci Atauriensis*. Madrid, Sesgo [most of the works contained in this volume, which are not listed, are by collaborators of the *NDHE* and deal with subjects related to this work].

—. (in print)*. "Sobre el léxico deportivo. A propósito de un corpus modular para el *NDHE*". [reworking of the lecture illustrated in *Reunión Científica en memoria de Luis Michelena*, June 2007].

Pascual, José Antonio / Domínguez, Carlos (in print)*. "Un corpus para un nuevo diccionario del español". [reworking of the lecture given in *Coloquio Internacional sobre Corpus Diacrónicos en Lenguas Iberorromances*, Palma de Mallorca, 25-27 October 2007].

Pascual, José Antonio / García Pérez, Rafael (2006)**. "Un Nuevo diccionario histórico de la Lengua Española", in *Aprendizaje de lenguas, uso del lenguaje y modelación cognitiva: perspectivas aplicadas entre disciplinas*. [Proceedings from the *XXIV Congreso Internacional de la Asociación Española de Lingüística Aplicada*. Madrid, Head Office of the Universidad Nacional de Educación a Distancia. Published in CD-Rom].

Pascual, José Antonio / García Pérez, Rafael (2006b)**. "La organización de los materiales en un diccionario histórico: las formas de interés filológico", in Bernal, Elisenda / De Cesaris, Janet (eds). *Palabra sobre palabra. Estudios ofrecidos a Paz Battaner*. Barcelona, Institut Universitari de Lingüística Aplicada / Universitat Pompeu Fabra: 189-200.

Pascual, José Antonio / García Pérez, Rafael (2007)*. *Límites y horizontes en un diccionario histórico*. Salamanca, Diputación Provincial.

Pascual, José Antonio / García Pérez, Rafael (2007b)**. "Las relaciones entre las palabras en un diccionario histórico. La relación genética", in Campos, Mar / Cotelo, Rosalía / Pérez Pascual, José Ignacio (eds). *Historia del léxico del español. Anejos de la Revista de Lexicografía* 5: 109-124.

Pena, Jesús (2008)*. "La información morfológica en los diccionarios", in Garcés, Pilar (ed.) (2008): 19-40.

Pérez Pascual, José Ignacio (2008)**. "Sinónimos y diccionario histórico", in Garcés, Pilar (ed.) (2008): 149-175.

Real Academia Española (1933-1936). *Diccionario histórico de la lengua española* [*DH*], 2 vols [*A-Cevilla*]. Madrid.

—. (1960-1994). *Diccionario histórico de la lengua española* (*DHLE*). [*A-Apasanca*; *B-Bajoca*]. Madrid.

—. (2001). *Diccionario de la lengua española* [*DRAE*]. Madrid, Espasa Calpe.

Salas, Pilar (2007)**. "Amato Lusitano y su Dioscórides: Léxico español y portugués", in *Historia de la Lexicografía española, Anexos Revista de Lexicografía* 7: 163-171.

Sánchez, Santiago U. (2008)**. "La creación de un marcador del discurso: *naturalmente*", in Javier, Elvira / Inés Fernández-Ordóñez, Inés / García, Javier / Serradilla, Ana (eds). *Reinos, lenguas y dialectos en la Edad Media ibérica. La construcción de la identidad. Homenaje a José Ramón Lodares*. Madrid / Frankfurt, Vervuert Iberoamericana: 425-458.

—. (2008b)*. "El significado de los verbos: sintaxis y semántica", in Garcés García, Pilar (ed.) (2008): 67-94.

—. (2009)**. "*Hacer*: un verbo que sirve para casi todo", in de Miguel *et al.* (eds): 195-232.

Tesoro della lingua italiana delle origini. [http://tlio.ovi.cnr.it/TLIO].

Trésor de la langue française (1971-1994). París, Gallimard. [http://atilf.atilf.fr/tlf.htm].

Varela, Diego (in print)*. "La presentación del lema en el Nuevo diccionario histórico de la lengua española (*NDHE*)", in *Revista Iberoamericana de Lingüística.*

Woordenboek der Nederlandsche [http://gtb.inl.nl/?owner=WNT].

THE LEXICOGRAPHY OF EARLY ITALIAN: ITS EVOLUTION AND RECENT ADVANCES (*TESORO DELLA LINGUA ITALIANA DELLE ORIGINI*)

PIETRO G. BELTRAMI

The *Tesoro della Lingua Italiana delle Origini* (*TLIO*) is a historical dictionary of early Italian. Edited by the *Istituto Opera del Vocabolario Italiano* (*OVI*) of the Consiglio Nazionale delle Ricerche (CNR) and published on the Institute's website (www.vocabolario.org), it covers a period from the earliest records of the language until the end of the fourteenth century; the symbolic cut-off point being 1375, the year of Boccaccio's death. The *TLIO* aims to provide comprehensive information relating to early Italian vocabulary before 1375; any illustrative quotations from after this date are chosen from a select portion of the available material. By the end of 2008, 19,000 entries (out of an expected final total of about 50,000) were available for online consultation.[1]

The first section of this article will discuss the context in which the work of the *TLIO* takes place, while the second section will focus on some of the typical problems which can arise during the editing process.

1. Unlike dictionaries of current usage (which focus primarily on contemporary language), historical dictionaries contain features which reflect a different approach to the study and presentation of lexicon.

As far as its sources are concerned, the historical dictionary is based on documentary evidence obtained through the close scrutiny of texts. For dictionaries dealing with the earlier stage of a language, this evidence is exclusively written documentation; while, typically, the material published in existing dictionaries is also included. It is worth noting that a dictionary

---

[1] For a more complete account of this work and its history, see also Beltrami 1997, 1999, 2001, 2004a, 2004b, 2004c, 2005, 2007, Beltrami / Fornara 2004, Beltrami / Boccellari 2006.

of current usage draws upon a multitude of resources, including the mother-tongue competence of its editors, as well as existing dictionaries and a variety of non-philological linguistic databases (i.e. those which do not place a particular emphasis on the provenance of each quotation).

With regard to its lexicon, a historical dictionary includes all the words contained in the source material, without subjecting them to editorial selection. The *Oxford English Dictionary*, a historical dictionary which also deals with the language in its current form, has set certain criteria for the selection process of its vocabulary[2] and modern-day Italian dictionaries would do well to follow its example, since their eagerness to include neologisms is a decision made mainly for commercial reasons. Dealing exclusively with the early language, the *TLIO* also cites unique attestations. By contrast, a dictionary of the current language includes those words considered (at least potentially) to be in current use, as well as a selection of technical and scientific terms which may also be used or understood by non-specialists. Such terms might include a selection of obsolete words, a knowledge of which may be regarded as necessary to the speaker of the contemporary language (in particular, words used by ancient authors who form part of the school curriculum), as well as a selection of neologisms, including foreign loan-words, which occupy an important place in modern-day Italian.

As for the content of its entries, the historical dictionary derives its meanings from the collected documentation (primary material obtained through the scrutiny of texts, or secondary material from existing dictionaries, glossaries, and studies), and presents them alongside contextual examples of usage which substantiate these meanings. Above all, it furnishes detailed information relating to the chronological sequence and development of the meanings, ordering definitions according to the date of their first attestation (the basic method of the *OED*), or to other methods (such as those employed by the *Trésor de la Langue Française*). In particular, it presents the earliest known attestation of each word for each of its meanings (for obsolete words, the *OED* provides the most recent one as well). The linguistic information provided for both meaning, as well as syntactic constructions, morphology, and spelling, can be described as descriptive and historical, as opposed to normative or prescriptive. For example, the historical dictionary does not specify how a given word should be spelled (which is one of the most frequent reasons

---

2 «To determine whether a word has caught on, we normally require several independent examples of the word being used, and also evidence that the word has been in use for a reasonable span of time» (from the web site of the *OED* Online, http://dictionary.oed.com).

for consulting a dictionary of the current language), but it reports objectively on the ways in which the word has been spelled according to the historical source material.

The *OED* and the *TLF* embody two impressive methodologies employed in the preparation of a historical dictionary: the *OED* as a dictionary documenting the history of the lexicon from its origins to the present day, and the *TLF* as a synchronic dictionary of the language of a specific historical time period (in this case covering French vocabulary from the era of the French Revolution until 1961).

The *Vocabolario degli Accademici della Crusca* of 1612, the first benchmark for modern monolingual lexicography in Europe, documents most of its words and definitions with examples taken from selected authors of the fourteenth century. Although it deals with a specific period in history, it may not be considered a historical dictionary, since it does not attempt to describe the evolution of its lexicon, but rather, bases the substance of its vocabulary on the literary authorities of fourteenth-century Florence. As recent studies have shown, it also introduces influential lexicon from the contemporary language not yet documented in the illustrative quotations, but which, nevertheless, constitutes a rich source of material for the dictionary's definitions. Until the fourth edition of 1729-1738, subsequent editions increasingly widened the canon of authors cited, although in the view of the dictionary's critics, their development did not extend far enough. Notwithstanding, there is no comparable expansion in terms of its historical approach to the lexicon and any historical annotations simply serve as a warning that some words, even if cited in the dictionary, remain obsolete. In the fifth edition, left unfinished at the end of *O* in 1923, it was intended that the obsolete words should be collected into a *Glossary* (the *A-B* fascicle of 1867 was the only one actually published), and it can thus be regarded as an example of a "lexicography of obsolete words", rather than as a lexicography of early Italian. This is worthy of note, since the Crusca's style of dictionary and exemplification remained prevalent not only until the publication of the *Tommaseo-Bellini*, but in many respects also until the appearance of the *Grande dizionario della lingua italiana* (*GDLI*, popularly known as the *Battaglia*).

Historical lexicography presupposes the existence of the science of historical linguistics. This plant, nurtured in the nineteenth century, was late in putting down roots in Italian lexicography, for the simple reason that Italy was slow to absorb the principles of Romance philology. A few dates will demonstrate this. Ugo Angelo Canello was not appointed to the position of "private professor" of Romance philology at Padua until December 1872, and it was only in 1876 that he was assigned the task of teaching the comparative history of neo-Latin literature. In 1873-1874 Pio Rajna started teaching at the Accademia di Milano[3] and the *Tommaseo-Bellini* was published from 1861 to 1879, while the fifth edition of the *Vocabolario degli Accademici* had been in preparation from the second decade of the century (its first fascicle was released in 1843 and the first volume was published in 1863).

The *GDLI* project, which was established in 1951 (the first volume being published in 1961), took advantage of textual editions based on philological studies from the first half of the twentieth century in order to reverify the illustrative quotations included in the most important dictionaries of the Italian lexicographical tradition, from the *Crusca* to the *Tommaseo-Bellini*. The scrutiny of new editions continued throughout the process of compiling the *Battaglia*, with the twenty-first and last volume being released in 2002. The *Battaglia*, however, was not projected by its compilers as a philological or historical dictionary, and if it is treated as such then the studies of Francesco Bruni[4] at least strive to attest that this was not the original intention. In fact, from the very beginning, the *Battaglia* has been considered and used as a historical dictionary, and it remains the source for most of the dating of early terms cited by other lexicographical volumes.

From a different perspective, the lexicography of early Italian – as distinct from that of modern and contemporary Italian – requires a historical-philological approach which not only relies, in an ideological sense, on the notion of the continuity of Italian, but also takes into account those features peculiar to early Italian. As Massimo Fanfani wrote: «l'idea di compilare un dizionario dell'italiano antico o, per meglio dire, dei volgari italiani antichi, data la particolare impostazione ideologica che ha permeato per secoli la nostra lessicografia e la natura stessa della nostra storia linguistica, è affiorata solo a tratti e piuttosto tardi».[5]

During the period which extends from the origins of the language until the end of the fourteenth century and beyond, "Italian" should be essentially regarded as "Italo-Romance"; that is to say, a unified national language was yet to emerge. With Florentine and Tuscan, whose significance was evident from the end of the thirteenth century and which

[3] Cf. Crescini 1886. Until the last decades of the twentieth century, the *Tommaseo-Bellini* remained the most important work on Italian lexicography in existence.

[4] Cf. Bruni 1992. With reference to this see: Beltrami 2005.

[5] Fanfani 2004: 90 [The idea of compiling a dictionary of early Italian, or rather of the early Italian vernaculars, emerged somewhat late, hindered by the particular ideological approach which has for centuries permeated Italian lexicography and Italian linguistic history].

began to emerge as important varieties during the fourteenth century, there exists a great variety of Italian languages, which include Lombardic, Venetian, Umbrian and Sicilian, amongst others. These were languages in the full, functional sense of the term which, for a certain time, were all equally important, being employed in the preparation of public records, legislative acts, city and guild statutes, as well as literary and scientific works. At least some of what was written during the second half of the thirteenth century in languages other than Florentine and Tuscan needs to be included in the history of Italian lexicon. Indeed, the *Battaglia*, whose main focus is the national language, cites the Milanese Bonvesin da la Riva and the Umbrian Iacopone da Todi without warning its readers that their languages were different; and when reporting early non-Tuscan forms (for example, the northern form *radixe* under the entry for *radice* 'root'), it labels them as "ancient forms", itself a misleading description in this context.

The lexicography of early Italian consisted for a long time mainly in glossaries to textual editions. I refer primarily to texts of linguistic interest, which could be defined as largely "practical" or documentary in nature. These include the series of editions furnished with linguistic commentaries who took as their model Arrigo Castellani's *Nuovi testi fiorentini del Dugento e dei primi del Trecento* (Firenze, Sansoni, 1952), followed by the work of a number of illustrious editors including Stussi and Serianni, as well as edited anthologies of great historical significance such as the *Crestomazia* by Monaci and Arese. There are, of course, numerous other studies on different features of the early language, which also concern the lexicon.

The *Concordanze della Lingua Poetica Italiana delle Origini* project (*CLPIO*), the brain-child of d'Arco Silvio Avalle, was established towards the end of the 1960s. The project did not simply concern a single linguistic variety of Italian, but rather, the entire corpus of early Italian poetry. A volume containing the texts, linguistic commentary and the so-called *omofonario* (concordance of rhymes) was published by Avalle in 1992. The project interweaves lexicography and philology in an exemplary and unique way. It includes all poetic works prior to the end of the thirteenth century recorded in contemporary manuscripts, and no later than the beginning of the following century. With the contribution of a team of collaborators, Avalle prepared new critical editions of all the texts, or better of all the manuscripts (poems which appear in different manuscripts being printed each time); and it was these editions which set the standard for future lexicographical studies. In light of this, even the concept of a "critical edition of manuscripts" can be considered an innovation, and one which ultimately merits a more in-depth analysis and discussion. The aim was not to compile a dictionary, but rather to provide an exhaustive lemmatisation of occurrences, conceived as the kernel of a coherent reconstruction of the linguistic system in operation during the thirteenth century. Furthermore, because much of the material comes from the three main *canzonieri*, it also became a study of the language of the first Italian lyric poetry. The principal concept behind Avalle's reconstruction is that the evidence for the early language clearly reveals a linguistic system distinct from that of the "national" Italian of the following centuries. The lemmatisation was carried out using the computational technologies of the 1960s and 1970s, but it will be published in a modern electronic format by Lino Leonardi, who took over as supervisor of the project after Avalle's death. While the computational system was used for data processing and research, its input was rigorously "manual", deriving from an accurate and scholarly interpretation of the texts.

When Avalle embarked on the *CLPIO* project, the new historical dictionary of the *Accademia della Crusca* was still in its early stages. The idea of a historical dictionary which would displace the traditional *Vocabolario degli Accademici*, interrupted in 1923, had long been in the works.[6] The crucial impetus was given by Giacomo Devoto, who took advantage of the opening of the humanities division of the CNR in 1963, and it was the CNR that provided the necessary grants for the project. From the minutes of the plenary meeting of the Accademia on 31 October 1964[7] – which approved the inauguration of the project – it emerges that the final decision as to whether it would be a historical dictionary covering the whole history of Italian or only of its early centuries, had yet to be decided. The main project was started in 1965, but in 1972 it was decided to concentrate only on the early study, while postponing the rest. This is how the *TLIO* project started, but we will return to a more detailed examination of its conception later in this paper.

The Accademia della Crusca conducted a significant amount of preparatory work on the processing of *TLIO* material up to the end of the 1970s, digitising and lemmatising texts containing some 14 million word occurrences in total. However, this never developed into an editorial project for the compilation of a dictionary (in fact, the editorial work was never begun), and neither did it provide scholars with easy access to the data, which, as a result, remained largely unexamined.[8] This was why

[6] Cf. Barbi 1935; Pasquali 1941; Nencioni 1955.

[7] Published in Mastrelli / Parenti 1999: 221-24.

[8] Reflecting the computational technologies of the time, the output consisted of many complex yet muddled tabulations, which, given the size of the *TLIO*, were

when Giorgio Colussi published a book about the infinitive construction in early Italian based on the remarkable lexical evidence he had collected,[9] he correctly believed himself to be working in a vacuum.

The *GAVI* (vol. 1 published 1983) constitutes the first attempt to create a dictionary of early Italian, although its general shape and objectives changed frequently during the process of its compilation. It began life as a kind of super-glossary, and its aim was to collect together data from the glossaries and indices of the major editions of early Italian texts encompassing all the Italian linguistic varieties. Colussi's decision to address Italo-Romance in general, rather than simply the varieties from which the national language originated, seems to have come naturally to him because of his philological approach; whereas, such an approach remained problematic within the Crusca. From the start, the intention was to produce a versatile working tool within a reasonable time frame. This had a bearing both on the choice of the material addressed and on the processing methods employed, which were influenced by the fact that Colussi continued to work without collaborators. The project was to all intents and purposes proceeding in a vacuum and one which no one imagined that the *TLIO* could fill; the first *TLIO* entries being published online in October 1997. So it was that Colussi, encouraged by the appreciation which his work had received from scholars, became more ambitious and enriched his entries with a wider range of material, thus improving the quality of the work at the expense of its progress. At this point, he decided to move ahead and compile the final alphabetical sections, those which were still incomplete in the *Battaglia* (which was, at that stage, still proceeding somewhat slowly, eventually reaching completion in 2002 after a considerable change of pace towards the end). When, in 1998, it became possible to consult the *OVI* database of early Italian on the Internet,[10] Colussi, using this enormous wealth of new material, decided to re-examine and enhance the entries of *GAVI*, starting once again with the letter *A*. In the years that followed, he found that he also had to take into consideration the entries of the *TLIO* which, from 1999 onwards, had started to appear at the rate of 2000 per year. Many of these revised *GAVI* entries became, at least in part, commentaries on the corresponding *TLIO* entries, with further studies added to the database in

---

impossible to use efficiently. The data conversion from the older tape formats to new interactive formats (*DBT*, then *GATTO*) was conducted gradually during the second half of the 1980s and processed mainly between 1992 and 1995.

[9] Colussi 1978.

[10] Colussi's speech at the presentation of online databases, 20 May 1998 at Villa Reale di Castello, is now in Colussi 2007.

the form of annotations. The *GAVI* is an idiosyncratic work in many ways, both with regard to its distinguishing features, as well as its merits and shortcomings (which are beyond the scope of this article). It is partly a dictionary, partly a collection of essays, partly a "conversation on the lexicon" between Colussi and his readers. Progress on the *GAVI* was eventually interrupted by the death of its creator and author, with whose personality it will forever be linked.[11]

2. The *TLIO*, now under the direction of the Consiglio Nazionale delle Ricerche which has taken over from the Accademia della Crusca,[12] is a historical dictionary similar to the *TLF* in some respects: it covers a limited period of the language's history, its definitions are presented in a non-chronological order, but an exact chronological indication of the entry and of each meaning is available. The contribution that existing dictionaries can give to the redaction of the *TLIO* is very limited; apart from the mandatory double-checking and integrations, the *TLIO* is edited from scratch and is based on the *OVI* database (early Italian *Corpus OVI*).[13]

2.1 Developed in conjunction with the dictionary, the database has had a complex history, which we will necessarily exclude from these pages.[14] At the moment it contains a total amount of 21,779,245 occurrences taken from 1960 published texts,[15] written in all Italian language varieties before

---

[11] An excellent outline of the *GAVI*'s history until 2003 can be found in Fanfani 2004.

[12] A first version of the database for Early Italian – which has since been greatly expanded – was ready in 1995, but the project had been shelved many years earlier by the Accademia della Crusca, with which the editing team now shares only the headquarters and the library. The *OVI* had become a research centre (1985) and then an Institute within the Consiglio Nazionale delle Ricerche.

[13] Every citation taken from a different source is marked with *f* ("fuori" [outside the corpus]) if it is second-hand information (taken from a dictionary, which is, therefore, quoted) or with *F*, if the text has been directly consulted (even if the team has found that text thanks to a citation in a dictionary or in another source).

[14] On the very first period see Beltrami 1995; on the encoding criteria adopted today see Pollidori 1999.

[15] Unpublished texts are not taken into account, with the exception of some temporary or soon-to-be-published editions, and of editions compiled especially for the corpus (as, for example, the partial collection of the works of the fourteenth century northern Italian poet Antonio da Ferrara, edited by Roberta Manetti). Due to the elaboration process, a text is a file that contains either one text, regardless of its size, which is classified singularly according to its date or language variety (for instance, Dante's *Comedy*, Boccaccio's *Decameron*, but also an anonymous sonnet or a brief notarial document) or a series of texts that are classified all together (for

the end of the fourteenth century; although some texts from the fifteenth century are also included.[16] The texts written in the Tuscan dialect number 1200, with 17,600,574 occurrences (eight Corsican texts with a total of 4146 occurrences are included among the Tuscan texts). On the one hand, this data shows that medieval Tuscany was more productive than other linguistic areas, while on the other, that the choice of publishing fourteenth century Tuscan texts was predominant for a long time (the fourteenth century is also known as "the golden age of our language" according to the old tradition inaugurated by Pietro Bembo, which was rekindled in the nineteenth century). Non-Tuscan texts can be divided according to their linguistic features into northern (525 texts with 2,186,556 occurrences), central and southern (178 texts with 1,342,849 occurrences), and Sicilian (47 texts with 537,103 occurrences).[17] With regard to their chronology, the texts of the *corpus* date mainly from the thirteenth and fourteenth centuries: there are 535 thirteenth-century texts with 2,628,521 occurrences, and 1384 fourteenth-century texts with 18,226,553 occurrences (an approximation, due to dating uncertainties, has been made for some texts straddling the two centuries).

These figures are a record of the corpus as it stood in 2007 and will necessarily change with time. The database is intended to be added to continually, and it contains not only all published texts written before the end of fourteenth century (at the moment it contains all essential texts, which are largely sufficient for the redaction of a dictionary), but also

---

instance, the 52 poems in the *Rime* by Guido Cavalcanti, or the 366 compositions in the *Rerum vulgarium fragmenta* by Petrarca). The significant quantitative gauge is the amount of occurrences, not the number of texts. Some texts may also appear twice and therefore be counted twice in the corpus.

[16] In particular, the vernacular Bible based on an *incunabulum* dating back to 1491, edited by Carlo Negroni (Bologna, Romagnoli, 1882-1887). Texts of this kind are quoted in the *TLIO* mainly in less attested entries or when they contain first attestations of words and meanings.

[17] There are also ten texts with 108,026 occurrences which could not be classified in the four categories. In this classification the term *northern* identifies those varieties spoken to the north of the Tuscan-Emilian Appennine, *central* and *southern* as those spoken in southern Italy (excluding Sicily and Sardinia). *Middle* is a synonym for "central", "central Italy", but the former is favoured due to the fact that, even though it belongs to that geographical region, the Tuscan language variety has particular features and a special social role in the history of the Italian language which places it in a category of its own. Texts written in the language varieties spoken in Sardinia and Friuli (with the exception of a few texts) are excluded from the dictionary because they are considered to be proper independent languages.

future editions of currently unpublished texts, as well as new, more reliable editions of already published texts. The initial criteria adopted in the selection of texts permitted only philologically reliable editions, or editions that could be revised by the editors (various texts, especially documentary texts, or texts existing only in a single manuscript, were revised directly from their manuscripts).[18] The work of revision was gradually abandoned with time owing to the sheer amount of effort which the process entailed. It became clear that the compilation of the dictionary would not be comprehensive without the presence of a certain number of texts still lacking a philologically reliable edition; for example, Brunetto Latini's *Tesoro* in the Tuscan translation, whose presence in the database was essential in order to avoid significant blank spaces in comparison to the lexicographic tradition. This can, therefore, explain the decision to include these texts and mark the ones which are published in less reliable editions by putting their bibliographic abbreviations within angulated brackets (< >), both in the database as well as the dictionary. Every text has a bibliographic abbreviation where the indication of its supposed linguistic origin and dating can be found.[19] The database automatically links the bibliographic abbreviation to all its occurrences and it is possible, with a little editorial adjustment, to paste the output into the dictionary as it stands.

In order to ensure the linguistic reliability of both the database and dictionary, the label *TS* ('texts significant for the documentation of the specific language variety') can be found in the index reference of those texts written in a homogeneous and perfectly definable language (these texts include, amongst others, practical texts, notarial acts, and confraternity or town statutes). These texts are available in editions either specifically created for history (such as, for example, the aforementioned *Nuovi testi fiorentini del Dugento e dei primi del Trecento*, edited by Castellani, 1952), or in any case reproducing the linguistic form of the manuscript (for example, Brunetto Latini's *Rettorica*, edited by Francesco Maggini, new edition by Segre 1968).[20] The label *TS* can be found on the bibliographic information line of all online database quotations on *GattoWeb* (the search engine powered by the *OVI*) and it is possible to

---

[18] Cf. De Robertis 1985.

[19] Since it seemed superfluous to explicitly qualify the language of Dante, Petrarca and Boccaccio, the quotations taken from their texts do not contain an indication of their linguistic origins; it is, however, implicit that they be labelled *Fior.* ("Fiorentino" [Florentine]).

[20] Brunetto Latini, *La Rettorica*, edited by Francesco Maggini, Firenze, Galletti e Cocci, 1915 (new edition by Cesare Segre, Firenze, Le Monnier, 1968).

select this among the criteria for the creation of subcorpora in searches limited to these kinds of texts. Moreover, *TLIO*'s entries must quote the oldest TS text that contains the first attestation of the word in that variety[21].

The database was published in 1998 using *GATTO*, software created by Domenico Iorio-Folio and still in development at the *OVI*.[22] Since 2005, the database can be consulted online, thanks to the *GattoWeb* software created by the same author.[23] It was already – and still is – available online in its ItalNet version, as created by Mark Olsen using *Philologic* (University of Chicago software); however, using this version it is only possible to consult the word forms (i.e. lemmatisation is not carried out).

On the whole, the lemmatisation of the database still respects the criteria formulated by d'Arco Silvio Avalle in the 1970s and published in Piero Esperti (1979), although with some exceptions which include, for example, the absence of compounds.[24]

From a linguistic point of view the most remarkable aspect of the *TLIO* is its lack of distinction between adjectives and pronouns; the label *agg.* is assigned to qualifier adjectives, while the labels *dim.* [demonstrative], *indef.* [indefinite], *interr.* [interrogative], *pers.* [personal], *poss.* [possessive], *rel.* [relative] are assigned to both pronouns and adjectives without further distinction. Notwithstanding the theoretical implications of this functional approach, the choice to exclude further distinction markers has proved not only practical, but also successful.

Another practical choice, linked to the fact that the database was originally aimed primarily at the dictionary, is the decision to mark only a verb's grammatical category and not its conjugation (verbal forms are

[21] Being a newly adopted rule, it has been applied only to recent or re-edited *TLIO* entries, but will be soon applied to all entries at the end of a substantial edition currently in progress.

[22] Cf. Iorio-Fili 2007. *GATTO* can be downloaded from the *OVI* website in its newest version. It is free and can be used for non-profit research; a large didactic handbook is also available. The first implementation of the *OVI* corpus dates back to the end of 1995 (*DBT* by Eugenio Picchi).

[23] Cf. Iorio-Fili 2006.

[24] For example, in the sentence: «e come a maggiore pericolo credevano venire per causa di Pompeo e di Cesare» [since they feared themselves in greater danger because of Pompeo and Caesar] (in *Fatti di Cesare*, Sienese text from the end of thirteenth century), the three elements of the locution *per causa di* have been separately lemmatised and the phrase is registered under the entry "causa s.f." 1.3 and can be located by looking for one of the three elements (for example *causa*) in the list of compounds which links its items to the entries.

marked only with *v.*, without further distinctions of mood, tense, and person); pronominal usage of verbs, however, is expressed.[25]

Another difficulty that cannot be avoided and is often the source of uncertainties is the distinction between participles with verbal and adjectival function; for example, *dettato/dettata* [dictated] is lemmatised as "dettare v." in: «trovai il suo latino in tal modo dettato, che...» [I found his Latin dictated in such a way, that…], taken from the *Dialogo di santo Gregorio* translated by Domenico Cavalca,[26] but as "dettato agg." in: «Ma perciò che lla pistola, cioè la lettera dettata...» [But because the epistle, that is the dictated letter…], from the *Rettorica* by Brunetto Latini. These uncertainties affect the wordlist of the dictionary, where adjectival participles have their own entry.

With regard to the procedure for compilation, the system requires that when using the lemmatisation software (included in the *GATTO* software), the operator manually inserts the information that a certain attested graphic form is an occurrence of a certain lemma; for example, in the first aforementioned sentence, that *dettato* is an occurrence of "*dettare* v.", and in the second, that *dettata* is an occurrence of "*dettato* agg.". Having acquired this information regarding a precise section of the text, the system creates a pair comprising of a word form and a lemma in the machine dictionary (e.g. "*dettato* – *dettare* v."). Following the lemmatisation of every passage, a list of the lemmas present in the machine dictionary and a list of the lemma's various forms will be available.

As the lemmatisation of the corpus currently stands, the list of the lemma "*dettare* v." presents the following forms:

> detò, detta, détta, dettando, dettano, dettar, dettare, dettasse, dettata, dettate, dettati, dettato, dettava, dettavano, detti, dettò, dicta, dictale, dictano, dictante, dictar, dictare, dictato, dictau, dictava, dictiria, dictoa, dictone, dita, dità, ditade, ditadi, ditar, ditare, ditarla, ditasse, ditava, ditó, ditta, dittan, dittando, dittano, dittar, dittare, dittasse, dittasti, dittata, dittate, dittato, dittava, dittavan, dittò, dittoe, dittòe.

---

[25] For example in: «Democlito fu eccellente filosofo ed elli stesso s'abbacinò degl'occhi per avere più sottile intelletto nello studio» [Democritus was an excellent philosopher and he blinded himself in order to have a more subtle awareness in his studies] (from Antonio Pucci, *Libro di varie storie*, edited by Alberto Varvaro, *Atti dell'Accademia di Scienze Lettere ed Arti di Palermo* 16, part II, fasc. II [1957]) the word *abbacinò* is lemmatised under "*abbacinare(-si)* v.". In the *TLIO* pronominal verbs are to be found in the non-pronominal form ("*abbacinare* v.").

[26] Domenico Cavalca, *Dialogo di santo Gregorio volgarizzato*, edited by Carlo Baudi di Vesme, Torino, Stamperia Reale, 1851.

It does not contain either *dettiamo* or *dettassimo* because, even if these forms of *dettare* could in theory have been used, they are not present in the corpus.

This "bottom-up" lemmatisation (from the text to the machine dictionary) is the opposite of a "top-down" rendition, which would consist in creating beforehand a machine dictionary that contains all the lemma's possible forms («dettare: detto, detti, detta..., dettavo, dettavi, dettava...»), then asking the system to examine the texts, register which lemma the forms found in the texts can belong to and, if needs be, also decide between the various possibilities (e.g. are *debbe*, *debbono* forms of *dovere* in the present tense or, are they as they appear in the chronicles written in the Pisan language by Ranieri Sardo, past forms of *avere*? It should be noted, however, that the large majority of such ambiguities are less irregular in nature). The latter method could not be applied to a corpus like the *OVI*'s, which contains texts written in very different language varieties and with a multitude of graphic uses (partly linked to the ancient copyists' choices and partly to the modern editions' graphic criteria) which are often difficult to interpret. The list of a lemma's possible graphic forms in a certain language variety is more a research topic than an initial concept.[27]

At the moment, more than 3,5 million occurrences have been lemmatized, for a total amount of more than 115,000 lemmas.[28] Almost every graphic form present in the corpus has been lemmatised at least once[29]; therefore, the machine dictionary essentially contains a complete list of all forms of a lemma present in the corpus, and as a result, a search by lemma will offer a reliable list of forms. With this type of search it is possible to obtain only the locations in which the selected forms have been lemmatised (for example "*dettare* v."= 178 occurrences) or to extend the

[27] Automatic lemmatisation makes use of complex tools, of which the machine dictionary is one, and requires as a minimum condition that the lemmatised texts be written in a homogeneous language; in other words, we would need an automatic lemmatising tool for each language variety present in the corpus. Lately, the research at the *OVI* has also been widened in this direction.

[28] For various reasons, the amount of lemmas does not correspond to that of the *TLIO* entries, which at the end of the compilation will be around 50,000. The procedure of lemmatising single occurrences was conceived in the earliest phase of the work (the second half of the 1960s and 1970s) when, without the technology available today, this procedure was considered useful in order to create, for future editors, a collection of selective cards not significantly different from those used in traditional lexicography, but based on exhaustive text processing. An exhaustive lemmatisation of the database would be welcome but it requires a commitment beyond the *OVI*'s current resources.

[29] With a total of 3000 forms out of 442,770 remaining.

search to find the occurrences of all the forms that appear on the list, homographs included; the case of the word "*dettare* v." is particularly complex because there are homographic forms belonging to the lemmas *dire* and *dito* (29,717 occurrences). *Moderno*, however, is a different, but no less significant example ("*moderno* agg." and "*moderno* s.m.", plus one lemmatised occurrence "*moderno* avv." as part of the adverbial locution *per moderno*):[30]

> 71 lemmatised occurrences;
> List of forms: "moderna, moderne, moderni, moderno, modernu, mudernu";
> 154 occurrences can be retraced in the texts through a search by forms where none are ambiguous, or otherwise impossible to confuse with other lemmas.

2.2 The database may be used for every type of linguistic research, especially lexical, but its main aim is to help the *TLIO* editors in the compilation of the dictionary entries. There can be said to be a two-way relationship between the database and the dictionary; on one hand, the entry is created on the basis of the attested meanings found during the exhaustive processing of the corpus' available occurrences, with every possible meaning of the entry being followed by a selection of such occurrences, while on the other, every entry is linked to the database in such a way that it is possible to verify the work carried out by the editor. The link between the two tools is the list of forms, which can be found at paragraph 0.1 of the entry (cf. "*moderno* agg./s.m.", where the above-mentioned list can be found). By clicking on the GattoWeb icon (a yellow cat in front of an open book) on the left frame of the online dictionary the programme starts up and automatically carries out the search of such forms.

We can now take a closer look at the structure of the entry (which can be found further on).[31] Lemmatisation has shown that *moderno* can be either an adjective or a noun, and since, in this case, we are dealing with a nominalised adjective, its grammatical category will be marked as "agg./s.m.". The etymological information is usually limited to a cross-

---

[30] The lemmatisation of a locution's elements is now under revision; *moderno* taken from *per moderno* will later appear lemmatised as "*moderno* s.m." (while the locution will remain in the *TLIO*'s list of compounds).

[31] The pdf redaction guidelines of the *TLIO* (a handbook for editors) can be found on the first page of the online dictionary. Nevertheless, experience has shown that very frequently, cases are encountered which cannot be manipulated by exclusively following the guidelines, and which, therefore, often need to be adjusted; in those cases, the editors turn to the supervisors for advice.

reference to an etymological dictionary, preferably the *LEI* or, when absent, the second edition of the *DELI*; further etymological research seemed futile with the important developments currently taking place in this field.

Having automatically extracted the list of forms in order to insert it into paragraph 0.1, the editors examine the list of the texts where these forms appear (this list is also retraceable through a search tool in the programme), and from this create a chart of texts in paragraph 0.4 where the first attestations of the word in different varieties have been found. For the compilation of this chart, editors only take into account those texts written in a language whose linguistic origin is well-defined (texts written in a mixed language or copied in a linguistic form different from its original are therefore excluded). Furthermore, every text is double-checked before being inserted into the chart in order to make sure that it contains an occurrence of a certain lemma and not a homograph of one of the lemma's forms.

The oldest attestation of the word *moderno* among the 154 forms traceable in the database is taken from Dante's *Convivio* (roughly dating to 1304-1307);[32] this text will be quoted both in paragraph 0.4, whose first subparagraph is dedicated to Tuscan texts (or Tuscanised texts, such as those written by Sicilian poets and translated into Tuscanised versions, or Corsican texts), and in paragraph 0.3, which reproduces the oldest attestation of all the texts concerned.[33]

Since Dante's text is in the Florentine dialect, no further Florentine texts or texts marked as generally Tuscan will be quoted in paragraph 0.4 (e.g. the next text after Dante, *Documenti d'Amore* by Francesco da Barberino).[34] However, because this first text from the list (Dante's *Convivio*) is not marked as *TS*, the editors have added to the subparagraph dedicated to Tuscan texts the quotation from the first Florentine *TS* text (in

[32] Approximate datings must be turned into formalised expressions for the dictionary's management. This list of datings can be found on the *Sistema di Datazione* webpage whose link is on the *TLIO's* homepage. In the entries the quoted contexts are listed in the same order as they appear in the database.

[33] Since the definitions are not necessarily in chronological order, paragraph 0.3 will also provide an indication of the first definition or subdefinition under which the text with the first attestation is quoted. The last attestation in chronological order is not mentioned because the *TLIO* is supposed to be followed by another historical dictionary covering the following centuries, in which it will be stated if a word is obsolete and how long it has been so.

[34] Francesco da Barberino, *Documenti d'Amore*, edited by Francesco Egidi, 4 vols, Roma, Società Filologica Romana, 1905-1927.

this case, *Stat. fior.* 1334),[35] which immediately follows the *Convivio*, the reason being that there are no more Tuscan texts to quote in this list from the period 1307 to 1334.

Following this criterion the editors complete the chart of the texts with the first attestations of the word in the different language varieties and split the texts into Tuscan, northern and Sicilian; it is worth noting that there are no attestations of the term in middle and southern texts.

The *Rima Lombarda de vallore* by Tommaso Fontana from Parma,[36] mentioned in the list, presents only one occurrence of *moderni* which is, however, part of a Latin citation. Text and examples are, therefore, not quoted in the list and under the definitions, but are mentioned in paragraph 0.6 dedicated to annotations in order to justify its presence in the database. Apart from cases like this, the editors make sure that at least one example taken from every text listed in paragraph 0.4 is quoted in the entry.

Going back to the list for *moderno*, the first entry to appear is the plural nominalised form *i moderni*, whose definition in reference to this attestation is «Sost. plur. Coloro che vivono e operano nel tempo presente» [Those who live and work at the current time]. This is the second definition.

The second occurrence on the list (which is also plural), taken from Francesco da Barberino's text, is dismissed; although the reader who seeks further clarification will be able to find it in the database.

The third occurrence is taken from Dante's *Comedy* and its definition is: «Che appartiene o si riferisce al tempo presente o al passato immediatamente prossimo» [Which belongs or refers to the present time or to the immediate past]. This definition is number one and finding it to be sufficient we have overlooked the *Battaglia*'s typical excess in offering for this entry a multitude of detailed definitions, which are generally to be read in context and do not always belong to the term which they describe.[37]

---

[35] *Statuto dell'Arte di Calimala del 1334*, in Paolo Emiliani Giudici, *Storia dei Comuni italiani*, vol. III, Firenze, Le Monnier, 1866: 171-367.

[36] Tommaso Fontana, *Rima lombarda de vallore*, in Ubaldo Meroni, Concetta Meroni Zanghi, "La più antica filigrana conosciuta (non posteriore al 1271) e una Rima volgare inedita del XIV sec. («Rima lombarda de vallore»)", in *Annali della Biblioteca Governativa e Libreria Civica di Cremona* 5, 1 (1952): 17-40.

[37] Its first definition will be explicatory: «Che è in vigore da poco tempo; che ha valore ed efficacia nel tempo presente; che rispecchia o è adeguato al gusto, alle esigenze, alla mentalità del tempo presente; che è proprio o caratteristico degli aspetti e delle manifestazioni della vita materiale, sociale, spirituale e culturale dei tempi attuali (e rappresenta di conseguenza un rifiuto, una rottura più o meno netta col passato: un costume, un'usanza, un atteggiamento mentale, un modo di essere,

Among other attestations of the term in Dante's *Comedy* the collocation *uso moderno* has to be isolated and is used as a subdefinition subordinated to definition number one (the editors did not consider it necessary to provide it with an explicit definition).

The texts by Jacopo Alighieri[38] present some examples of the term *moderno* used in contrast to *antico*, therefore providing another subdefinition for definition one: «In contrapposizione ad antico» [As opposed to what is ancient]; it will appear inside square brackets because it is a metalinguistic specification, as opposed to a proper definition.

The Tuscan version of the term found in Armaninno's *Fiorita* is dismissed because its date and content are very close to Dante's examples; therefore, the next quoted attestation of the term is its plural nominal form found in the Venetian version of the same text, the *Fiorita*.[39]

In Jacopo della Lana's text, classified as Bolognese, another example to be classified under definition number one can also be found; a further two are taken from Ugo Panziera's *Trattati*, classified as western Tuscan, and one from the *Ottimo commento*.[40]

The text *Statuto dell'Arte di Calimala* (*Stat. fior.*, 1334) presents the first attestation of *antico e moderno* employed in an unquantifiable form; this usage being marked in the entry by another subdefinition of definition one: «[Con valore cumulativo:] *antico e moderno*».

---

di pensare, una civiltà). – Anche: che seguita a destare interesse ed è tuttora sentito e considerato attuale, pur appartenendo al passato» [Which has recently come into existence; which has current effect and validity; which corresponds with or is adapted to current tastes, needs and attitudes; which is characteristic of the current material, social, spiritual and cultural life (and which as a result, represents a rejection or a comparatively clean break from the past: a custom, a habit, a mental approach, a way of feeling and thinking, a culture). – Also: which still arouses great interest and is still considered up-to-date even though it belongs to the past]. The first example quoted under this definition is taken from Dante's *Purg*. XVI 42: «Se Dio m'ha in sua grazia rinchiuso / tanto che vuol ch'i' veggia la sua corte / per modo tutto fuor del moderno uso...».

[38] Jacopo Alighieri, *Chiose all'«Inferno»*, edited by Saverio Bellomo, Padova, Antenore, 1990.

[39] Armannino giudice da Bologna, *Fiorita* (fragment of redaction A, Venetian disguise, cod. Marc. ital. VI. 50), in Paolo Savj-Lopez, *Storie tebane in Italia*, Bergamo, Istituto Italiano d'Arti Grafiche, 1905: 103-21.

[40] Jacopo della Lana, *Chiose alla "Divina Commedia" di Dante Alighieri. Purgatorio*, in Guido Biagi, G.L. Passerini, Enrico Rostagno (eds.), *La Divina Commedia nella figurazione artistica e nel secolare commento*, vol. II, Torino, UTET, 1931; Ugo Panziera, *Trattati*, Firenze, Mischomini, 1492; *L'Ottimo Commento della Commedia*, vol. II *Purgatorio*, edited by Alessandro Torri, Pisa, Capurro, 1827.

Giovanni Campulu's *Libru de lu dialogu de sanctu Gregoriu* presents the first attestation of a collocation that requires a subdefinition, together with other similar cases that will be found later in the list of examples: «*Tempi moderni*, *tempo moderno*, *età moderna*: il periodo cui appartiene il sogg. parlante o scrivente» [The period of time to which the writer or speaker belongs].[41]

The attestations found in the following texts from the list do not require specific definitions or subdefinitions, and a selection of them appear as examples of the various definitions which the dictionary provides of the presence of the term in texts from different eras and linguistic areas. The editors are therefore careful to include at least one example from each text listed in paragraph 0.4 in the entry. On the other hand, Sacchetti's *Trecentonovelle*[42] presents the locution *per antico e per moderno* which must be marked and as a result, made the object of a subdefinition registered at paragraph 0.5 of the entry. On the online *TLIO* the compounds (phrasal expressions or locutions)[43] are indexed at the end of paragraph 0.5, after the label *Locuz. e fras.* [locutions and idioms] and a separate chart classifying these expressions alone is available on the website; every expression contained in the chart is then linked to the entries where is it registered.

Every time the editors would come across a new meaning, a new locution or collocation of the term in the examination of the texts, the whole list of the contexts in the database was re-examined in order to make sure that the text quoted was actually the oldest one to provide that attestation.

After having checked the whole list, the editors then verified if other dictionaries contained definitions or samples that could not be found through the examination of the corpus, either because a text is not yet in the corpus, or because of a misinterpretation. If some of these definitions and samples found in the dictionaries add something necessary to the entry (this is not the case with *moderno*, however), they are added and marked as "fuori corpus".

Only after having made all these checks, the editors were able to set the definitions and subdefinitions in a certain order (first and second level definitions are listed in paragraph 0.7 in order to speed up the consultation

[41] Giovanni Campulu, *Libru de lu dialagu de sanctu Gregoriu*, edited by Salvatore Santangelo, Palermo, Boccone del Povero, 1933.

[42] Franco Sacchetti, *Il Trecentonovelle*, edited by Vincenzo Pernicone, Firenze, Sansoni, 1946.

[43] Further information concerning the classification of the compounds in the *TLIO* can be found in paragraph 15 of the aforementioned redaction guidelines.

of the entry). The result of this compiling process has the following layout:[44]

MODERNO agg./s.m.

0.1 *moderna, moderne, moderni, moderno, modernu, mudernu.*
0.2 DELI 2 s.v. moderno (lat. tardo *modernum*).
0.3 Dante, *Convivio*, 1304-7: **2**.
0.4 In testi tosc.: Dante, *Convivio*, 1304-7; *Stat. fior.*, 1334; *Comm. Arte Am.* (A), XIV pm. (pis.).

In testi sett.: Armannino, *Fiorita* (07), p. 1325 (ven.); Jacopo della Lana, *Purg.*, 1324-28 (bologn.); *Serapiom* volg., p. 1390 (padov.); Gid. da Sommacamp., *Tratt.*, XIV sm. (ver.).

In testi sic.: Giovanni Campulu, 1302/37 (mess.); Accurso di Cremona, 1321/37 (mess.); Simone da Lentini, 1358 (sirac.).
0.5 Locuz. e fras. *per antico e per moderno* **1.4.1**.
0.6 **N** L'occ. di *moderni* in Fontana, *Rima lombarda*, 1343/46 (parm.) è in lat.
0.7 **1** Che appartiene o si riferisce al tempo presente o al passato immediatamente prossimo. **1.1** Uso moderno. **1.2** [In contrapposizione ad antico]. **1.3** Tempi moderni, tempo moderno, età moderna: il periodo cui appartiene il sogg. parlante o scrivente. **1.4** [Con valore cumulativo:] antico e moderno. **2** Sost. plur. Coloro che vivono e operano nel tempo presente.
0.8 Pietro G. Beltrami 12.05.2006.[45]

1 Che appartiene o si riferisce al tempo presente o al passato immediatamente prossimo.

[1] Dante, *Commedia*, a. 1321, *Par.* 16.33, vol. 3, pag. 260: con voce più dolce e soave, / ma non con questa **moderna** favella.

[2] Jacopo della Lana, *Purg.*, 1324-28 (bologn.), c. 28, 88-102, pag. 599, col. 1.6: com'è dicto, tal logo in lo stado de l'inocenzia era partí dai **moderni** atti e costumi, e però 'l demostra sovra omne impressione elementale.

[3] Ugo Panziera, *Trattati*, a. 1330 (tosc.occ.), 11, pag. 75, col. 22.8: Se io trovassi creatura alcuna la quale fusse di sensata ragione vestita perfectamente virtuosa, in croce con

[44] The various graphic and formal characteristics, and codifications that will have to be introduced in the entry (or that come directly from the database) for the future completion of the dictionary's software dedicated to its edition and publication (currently under development) will not be dealt with here.

[45] The entry is noted in paragraph 0.8 by the first editor and possibly by the others who have implemented substantial modifications, regardless of the level to which the entry has been modified in the standard revision process. The given date attests to the corpus' state at the moment of its redaction and will be changed after revisions (including those made subsequent to the publication) that have required a re-examination of the corpus. Revisions carried out without a new consultation of the corpus are marked in the online edition as "u.r." followed by the date at the end of the entry.

Christo crocifissa, senza niuna altra prerogatione, contenta di sua povertade, di lei farei quasi uno mio Dio: tanto mi sono li sancti **moderni** sospecti.

[4] *Ottimo*, *Purg*., a. 1334 (fior.), c. 26, proemio, pag. 478.23: e commenda il nuovo stilo de' trovatori **moderni**.

[5] Accurso di Cremona, 1321/37 (mess.), L. 5, cap. 8, vol. 2, pag. 56.13: furtiza virtuusa; volciru muriri di duluri apressu di li loru filloli; et zò avimu exemplu **mudernu** di misèri Antonula...

[6] Giovanni Villani (ed. Porta), a. 1348 (fior.), L. 2, cap. 6, vol. 1, pag. 72.18: assai avemo detto sopra il nostro fiume d'Arno, per trarre d'ignoranza e fare avisati i presenti **moderni** viventi di nostra città, e gli strani che sono e saranno.

1.1 Uso moderno.

[1] Dante, *Commedia*, a. 1321, *Purg*. 26.113, vol. 2, pag. 453: «Li dolci detti vostri, / che, quanto durerà l'uso **moderno**, / faranno cari ancora i loro incostri».

[2] Tommaso di Giunta, *Conc. Am*., XIV pm. (tosc.), prosa 7, pag. 25.3: Secondo che ragione mostra, l'uso **moderno** si divide in due parti: la prima parte si è l'essere rozzo et poco usante; la seconda parte si è amare.

[3] Gid. da Sommacamp., *Tratt*., XIV sm. (ver.), cap. 5, parr. 2-7, pag. 134.6: Onde, li marigali se debbonno compillare con parole vulgare e grosse ma lo sòno, osia lo canto, deli dicti marigali, secondo l'uso **moderno**, dée essere belletissimo.

1.2 [In contrapposizione ad antico].

[1] Jacopo Alighieri, *Inf*. (ed. Bellomo), 1321-22 (fior.), 5, pag. 107.15: tra' quali d'alquanti antichi e **moderni** per exempro degli altri nelle seguenti chiose procedendo si conta.

[2] Boccaccio, *Fiammetta*, 1343-44, cap. 5, par. 27, pag. 145.14: non dubito che qualunque forestiere [[...]] non giudicasse noi non donne **moderne**, ma di quelle antiche magnifiche essere al mondo tornate...

[3] Fazio degli Uberti, *Dittamondo*, c. 1345-67 (tosc.), L. 4, cap. 20.3, pag. 310: Da Parigi partiti, com'io dico, / ragionando m'andava la mia scorta / or del tempo **moderno**, or de l'antico.

[4] Petrarca, *Trionfi*, 1351(?)-74, *T. Cupidinis* III.12, pag. 209: Mentre io volgeva gli occhi in ogni parte / S' i' ne vedesse alcun di chiara fama, / O per antiche, o per **moderne** carte...

1.3 *Tempi moderni, tempo moderno, età moderna*: il periodo cui appartiene il sogg. parlante o scrivente.

[1] Giovanni Campulu, 1302/37 (mess.), L. 3, cap. 25, pag. 109.7: ma eu vollu recuntare li miraculi li quali foru facti pir alcuni patri sancti, in kisti tempi **moderni**, intra Ytalia».

[2] *Comm. Arte Am*. (A), XIV pm. (pis.), ch. 384, pag. 596.6: Mostra l'autore le cagione per le quale a llui piace la **moderna** età.

[3] Simone da Lentini, 1358 (sirac.), cap. 22, pag. 103.10: et chi Missina non era cussì grandi terra, nè cussì populata comu esti hora, lu tempu **modernu**.

[4] Boccaccio, *Decameron*, c. 1370, Proemio, pag. 5.2: Nelle quali novelle piacevoli e aspri casi d'amore e altri fortunati avvenimenti si vederanno così ne' **moderni** tempi avvenuti come negli antichi...

[5] *Stat. fior*., 1374, pag. 66.24: come al tempo **moderno** laudabilmente è consueto...

1.4 [Con valore cumulativo:] *antico e moderno*.

[1] *Stat. fior*., 1334, L. III, prol., pag. 325.8: Infrascritti sono ordinamenti che parlano sopra i fatti dell'Opere di san Giovanni, e di san Miniato predetti, e dello spedale overo

magione di santo Jacopo a santo Eusebio, retti e governati sotto l'antica e **moderna** difensione e ferma guardia della lodevole Arte e Università de' Consoli e de' mercatanti dell'Arte di Calimala della città di Firenze.

[2] Giovanni Villani (ed. Porta), a. 1348 (fior.), L. 13, cap. 44, vol. 3, pag. 400.20: e per tanti benefici fatti per lo Comune e popolo di Firenze, antichi e **moderni**, non volere esere udite niuna loro ragione...

[3] Sacchetti, *Trecentonovelle*, XIV sm. (fior.), *Proemio*, pag. 3.5: e raccogliere tutte quelle novelle, le quali, e antiche e **moderne**, di diverse maniere sono state per li tempi...

1.4.1 Locuz. avv. *Per antico e per moderno.*

[1] Sacchetti, *Trecentonovelle*, XIV sm. (fior.), 158, pag. 381.19: come sempre e per antico e per **moderno** s'è veduto nel mondo.

2 Sost. plur. Coloro che vivono e operano nel tempo presente.

[1] Dante, *Convivio*, 1304-7, IV, cap. 15, pag. 356.4: per che tale quale fu lo primo generante, cioè Adamo, conviene essere tutta l'umana generazione, ché da lui alli **moderni** non si puote trovare per quella ragione alcuna transmutanza.

[2] Armannino, *Fiorita* (07), p. 1325 (ven.), pag. 112.5: Adonca vui **moderni** non seguì le voie desolute de color che solo per cadar defende soa tinçon, mo voiè creder a queli che li suo fati guida con raxon e fermeça.

[3] *Serapiom* volg., p. 1390 (padov.), *Erbario*, cap. 347, pag. 387.16: E segondo la sentencia de li **moderni**, grani cinque basta.

The process of compilation which I have described above works well for entries with up to a thousand attestations in the corpus. For terms with a very high number of attestations, the editor is required to use his skills in order to find some method of simplification which results in an exhaustive entry that does not require too much time to create.

2.3 The redaction process that has been described in this paper gives form to an autonomous and noteworthy dictionary, but it remains temporary. Despite the many difficulties encountered, we have tried to take advantage of all the possibilities that the online version can offer[46] in order to both make this tool available to researchers as soon as possible, as well as keep the initiative afloat. And more, the online dictionary allows the editor full control on his work, i.e. the possibility of correcting, integrating and completing what he has already edited. The dates which appear in the entry allow the reader to evaluate the dictionary's process of development. Much work, however, remains to be carried out, both in increasing the number of entries and in revising and completing those which have already been compiled.

[46] The difference between dictionaries deriving from digitalised printed versions (where the online edition becomes an alternative publishing and consulting method) and online dictionaries (where the online edition is first and foremost a working method) is evident.

The dictionary's final project includes a section dedicated to the derivational, synonymic and antonymic relationships in Early Italian Lexicon, and most importantly, a section on syntactic notes;[47] however, both of these initiatives have been postponed for the time being. Due to the absence of these syntactic notes, for now the dictionary's fundamental semantic orientation remains slightly unbalanced, especially when one considers that the definitions of verbs are, for example, divided into meanings which do not take into account their intransitive, transitive or pronominal/reflexive use.

The bibliography is yet to be completed and is intended to register the presence or absence of the *TLIO*'s entries in important lexicons by comparing their dating. For the moment, the absence of this kind of annotation in the entries makes it impossible for the reader to effectively access many backdatings that could otherwise be obtained thanks to the editors' use of both first-hand sources, in addition to an exhaustive processing of electronic text in place of lexicographic sources, as well as a selective text processing. It is highly probable that future paper dictionaries will present revised dating, given that they already have access to the online *OVI* early Italian database and to at least a third of the *TLIO* published so far.

References

Barbi, Michele (1935). "Crusca Lingua e Vocabolari", in *Pan* 3, 9: 13-24 [now in *Per un grande vocabolario della lingua italiana*, Firenze, Sansoni, 1957].

Battaglia, Salvatore (1961-2002). *Grande Dizionario della Lingua Italiana*. Torino, UTET [from volume VII onwards under the direction of Giorgio Bàrberi Squarotti].

---

[47] Until summer 2004 the redaction of syntactic notes was contemporary to the compiling process, in particular those regarding verbal constructions (included in paragraph 0.5: the essay *«A» preposizione e altri problemi di sintassi* deals with these kinds of notes). Examples of such entries can be seen in the *Bollettino dell'Opera del Vocabolario Italiano* until volume VIII, 2003 and in the note at the end of § 10.1 of the editing guidelines accessible on the dictionary's website. The decision to postpone this part of the editing was due on one hand to the intention to accelerate the enlargement of the dictionary and on the other the need to re-elaborate the criteria regarding a wide and compact corpus of entries; the decision to leave these notes out of the online dictionary came later and, for this reason, they are not contained within the re-edited entries.

Beltrami, Pietro G. (1997). "Sogni e realtà della lessicografia assistita dall'informatica: il caso del *Tesoro della lingua italiana delle origini*", in *Lessicologia e lessicografia. Atti del Convegno della Società Italiana di Glottologia (Chieti-Pescara, 12-14 ottobre 1995)*. Roma, Il Calamo: 223-253.

—. (1999). "Il *Tesoro della Lingua Italiana delle Origini* e l'onomastica", in *Rivista Italiana di Onomastica* 5, 2: 349-361.

—. (2001). "L'etimologia nel *Tesoro della Lingua Italiana delle Origini*", in Benedetti, Marina (ed.). *Fare etimologia. Passato, presente e futuro nella ricerca etimologica. Atti del Convegno (Università per Stranieri di Siena, 2-3 Ottobre 1998)*. Roma, Il Calamo: 123-146.

—. (2004a). "The CNR On-line Historical Dictionary and its Tools", in Bozzi, Andrea / Cignoni, Laura / Le Brave, Jean-Louis (eds). *Digital Technology and Philological Disciplines*, Pisa, Istituti Editoriali e Poligrafici Internazionali: 21-30.

—. (2004b). "«A» preposizione e altri problemi di sintassi nel *Tesoro della Lingua Italiana delle Origini*", in *SintAnt. La sintassi dell'italiano antico. Atti del Convegno internazionale di studi (Università 'Roma Tre', 18-21 Settembre 2002)*. Roma, Aracne: 65-78.

—. (2004c). "Il *Tesoro della Lingua Italiana delle Origini* (*TLIO*) per il lessico scientifico", in Corradini, M. Sofia / Periñan, Blanca (eds). *Giornate di studio di lessicografia romanza. Il linguaggio scientifico e tecnico (medico, botanico, farmaceutico e nautico) fra Medioevo e Rinascimento. Atti del convegno internazionale (Pisa, 7-8 Novembre 2003)*. Pisa, ETS: 47-59.

—. (2005). "Il *Battaglia* visto dal cantiere del *Tesoro della Lingua Italiana delle Origini*", in Beccaria, Gian Luigi / Soletti, Elisabetta (eds). *La lessicografia a Torino dal Tommaseo al Battaglia. Atti del Convegno (Torino-Vercelli, 7-9 Novembre 2002)*. Alessandria, Edizioni dell'Orso: 309-321.

—. (2007). "La lessicografia italiana a Firenze e l'Opera del Vocabolario Italiano", in Maraschio, Nicoletta (ed.). *Firenze e la lingua italiana fra nazione ed Europa. Atti del Convegno di studi (Firenze, 27-28 maggio 2004)*. Firenze, Firenze University Press: 181-188.

Beltrami, Pietro G. / Boccellari, Andrea (2006). "Banche dati e dizionari on-line. Il *Tesoro della Lingua Italiana delle Origini* e la banca dati dell'italiano antico dell'Opera del Vocabolario Italiano", in Schweickard, Wolfgang (ed.). *Nuovi media e lessicografia storica. Atti del colloquio in occasione del settantesimo compleanno di Max Pfister (Saarbrücken, 21-22 aprile 2002)*. Tübingen, Niemeyer: 3-14.

Beltrami, Pietro G. / Fornara, Simone (2004). "Italian Historical Dictionaries: from the Accademia della Crusca to the Web", in *International Journal of Lexicography* 17, 4: 357-384.

Bruni, Francesco (1992). "La preparazione del *Grande dizionario della lingua italiana* nel carteggio tra Salvatore Battaglia e Carlo Verde", in *Medioevo Romanzo* 17: 99-133.

CLPIO = Avalle, d'Arco Silvio (ed.) (1992). *Concordanze della Lingua Poetica Italiana delle Origini*. I, Milano / Napoli, Ricciardi.

Colussi, Giorgio (1978). *Ricerche sulla lingua del Duecento e del primo Trecento: Reggenza infinitiva e temi afferenti*. Helsinki, Helsinki University Rapid Manuscript Reproduction.

—. (2007). "Il *Glossario degli Antichi Volgari Italiani* fra vecchi e nuovi strumenti", in *Bollettino dell'Opera del Vocabolario Italiano* 12: 247-254.

Crescini, Vincenzo (1886). "Ugo Angelo Canello", in *Miscellanea di filologia e linguistica dedicata alla memoria di Napoleone Caix e Ugo Angelo Canello*. Firenze, Le Monnier: 25-35.

DELI = Cortelazzo, Manlio / Zolli, Paolo (1999). *Dizionario etimologico della lingua italiana*. Bologna, Zanichelli [second edition by Manlio Cortelazzo, Michele A. Cortelazzo].

De Robertis, Domenico (1985). "L'ufficio filologico dell'Opera del Vocabolario", in *La Crusca nella tradizione letteraria e linguistica italiana*. Firenze, Accademia della Crusca: 443-451.

Esperti, Piero (1979). "Grammatichetta della lingua italiana ad uso del calcolatore", in Avalle, d'Arco Silvio (ed.). *Al servizio del vocabolario della lingua italiana*. Firenze, Accademia della Crusca: 123-187.

Fanfani, Massimo (2004). "I vent'anni del *GAVI*", in *Lingua Nostra* 65, 3-4: 89-92.

Iorio-Fili, Domenico (2006). "Per un nuovo approccio alle banche testuali online. Estratto dalla Guida di GattoWeb", in *Bollettino dell'Opera del Vocabolario Italiano* 11: 273-397.

—. (2007). "Breve storia, stato attuale e prospettive del software GATTO", in *Bollettino dell'Opera del Vocabolario Italiano* 12: 365-386.

LEI = Pfister, Max (ed.) (1979–). *Lessico Etimologico Italiano*. Wiesbaden, Reichert. [now co-directed by Wolfgang Schweickard].

Mastrelli, Carlo Alberto / Parenti, Alessandro (eds) (1999). *Giacomo Devoto nel centenario della nascita. Atti del Convegno 'Giacomo Devoto e le Istituzioni' (Firenze, 24-25 ottobre 1997)*. Firenze, Olschki.

Nencioni, Giovanni (1954). "Relazione all'Accademia della Crusca sul vocabolario della lingua italiana", in *Studi di Filologia Italiana* 13:

395-420. [now in *Per un grande vocabolario della lingua italiana*, Firenze, Sansoni (1957)].

Pasquali, Giorgio (1941). "Per un Tesoro della lingua italiana", in *Atti della R. Accademia d'Italia. Rendiconti della Classe di scienze morali e storiche*, serie 7th, 2: 490-521. [now in *Per un grande vocabolario della lingua italiana*, Firenze, Sansoni (1957)].

Pollidori, Valentina (1999). "Analisi, trattamento e codifica dei dati testuali per la base di dati del *Tesoro della Lingua Italiana delle Origini*", in *Bollettino dell'Opera del Vocabolario Italiano* 4: 375-406.

Tommaseo-Bellini = Tommaseo, Niccolò / Bellini, Bernardo (1861-1879). *Dizionario della lingua italiana*. Torino, UTET.

THE OXFORD ENGLISH DICTIONARY: WHAT DOES THE FUTURE HOLD FOR HISTORICAL LEXICOGRAPHY?

JOHN SIMPSON[1]

From the middle of the nineteenth century until the late twentieth century the models for historical lexicography, building on the developments in comparative philology, were largely static. In general, the style of historical dictionaries (including the *Deutsches Wörterbuch*, the *Woordenboek der Nederlandse Taal*, and the *OED*) reflected the scholarly and cultural perspectives of the nineteenth century.

In the last decades of the twentieth century the technology available to lexicographers began to change, and historical lexicography has subsequently been adapting to this. We are seeing significant changes in a number of different (and important) areas: in the availability of lexical data, in the ways in which this data can be processed, in the editorial techniques used to compile dictionaries, and in the mediums by which users (or readers) can interact with dictionaries.

This paper concentrates on three issues. Firstly, how will the ready availability of historical data change historical lexicography? Secondly, how will a shift away from the individual entry as the focus of lexicography affect our view of language? And thirdly, where do the lexicographer and the historical dictionary now stand in relation to the dictionary user?

All of these features are currently undergoing a profound shift. We are standing at the foothills of this change. Where will it end, and what will the lexical landscape look like once these changes have started to resonate through the world of historical lexicography?

---

[1] Images from the *OED Online* web site (http://dictionary.oed.com/) are copyright to Oxford University Press and are reproduced by kind permission of the Secretary to the Delegates of Oxford University Press.

1 Availability of Data

The examples in this paper are taken from English lexicography, but similar developments are of course occurring in the lexicography of other languages. The dominant aspect as regards data availability is the large amount of searchable text accessible online today to the lexicographer.

Traditionally, historical dictionaries have engaged in extensive sampling programmes, basing their analysis of the language on thousands or millions of index cards or slips. The relevance of the terms extracted by this technique has been dependent upon the reliability of readers and upon the accuracy of guidelines for reading laid down by lexicographers.

This reliance on human readers is necessarily flawed, and has been assessed statistically. Jürgen Schäfer's *Lexicography and the OED*,[2] for example, submitted several key historical texts to a word-by-word reading against the first edition of the dictionary, and found many occasions when readers had apparently overlooked earlier usages of words or senses of words, or had missed terms which were not in the dictionary. He provided a reader reliability rating for each text, as well as publishing apparent omissions so that lexicographers could rectify these errors. He followed this up with two substantial volumes providing information about similar errors and omissions extracted from a wider range of historical texts.[3]

The traditional reading of texts is still a significant weapon in the lexicographer's armoury. The principal reason for this is that it makes optimum use of a precious resource: the human reader. The dictionary reader brings a wealth of experience to the task. He or she is alert to the regularities and irregularities of language. When reading a contemporary text, the reader is able to identify terms which may not already be in the dictionary, and can consult the dictionary itself to ensure that a particular term is already covered, is completely new to it, or suggests a shade of meaning which appears to be emerging from those already recorded. Importantly, the reader can identify new meanings which the computer is not able to distinguish from existing senses.

Furthermore, the reader is able to judge which of several instances of a term found in a single passage is most relevant for the dictionary, as a helpful exemplar. An article on a new medicine, for example, may use the keyword frequently, but the reader is able to save the lexicographer time by reporting only on that sentence that best fits the dictionary's needs. The reader, at least in the case of experienced readers, is a vital time-saver for the lexicographer, whereas a computer is best suited to supply material in

[2] Schäfer 1980.

[3] Schäfer 1989.

quantity. It may seem strange, but "quantity" is the last thing that the hard-pressed lexicographer requires. The more there is to review, the slower the lexicographer is able to proceed. By offering a digest of the source material, the reader is able to give the lexicographer an overview without swamping him or her with too much information.

When confronting historical text, the reader needs to wear a different hat. Historical reading is complex, but rewarding, both for the reader and for the dictionary. The reader needs to be alive to the typical vocabulary of the text being read, so that any deviation from the regular triggers an alert in the reader's head which prompts him or her to consider whether this irregularity indicates a new or perhaps an obsolescent term or phrase which may be worth recording for the dictionary. On the other hand, regularity can mean that the reader should record a typical example of usage, particularly if it is the source that is noteworthy. A reference for a household term from a personal document (such as an inventory) may be more valuable to the lexicographer than one from a more stylised genre of text.

The lexicographer and reader work together to identify texts which fill gaps in the dictionary's coverage of genre. With pinpoint accuracy the lexicographer-reader combination is able to ensure that coverage of specialist areas (perhaps areas not satisfactorily or easily covered by electronic reading) is comprehensively sampled.

Traditional reading methods are nowadays used alongside computer searching, and both have their own advantages. Reading requires that enormous effort be expended on analysing a small fragment of the available data. Nowadays we are familiar with the practice of searching electronic texts, which offers some significant advantages over traditional reading. Two of the most important historical databases for English available today are the *Early English Texts Online* database[4] (*EEBO*), containing scanned and in many cases fully searchable texts from the dawn of the printed book in England in the late fifteenth century up until 1700. Following on from this database, we have the *Eighteenth Century Collections Online*[5] database (*ECCO*), which contains fully searchable texts from thousands of eighteenth-century works. *ECCO* currently has 150,000 books scanned, searchable, and available on-screen in facsimile. A search for the word *European* on this database provides 18,531 results from the eighteenth century: certainly enough to give the lexicographer a very good idea of how the word *European* operated at the time.

---

[4] http://eebo.chadwyck.com/home.

[5] http://gale.com/EighteenthCentury/.

These resources may be supplemented by many other searchable historical databases of different registers and genres of English. As time goes by, we must expect the coverage offered by databases of this type to expand, perhaps bringing the majority of printed (and even manuscript) text within the scope of the lexicographer's radar. The most significant database to appear on the scene recently is perhaps *Google Books*,[6] which offers a wide range of texts but must be used cautiously by the lexicographer because of problematic bibliographical information, copyright issues on the display of data, and the restrictive syntax of Google searching.

The emergence of such databases has had a profound effect on the revision of the *Oxford English Dictionary*, on which I and over sixty colleagues are involved in Oxford and New York. We started the revision and update in earnest in the mid nineties, when the first small historical databases were beginning to appear, in fits and starts, on the Internet. Previously our access to machine-readable texts had been primarily through computer concordances – some of which had been available in one form or another since the late 1960s.

The results from these emergent resources caused us to review the early draft revisions we had made to the *OED* in the 1990s and, after examining many of the databases then available, to re-edit entries in the light of this new historical material. The results were astounding. We were able to find considerably better documentation for many words, and thereby to improve substantially the record of the language we were documenting.

The strengths of computer searching, when compared with the human reader, are mainly in terms of the quantity of material that can be processed, the speed of that processing, and (to some extent) the variety of lexical patterns that the computer can identify. In addition, the computer is able to report suggested items for inclusion which do not seem to be already covered in the dictionary. The computer makes a broad sweep of the available data, and in doing so produces many useful results. The human reader makes a smaller, but in some ways more comprehensive, search.

Computers are strongest, at present, when processing modern text. They have more problems with the variable spelling of texts in the past. They are also less able to process historical texts of poor print quality which have been bulk-scanned. Although human readers miss things, computers, paradoxically, miss more.

---

[6] http://www.google.co.uk/books.

The various historical databases available to the editors of the *OED* today complement the older traditional methods of data collection by readers. Taken together, both methods enable the editors to establish earlier usages for between 40 and 50% of all of the terms (words, meanings, phrases, etc.) that have been revised to date (just under one quarter of the dictionary).

A case in point is the entry for the word *prescriptive*. In the first (and consequently in the second) edition of the *OED* the word *prescriptive* has the look of being a term which arose in English firmly in the middle of the eighteenth century. The evidence for the use of the earliest five senses of the word date respectively from 1748 (Samuel Richardson's *Clarissa*), 1765 (Blackstone's commentaries on the laws of England), 1765 (Samuel Johnson's prefaces to Shakespeare), 1766 (Blackstone again), and 1785 (Edmund Burke). No new senses are recorded during the nineteenth century, and two technical uses (in philosophy and anthropology) arise in the twentieth century.

One might imagine that *prescriptive* was indeed a word of eighteenth-century origin. The mid eighteenth century was a time at which, in the field of language, there was a feeling that English should be "fixed" at what was then considered to be its prime. This notion of authority and prescription permeates mid eighteenth century thought. But research using the *Early English Books Online* database allows the *OED* to show that the origins of the word *prescriptive* do not lie in the eighteenth century, but in the seventeenth. The first occurrence of the word currently dates from 1663, eighty-five years before Samuel Richardson's *Clarissa*, in the sense 'that prescribes or directs; giving definite, precise directions or instructions'. *EEBO* provided an example of the word in this meaning from *Fortescutus illustratus, or a commentary on that nervous treatise De laudibus legum angliae, written by sir John Fortescue*, by Edward Waterhouse:

> He proposes the Laws of Government, as founded upon the Law of God, Nature, and Nations, to be prescriptive of all virtue, accumulated in the fear of God.[7]

Once the word can be regarded as one originating in the seventeenth century, it is no surprise, perhaps, to find another meaning antedated to the same century. *OED*'s third sense, a legal meaning 'derived from or based on prescription or lapse of time', dated by the first edition of the *OED* from Blackstone in 1766, now appears seventy-seven years earlier in an

[7] Waterhouse 1663: 56.

account of some proposals made by the then Bishop of Salisbury, Gilbert Burnet, in his *Collection of eighteen papers, relating to the affairs of church & state, during the reign of King James the Second*:

> Upon the Restoration of Corporations to their Ancient Charters, and Burroughs to their Prescriptive Rights, He would Order Writs to be issued out for a fair and free Parliament.[8]

Several of Waterhouse's works had been read by volunteer readers for the *OED* in the nineteenth century, and he was at the time credited with the first recorded use of several words (*conferrable*, *magneticness*, etc.), but the reader who was allocated his *Fortescutus Illustratus* had overlooked the occurrence of *prescriptive*. He or she had also overlooked earlier usages by Waterhouse (1663) for other words, including *pileus* (in classical history a 'felt hat without a brim', previously dated to John Adams in 1776), *prepollency* ('predominance', dated to 1681), and the earliest recorded sense of *promiscuity* ('indiscriminate order', known earliest to the first edition of the *OED* from the work of Edgar Allan Poe in the mid nineteenth century).

There are problems with these new resources. The databases themselves are continually growing, and so they need rechecking regularly to collect new discoveries. We are finding that once we publish an entry online users search these databases themselves and send us additional findings, sometimes from online resources and sometimes from their own reading.

Recent additions to the *OED* submitted to the dictionary from such sources include some remarkable material. *OED3* had entered the term *money-changing* from 1699 (which itself was a considerable improvement on the date of 1938 provided in the relevant volume of the *Supplement to the OED* in 1976): a correspondent alerted the editors to an example from 1623, which is now in place in the online dictionary. The term *moreish* (relating to tasty food) has a modern ring to it: the *OED* dated it from Jonathan Swift's *Polite Conversation* of 1738, but a correspondent found an example forty-seven years earlier, in 1691. Predictable derivatives are often hard to track down in early uses: the *OED* had found *old-maidishness* in 1824, but again a correspondent pointed out evidence for the use of the term twenty-eight years before this, in 1796. One of the features of the online dictionary is that it continues to grow both in size and in accuracy as a result of findings supplied to the editors once each section has been revised and published online.

---

[8] Burnet 1689: 10.

The technique of searching historical and modern databases is still reliant on the human reader, even though the databases are searchable electronically. Complex computer tools are certainly available for modern text, but adequate search software is not yet available which reliably handles historical text-searching.

Furthermore, the databases which provide historical data are typically not presented with lexicographers in mind. From a historical lexicographer's point of view a simple keyword-in-context format of results (sortable according to various criteria) offers the best initial view for lexical analysis, but on most historical databases the searcher is presented with a list of texts in which the search string may be found, and then has to manoeuvre through one or more further clicks and stages to find out whether the particular hit in question is of relevance to the enquiry. It is time that a standard for the lexicographical use of historical databases was developed.

In addition, there is a problem with the scanning of older text. Some historical databases allow the user to move directly from the search results to a facsimile of the source cited. Although this is extremely useful to the lexicographer, it sometimes masks the fact that the text has not been well scanned, and so some instances of the search term may be missed during the search. Generally, those databases (such as *Early English Books Online*) which allow access to the scanned text in character form (often as well as in facsimile) are likely to contain more accurately scanned and often proofread text.

The publishers of historical text databases do show some awareness of searchers' needs. When *EEBO* first went online, simple text searching resulted in a display of texts in which the search word could be found. More recently the search output has been modified so that the user sees the details of the work as well as a string of text including the search word, in context. This is extremely helpful for the lexicographer, but is still not as useful as a keyword-in-context display, in which a screenful of text strings including the keyword is presented, with the key words aligned in a central column. Once these search lines are sorted according to relevant criteria (for example, by the following word, in alphabetical order), the linguist is more easily able to identify syntactical patterns. The fact that these databases are so large means that any means of simplifying the task of analysis is very welcome.

A key shortcoming at the moment is that computer-based resources are most helpful in researching lexical items which the lexicographer has already identified. The traditional reading of texts has the benefit that the reader can address texts which are not (yet) available online, and can identify new meanings in a source – something that computer programmes are not particularly adept at accomplishing. It should also be noted that unqualified, amateur readers are likely to misinterpret evidence, so that the lexicographer has to reject some offerings. There is still a valuable place for the traditional reading of texts by eye, by expert, trained readers, in search of new lexical features which the computer is less able to recognise.

A brief survey of documentary material entering the revised *OED* through the dictionary's reading of historical sources in printed format shows the value of this time-honoured technique. The first documented example of the word *Nuremberger* (a native or inhabitant of Nuremberg) in the first (and consequently the second) edition of the *OED* comes from John Ray's *Observations Made in a Journey through Part of the Low Countries, Germany, Italy, and France* (1673). This seems a credible source for a first reference: a travel text which describes a journey outside Britain. And yet the reading of historical sources for *OED3* reveals that the term (in the form *Norimberger*) appears forty-one years earlier in the *Swedish Intelligencer* of 1632 (again a text dealing with matters outside Britain). But predatings are often found on home turf. *OED1* documents the term *pig market* from 1681 (in an extended use foreshadowing a meaning specific to Oxford University). But *OED3*'s reading of *Mercurius Electicus* (1647) provides a thirty-four year antedating:

1. A market held for the sale of pigs; a place where such a market is held; (also) the trade in pigs generally.

1647 *Mercurius Electicus* 12–19 Nov. 23 This unworthy fellow Lilly: who deserves..to be whipt about the Pig-market. ***a*1679** R. Wild *Benefice* (1689) I. 8 A Discourse like that between Dr. Faustus and the Devil, or two or three Men in a Pig-Market.—That's a Dialogue. **1701** *Refl. on Jacobite Plot* 19 K. James will whip him about the

The same story continues throughout the revised section of the dictionary: discoveries made through an examination of online historical texts are counterbalanced by discoveries unearthed by traditional reading (see also, for example, *maladministration*, *misintelligence*, *officiate*, *post-free*, etc.). And while the sum total of printed historical texts remains constant, new texts are constantly being made available from manuscript, and the dictionary's readers can search through these looking for new material for the *OED*. Two excellent sources of this type which have been published recently are H.L. Blackmore's *Armouries of the Tower of London* (1976), full of the vocabulary of soldiery (and many other matters), and David Starkey's *Inventory of King Henry VIII: Society of Antiquaries MS 129 and British Library MS Harley 1419* (1998), documenting an extensive list from the household material possessed by

Henry VIII. Neither of these texts make easy reading for the novel-lover, but both contain a mass of vital information on vocabulary and spelling variation for the historical lexicographer.

To summarise this section on the availability of data: there is plenty of scope for improvement in the future. More texts will become available, which will tend to make lexicographers' online searches (and their subsequent entries) more complete and accurate. The types of text available will expand, taking in more ephemeral and manuscript sources, documenting local and informal vocabulary much more extensively than the range of more formal texts currently available. Alongside this, the human reader will continue to provide a valuable service to the lexicographer, highlighting nuances which evade the computer's processing, and working through important records which are not available for computer scanning. By using both of these methods, lexicographers and historical dictionary users will see further into the lives of everyday people through their vocabulary as more of these informal and personal documents become readily accessible. Entries for individual words will become more accurate reflections of the language.

But where does this mass of available data leave the lexicographer? With better data with which to construct entries, the lexicographer is now much more able to concentrate on the central aspects of lexicography: analysing meaning from evidence, preparing accurate and elegant definitions, and thinking more widely about the words under review and their place more generally within the language.

2 The Shift in Focus from the Dictionary Entry to the Language Itself

The second area of change that can be identified is a shift in focus from the individual dictionary entry to the network of words included in a dictionary, and hence to the whole assemblage of words in the language. Traditional lexicography is very entry-based. Lexicographers have stored information alphabetically, and have worked in a relentless alphabetical progression through the lexicon. The lexicographer responds to the evidence about each term, and reflects that in the resultant entry.

Traditional lexicography has certainly developed strategies for linking words together, and the most successful of these is the cross-reference, whether it appears in an etymology, a definition, or elsewhere in an entry. In outline form the cross-reference enables all readers to move rapidly around the network of links, in their online version possibly allowing them to recognise connections far more readily than in print. In a similar but more far-reaching way, modern tools for lexicographical editing have allowed the editor to break out of the alphabetical strait-jacket, and to compare and edit clusters of related words at the same time.

The individual entry is still, of course, a major focus of interest for the user, but historical dictionaries present information not only about particular words, but also about the language as a whole. Before the advent of the CD-ROM, and subsequently the Internet, much of this information was locked inside the dictionary and was therefore inaccessible to users. Users (and indeed lexicographers) were so used to regarding a dictionary simply as a repository of information about individual words that this wider perspective was often forgotten.

In future we can expect to see this situation change dramatically, and this change will be led by lexicographers and linguists. Once users realise the wealth of information that is locked away in a dictionary, their appreciation of the depth of information presented will shift significantly. But lexicographers cannot expect users to master the techniques needed to uncover this hidden information themselves. It will have to be presented to them easily by means of a helpful interface.

One of the advantages of the use of corpus tools in lexical analysis is that they broaden the perspective of the lexicographer, and hence of the dictionary user. The problem with data is that there is typically too much of it. Even the old-fashioned reading programmes were based on a system of sampling. Sampling continues, necessarily, in the computer analysis of modern text, but the results of analysis by computer tools allows the lexicographer to pick up lexical trends based on a far larger sample of data than was imaginable only ten years ago.

Once again, this highlights the language rather than the entry. By seeing with which other words a given term interacts (through proximity, syntax, or any other feature that the tools are written to investigate), the lexicographer is continually reminded that words do not exist in isolation, but are part of a network stretching across the language, and across linguistic boundaries into other languages. Our ability to regard a word as part of such a network will be crucial to how we regard dictionaries, and language, in the future.

Historical dictionaries contain much more than information about individual words. As noted above, the key word here is "trend". And the key aspect of user access is simplicity. The user needs to be presented with easy ways to analyse these trends and patterns.

Historical dictionaries typically hold information about when a word, or a sense of a word, was first recorded in the language. By processing this information locked inside the dictionary, it is relatively simple to provide a listing of words which entered the language in a particular year or other time period. Instantly, the user is presented with food for thought. This type of word was entering English in the early sixteenth century. Why was that? What were the social and cultural conditions which tended to promote this type of borrowing at this particular time? Was this perhaps a period in which borrowing was on the decrease, and native formations were on the increase? How was the profile of the language affected by external events: travel, wars, developments in the arts or sciences, etc.? The dictionary will not give the answers, but it will provide substantial data for analysis.

The following charts give some impression of one type of graphic illustration which a historical dictionary can provide.[9] The data is taken for a small subset of the revised *Oxford English Dictionary*: specifically the range of words between *pomander* and *prajnaparamita* first published online in December 2006.

The first chart below shows how many senses (and then words) entered English in each of the listed time frames, according to new *OED* evidence. Note the low figure for Old English (few words in Old English begin with the letter *P*), and the drop illustrated in the eighteenth century (a real fact of language use at the time or a curiosity of *OED*'s data?).

	senses	**words**
Old English	44	27
Middle English	779	348
1500-99	870	343
1600-99	1141	444
1700-99	859	257
1800-99	2556	688
1900-	1967	551

Tagging embedded within the dictionary text has been used to extract information relevant to the etymologies of the 2,500 or so words in this alphabetical range. As a result of this, we can see that out of 2,658 main

9 http://dictionary.oed.com/news/updates/revisions0612.html (*OED Online* December 2006). I am indebted to my colleague, Dr Philip Durkin, the *OED*'s Chief Etymologist, for assistance in analysing the data used in these illustrations.

entries, 820 are borrowed into English (wholly or partly) from another language (= 31% of the total):

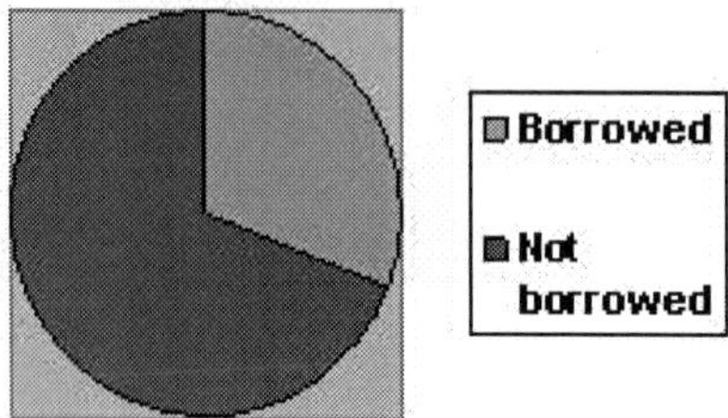

In addition, 103 main entries are borrowed (wholly or partly) from personal or place names, and 70 further entries are (wholly or partly) calqued on models in foreign languages.

Within this revised range the number of borrowings from various languages is as follows:

Latin	347
French	265
Latin and French jointly	47
Greek	44
German	29
Italian	22
Spanish	16
Dutch	15
Portuguese	9
Other	65 (in no case more than 5)

Yet again the numbers show that the borrowed words in this range are dominated by those from Romance languages, with Latin and French derivations leading the group.

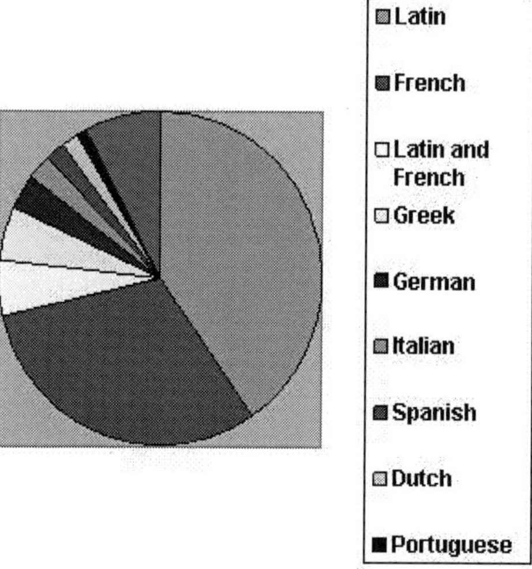

It is also possible to examine the data by time period. The following charts shows activity in the sixteenth century (351 main entries, of which 125 (36%) are borrowings) contrasted with the twentieth century (538 entries, of which only 56 (10%) are borrowings):

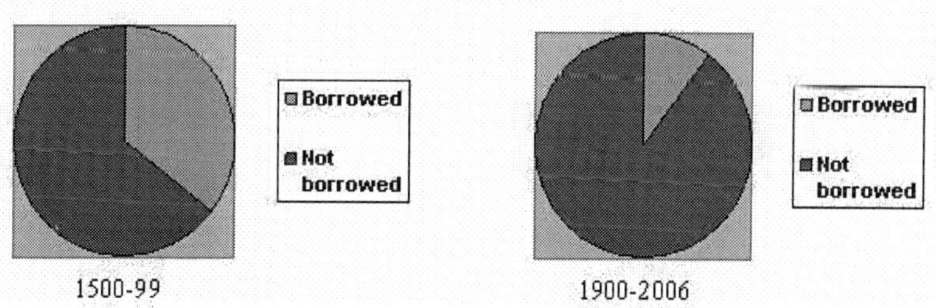

As work on the dictionary progresses, it will be fascinating to see how these figures change: whether, for example, modern words are much less likely to be borrowed, or what percentage the dictionary eventually gives (when fully revised) for the relative balance of Romance- and Germanic-based words.

Let us take a specific example. The word *powder* has a long history in English. It is one of the many words which entered English in the Middle Ages. The etymology for the revised entry for the word in *OED3* shows this network of relationships prior to English. Etymology is currently the most advanced area of historical lexicography in terms of links outside an entry. The etymology of an entry, if sufficiently comprehensive, can take the reader on a journey back through time amongst numerous languages, linking English, for example, with French, German, Italian, Spanish, and even further afield into languages which are more "exotic" (from the European perspective).

The example below shows the etymology of the word *powder* as it appeared in the first edition of the *OED* (1907):

> [ME. a. F. *poudre* (13th c.):—earlier OF. *poldre, puldre*:—*polre* (11-12th c.):—L. *pulver-em* (in nom. *pulvis*, whence It. *polve*, Sp. *polvo*, Pr. *pols*) dust. In 15-16th c. F. usually spelt *pouldre* (*l* re-inserted after L.); so, in 15-17th c. Eng., *poulder*, etc. With *pouther* cf. Sc. *shouther* = *shoulder*; also *father, mother, gather, hĭther*, with ð for d before *-er*.]

The original derivation takes the reader backwards from the point of entry into English. The immediate donor language is stated as French (where the older French forms with *–ld-* help to explain early variant spellings in English such as *poulder* and *pulder*). But the etymology takes the reader back yet further, to the Latin source of the French word. Links are then demonstrated in the entry to those other Romance languages which are indebted to Latin for their version of the word, parallel to its emergence in French. These parallel Romance forms appear in Italian (*polve*), Spanish (*polvo*), and Portuguese (*pols*). The remainder of the etymology concentrates on an analysis of various variant spellings found in English.

This example shows clearly the scope for linkage between the *OED* and other national dictionaries at the level of etymology.

The revised etymology of the word *powder* in *OED3* (2007) takes this analysis several stages further:

> [< Anglo-Norman *pudre, podre, poudre, poudere, pudere, poure, puldre* and Old French *poldre, puldre, pulre*, Middle French *poudre, pouldre, poulre, poure* (French *poudre*) dust (1100-71), finely ground substance (*a*1190-71), medicinal powder (13th cent.), cosmetic in powder form (1328-71), gunpowder (1361-71; 1367-71 in *poudre à canon*; 1690 in *sentir la poudre à canon* (of a geographical area) to stand in extreme danger at the first declaration of war) < classical Latin *pulver-, pulvis* dust (see PULVER *n.*). Cf. Old Occitan *polvera* (early 13th cent.; also *poldra* (14th cent. in an isolated attestation, prob. < French)), Catalan *pólvora*, †*pólvera* (both 13th cent.), Italian *polvere* (12th or 13th cent.); cf. also Middle French *poulce* POUCE *n.* and cognates cited at that entry.
>
> With the change of postvocalic /d/; to /ð/; before /ər/ in *β* forms cf. note at MOTHER *n.*'
>
> Recorded in surnames in the late 13th cent. (William *le Poudre* (1260-7), Johannes *le Poudere* (1294-7), Galfrido *pouder* (1296-7)), but these more probably reflect the Anglo-Norman than the Middle English word.]

The immediate donor language for English is now seen to be Anglo-Norman, the variety of French used especially in courtly, administrative, and legal contexts in England after the Norman Conquest. The forms documented here tie in with the variant spellings found in early English, emphasising the essential continuity of the word. Old French and Middle French are also given as parallel sources, reminding the reader that etymology is not a simple science, and that words can have more than one source during their complex passage from one language to another. Furthermore, as far as is possible the dating of the relevant senses of the word in these languages is provided, so that the reader can start to plot the detailed relationship between English and various varieties of French at the point of transmission and afterwards. Yet again the source of the French word is shown to be Latin (this time clarified as classical rather than later Latin), and parallel developments from the Latin elsewhere in Europe are documented. Tellingly, the revised etymology also points out several words ultimately derived from Latin *pulvis* which have also found a place in English (the nouns *pouce* and *pulver*), which assists in broadening the network of *powder* in English: in the case of the cross-reference to *pouce* this introduces a group of words derived from the nominative stem of Latin *pulvis*, a link which is missing from *OED1*.

At present most dictionaries are stand-alone texts. And yet etymologies bridge the gap between one language and those from which it has borrowed words. It is not difficult to envisage an environment in which an etymology in one dictionary is linked through the Internet to related etymologies (and hence related words) in the national dictionaries of other languages. Immediately the focus changes from the individual entry to language as a whole, and the reader is made much more conscious of the interrelatedness of national lexicons.

The *Oxford English Dictionary* is moving along these lines at the moment, though only in a small way. Through collaboration with the *Dictionary of Old English* at Toronto we have been looking forward to the time when entries in the 'Old English dictionary' will be linked online to the equivalent *OED* entry. The linkage became live in January 2008, and users of the online *Dictionary of Old English* (currently available from the letters *A* to *G*)[10] are able to move easily from the entry for a word in the 'Old English dictionary' to its equivalent entry in the *OED*. This process could doubtless be extended in the future to many other dictionaries.

To help bring this about, the *OED* might seek to develop closer relationships with other national dictionaries, so that the user can pass from one entry in the *OED* to equivalent entries elsewhere. Etymologies

---

[10] http://www.doe.utoronto.ca/.

are the most obvious links. It would be possible to imagine establishing a central master list (or union list) of words, from which links could go to any historical (or other) dictionary which contains the word. But we probably don't need to go this far, as it would be relatively easy to link the relevant entries programmatically, so that the user is taken from the *OED*'s entry for, say, *magazine*, to the equivalent entry (*magasin/magazin*) in the *Trésor* and the *Deutsches Wörterbuch*. That would be a great step forward for users of online dictionary resources. Once at the target dictionary, the user should then be able to track equivalent links within the target language (and outwards again to other dictionaries and associated resources).

This of course puts a further burden on (or presents a further challenge to) the lexicographer. If users can access, through a chain of links, a number of other dictionaries edited at different times by different editors or editorial teams, then the user will expect consistency between the information provided by the various linked dictionaries. Lexicographers will need to make sure that their dictionaries remain up to date. Indeed, this may bring a further convergence in styles between the various national and other dictionaries, facilitating easier comprehension by the external user of the various dictionaries' contents.

The English word *powder* can stand as a good example of links possible "within" a language, and these links often represent starting points for further language research and appreciation. The noun *powder* stands at the centre of a network of related English words. Those words which are alphabetically adjacent are easy to find in a printed and online dictionary. Some are nested within the same entry (*powder canister*, *powder charge*, *powder maker*, *powder mark*, *powder measure*, *powder scales*, etc.): there are almost 90 such terms listed in the *OED*'s entry for *powder*. Each is provided with documentation showing the extent of the term's life in English.

One such example is *powder house*, recorded from the mid fifteenth century to the present day:

powder house *n.* a building for storing gunpowder or other explosive material; also *fig.*

1461 in *Cal. Patent Rolls Edward IV* (1897) I.23 *Powederhous. **1626** in B. W. Quintrell *Maynard Lieutenancy Bk.* (1993) I. 143 Wee finde..an intention to build..a second powther house. **1720** in *Mass. House of Representatives Jrnl.* (1921) **2** 288 Daniel Powning, keeper of the Powder-House. **1848** *Knickerbocker* **18** 216 The powder house, the pound, the poor-house and the county-house, are all objects of notice to the traveller. **1928** *Manch. Guardian Weekly* 7 Sept. 181/4 The spark that fired this powder-house was a letter protesting against the 'constant criticism' of the methods of Lancashire cricketers. **1997** *Archaeology* Sept.-Oct. 100/2 It was a self-sufficient complex that included a..powder house and proofing house (where the muskets were test fired).

Another is *powder-mill*, noted in English from the mid seventeenth century until the present day, and with a French parallel form from the seventeenth century:

powder-mill *n.* [cf. French *moulin à poudre* machine for grinding an explosive mixture of saltpetre, sulphur, and charcoal (*a*1630)] now chiefly *hist.* a mill for making gunpowder.

1650 R. STAPYLTON tr. F. Strada *De Bello Belgico* VII. 40 These *Powder-Milles used to be distant from Townes. **1772** G. WHITE *Jrnl.* 5 Jan. (1970) v. 47 The concussion felt Jan.: 6..was occasioned by the blowing-up of the powder-mill near Hounslow. **1856** R. W. EMERSON *Eng. Traits* xv. 264 We walked with some circumspection, as if we were entering a powder-mill. **1951** N. PEVSNER *Middlesex* 115 The famous old powder mills have alas been pulled down. **2004** *Kent & Sussex Courier* (Nexis) 19 Mar., It is 70 years since the production of gunpowder stopped at Leigh powder mills, costing many local jobs.

The possibilities for linkage between the various component parts of these compounds, on a journey of discovery through English vocabulary and its associated culture, are almost endless.

From the point of view of the individual word, the network of language expands in ever-increasing circles. The items listed above are nested within the entry for *powder*. Alongside these, there are many more which do not form part of the same entry, but are found alphabetically adjacent to *powder*. This new circle of words includes more significant compounds which have headword status in their own right, and derivative terms which have arisen from the base noun *powder*.

Amongst this set may be found the verb *powder*, which is first recorded in Middle English slightly after the noun, and may be in part derived from the equivalent Anglo-Norman verb. In addition, we find *powderable*, *powderal*, *powder bag*, *powder barrel*, *powder blue*, etc. As one would expect, these arrive in English after the noun *powder*, on whose existence they depend. Their arrival can be plotted in a "genealogical" tree with the noun at the head, demonstrating the immediate network of words dependent upon *powder*. An analysis of these adjacent terms is necessary to enlarge our understanding of the place of *powder* in the dictionary and in the language. Examination of the second elements of these compounds and derivatives also extends the network of linkage significantly.

The next formal circle to which the reader can move involves compounds and other terms which include the element *powder*, but which are not physically adjacent to the base noun in the dictionary. The language is not bound by alphabetical order, and so their position elsewhere in the alphabet is largely irrelevant in terms of our understanding of the significance of *powder* in the language.

Members of this third-level set of terms include *baby powder*, *baking powder*, *bepowder*, *to beat to a powder*, *cubical powder*, *custard powder*, and *empowder*. In fact, the *OED Online* shows 218 such terms lurking quietly in the dictionary at some distance from the base *powder*.

The network of links can expand rapidly for major words in the language. If the genealogical tree were expanded to include all of these, then it would have extensive ramifications, both literally and in terms of lexical influence.

But the formal existence of this network is only the start of any analysis. There are many further implications which can be investigated. Chronologically, the existence of this network allows the reader to determine periods and spheres of importance for the set of terms. Perhaps more significantly, the changing subjects with which many of these terms are associated suggest to the user how the words interact with the culture of the times in which they were first used and subsequently developed. For *powder* we see that the word is important, for example, in the technical world of chemistry and pharmacy. But more importantly we see the word emerging from technical use into the routine, everyday life of speakers of English (baby-care, cookery, etc.).

Formal links based on orthography are only one way in which the reader can explore the network of associations building outwards into the language from a particular word. Another branch of the network is the chronological one, and this is an especial feature of historical dictionaries.

The entry for *powder*, to continue the analysis with this word, indicates that it was first recorded in English around the year 1300. The historian of language and culture immediately asks why the word was found necessary at this time, and what were the conditions of its arrival. Some of this information is obscure to the modern-day reader; other facets have been glimpsed from the etymological details of the word. But the historian can also look sideways, at other words which entered English at around the same time, in order to see whether some form of pattern emerges which bolsters other information about the word.

In the case of *powder* we find, from the *OED Online*, a large number of other words which entered English at the end of the thirteenth century. Examples include *madam*, *majesty*, *manor*, *mariner*, *marvel*, *mattress*, *maudlin*, *maugre*, *melody*, *member*, and *message*. This selection is just a short sample of the many words first recorded from this period in the history of English. It serves to remind the reader of the principal concerns of the English-speaking peoples at the time, when Anglo-Norman and French words from the ruling tier of society were passing easily into the language, often at the expense of, or in parallel with, other native Germanic words. A similar synchronic slice can be obtained from any other period of English, testifying to the concerns of language-users at any era of their history. The interconnectedness of language and society gradually becomes more apparent the wider we throw our net across the language.

The foregoing examples take etymology, orthography, and chronology as their starting points. There are other strands which can also be explored. It would be surprising if the reader of a dictionary were not able to follow a semantic trail, and the results here open up other areas of investigation.

One of the key words in the primary definition of *powder* is 'dust'. We can take this term as our lead. The *OED* contains 464 definitions in which the term 'dust' is used. The words defined take the reader into another area of the influence of *powder* on the language. A selection of these words includes *angel*, *ash*, *brush*, *cloud*, *grain*, and *gun*. Needless to say there are many other more obscure words which interrelate with 'dust' semantically, either as direct semantic parallels or as terms for which 'dust' occurs as a less significant aspect of the definition (a potential object of a transitive verb, for example). In the same way that it is often said that any two humans can be linked genealogically or by some other form of association in a remarkable short number of links, so the same – it is beginning to appear – may be said of words.

The *OED* also allows various other forms of linkage (by cited work or author, by subject labeling, etc.). The upshot of this analysis is that we should not focus our attention exclusively on the insular details of a particular word, but should look at words not just in the context of the text in which they occur, but also in that of the wider language (and the languages with which English interacts).

We can extend this type of analysis to other areas: to synonyms, perhaps. How does a language cope not just with change of meaning, but with the introduction of new words to replace or supplement older ones with the same meaning? For English, the *Glasgow Historical Thesaurus of English*[11] (largely based on the *OED*) offers the prospect of links between semantically related words. If this concept were extended to other dictionaries (by manual or computational methods) then we would be in a much better position to observe types of semantic change over time.

Much the same might be said about the links between subject, register, and other characteristics to which we apply labels in a dictionary, or between words typically used by particular writers or genres. Although this information can provide data about the individual dictionaries in which it is contained, it can offer far more information about the interrelationship of words and their use and the language as a whole.

---

[11] http://www.arts.gla.ac.uk/SESLl/EngLang/thesaur/homepage.htm.

In summary, once we have established the notion of the dictionary as an index to the experience of language users, we can start to see the dictionary as a central resource or hub in a network of texts. Historical dictionaries cite excerpts of the data on which they are based. We are beginning to see links outwards from dictionaries to these and other texts. The user will be presented with a historical dictionary which is a portal to a much wider world of information. This may be a scanned and searchable version of a text cited in the dictionary, or it may be information of a different type: not just encyclopaedic and bibliographical sources, but even stock exchange data or astronomical tables. The dictionary contains information on all subjects, and any external source becomes relevant to our experience of the language.

So having looked at the availability of data and a proposed shift of interest away from the dictionary entry as a focus of concern towards the language as a whole, we can now ask what effect this will have on the relationship between the lexicographer, or the linguist, and the ordinary or academic user.

3 The Changing Relationship between the Lexicographer and the User

The last section placed the lexicographer at the centre of a nexus of dictionaries, texts, analytical software, and the real world. In the past, the user had little direct communication with the lexicographer, except in the case of those few scholars who were kind enough to send the lexicographers their proposed corrections.

But nowadays the large national dictionaries are available, for the most part, through the Internet. The audience is suddenly much wider: not just scholars and students in libraries, but anyone who can (and wishes to) access the dictionary.

For lexicographers and publishers this accessibility brings with it a challenge: to present these complex texts in such a way that the enlarged readership can understand, while at the same time not oversimplifying or "dumbing down" the content.

Fortunately this increased accessibility comes at a time when the role of the dictionary is changing, from a single look-up resource to one which links together words, language, and the wider world of language use. By introducing new interfaces to query the dictionary data, lexicographers can make it easier for users to find and extract information which they previously did not realise was locked inside the dictionary.

The reach of the dictionary as a pedagogical tool in schools and colleges will expand significantly, as students (and teachers) see how information about words can inform their understanding of other disciplines. Students will start to see the historical dictionary as an approachable resource, rather than one which is academic and rather forbidding.

At the same time, the amount of two-way communication between lexicographers and users will increase, and this is of particular benefit for the dictionary, as users often have specific information which would be of use to the dictionary.

The beginnings of this process can be seen in an initiative which the *Oxford English Dictionary* recently established. There is now a web site containing information about science-fiction terms in the *OED*,[12] and inviting readers to submit better information – earlier examples, sharper information on definitions, etc. The results have been excellent, and they are being incorporated in the *OED* as it is being revised. In addition, a book of these findings, *Brave New Words*, was published in 2007.[13]

Here are some of the references earlier than those currently in the *OED* for words from the area of science fiction. *Lunarscape* is recorded in the *OED* from 1965 («No one knows in detail what the lunarscape is like»: *Newsweek* 25 Jan., p. 89). It means 'a picture or view of the moon's surface; the lunar landscape'. The following text now appears on the *OED*-related science-fiction site:[14]

Earliest cite	Bernard I. Kahn, 'For The Public'
Comment	Mike Christie submitted a 1946 cite from Bernard I. Kahn's "For The Public". (Earliest cite in OED2: 1965).
Last modified	4 June, 2006

Citations for lunarscape n.

click here for more information about the citation list

1946 B. I. Kahn *For Public* in *Astounding Sci. Fiction* Dec. 94/2	I don't want to chase the thing over the lunarscape to find a test-tube.

Another page evidences even more activity. The term *earthgirl* is not yet entered in the *OED*. Readers of science fiction clearly feel that it should be there:[15]

---

[12] http://www.jessesword.com/sf/home.

[13] Prucher 2007.

[14] http://www.jessesword.com/sf/view/2069 (site visited 26 January 2008).

[15] http://www.jessesword.com/sf/view/2069 (site visited 26 January 2008).

Definition	a girl or woman from the planet Earth
OED requirements	antedating 1936
Earliest cite	A. Macfadyen, Jr., 'The Time Decelerator'
Comment	Fred Galvin submitted a 1942 cite from Ray Cummings's "Gods of Space". Fred Galvin submitted a 1950 cite from John D. MacDonald's "Shadow on the Sand". Fred Galvin submitted a 1955 cite from Jack Vance's "Meet Miss Universe". Fred Galvin submitted a cite from a 1982 reprint of Jack Vance's 1945 "The World-Thinker"; Mike Christie verified it in the original magazine appearance. Fred Galvin submitted a 1947 cite from "James MacCreigh's" "Donovan Had a Dream". Fred Galvin submitted a 1947 cite from Henry Hasse's "Trail of the Astrogar". Fred Galvin submitted a cite from a 1975 reprint of A. Macfadyen, Jr.'s 1936 "The Time Decelerator"; Mike Christie verified the first magazine appearance in the July 1936 Astounding Stories. Fred Galvin submitted a cite from a 1959 reprint of Robert Silverberg's "The Planet Killers" (originally published in 1957 as "This World Must Die!". Fred Galvin submitted a 1946 cite from John Douglas' "Futura". Fred Galvin submitted a 1949 cite from Thornecliffe Herrick's "The Lost World". Fred Galvin submitted a 1956 cite from Milton Lesser's "Meet Miss Solar System". Fred Galvin submitted a 1951 cite from Sylvia Jacobs's "The Pilot and the Bushman". Fred Galvin located a reference to the story "The Earth Girl" by Carroll K. Michenor (Weird Tales, 12/1924); we would like to obtain a cite from this story.

Such a mass of early evidence does indeed suggest that the editors of the dictionary should turn their attention to *earthgirl*, as there is little doubt that it has a firm place in the vocabulary of science fiction.

It would be good to see this sort of research extended to other areas. The idea has been mooted for some time now of the *OED* supporting a "wiki", allowing general access to all users. Such a facility could permit users to enter potential antedatings, new words or meanings, suggested amendments to definitions, etc. in such a way that other users (as well as the editors) could immediately benefit. Lexicographical teams do not have the resources to search every available book and online database for better evidence of the words on which they are working. They publish what they can find, and users (who often have parallel access to these resources) search through them and send their findings to the lexicographer for analysis and incorporation in the dictionary. The ordinary user thus becomes in some sense a part of the lexicographical team, working remotely and supplying additional information, in much the same democratic way in which volunteer readers have contributed to the development of the dictionary over the past century by providing material for the editors to review. The basic dictionary text needs to remain under the control of the lexicographers, but it is certainly possible to imagine establishing a site at which anyone can add their discoveries for others to see and for the lexicographers to review and incorporate as appropriate.

In passing it is relevant to note that the *OED* has, for the past two or three years, accepted quotations from web sources – even, on rare occasions, from blogs. So language users do not need to be traditionally published authors to see their contribution to the language reflected in the dictionary.

A good example of this occurs at the *OED*'s revised entry for the informal noun *pore* ('a careful or close examination'). The word is rarely encountered in written text, and so it was difficult for the dictionary to find a modern example of the term to demonstrate that it was not obsolete (or a nonce-use). The first edition of the dictionary had, over a hundred years ago, only been able to find one example, from a daily newspaper of 1871. As today's editors were not able to provide any further examples from traditional printed text, they turned to the Internet, and the (occasional) modern history of the colloquial term *pore* in this sense is now instanced by a quotation taken from the net:[16]

2006 *www.dogbomb.co.uk* (O.E.D. Archive) 18 May, Having had a pore over the BB website, both..went on record saying they wouldnt have taken the money.

A copy of this quotation was retained in the *OED*'s archive, in case (as often happens in such instances) it should disappear from the Internet, and not be available for verification by subsequent researchers. In the case of this quotation, though it is no longer part of an active web discussion, it has been archived on the Internet, and so it still available for general review.

Another aspect to be borne in mind is the changing expectations of users. As access to dictionary resources grows, lexicographers will need to appreciate that users typically want a one-stop resource, and they want to key in a simple string and to receive the results that fit with what they are researching. They will not want to scroll through many pages to refine their results. This again is something that lexicographers need to bear closely in mind when designing online enquiry systems.

But the biggest change for the user in the future may be that access to the dictionary will not necessarily come about through direct access to the *OED* or another major dictionary resource. The dictionary will stand as a gatehouse offering access to many different types of texts. The user may be researching one line of enquiry, and find that the next link will be through the dictionary, to collect a piece of information (on a word, or on a pattern or trend of language, perhaps), before moving on elsewhere in the dictionary or on and out into a different resource.

National historical dictionaries now have, therefore, a great chance to expand their utility. They can break away from being simple look-up points for information, and can become the centre of a much wider world of information and knowledge, in the hands of users and readers who appreciate the need to see things from a new, higher perspective. Anything lexicographers and students of lexicography can do to further this

[16] http://dictionary.oed.com/cgi/entry/50184282 (site visited 26 January 2008).

objective will be of substantial service to the academic and general community of users.

References

Primary Sources

Burnet, Gilbert (1689). *Collection of eighteen papers, relating to the affairs of church & state, during the reign of King James the Second.* London, John Starkey and Richard Chriswell.

Waterhouse, Edward (1663). *Fortescutus illustratus, or a commentary on that nervous treatise De laudibus legum angliae, written by sir John Fortescue.* London, Roycroft.

Secondary Sources

Prucher, Jeff (2007). *Brave New Words:The Oxford Dictionary of Science Fiction.* Oxford, Oxford University Press.

Schäfer, Jürgen (1980). *Documentation in the O.E.D: Shakespeare and Nashe as Test Cases.* Oxford, Clarendon Press.

—. (1989). *Early Modern English Lexicography*, 2 vols. Oxford, Clarendon Press.

RESEARCH AND RESOURCE ENHANCEMENT IN FRENCH LEXICOGRAPHY: THE ATILF LABORATORY'S COMPUTERISED RESOURCES

JEAN-MARIE PIERREL AND ÉVA BUCHI

1 Introduction

During the second half of the twentieth century, a number of major contributions to French lexicography were developed in Nancy, first within the *Centre de Recherche pour un Trésor de la Langue Française* (CRTLF), then within the *Institut National de la Langue Française* (INaLF). The present research institute, *Analyse et Traitement Informatique de la Langue Francaise* (ATILF, www.atilf.fr), aspires to become the latter's rightful successor.

Initiated as a result of the *Trésor de la Langue Française* project (*TLF*) – the main lines of which we return to in section 2.1 – the work carried out in Nancy on French lexicography has now gone further. Beyond the compilation of the TLF, research has gone in two additional directions: historical lexicography and the computerised enhancement of existing resources. In the following pages, we assess the results of this work by presenting, in order:

- The *Trésor de la Langue Française Informatisé* (*TLFi*), which is the computerised enhancement (on CD-Rom and on the Web) of the authoritative *TLF* dictionary (see paragraph 2.1). But it goes far beyond the simple computerisation of the *TLF*'s printed version. This project has laid the foundations for a new way of exploring lexicographical data, giving rise to genuinely innovative modes of interpretation. It has injected new life into this great dictionary, now undoubtedly the most widely consulted institutional French dictionary on the Web.
- The *Dictionnaire du Moyen Français* (*DMF*), decisively links computerised development with historical lexicography (see section 3). It aims at filling the gap left between Tobler / Lommatzsch (for the earlier period) and Huguet (for classical French). It describes French

vocabulary between 1330 and 1500, and is based on a concept of *evolving lexicography* (Martin 2007:1), made possible nowadays by computerisation.

- Other recent developments in historical lexicography (see section 4), more precisely the *TLF-Étym* programme, which aims at progressively revising the *TLF*'s "Etymology and history" sections; the *Base des Mots-fantômes*, a critical metalexicographical project seeking to list the *ghost words* or *fantasmas lexicográphicos* (Pascual Rodríguez / García Pérez 2007:170), i.e. all the pseudo-lexemes with an erroneous lexicographical status ("the words that do not exist"), the ghost meanings and the wrong lemmatisations found in French historical and etymological reference dictionaries; finally, the *Bibliographie Godefroy*, which aims to identify the obscure sigla within the immense documentary bulk of the Godefroy dictionary. It does so either by cross-referring to more explicit abbreviations, or by philological work on the publications – and even the manuscripts, though more rarely – which include the various texts concerned.
- Finally, the *Portail Lexical* of the Centre National de Ressources Textuelles et Lexicales (CNRTL), created two years ago by the CNRS within our institute (see paragraph 5). This lexical portal seeks to enhance and share (in the first instance, with the scientific community) a collection of data gathered by researchers working on French lexis. As an ongoing project, this lexical database seeks to offer as much information as is available for each individual lexeme.

As will become clear through our presentation of each element, these varied contributions to French lexicography are based on common objectives, and depend centrally on our concern to enhance and to make available (thanks to computerisation and the availability of information on the Web) the collection of lexicographical and historical data on French lexis which has been assembled and produced by our institute, and, more generally as far as the CNRTL is concerned, by the French language community.

2 From the *Trésor de la Langue Française* to the *Trésor de la Langue Française Informatisé*

2.1 The *Trésor de la Langue Française*

The *Trésor de la Langue Française*, a nineteenth- and twentieth-century language dictionary (Imbs / Quemada 1976-1994; cf. Radermacher 2004), is the result of a great lexicographical adventure which brought together more than one hundred contributors over thirty years, first under the direction of Paul Imbs, Recteur of the Académie of Nancy (regional education authority), then under that of Professeur Bernard Quemada.

Thus it was that by legislation enacted on 20th December, 1960, a research institute was created in Nancy with the aim of establishing the documentation, editorial process, and publication of a *Trésor de la Langue Française*. This project had been prepared and the decision had been taken, three years before, by an international conference on French and Romance lexicology and lexicography, organised by the head of the *Centre de Philologie Romane de Strasbourg*, Paul Imbs (cf. Imbs 1961: 285-289). Littré's dictionary (1863-1873) being then free of copyright restrictions, an interesting if controversial discussion ensued: one option was to republish that famous dictionary – because of its status of "monument" belonging to the science of its time – but the counterview prevailed, that the time had come to start building something entirely new. This new project would have to take into account the findings of twentieth century lexicology and lexicography, new possibilities regarding available documentation, and of course the changes which had arisen in the French language since the mid nineteenth century. The findings of the Strasbourg colloquium were very clear on the last point:

> Instrument de travail, le *Trésor* poursuivrait donc un double but: être le témoin objectif et impartial du vocabulaire français, mieux connu parce que mieux inventorié; être ce qu'avait été le Littré pour son temps: un exemple-type de lexicographie scientifique moderne [The TLF, as a tool, has two aims: to offer an objective and impartial survey of the vocabulary of French, which will be better known if it is better indexed, and to be what Littré was in its era: an exampe of the best of modern scientific lexicography].

If, today, one were to resituate the *Trésor* in relation to the demands of lexicography, it would still be appropriate to reiterate its initial aims as defined by Paul Imbs. Hence, the *Trésor* was to be:

- A dictionary of the French-speaking world. France had indeed to catch up with other countries in this matter. Twenty-five years earlier, England had compiled its *New English Dictionary* (Oxford Dictionary), and other Latin, Germanic or Slavic countries had already been working on the publication of a national dictionary.
- A historical dictionary. The *Trésor* would not limit itself to only the current usage of words, but it would include, for each word, an "etymological and historical" section, fully reflecting current knowledge in that field.
- A linguistic dictionary, or dictionary of the language. As opposed to other dictionaries with an encyclopaedic perspective, the *Trésor* would

try and define each word by its linguistic characteristics: its form, its meaning, and its stylistic and syntactic usages.
- A dictionary that has been the work of an entire generation. The creation of a research centre for a *Trésor de la Langue Française* coincided with the beginning of the use of mecanographic and computerised tools of documentation in the field of humanities. Hence, from 1964 onwards, thanks to powerful computer facilities, more than 1000 literary works were exhaustively analysed. This enabled the editors to draw on an immensely rich collection of examples of usage (430,000 examples), which gave birth to what is undoubtedly the biggest textual database for a specific language: *Frantext* is regularly updated and nowadays covers more than 4000 works at the ATILF (around 80% French literary works and 20% technical works).

The *Trésor de la Langue Française* is the first dictionary to use a systematic methodology to analyse the real usages of the words in our language/French, through the use of a vast textual database. The compilation of that database started in the 1960s, and its chief aim was to provide the *TLF* dictionary's publishers with properly-organised data. Thus, when an editor had to write an article, he was provided with the systematic concordanced occurrences of that word, sorted by different criteria: the sources arranged in chronological order, equipped with left and right contexts in alphabetical order, in documents focusing on co-occurrences ("binary groups", cf. Gorcy *et al.* 1970), but also syntactic constructions belonging to each discourse component in a specific order. Those concordances were used in order to effect a preliminary classification of the available documentation, and they then enabled the editors to obtain enlarged contexts, from which the examples which were to appear in the dictionary were selected.

2.2 *Le Trésor de la Langue Française Informatisé*, a Computerised Version of the TLF

2.2.1 What are the Characteristics of the *TLFi*?

The *TLFi* (www.atilf.fr/tlfi) remains a faithful image of the printed version of the *TLF*, even in its on-screen typography. Like the *TLF*, it is characterised by its rich and varied material, and by its complex structure:
- Importance of the nomenclature: 100,000 words with their etymologies and their history, along with 270,000 definitions.
- Variety of meta-textual objects included in each article (headwords, grammatical information, semantic or stylistic markers, field markers, definitions, documented examples).

- Wealth of examples: 430,000 quotations from French (mainly literary) works from the last two centuries.
- Diversity of sub-sections: a section dedicated to synchronic semantic analysis (from 1789 onwards), a "pronunciation and spelling" section, an "etymology and history" section, a section devoted to lexical statistics and a bibliographical section for the main articles.

Moreover, the computerised version of the *TLF* (Dendien / Pierrel 2003) features access with a high level of sophistication (ability to disregard accents, tolerance of common spelling mistakes, phonetic and morphological treatment). Thus spelling mistakes are automatically corrected, and access to articles is possible by typing a form and not necessarily a lemma or a headword; hence a range of means of access is available.

We will not go back over the different phases of the computerisation of the *TLF*, already discussed elsewhere (Dendien / Pierrel 2003), but will limit ourselves to a review (via examples) of different forms of access which the computerised version of the *TLF* provides.

2.2.2 Access to the *TLFi*

The *TLFi* is a retro-conversion of the *TLF*'s printed version. By introducing processes involving semi-automatic identification of the textual formats of the dictionary's articles, detailed tagging has been introduced, both typographical (so we could keep a 100% faithful image of the *TLF*) and semantic (identification of the main textual forms within each article). Some figures regarding the precision of the tagging process: after validation of all sixteen volumes, 36,613,712 XML tags were in place, i.e.: 17,364,854 typographical tags, 1,070,224 hierarchical tags, 18,178,634 tags tracking textual objects, among which were 92,997 entries and 64,346 phrases accompanied by their 271,166 definitions and illustrated by 427,493 examples.

The *TLF*'s detailed tagging and the using of the corresponding XML document has enabled us to provide access to the whole dictionary. It thus combines all the advantages of a dictionary with those of a textual resource and a proper lexical database:

- Word, phrase or lexical form search, more or less correctly spelled, along with the possibility, through the use of a special "control panel", of highlighting various fields in the search result (definitions, grammatical category, notional domain, example, author of an example, construction, marker, etc.).
- Possibility of hyper-navigation within the dictionary, enabling the user to move from one word of the meta-language to its lexicographical description (and more importantly its definition) in one click.

- Assisted searches or complex requests, exploiting the whole of the dictionary's structure through the combined application of various criteria.

2.2.3 Examples of Searches in *TLFi*

The Web site www.tlfi.fr offers an introduction to the *TLFi* and displays its different search modes; yet the best way to appreciate the effectiveness of the computerisation of the *TLF* is either to use the *TLFi* CD-Rom (*ATILF* 2004), or to go directly to the address: www.atilf.fr/tlfi.

Three main types of access to articles are proposed: word search, assisted search and complex search.

Word Search

This search enables the user to access a word through a system of correction and automatic lemmatisation (artificial or not): hence, a search for the word *etique* (without the accent), leads to the two corresponding articles *étique* or *éthique*; likewise, typing the form *sussiez* enables the user to be automatically redirected to the article *savoir*. It also offers the possibility of directly getting the definitions and the conditions of use:

- A lexical unit which is not the object of an independent lexicographical treatment (for instance, the masculine noun *trompette* is found via the request "le trompette", in a macro-article *trompette* including both the masculine and the feminine).
- A phrase such as *battre la mesure*, focusing on the relevant element that was requested, and offering the possibility of highlighting a given textual object, thanks to a sort of electronic "coloured highlighter". This can be seen in the following definition:

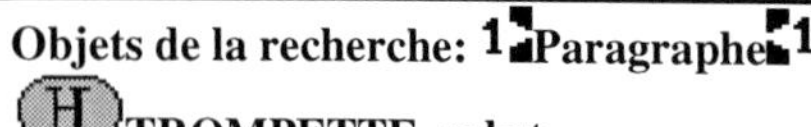

Objets de la recherche: 1 Paragraphe 1

H TROMPETTE, subst.

II. — *Subst. masc.* Personne qui joue de la trompette.
1 A. — Soldat chargé d'exécuter les sonneries. ***Le trompette*** *de l'escadron, d'un régiment de cavalerie. Tu seras capitaine, avec une nuée de trompettes courant et sonnant devant toi* (HUGO, *Légende*, t. 3, 1877, p. 390). 1
— *Loc. fam., vieilli. Il est bon cheval de trompette.* Il ne se laisse ni effrayer, ni intimider. *Son air, un air de bon cheval de trompette qui ne craignait pas le bruit* (A. DAUDET, *Tartarin de T.*, 1872, p. 13).
B. — Musicien jouant dans une fanfare, un orchestre. Synon. *trompettiste* (*infra* dér.). *Le trompette noir du dancing* (BEAUVOIR, *Mandarins*, 1954, p. 306).

Assisted Search

The second type of search offers, for instance, a means of establishing a list of all the compounds including a given element; thus an enquiry which looks up compounds including the lexeme *queue*, generates 35 results, including:

COURTE-QUEUE, adj. et subst.
DEMI-QUEUE, subst. fém.
HOCHEQUEUE, HOCHE-QUEUE, subst. masc.
PAILLE-EN-CUL, PAILLE-EN-QUEUE, subst. masc.
PORTE-QUEUE, subst. masc.
QUEUE(-)D'ARONDE, voir ARONDE.
Etc.

The assisted search also enables the user to look up «verbs which in nautical usage, pertain to the handling of sails». The user needs only to specify a search, in the category of verbs, for those verbs which belong to the notional domain of "nautical activity" and which correspond to a definition that includes an inflectional form (singular or plural) of the word *voile*, i.e. more concisely formulated: [grammatical code: *verbe*; domain: *sailing*; object type: *definition*, content: &m*sail*[1]]. Below are the 61 results thereby generated:

ABRIER, ABREYER, verbe trans.
3Empêcher le vent, en l'interceptant, de passer jusqu'à (une autre **voile**) :3
AGRÉER[2], verbe trans.
3,,Préparer ou travailler à la garniture, aux agrès d'un bâtiment, fourrer les dormans, estroper les poulies, garnir **voiles**, vergues, etc. : `` (WILL. 1831) :3
AMURER, verbe.
3Fixer l'amure d'une **voile** pour l'orienter selon le vent :3
ETC……

[1] &msubs enables us to try all the forms of a substantive, just as &cverbe enables us to try all the forms of a verb.

To take another example: for all the words whose definition includes the noun *liberté* [object type: *definition*; content: &m*liberté*], there are 306 results, including:

Objets de la recherche: 1Définition1

ABUSER, verbe trans.
1Exagérer dans l'usage d'une possibilité, d'une **liberté:**1
AFFRANCHI, IE, part. passé, adj. et subst.
1(Celui) à qui on a donné la **liberté.**1
AISE[1], subst. fém.
1Grande **liberté.**1
ALIÉNANT, ANTE, part. prés. et adj.
1Qui prive l'homme de son humanité, de sa **liberté:**1
Etc.....

Complex Search

Consulting the dictionary can entail even more complex processes. Thus it is possible to launch the following request: "What nouns are borrowed from an (undefined) foreign language and used in the terminology of cooking?". This involves simply using the "complex search" rubric and specifying:

Object 1: type *Entrée*;
Object 2: type *Code grammatical*, content "substantif", relationship 'inclus dans l'objet 1';
Object 3: type *Domaine technique*, content "art culinaire", relationship 'dépendant de l'objet 1';
Object 4: type *Langue empruntée*, relationship 'dépendant de l'objet 1'.

The relationship 'inclus dans l'objet 1' of *Object 2* means that the entry is a substantive; the relationship 'dépendant de l'objet 1' of *Object 3* suggests that the technical domain marker is within the scope of *Object 1*; and the relationship 'dépendant de l'objet 1' of *Object 4* means that the object is in the article whose entry is *Object 1*.

Such a request gives us 42 results, including:

Objets de la recherche: **1 Entrée 1 2 Code grammatical 2 3 Domaine technique 3 4 Langue empruntée 4**

	BOR(T)SCH, subst. masc.
1	**4** Empr. au russe **4**
	CARAMEL, subst. masc.
2	**4** Empr. à l'esp. **4**
	CAVIAR, subst. masc.
3	**4** Empr. au vénitien **4**
	CONDIMENT, subst. masc.
4	**4** Empr. au lat. class. **4**
	ESSENCE^{3}, subst. fém.
5	**4** Empr. au lat. class. **4**
	ESTOUFFADE, subst. fém.
6	**4** Empr. à l'ital. **4**
	GANACHE, subst. fém.
7	**4** Empr. à l'ital. **4**

3 *Dictionnaire du Moyen Français (DMF)*

3.1 Methodological Characteristics

3.1.1 A New Concept: Evolving Lexicography

The idea of a *Dictionnaire du Moyen Français* (*DMF*) was first mooted in 1980 on the occasion of the Third International Conference on Middle French (cf. Wunderli 1982). It was developed by Robert Martin, who directed it from 1982 (the beginning of the preliminary work) until 2000. The *DMF* was then overseen by Bernard Combettes (2000-2002) and Hiltrud Gerner (2003-2007), and continues to develop under the direction of Sylvie Bazin-Tacchella (from 2008).[2]

After the publication, in 1998, of an experimental "pre-publication" volume covering the alphabetical section A-AH (DMF^0), the project took on another form, although it kept the same goal. The hardcopy version was – at least provisionally – dropped in favour of an electronic publication that would be produced in successive phases. It takes the form of an evolving lexical database encoded in XML format (cf. http://www.atilf.fr/dmf). The architect of the *DMF* has thus described the advantages of this solution:

[2] Robert Martin and Hiltrud Gerner are still significantly involved in the editorial process.

> L'idée centrale qui guide le projet du DMF est que l'informatique autorise désormais une lexicographie évolutive: il ne s'agit plus de rédiger le dictionnaire lettre par lettre, ce qui le laisserait dans l'inachèvement aussi longtemps que la lettre ultime n'est pas atteinte, mais plutôt de procéder par une suite d'étapes dont chacune possède sa propre clôture tout en restant ouverte à tous les développements ultérieurs. La facilité avec laquelle les outils informatiques permettent d'augmenter, de corriger, de restructurer les données ne peut rester sans incidence sur la technique lexicographique. L'option choisie pour le DMF s'appuie fortement sur l'idée que les dictionnaires d'aujourd'hui, non pas commerciaux mais scientifiques, ne devraient plus être des produits figés que seules peuvent modifier d'hypothétiques rééditions, inévitablement coûteuses et elles-mêmes figées pour longtemps, mais au contraire des bases informatisées, faciles d'accès et ouvertes à peu de frais à tous les enrichissements et à toutes les améliorations que l'on peut estimer souhaitables (Martin 2007: 1) [The central idea behind the *DMF* project is that computerisation henceforth permits 'evolving lexicography': it is no longer necessary to edit a dictionary letter by letter, which means that it is not finished until the end of the alphabet is reached, but it becomes possible to proceed instead in a series of phases, each of which can be completed whilst still allowing for further development. The ease with which, thanks to computerisation, data can be expanded, corrected, and restructured is bound to impinge on lexicographical methodology. The system chosen for the *DMF* is based on the idea that modern scholarly (rather than commercially-produced) dictionaries, should not be finished products which can only be altered via putative revised editions which are inevitably expensive and which themselves are then fixed for a long period of time, but should instead be easily accessible computerised databases which can be subsequently enriched and improved at will for minimal cost].

It is thus necessary to distinguish *DMF1*, available on the internet since 2003, from *DMF2* (the current online version) and *DMF3*, still a work in progress (to say nothing of future versions and developments). *DMF1* (cf. Gerner 2005) assembled thirteen lexica, each of them analysing the vocabulary of a defined corpus. Those lexica cover either a representative text of the time (such as that which Jean-Loup Ringenbach produced for the *Passion d'Auvergne*), or again, the whole of a key Middle French author (for instance, Andrieu de la Vigne, available thanks to Annie Bertin); the lexica can, equally, cover the vocabulary pertaining to one specific genre (such as the *Lexicon of didactic texts* by Hiltrud Gerner). Preliminary lemmatisation ensures that all thirteen lexica can be simultaneously consulted (32,779 lemmas are dealt with in 84,778 articles: one lemma is thus dealt with in an average of two to three different lexica).

DMF2, the currently-available online version (cf. Gerner 2007a; Martin *et al.* forthcoming) gathers together seventeen lexica. Among them, of particular importance is the *Lexique complémentaire*, which is based on a very large corpus consisting – among others – of texts digitised at the ATILF, of gleanings from published editions, and of dictionaries of medieval French as well as historical dictionaries. This *Lexique complémentaire* (in itself containing 35,000 lemmas), deals mainly with rare lexical units (missing from the thirteen lexica of the *DMF1*): hapaxes, authorial inventions, one-time Latinisms, ghost-words (see below, 5.2) that are identified as such. But it also contains lexemes that are still in use in contemporary French, such as *cécité* or *palissade* (Gerner 2007a: 71). The nomenclature of *DMF2* is thus almost twice the size of the *DMF1*, with the number of lemmas increasing to 60,241 (discussed in 117,723 articles, which corresponds to an average of fewer than two articles per lemma).

DMF3 is deliberately intended to fit in with the project's own internal coherence and planning: its additional contribution will chiefly be in the provision of a significant number of synthetic meta-articles, established on the basis of several articles devoted to one single lemma.

3.1.4 Larger-scale Objectives

Scholars are unable to agree on the chronological boundaries of Middle French. Those that were fixed for the *DMF* (1330-1500) are justified by reasons which are both historical (the accession of the Valois to the throne in 1328; the beginning of the Italian wars in 1497) and linguistic (such as the appearance of a proclitic subject pronoun, compulsory in the main clause, cf. Posner 1997: 378-388). But they are also justified by the complementary nature of the *DMF* and Tobler/Lommatzsch for the earlier period, and Huguet in the aftermath Middle French. Although a variationist perspective is taken into account by the *DMF* (see for instance its careful approach to diatopia), the period under scrutiny in the dictionary is treated as a broad synchronic sweep, similar to that of the *TLFi* (and not as a narrow diachronic selection).

The nomenclature of the *DMF* takes into account all the lexical units (nouns, adjectives, verbs, adverbs, interjections and numerals) of the corpus, including the hapaxes. For the time being, it leaves out grammatical units (*DMF2*). In order to maintain some semblance of control over the immense formal variety presented by the vocabulary of a non-standardised period of a language such as that of Middle French, Gilles Souvay devised for the *DMF* the *LGeRM* lemmatiser (*Lemmes, Graphies lemmatisées et Règles Morphologiques*; cf. Souvay 2007). This instrument[3] connects each word (or noun-form) from a Middle French text (and specifically, from a quotation in the *DMF*) to the lexeme of which it

[3] For it is an instrument, not a simple tool (for further reading on the distinction of those two notions, cf. Habert 2005).

is a graphical or morphological variant. This enables the *DMF* user to access the relevant lemma from any inflectional or graphical variant, and to navigate (by double-clicking) inside the dictionary, including between the Frantext database and the *DMF*. The *LGeRM* lemmatiser «opère avec une probabilité de réussite qui dépasse à présent les 90%» [is probably 90% accurate]" (Martin *et al.* forthcoming: 1); this level of accuracy is impressive.

As well as the central position occupied by the *DMF* in research into Middle French lexicology and synchronic lexicography, it is impossible to overstate its enormous heuristic potential for diachronic lexicology and etymology. Indeed, the vocabulary dealt with in the *DMF* refers to etymology – briefly but systematically – by reference to the *FEW* (*Französisches Etymologisches Wörterbuch*). This is not only the case where the *FEW* deals with the lexical unit under scrutiny, but also when the *DMF* entry is an addition to the *FEW*'s nomenclature, in which case this is indicated by **FEW*. Cases of this are far from rare: a quick survey reveals that the *DMF1* includes 97 etymological references to the alphabetical section *B-* in the first volume of the *FEW*. Among those, 43 can be linked to articles that are due to appear in the new version of the *FEW* (see above, 2).[4] The *DMF* thus emerges as *the* Middle French etymological dictionary, a feature which has tended to be overlooked.

A further example might be the lexicon of scientific language compiled by Danièle Jacquart and Claude Thomasset; in comparison with the *FEW*, this lexicon offers 339 new lexemes, 74 new etyma, along with hundreds of antedatings of individual words (Gerner / Martin 2007). The lexicon of the *Miracles de Nostre Dame par personnages*, compiled by Pierre Kunstmann, included 29 antedatings and one postdating (Gerner forthcoming). These figures suggest that the future use of the *DMF* for historical lexicology is very promising.

---

[4] The additions deal with 22 *FEW* articles: *BABA (*DMF* s.v. *débaver*, *débaver [soi]*), BAJULARE (s.v. *baillable*, *baillette*, *baillie*[2]), BALBUS (s.v. *bauberie*, *baubie*, *bauboiement*), BALNEARE (s.v. *baigneresse*, *baigneur*, *baigneux*), BARBA (s.v. *barbelé*, *barbière*, *barbillonner*), BASSUS (s.v. *basser*, *subaste*), BASTUM (s.v. *bastorné*), BATARE (s.v. *baie*[2]), BLASPHEMARE (s.v. *blasphemeur*), BOS (s.v. *bouvatier*), BRACHIUM (s.v. *bracelette*, *bracelot*, *brasset*, *brassière*), BRANCA (s.v. *brancherie*, *branchier*), BREVIS (s.v. *desbreveter*), BRITTUS (s.v. *breton*, *bretonnant*), BROCCUS (s.v. *brochardre*), *BRUSCIA (*brousser*), BŬCCA (s.v. *bellebouche*, *embouchoir*), BULLA (s.v. *billette*, *billeter*, *boulonnet*), BŬRRA (s.v. *bourrée*, *embourroumer [s']*), BŪTYRUM (s.v. *butirosité*, *butyreux*), BŬXUS (s.v. *buissière*), BYRSA (s.v. *boursal*, *boursière*).

3.1.3 Strategic Position on the International Stage

It is not particularly surprising that the analysis offered by the *DMF* should overwhelmingly supersede Godefroy (1881-1902). Godefroy is the only dictionary to cover (albeit only partly) the same period of the history of French. During the last century, lexicographical techniques and, above all, much more sharply-focused lexicological analysis (notably in the field of semantic description) have made substantial progress. In comparison with its illustrious ancestor – which is nonetheless still very useful (see below 5.3) – the *DMF*'s contribution is particularly striking in terms of both quality and quantity. Hence for the alphabetical range *I-*, Martin / Souvay (2003: 398) provide 300 additional lexemes in comparison with Godefroy.

Twenty years after its launch, the *DMF* is clearly "the" authoritative reference-work in the field of Middle French lexicology. Each new finding which emerges in the area (discovery of lexemes thus far undescribed; antedatings and postdatings; improved semantic analysis; attribution of a lexeme to a language variety) refers of necessity to the information available in the *DMF*'s columns. Another invaluable asset is its productive relationship with the other two giants of medieval French lexicography, the *DEAF* (*Dictionnaire Etymologyque de l'Ancien Français*) and the *AND* (*Anglo-Norman Dictionary*).

In addition, at the beginning of the twenty-first century, the *DMF* is a natural focal point for the best research in lexicology, concentrating on the fourteenth and the fifteenth centuries. Mention should be made in this context of the enrichment of the *DMF* by Frédéric Duval's study of classical Latin and Greek terminology, or the contribution made by Yan Greub's 2003 thesis on the localisation of Middle French farces.

3.2 Computerised Resource Enhancement

3.2.1 An Unrivalled Variety of Use

The *DMF* allows for a range of types of interrogation (cf. Gerner 2005: 159-161; Martin *et al.* forthcoming) which are unprecedented for a historical period of French (and perhaps for a historical period of any language). In what follows, we discuss only a few of the multidirectional modes of interrogation which are available: a complete etymological family is available via a single click on a *FEW* etymon; the computerised interrogation of definitions allows onomasiological access to the underlying data; and a specific menu is dedicated to the retrieval of locutions, much to the delight of phraseology scholars. Moreover, hyper-navigation does not stop where the dictionary *stricto sensu* ends, since the

DMF is now at the centre of an increasingly dense interconnected network of research (cf. Gerner 2007b).

We illustrate below three types of interrogation that are of considerable value to scholars in historical linguistics. The examples derive from research undertaken at the ATILF. Our three examples deal with lexicology (3.2.2), pragmatics (3.2.3) and constructional morphology (3.2.4). Suffice it to say that any number of other types of enquiry are possible.

3.2.2 Lexicology

The *DMF* was first and foremost designed to produce a description of the phonetic, semantic, morphosyntactic and variational aspects of the vocabulary of Middle French. It goes without saying that the dictionary's contribution is particularly significant in the field of lexicology, whether synchronic or diachronic. One brief example demonstrates this obvious use of the *DMF*.

When the *TLFi* etymological notices of the articles *adresse*^{1}, *adresse*^{2}, and *adresse*^{3} were revised as part of the *TLF-Étym* research programme (see section 4.1 below), one of the aims was to check the accuracy of the date "since 1559" suggested by the *TLFi* for meaning I.A. under *adresse*^{3}: «qualité d'une personne […] parvenant aisément à atteindre un but ou à obtenir un résultat (le but visé est la réussite dans des actions nécessitant l'utilisation du corps et en particulier des mains) [synonymes: *habileté*, *dextérité*]». The *FEW* (von Wartburg 1928 in *FEW3*, 84b, *DIRECTIARE I), Godefroy and Tobler / Lommatzsch (neither gives this meaning s.v. *adrece*), and the *AND* (which has no entry for this lexeme) yielded no information beyond that already available in the *TLFi*. Hence the *TLF-Étym* editors turned to the *DMF*: the choice of *Recherche d'une entrée* in the dictionary leads to nine articles for *adresse*, taken from nine different lexica. These include the following, an extract from the Christine de Pizan lexicon, compiled by Joel Blanchard and Michel Quereuil:

ADRESSE	**FEW III** **DIRECTIARE*
ADRESSE, subst. fém.	
I. -	"Chemin, direction": Mais bien traihoit [Paris] en une adresce Fleches empanees d'un arc (CHR. PIZ., *M.F.*, III, 1400-1403, 54). ...tant veoir vous desiroye Que j'en ay empris longue voye, Par le renom de vo proece, Qui de ce me mit en l'adrece (CHR. PIZ., *M.F.*, III, 1400-1403, 143).
II. -	"Art" : La roÿne d'Amasonie (...) D'armes savoit toute l'adrece. (CHR. PIZ., M.F., III, 1400-1403, 141).
III. -	"Celle qui montre le chemin, guide" : Philosophie y vi assise Moult haultement, en tel devise Que bien semble haulte maistresse Et des autres toutes l'adresse (CHR. PIZ., *M.F.*, II, 1400-1403, 104).
Pizan	Joël Blanchard / Michel Quereuil

The reader will immediately spot the fact that the attestation given under II. with the gloss "art" antedates the occurrence of the meaning 'habileté manuelle' of *adresse* by one and a half centuries (1559 → 1400-1403), which is itself worthy of attention. Two other datings emerging from this collection of articles also originate in the *DMF*: before 1343 (Guillaume de Machaut) for 'destination' (in fixed locutions such as *arriver à son adresse*, cf. Petrequin / Buchi in *TLF-Étym* s.v. *adresse*[1] I. A.) and ca. 1400 (Froissart) for «moyen ou ensemble de moyens mis en œuvre par une personne pour atteindre un but (synonymes: *diplomatie*, *doigté*, *finesse*, *manœuvre*, *procédé*, *ruse*)» (cf. Petrequin / Buchi in *TLF-Étym* s.v. *adresse*[3] II).

3.2.3 Pragmatics

Despite what readers might expect, the interest of the *DMF* is not restricted to the purely lexical, even in its currently available version (*DMF*2). Even though the treatment of grammatical units has been set aside for later, consultation of the dictionary has become a requirement for any scholar with an interest in the evolution of grammatical units and for that matter of discourse markers (or pragmatic units) in the French language.

In a recent publication, Mosegaard Hansen (2005: 47) dates the first occurrence of the marker *enfin* with the meaning «marking the final element of a series of items quoted» (for instance in *Il y a à Paris trois polices: primo: la police du royaume* [...] *secondo: celle du régent* [...] *enfin celle de Dubois*) to the second half of the sixteenth century. Anyone who wants to check the accuracy of the dating of *enfin* will turn to the *DMF*, even though the dictionary does not include – for the time being – the entry *enfin*. But as chance would have it, the dictionary has a search function *Recherche plein texte*, which offers 58 results for *enfin*. Among them, we find the following: Article 7/58 *1 attestation*

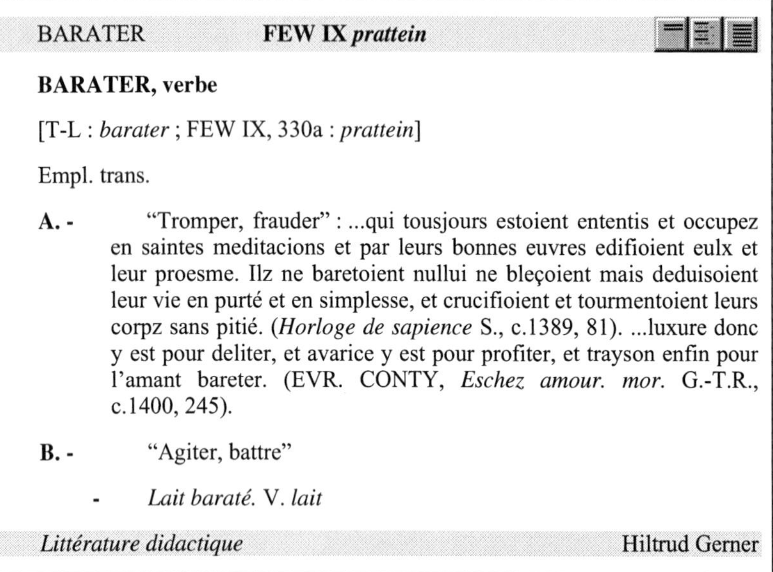

BARATER **FEW IX *prattein***

BARATER, verbe

[T-L : *barater* ; FEW IX, 330a : *prattein*]

Empl. trans.

A. - "Tromper, frauder" : ...qui tousjours estoient ententis et occupez en saintes meditacions et par leurs bonnes euvres edifioient eulx et leur proesme. Ilz ne baretoient nullui ne bleçoient mais deduisoient leur vie en purté et en simplesse, et crucifioient et tourmentoient leurs corpz sans pitié. (*Horloge de sapience* S., c.1389, 81). ...luxure donc y est pour deliter, et avarice y est pour profiter, et trayson enfin pour l'amant bareter. (EVR. CONTY, *Eschez amour. mor.* G.-T.R., c.1400, 245).

B. - "Agiter, battre"

- *Lait baraté.* V. *lait*

Littérature didactique Hiltrud Gerner

DMF2's article for *barater* includes, under *A.* "tromper, frauder", an attestation from Evrart de Conty antedating *enfin* "énumératif" by nearly two centuries (1587 → ca. 1400).[5] This undoubtedly has implications for our understanding of the historical development of this marker, whether aspectual or enunciative (cf. Buchi / Städtler in progress).

3.2.4 Constructional Morphology

It may be even more surprising to discover that the *DMF* is of considerable use for another linguistic sub-discipline, i.e. constructional morphology.

A stimulating study produced by our colleague Denis Apothéloz (2003) highlights the dual nature of the prefix *IN-* in contemporary French.

---

[5] The continuity of the tradition is guaranteed by an intermediary attestation, in 1452, proposed by the *DMF2* s.v. *tare*.

On the one hand, Apothéloz distinguishes a "basic" prefix *in-*[1], characterised by allomorphism: /in-/ before a basic form starting with a vowel (*inutile*), /ɛ̃-/ before a basic form starting with an obstruent consonant (*imbattable*), and /i-/ before a basic form starting with a resonant consonant (*illégal*). *In-* has either a negative meaning (*inutile* 'not useful') or a superlative meaning (*inqualifiable* 'extremely bad or poor'). Regarding the second term of the pair, *in-*[2], it only arises with basic forms starting with an obstruent consonant, and it is always (in Apothéloz's findings) realised as /ɛ̃-/ ([ɛ̃nɔmabl]); its meaning is exclusively negative (*inréparable* 'irreparable, unable to be repaired'). Apothéloz (2003: 43) asks the question as to when the pairs in /ɛ̃-/ of the derivatives starting with /i-/, and formed on a basic form with an obstruent consonant, evolved. Can the *DMF* answer this question? Does it include lexemes with the prefix *in-* (/ɛ̃-/) before roots in *r-* or *l-*? For this kind of oblique interrogation, the *DMF* offers, under the heading *Recherche sur les entrées*, a "+ options" button which enables the user to select, in order to filter the entries, an option to look up a character string via the initial letters of a series of words. This is different from the default mode "texte exact". Here is a sample of the results for *inr-*:

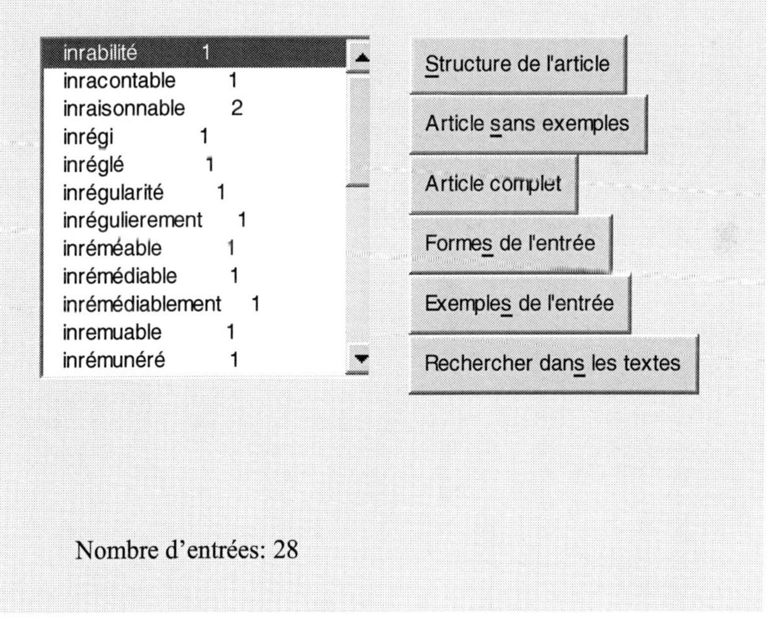

The result of such a request is surprisingly rich: it highlights 28 forms starting with *inr-*, and the majority of them are not listed in other lexicographical sources. The *DMF* data will thus prove to be crucial in answering Apothéloz's question concerning the chronology of this complex morpho-semantical system (cf. Buchi forthcoming).

4 Recent Developments in Historical Lexicography

4.1 *TLF-Étym*

4.1.1 Methodology of *TLF-Étym*

The *TLF-Étym* research project (cf. http://www.atilf.fr/tlf-etym, and Buchi 2005) is directed by Gilles Petrequin. Its aim is to progressively revise the sections entitled *Étymologie et Histoire* in the *TLFi*. There can be no question of revising all the 54,000-odd historical notices of the *TLFi*. On the one hand, the project endeavours to incorporate work by various researchers in their different fields; on the other hand, it will attempt a systematic revision of etymological notices in certain categories which are recognisably deficient (for instance, those which deal with Anglicisms and deonomastic words).

The methodological framework of the *TLF-Étym* project is based on the history and etymology of each word: this conception stems from the idea that etymology is not simply the identification of an etymon. It sets out to clearly state the formal and semantic link between the etymon and the lexeme under examination; the particular history of each word thus plays an integral part in etymology. This conception derives ultimately from Schuchardt, Meillet, Ernoult and above all von Wartburg. But Baldinger (1959: 239) probably put it best: «l'étymologie, [...] c'est [...] la biographie du mot [etymology is the biography of a word]».

Indeed, a proper methodology lies at the core of the elaboration of this programme:

> TLF-Étym a la chance de pouvoir bénéficier des réflexions méthodologiques des meilleurs spécialistes qui se sont exprimés lors des séminaires de méthodologie en étymologie et lexicologie historique qui se sont déroulés de septembre 2005 à juin 2006 (Chambon / Carles 2007: 315, n. 2).

The proceedings of these seminars can be downloaded from the *TLF-Étym* website (under the heading *En savoir plus*). Such an initiative from the ATILF has thus made it possible to associate with our research institute, the main contemporary experts in French etymology from around the world (foreign researchers such as Thomas Städtler and the *DEAF* team from Heidelberg, Franz Rainer in Vienna and Takeshi Matsumura in Tokyo, for instance, are closely involved in the project). It has also helped to revitalise this specific field of French historical linguistics. It is also important to note that the elaboration of etymological notices is often accompanied by explicit, independently-published theoretical commentary:

- *anil* and *indigo* (Benarroch forthcoming);
- *casuel*[2] and *défectif* (Andronache in progress);
- *cheire* (Chambon / Grélois 2007; cf. also Gouvert 2007);
- *claie* (Chambon forthcoming and Petrequin / Andronache in progress);
- *défectif*, *différer*, *obole* (Steinfeld / Andronache forthcoming);
- *lucarne* (Pitz 2006).

The revised notices can be downloaded from the *TLF-Étym* website; they include unpublished etymologies (Turcan s.v. *bienfaisance*: calqued on Latin, rather than generated within French; Chauveau s.v. *bigler*: continuation of proto-Romance, rather than a borrowing from Latin; Buron / Baudinot s.v. *fare*: borrowing from Breton instead of "unknown origin" etc.), antedatings (Stumpf/Evrard s.v. *fabulateur*: 1541 → ca. 1360/1380; Städtler s.v. *laconique*: 1529 → ca. 1372/1374; Petrequin s.v. *ostensoir*: 1771 → 1673; etc.), and ultimately, postdatings (Koehl s.v. *iota*: ca. 1240 → ca. 1300: Steinfeld s.v. *féodalement*; 1483 → 1514; Robin / Buchi s.v. *vélocipède*: 1804 → 1818; etc.). Nevertheless, a reasonable conclusion is that the greatest value of the *TLF-Étym* project will be the precision and coherence of the models of analysis developed for the twenty-two etymological sub-classes, whether with regard to inherited vocabulary (Steinfeld s.v. *claie*: «Continuateur régulier du protoroman régional */'kleta/» [*TLFi*: «du gaul. *cleta*»]), lexical borrowings (Navrátilová s.v. *riesling*: «emprunt à l'allemand» [*TLFi*: «mot all.»]) or French developments (Leroy s.v. *cerbère*: «Formation française: translation déonomastique du nom propre de créature mythologique *Cerbère*» [*TLFi*: «Empr. au lat. *Cerberus*»]).

4.1.2 Example

Moreover, the *TLF-Étym* forms a natural home for the etymological notices currently being revised as part of the DETCOL project (*Développement et Exploitation Textuelle d'un Corpus d'Œuvres Linguistiques*), directed by Bernard Colombat (cf. http://ctlf.ens-lsh.fr/documents/ct_projet_detcol.pdf). The website thus offers a renewed panorama on etymology and the history of technical grammatical terms, such as *antécédent*, *conjonction*, *gémination*, *gérondif*, *négation*, *parfait*, *pluriel*, *pronom* or *temporel*. The reader can compare, below, the etymological notice for the article *parfait*[2] in the *TLFi* with its revised version in *TLF-Étym*:

TLFi:

Étymol. et Hist. XIV^{e}s. gramm. adj. *prétèrit parfait* (*Ms. Fonds St Victor 867. Doctrinal avec glose, Anonyme du XIV^{e}s.* d'apr. Ch. THUROT ds *Notices et Extraits des mss de la bibl. impériale et autres bibl.*, XXII, 2, p.184); 1596 gramm. subst. «temps qui marque un passé accompli» (HULSIUS, introd.). Représente la trad., par la forme *parfait*, du lat. *perfectum tempus* ou, plus brièvement, *perfectum* p. subst. de l'adj. *perfectus*, terme de gramm. du lat.

TLF-Étym:

parfait2, *subst. masc.*

Étymologie
Histoire:

C. *prétérit parfait* loc. nom. masc. «temps verbal présentant le procès comme accompli et l'envisageant dans son résultat actuel». Attesté de la fin 12e siècle [par référence à la grammaire latine] (AelfricfH, page 102, in Städtler, *TraLiPhi* 37, page 128: tempore preterito perfecto: *par le* ***preterit parfet***, et plusquamperfecto: *et plusqueparfet*) à 1878 (*Ac^{7} s.v. parfait*: En Grammaire, ***Prétérit parfait***, ou substantivement, *Parfait*, Le prétérit qui marque une chose parfaite, une chose arrivée dans un temps qui n'est ni précis ni déterminé, comme *J'ai aimé, j'ai dit* [...]. L'emploi de *Parfait* [...] comme substantif[s] est le plus ordinaire). *Cf.* Städtler, *Grammatiksprache*, page 270 pour des attestations des 13e–15e siècles. Dernière attestation textuelle: 1775 (Condillac, *Cours d'étude*, volume 1, partie 2, chapitre 10, page 196, *in* Gallica = Frantext: On appelle *je ferois*, *prétérit imparfait* ; *je fis* & *j'ai [fait]*, ***prétérit parfait***; & *j'avois fait*, *plusque parfait*). –

A./B. *parfait* subst. masc. «temps verbal présentant le procès comme accompli et l'envisageant dans son résultat actuel». Attesté depuis 1596 (Hulsius[1], introduction grammaticale: Des Verbes [...] Present. Die zeit die jetze da ist / als: Ie mange, ich eß. / Imparfait. Zeit die halb fürüber ist / Ie mangeoye, ich aß / Indiffinit. Zeit so auch fast fürüber / Ie mangeay, ich aß / **Parfait**. Zeit die gar fürüber ist / I'ai mãgé, ich hab gessen. / Advenir. Zeit so noch zukünftig ist / Ie mangeray, ich werde essen). Première attestation dans une grammaire française: 1606 (Masset, *Acheminement*, page 11: Nos verbes ont cinq modes. Indicatif, imperatif, optatif, subiunctif, & infinitif: Trois temps principaux, present, passé & futur. Le passé se diuise en imparfait, aoriste simple, **parfait**, plus que parfait, aoriste composé, & parfait, tres-parfait; cf. aussi Maupas, *Grammaire*[2], page 92 v° /93 v°).-

Origine:
C. Transfert linguistique: calque du latin *praeteritum perfectum* loc. nom. neutre «temps verbal présentant le procès comme accompli et l'envisageant dans son résultat actuel (terme de grammaire)» (attesté depuis Quintilien, TLL 10/1, 1378, *s.v. perficio*), *cf. prétérit** et *parfait*[1]*. À ajouter FEW 9, 322b, praeterire 1 a β; *cf.* Städtler, *Grammatiksprache* 270.
A./B. Formation française: ellipse de *prétérit parfait* (*cf.* ci-dessus C.). Cette analyse se recommande en raison des témoignages explicites des sources lexicographiques (*cf.* "ou substantivement" dans la citation ci-dessus C.) ainsi que du parallélisme d'*imparfait* (< *prétérit imparfait*, *cf. imparfait** et *prétérit**). *Cf.* von Wartburg *in* FEW 8, 237b, pĕrfĕctus I 1 b α, qui avance à tort l'hypothèse d'un calque du latin *perfectum* subst. neutre «temps verbal présentant le procès comme accompli et l'envisageant dans son résultat actuel (terme de grammaire)» (attesté depuis Varron, TLL 10/1, 1377, *s.v. perficio*) sur *parfait*[1]*. On écarte de même l'hypothèse d'un emprunt à l'allemand *Perfekt* subst. neutre «temps verbal présentant le procès comme accompli et l'envisageant dans son résultat actuel» (attesté depuis le 17e/18e siècle seulement, Schulz, *Fremdwörterbuch*[1]), même si la première attestation absolue se trouve dans un dictionnaire allemand-français.

Dès les premiers témoignages d'un discours grammatical français, on relève le latinisme *prétérit parfait* (ci-dessus C.). C'est seulement à la toute fin du 16e siècle (en 1550, Meigret, *Traité*, page 70 emploie encore *prétérit parfait*) que *parfait* (ci-dessus A./B.) vient concurrencer la locution nominale, avant de l'évincer complètement au 19e siècle. – L'adjectif *parfait* à sens grammatical (*cf.* Städtler, *Grammatiksprache* 250-251) n'a pas de rapport étymologique direct avec le lexème traité ici ; il serait à classer *s.v. parfait*[1]*.

Rédaction TLF 1986 : E. Ammann. – Mise à jour 2007: E. Buchi. - Relecture mise à jour 2007 : J-P. Chauveau; T. Städtler; J-P. Chambon; M. Lang; G. Roques; Y. Matsumura; G. Petrequin; N. Steinfeld.

4.2 *Base des Mots-fantômes*

4.2.1 Methodological Characteristics

The *Base des Mots-Fantômes* ('Database of ghost-words') is a resource in critical metalexicography, directed by Nadine Steinfeld. It sets out to list the *ghost words* or *fantasmas lexicográficos* (Pascual Rodríguez / García Pérez 2007:170), i.e. all the pseudo-lexemes of erroneous lexicographical status ("those words that do not exist"), the ghost meanings and the wrong lemmatisations that can be found in major French historical and etymological dictionaries.

4.2.2 Example

In Godefroy's dictionary there is such an entry *labaille*:

> LABAILLE, s. f., syn. d'*escope*, mod. *écope*, sorte de pelle creuse qui sert à vider l'eau entrée dans une embarcation:
> Et en doivent les vaisseaulx qui viennent esditz havres chargez de blez en grenier chascun vaissel plaine une escope ou *labaille* ou l'en puche l'eaue. (1413, *Denombr du baill. de Constentin*, Arch. P 304, f° 116 v°.)

Von Wartburg failed to supply an etymology for the word and relegated it (in 1968) to the "materials of unknown or uncertain origin" (*FEW* 23, 108b, s.v. *écope*). This incarceration in the *FEW*'s "purgatory" constituted an implicit appeal to the scientific community to come up with etymological hypotheses to clarify the origin of *labaille*.

The mystery was eventually solved in 2006: as part of the revision of the article BAJULA 'bonne d'enfants' of the *FEW*, Jean-Paul Chauveau (2006: 2 n. 4) identified the word **labaille* as a misreading, by erroneous agglutination of the definite article, of a form which should be attached to the lexeme *baille* n.f. «baquet de bois en forme de demi-tonneau ou de cône tronqué, spécialement utilisé sur les bateaux», attested since 1340.

Now, because of the semantic gap between *écope* and *bonne*, it is very unlikely that any reader of Godefroy who was interested in the etymology of **labaille* would automatically think of consulting the *FEW* s.v. BAJULA. This is precisely where the *Base des Mots-Fantômes* comes into play: it centralises in a very convenient way the identifiable ghost-words scattered across articles in scholarly journals, conference proceedings, notices and lexicographical studies, as well as establishing new hypotheses regarding connections between forms. This is how the entry *labaille* appears in this data base:

LABAILLE 

1331-1500
lexie

Source première:

Gdf 4, 686a
labaille, subst. fém.
«syn. d'*escope*, mod. *cope*, sorte de pelle creuse qui sert à vider l'eau entrée dans une embarcation »

Et en doivent les vaisseaulx qui viennent esditz havres chargez de blez en grenier chascun vaissel plaine une escope ou *labaille* ou l'en puche l'eaue 1413 (*Denombr. du baill. de Constentin*, Arch. P 304, f° 116v°)

Source(s) secondaire(s):
Source secondaire:

FEW 23, 108b
Concept : ÉCOPE

Anorm. *labaille* f. «sorte de pelle creuse qui sert à vider l'eau entrée dans une embarcation» (Coutances 1413)

Justification:

mélecture portant sur un phénomène d'agglutination liée à l'article *la*
1413

Il convient de lire *la baille* «le baquet»

Solution:

LA BAILLE
FEW 1, 206a BAJULA 2

Correction des sources:

Source à corriger:

correction, déplacement-S
GdfC 8, 273b
baille, subst. fém.
«baquet»
Rem.: *Baille*, dans l'attestation de J. Du Clercq, *Mém.*, l. V, ch. XVIII, III, 375, citée ici, a été interprété à tort par Gay comme signifiant «palissade».

Source à corriger:

correction, déplacement
FEW 1, 206a
BAJULA

2005: J.-P. Chauveau ; T. Städtler, T. Matsumura

This is, then, a nice example of reciprocal enrichment operating between the *FEW* and the *Base des Mots-Fantômes.*

4.3 *Bibliographie Godefroy*

4.3.1 Methodological Characteristics

> Les utilisateurs du dictionnaire de Godefroy sont partagés entre l'intérêt que présente l'immense masse documentaire contenue dans les huit mille pages de ses dix volumes et la frustration de ne pouvoir disposer d'une bibliographie des sources exploitées [The users of Godefroy are torn between fascination by the vast amounts of information contained in the 8,000 pages of the ten volumes of the dictionary, and frustration at the absence of a proper bibliography of sources used] (Ringenbach 2003: 191).

This observation was the starting point of the *Bibliographie Godefroy* project, in progress, thanks to Jean-Loup Ringenbach (cf. http://www.atilf.fr/BbgGdf; Ringenbach 2003; forthcoming). The sigla system used by Godefroy is, it has to be said, unreliable. One example: the *Dit de buffet* (mid thirteenth century) is sometimes referred to as "Dit de buffet" or "Dit du buffet", and sometimes as "Du Vilain au buffet", without a date being supplied. The unreliability of the dictionary's own reference system means that the *Bibliographie Godefroy* will become every bit as indispensable as the bibliography to the *DEAF*.

The methodology used in the production of the *Bibliographie Godefroy* consists in identifying obscure sigla, either by cross-reference to more explicit abbreviations, or by philological investigation of editions of texts – and even of manuscripts – which contain the texts concerned.

4.3.2 Example

As part of our research on the history of the prefix *IN*- in contemporary French (see above 3.2.4), the following attestation from *Godefroy* remained a puzzle: «*Quant est de toy, tu mors et pinces Par ton envye inraisonnable Plus c'un serpent* (*Envye, Estat et Simplesse*, p. 6, ap. Ler. de Lincy et Michel, *Farces, Moral. et Serm. joy*., t. I)». What was the source? How were we to date it? Thanks to the *Bibliographie Godefroy*, this text can now be identified:

Envye, Estat et Simplesse

Envye, Estat et Simplesse

1) Exemples:

- Gdf : *irraisonnable*: *Envye, Estat et Simplesse*, p. 6, ap. Ler. de 24341 et Michel, *Farces, Moral. et Serm. joy.*, t.I
- autres citations : Gdf: *grogneu*, *oppresse*, *ragace*

2) Bibliographie:

Moralité à troys personnages, c'est assavoir Envye, Estat et Simplesse

- Texte: milieu du 16e s.
- Manuscrit: PARIS BN fr 24341 (Recueil La Vallière), f° 50a-53b, ca 1575
Édition(s): *Recueil de farces, moralités et sermons joyeux*, éd. Leroux de Lincy et Francisque Michel, Paris, t. 1, 1837, n° 10.

Renvois :

- Bossuat: 5844
- Louis Petit de Julleville, *Répertoire du théâtre comique en France au moyen âge: histoire du théâtre en France*, Paris, 1886, 62-63.

Once the text *Envye, Estat et Simplesse* had been dated to the mid sixteenth century, we realised that this was the last occurrence of the adjective *inraisonable*, at a time when French was opting decisively for *irraisonnable* (attested from the fourteenth century). Conversely, the value of such an attestation for historical lexicography (and over and above that, for historical constructional morphology) would have gone unnoticed without the help of the *Bibliographie Godefroy*.

5 The CNRTL Lexical Portal

5.1 Objectives of the CNRTL

The *Centre National de Ressources Textuelles et Lexicales* (CNRTL: www.cnrtl.fr) was created in 2005 by the CNRS and is directly associated with our institute, the ATILF. It aims to gather together within one single portal as many computerised resources and consulting tools as possible for the study, understanding, and diffusion of the French language.

Because it results from the convergence of different studies undertaken in various research institutes, the CNRTL is able to maximise the production, verification, harmonisation, diffusion and sharing of resources – whether computerised lexical or textual data, or tools and instruments designed to facilitate informed access to their content.

The decision to create the CNRTL is part of CNRS policy, which aims to establish new infrastructures, which will be vital for research work involving the whole scientific community. It is also the consequence of a joint programme by the "Direction de l'Information Scientifique" and the "Département Homme et Société" within the CNRS. The acknowledged scientific expertise of the CNRTL, along with the numerous national and international collaborative projects run within the various research institutes of which it is part, have enabled the project to establish itself within European research, thanks to:

- direct collaborations with partner institutes, in Great Britain (University of Oxford), Germany (Computing centres in Trier and Würzburg, DFKI in Saarbrücken, MPI), and in the Netherlands (University of Nijmegen);
- participation in CLARIN (http://www.mpi.nl/clarin/), the European network of resource management and centres of linguistic technology.

5.2 Resources Located within CNRTL

The CNRTL revolves around five activities: a lexical portal for French; text and data corpora, annotated or not; encyclopaedic and linguistic dictionaries (old and modern); phonetic, morphological, syntactical and semantic lexica; linguistic tools (labellers, analysers, aligners, concordancers, annotation tools). Among the resources that are already part of the CNRTL – the lexical portal is further discussed in the following paragraph – the following should be noted:

- corpora of texts free of writers' and publishers' copyright (in the first instance, 500 texts taken from *Frantext*): selected according to their authors, titles, dates and genres, with the possibility of downloading selected texts in XML format – with a TEI-compliant DTD (www.tei-c.org);[6] the user thus has access to files including the DTD and the XML/TEI encoding of the texts. To the best of our knowledge, the CNRTL is the first website to offer a collection of French corpora in XML/TEI format with around 150 million characters;
- the Morphalou lexicon, derived from the *TLF* nomenclature, whose access is free for consultation and downloading: an open lexicon of French inflected forms, containing 524,725 inflected forms belonging to 95,810 lemmas. These have been linguistically validated (approved by an editorial committee) and conform to the proposal for normalisation of ISO lexical data (TC37/SC4);
- computerised versions of dictionaries, whether modern (*TLFi*; *Dictionnaire de l'Académie Française*: eighth [1932-1935] and ninth [1992–] editions) or older (Dictionaries of R. Estienne [1552], of Jean Nicot [1606], of Bayle [1740], of Féraud [1787-1788], of the *Académie*

[6] Nancy, thanks to the association of the ATILF with the INIST and the LORIA, is now the European support centre for the TEI.

[first edition, 1694; fourth edition, 1762; fifth edition, 1798; sixth edition, 1835]), along with the Diderot and d'Alembert *Encyclopédie*.[7]

The CNRTL also offers to the scientific community linguistic tools and instruments that can be used directly on the website, from a simple Internet browser. Among the different projects in progress or planned, we will be offering simple and user-friendly access to tools such as:

- *FLEMM*: a flexional analysis tool for French texts that have been previously tagged using one of the two taggers: *Brill* or *TreeTagger*.
- *POMPAMO*: a detection tool for potential cases of formal and categorical neologism, based on the use of restricted lexica. This project makes use of lexical resources such as *Morphalou* and offers the possibility of creating new resources as well.

5.3 The Lexical Portal, an Example of Lexical Data Integration

The CNRTL lexical portal aims to enhance and share – mainly with the scientific community – various types of data taken from research studies on the vocabulary of French. An ongoing project, this lexical data-base endeavours to provide users with as much available information as possible, the starting point of each enquiry being the individual lexical unit.

5.3.1 Lexicographical Information

Lexicographical data are the priority in our work. Thus far, we have managed to include in this portal all the information provided by the *TLF* (www.atilf.fr/tlfi) which appears by default when lexicographical information is requested. This information is supplemented by easily available information via a menu. This is taken from:

- the *Académie Française dictionary* (fourth, eighth and ninth editions) (www.atilf.fr/academie), which has been computerised within our institute as part of a partnership programme with the Académie.
- the *Base de Données Lexicographiques Panfrancophones* (*BDLP*: http://www.tlfq.ulaval.ca/bdlp/). This international-scale project is part of the *Trésor des vocabulaires français* enterprise originally initiated by Bernard Quemada in the 1980s. The aim of the *BDLP* is to construct and to assemble representative databases of French as spoken in each French-speaking area. The databases are designed in order that they can be consulted separately or at the same time, and so that they

[7] Most of the computerised versions of old dictionaries, along with that of the Diderot and d'Alembert *Encyclopédie* are the result of a partnership with the ARTLF (http://humanities.uchicago.edu/orgs/ARTFL/).

constitute a supplement to the *Trésor de la Langue Française Informatisé*. With an international perspective, the BDLP project is sponsored by the Agence Universitaire de la Francophonie, which supports it via its network for the study of French in the French-speaking world (http://www.eff.auf.org/).

– the *Base Historique du Vocabulaire Français* (*Datations et Documents Lexicographiques*: www.atilf.fr/ddl), made up of datings for French vocabulary, and based on the data found in the 48 volumes of the *Datations et Documents Lexicographiques* collection (Quemada 1970-1998).

All of these lexicographical data are also directly available, for any given form, at the address http://www.cnrtl.fr/lexicographie/, followed by the form which the user wishes to consult. Thus: http://www.cntrl.fr/lexicographie/aguerrit enables the user to access all available lexicographical information for the verb *aguerrir*.

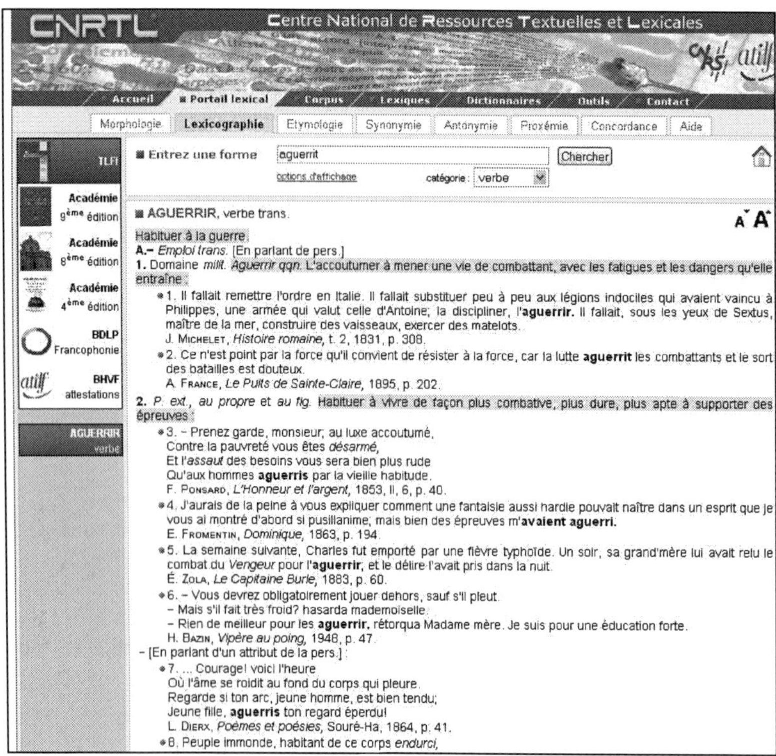

5.3.2 Morphosyntactical Information

Morphosyntactical data are taken from the *Morphalou* base (www.atilf.fr/morphalou), which was set up along with the *TLFi* nomenclature. This information is also directly available from any form of the paradigm, as in *aguerrit*, via: http://www.cnrtl.fr/morphologie/*aguerrit*.

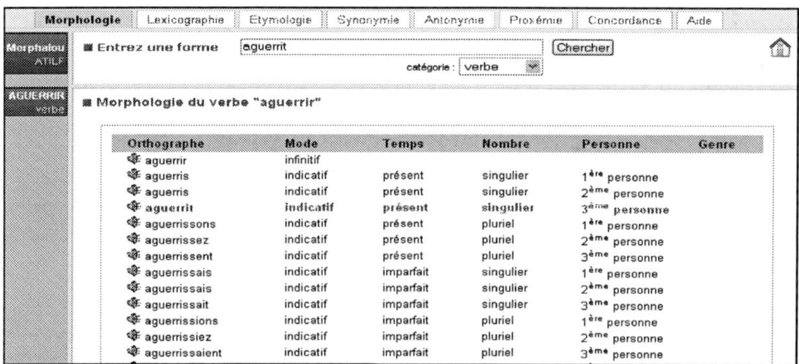

Orthographe	Mode	Temps	Nombre	Personne	Genre
aguerrir	infinitif				
aguerris	indicatif	présent	singulier	1ère personne	
aguerris	indicatif	présent	singulier	2ème personne	
aguerrit	indicatif	présent	singulier	3ème personne	
aguerrissons	indicatif	présent	pluriel	1ère personne	
aguerrissez	indicatif	présent	pluriel	2ème personne	
aguerrissent	indicatif	présent	pluriel	3ème personne	
aguerrissais	indicatif	imparfait	singulier	1ère personne	
aguerrissais	indicatif	imparfait	singulier	2ème personne	
aguerrissait	indicatif	imparfait	singulier	3ème personne	
aguerrissions	indicatif	imparfait	pluriel	1ère personne	
aguerrissiez	indicatif	imparfait	pluriel	2ème personne	
aguerrissaient	indicatif	imparfait	pluriel	3ème personne	

5.3.3 Etymological Information

Etymological data are taken from the *TLF* (www.atilf.fr/tlfi) and the *TLF-Étym*, which updates the etymological notices of the *TLF* (see above 4.1). They are directly available, for a given form, via: http://www.cnrtl.fr/etymologie/aguerrit.

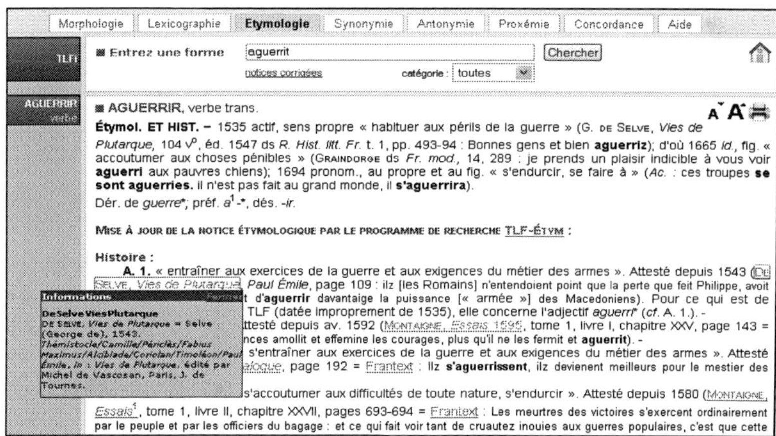

5.3.4 Synonyms and Antonyms

Data on synonyms and antonyms come from the *Caen dictionary of synonyms* (http://www.crisco.unicaen.fr/), which was set up on the basis of data from the INaLF. These data are also directly available via: http://www.cnrtl.fr/synonymie/aguerrit

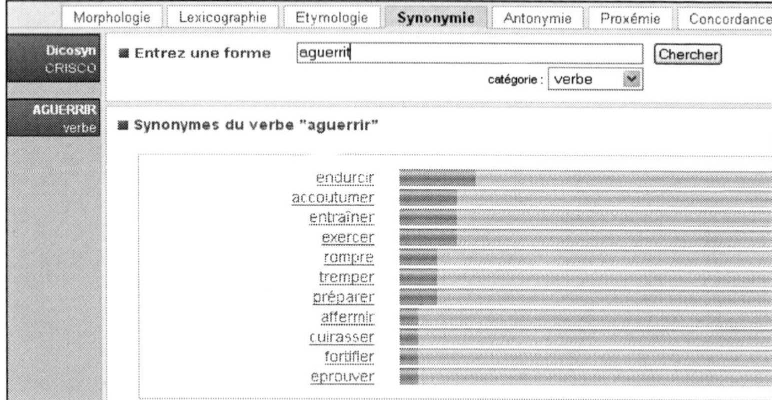

or http://www.cnrtl.fr/antonymie/aguerrit.

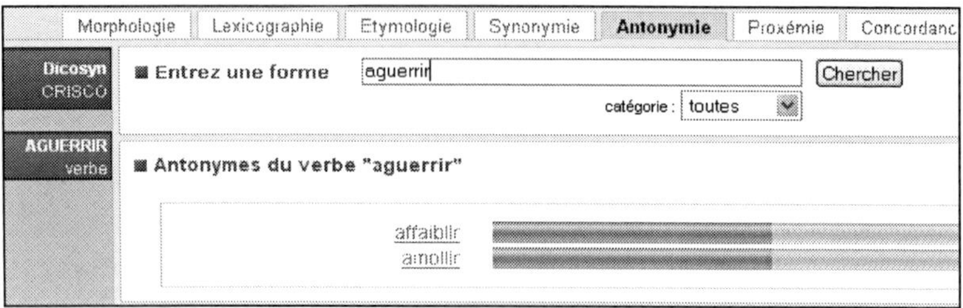

5.3.5 Concordance

This concordance makes use of the corpus of copyright-free texts on the *Frantext* database (www.atilf.fr/frantext); it also provides the option of converting the results of the concordancer into XML/TEI format. As far as we are aware, it is the only website which enables a user to convert a French concordancer of this size into a normalised format. The concordances are also directly available via: http://www.cnrtl.fr/concordance/aguerri.

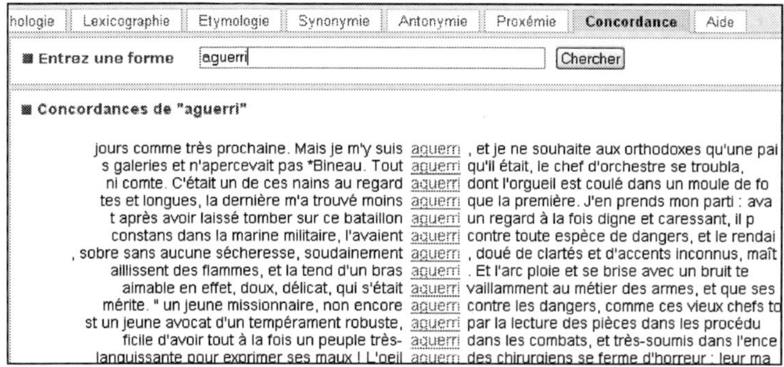

Moreover, the user only has to right-click on one of the examples to get its complete reference. Hence, for the first example:

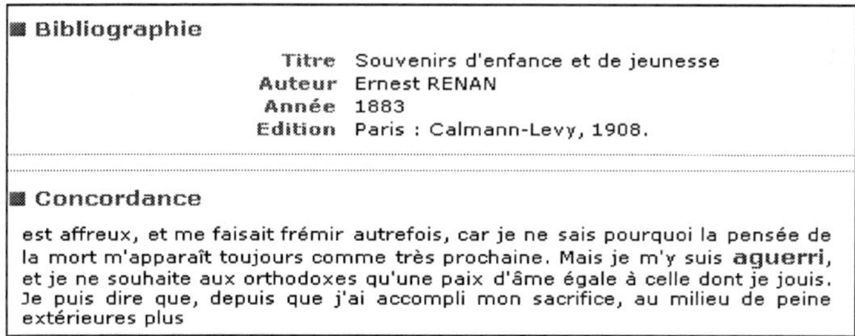

The lexical portal also permits double-clicking on a word-form and hyper-navigation to all the lexical data available regarding the given lexical unit. For instance, in order to get information concerning the form *apercevait*, from the second example in the concordance, a double-click on the word-form produces a new menu, directing the user towards all available data on this form and on the verb *apercevoir*:

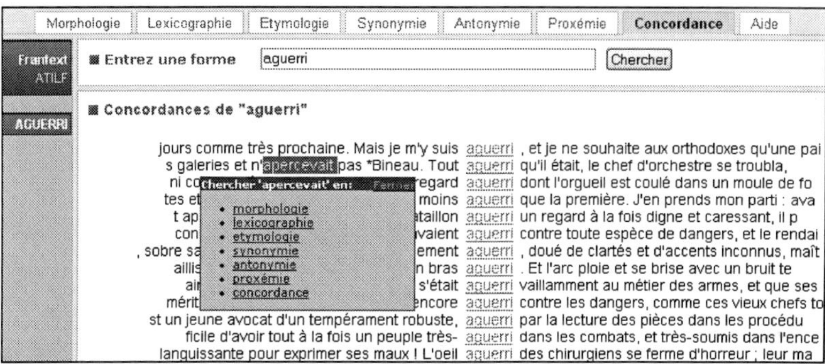

5.3.6 Proximity

Also available via the CNRTL is a 3-D display of proximity (a representation of all semantically-near terms) in the French language, the result of a joint project by IRIT and ERSS (http://Prox.irit.fr) (Gaume 2006): http://www.cnrtl.fr/proxemie/aguerrir.

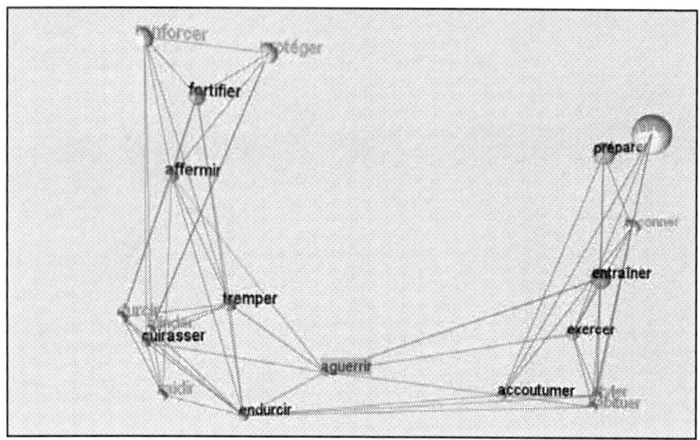

6 Conclusion

6.1 Computerisation as a Means to Enhance Lexicographical Research

As far as French is concerned, the *TLFi* has opened up ground-breaking perspectives, thanks to its rich content, entirely XML-encoded. For a long time, the *TLF* had been said to be a dictionary designed for an elite. Such a view of the *TLF* could be justified by at least three characteristics of the dictionary's printed version:

- its length, 16 volumes, each of them above 1000 pages;
- its descriptive richness, which could sometimes be viewed as an obstacle to casual reading, at least for the more complex articles; the article aimer, for instance, extends over 12 pages, or 24 columns, and it was not always easy for non-specialists to cope with such rich information;
- its cost, about 1500 euros, which prevented it being widely accessible.

Even though it soon became an authoritative reference work in the field of French lexicography, its publication was limited to a thousand or so copies, distributed to a limited public made up mainly of academics.

Its computerised version in the form of a CD-Rom (around 15,000 copies sold in less than four years) or as a freely-accessible, web-based database achieved great success among the general public, but also among scholars and language professionals. There are now 300,000 daily connections to its Web version from all around the world, and it is referenced in an innumerable range of sources. Its popularity makes it an effective means of promoting French.

Its more recent integration within the CNRTL lexical portal and its interconnections with other types of resources for French vocabulary studies place it at the core of a collection of resources on French in which it retains pride of place. It thus shows that its elitist reputation is clearly unjustified, and its diffusion on the CNRTL lexical portal (the target of around 300,000 daily hits from all around the world) makes it one of the most widely consulted dictionaries on the internet to date.

Finally, a comment on the fact that the diffusion of a computerised version of an authoritative scientific reference work now offers new scope for the production and dissemination of research findings. Beyond the purely scholarly world, new technology offers the opportunity to make our research findings available to society at large. The value of this is demonstrated by comments on the Web, on various institutional or professional websites.

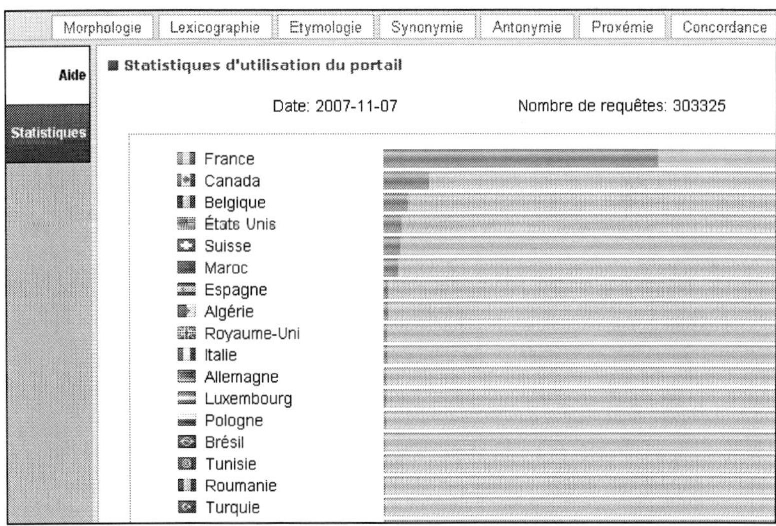

The increase in the use of enhanced, computerised versions is thus dramatically changing working methods, and the extent of collaboration, within the humanities and social sciences research communities.

6.2 From French to Romance Languages

The strategic position of the ATILF in the field of computerised lexicographical resources is, to date, chiefly of value for French alone. Nonetheless, this restriction is far from being set in stone: on the one hand, the CNRTL positively welcomes resources and instruments dedicated to languages other than French, and on the other hand, the ATILF is soon to move from French to Romance languages, at least in the field of historical lexicology.

This diversification mainly concerns Gallo-Romance languages in the first place: two types of computerised lexicography currently carried out within the *FEW* (cf. http://atilf.fr/few). The first part of this global enterprise is intended to lay the foundations of the future retroconversion of the dictionary (cf. Renders forthcoming; in progress); the second type of work concerns the computerisation of the editorial procedure (cf. Matthey / Nissille forthcoming).

A development encompassing the whole of the Romance language family is already under way thanks to the launch of the *DÉRom* project (*Dictionnaire Étymologique Roman*, cf. http://www.atilf.fr/derom and Buchi / Schweickard, forthcoming) in January 2008. The ideal might be, in the near future, the possibility of hyper-navigation between the *FEW*, the *LEI* and the *DÉRom*; only time will tell if such a goal can be achieved…

References

Andronache, Marta (2008) (in progress). "Le problème de la continuité en lexicologie historique. Réflexions à partir de la pratique lexicographique dans le cadre du projet DETCOL". [Proposal of communication submitted to the Congrès Mondial de Linguistique Française 2008].

ATILF (2004, 2005). *Trésor de la Langue Française informatisé*. Paris, CNRS Editions [with CD of the whole text, PC Version, ISBN 2-271-06273-X, Mac OX X Version, ISBN 2-271-06365-5].

Apothéloz, Denis (2003). "Le rôle de l'iconicité constructionnelle dans le fonctionnement du préfixe négatif *in-*", in *Cahiers de linguistique analogique* 1: 35-63.

Baldinger, Kurt (1959). "L'étymologie hier et aujourd'hui", in *Cahiers de l'Association internationale des Études françaises* 11: 233-264.

Benarroch, Myriam (forthcoming). "Le traitement des emprunts au portugais dans le TLFi", in Pierrel, Jean-Marie *et al.* (eds). *Actes du Colloque international "Lexicographie et informatique: bilan et perspectives" (Nancy, 23-25 janvier 2008).*

Buchi, Éva (2005). "Le projet TLF-Étym (projet de révision sélective des notices étymologiques du *Trésor de la langue française informatisé*)", in *Estudis romànics* 27: 569-571.

—. (forthcoming). "Réel, irréel, inréel: depuis quand le français connaît-il deux préfixes négatifs IN-?", in Brun-Trigaud, Guylaine *et al.* (eds). *Actes du colloque GalRom07. Diachronie du gallo-roman. Évolution de la phonologie et de la morphologie du français, du francoprovençal et de l'occitan (Nice, 15-16 janvier 2007).*

Buchi, Éva / Schweickard, Wolfgang (forthcoming). "À la recherche du protoroman: objectifs et méthodes du futur Dictionnaire Étymologique Roman (DÉRom)", in Iliescu, Maria *et al.* (eds). *Actes du XXVe Congrès International de Linguistique Romane (Innsbruck, 3-8 septembre 2007).* Tübingen, Niemeyer.

Buchi, Éva / Städtler, Thomas (in progress). "La pragmaticalisation de l'adverbe *enfin* du point de vue des romanistes ("Enfin, de celui des francisants qui conçoivent leur recherche dans le cadre de la linguistique romane")" [Proposal of communication submitted to the Congrès Mondial de Linguistique Française 2008].

Chambon, Jean-Pierre (forthcoming). "Pratique étymologique en domaine (gallo-) roman et grammaire comparée-reconstruction. À propos du traitement des mots héréditaires dans le TLF et le FEW".

Chambon, Jean-Pierre / Carles, Hélène (2007). "À propos du traitement des emprunts à l'occitan dans le *Trésor de la langue française*", in Rézeau, Pierre (ed.), *Richesses du français et géographie linguistique*, vol. 1. Bruxelles, de Boeck: 313-325.

Chambon, Jean-Pierre / Grélois, Emmanuel (2007). "Pour la révision de l'article *cheire* du *Trésor de la langue française*", in Rézeau, Pierre (ed.). *Richesses du français et géographie linguistique*, vol. 1. Bruxelles, de Boeck: 327-360.

Chauveau, Jean-Paul (2007). "FEW: article BĀJULA", in *ATILF* (2004, 2005) [http://www.atilf. fr/few/bajula.pdf].

DEAF = Baldinger, Kurt *et al.* (1974–). *Dictionnaire Étymologique de l'Ancien Français.* Québec / Tübingen / Paris, Presses de l'Université Laval / Niemeyer / Klincksieck.

Dendien, Jacques / Pierrel, Jean-Marie (2003). "Le Trésor de la Langue Française informatisé: un exemple d'informatisation d'un dictionnaire de langue de référence", in *Traitement Automatique des Langues* 44, 2: 11-37.

DMF[0] = Martin, Robert (dir.) (1998). *Dictionnaire du Moyen Français (DMF). 1330–1500, A-AH.* Nancy, INaLF.

DMF = *Dictionnaire du Moyen Français.* Nancy, ATILF/Nancy-Université & CNRS. [http://www.atilf.fr/dmf].

FEW = Wartburg, Walter von *et al.* (1922-2002). *Französisches Etymologisches Wörterbuch. Eine Darstellung des galloromanischen Sprachschatzes*, 25 vols. Bonn / Heidelberg / Leipzig-Berlin / Bâle, Klopp / Winter / Teubner / Zbinden.

Gaume, Bruno (2006). "Cartographier la forme du sens dans les petits mondes lexicaux", in *JADT*: 541-465.

Gerner, Hiltrud (2005). "La *Base des Lexiques du Moyen Français* (*BLMF*): *Première étape vers le DMF électronique*", in Kabatek, Johannes / Pusch, Claus D./ Raible, Wolfgang (eds). *Romanistische Korpuslinguistik II: Korpora und diachrone Sprachwissenschaft*, Tübingen, Narr: 155-162.

—. (2007a). "Le *Lexique Complémentaire*: deuxième étape vers le DMF électronique", in Trotter, David (ed.). *Actes du XXIV*[e] *Congrès International de Linguistique et de Philologie Romanes*, vol. 4. Tübingen, Niemeyer: 69-77.

—. (2007b). "Constitution et évolution des corpus textuels et lexicaux à l'ATILF. Interconnexion des ressources", in Kunstmann, Pierre / Stein, Achim (eds). *Le Nouveau Corpus d'Amsterdam. Actes de l'atelier de Lauterbad (23-26 février 2006)*. Stuttgart, Steiner:101-109.

—. (forthcoming). "Cueillette de quelques attestations intéressantes dans le Lexique des *Miracles Nostre Dame par personnages*".

Gerner, Hiltrud / Martin, Robert (2005). "Le lexique de la langue scientifique à l'aune du FEW", in Jacquart, Danielle /James-Raoul, Danièle / Soutet, Olivier (eds). *Par les mots et les textes. Mélanges de langue, de littérature et d'histoire des sciences médiévales offerts à Claude Thomasset*. Paris, Presses de l'Université de Paris-Sorbonne: 357-370.

Godefroy, Frédéric (1881-1902). *Dictionnaire de l'ancienne langue française et de tous ses dialectes du IX*[e] *au XV*[e] *siècle*, 10 vols. Paris, Vieweg.

Gorcy, Gérard / Martin, Robert / Maucourt, Jacques / Vienney, Roland (1970). "Le traitement des groupes binaires", in *Cahiers de Lexicologie* 2: 15-46.

Gouvert, Xavier (2007). "Le traitement étymologique des 'francoprovençalismes' dans le *Trésor de la langue française. Problèmes méthodologiques et étude de cas*", in Rézeau, Pierre (ed.). *Richesses du français et géographie linguistique*, vol. I. Bruxelles, de Boeck: 361-413.

Greub, Yan (2003). *Les Mots régionaux dans les farces françaises. Étude lexicologique sur le Recueil Tissier (1450–1550).* Strasbourg, Bibliothèque de linguistique romane.

Habert, Benoît (1995). "Traitements probabilistes et Corpus", in *Traitement Automatique des Langues* 36: 1-2.

—. (2005). "Portrait de linguiste(s) à l'instrument", in *Texto!*, 10, 4 [http://www.revue-texto.net/Corpus/Publications/Habert/Habert_Portrait.html].

Habert, Benoît / Nazarenko, Adeline / Salem, André (1997). *Les linguistiques de corpus*. Paris, Armand Colin.

INALF = Frantext (outil de consultation de ressources informatisées sur la langue française) (1992). Nancy, ATILF (CNRS & Nancy-Université) [http://www.frantext.fr].

Mosegaard Hansen, Maj-Britt (2005). "From prepositional phrase to hesitation marker. The semantic and pragmatic evolution of French *enfin*", in *Journal of Historical Pragmatics* 6: 37-68.

Huguet = Huguet, Edmond (1925–1967). *Dictionnaire de la langue française du seizième siècle*, 7 vols. Paris, Champion / Didier.

Imbs, Paul (ed.) (1961). *Lexicologie et lexicographie françaises et romanes. Orientations et exigences actuelles (12-16 novembre 1957)*. Strasbourg / Paris, Éditions du CNRS.

Imbs, Paul / Quemada, Bernard (eds) (1971–1994). *Trésor de la Langue Française. Dictionnaire de la langue du XIXe et du XXe siècle (1789–1960)*, 16 vols. Paris, Éditions du CNRS / Gallimard.

Laporte, Eric (1997). "Les Mots. Un demi-siècle de traitment", in *Traitement Automatique des Langues*, 38, 2: 47-68.

LEI = Pfister, Max / Schweickard, Wolfgang (eds.) (1979–). *Lessico etimologico italiano*. Wiesbaden, Reichert.

Martin, Robert (2001). *Sémantique et automate*. PUF, Paris.

—. (2007). *Dictionnaire du Moyen Français (DMF) (1330–1500)*. [Second version: DMF2] [http://atilf.atilf.fr/gsouvay/dmf2/ PresentationDMF2.pdf].

Martin, Robert / Gerner, Hiltrud / Souvay, Gilles (forthcoming). "Présentation de la seconde version du DMF (*Dictionnaire du Moyen Français*)", in Iliescu, Maria *et al.* (eds). *Actes du XXV*[e] *Congrès International de Linguistique Romane (Innsbruck, 3-8 septembre 2007)*. Tübingen, Niemeyer.

Martin, Robert / Souvay, Gilles (2003). "Quelle postérité électronique pour le Godefroy?", in Duval, Frédéric (ed.). *Frédéric Godefroy, Actes du X*[e] *colloque international sur le moyen français organisé à Metz du 12 au 14 juin 2002 par le Centre "Michel Baude, littérature et spiritualité" et par l'ATILF (UMR 7118)*. Paris, École des Chartes: 393-403.

Matthey, Anne-Christelle / Nissille, Christel (forthcoming). "L'irruption de l'informatique dans la rédaction d'un dictionnaire historique: l'exemple du FEW (*Französisches Etymologisches Wörterbuch*)", in Iliescu, Maria *et al.* (eds). *Actes du XXV*[e] *Congrès International de*

Linguistique Romane (Innsbruck, 3-8 septembre 2007). Tübingen, Niemeyer.

Pascual Rodríguez, José Antonio / García Pérez, Rafael (2007). *Límites y horizontes en un diccionario histórico*. Salamanque, Diputación de Salamanca.

Petrequin, Gilles / Andronache, Marta (in print). "Le projet TLF-Étym: apports récents de l'étymologie comparée-reconstruction". [Proposal of communication submitted to the XIII International Congress of Euralex, Barcelona, 15-19 July 2008].

Pierrel, Jean-Marie (2000). *Ingénierie des langues*. London, Hermès Science.

—. (2005). "Un ensemble de ressources de référence pour l'étude du français: TLFi, Frantext et le logiciel Stella", in *Revue Québécoise de Linguistique* 32, 1 ["Traitement Automatique des Langues Web et Corpus"]: 155-176.

Pitz, Martina (2006). "Pour une mise à jour des notices historiques consacrées aux emprunts à l'ancien francique dans le *Trésor de la langue française informatisé*", in Buchi, Éva (ed.). *Actes du Séminaire de méthodologie en étymologie et histoire du lexique, Nancy/ATILF, année universitaire 2005/2006*. Nancy, ATILF [http://www.atilf.fr/atilf/seminaires/Seminaire_Pitz_2006-11.pdf].

Posner, Rebecca (1997). *Linguistic Change in French*. Oxford, Clarendon.

Quemada, Bernard (ed.) (1970-1998). *Matériaux pour l'histoire du vocabulaire français. Datations et documents lexicographiques*, 2 series, 48 vols. Besançon / Paris, Centre d'Étude du Vocabulaire Français / Didier / Klincksieck.

Radermacher, Ruth (2004). *Le* Trésor de la langue française. *Une étude historique et lexicographique*. [thesis, Université de Strasbourg].

Renders, Pascale (forthcoming). "L'informatisation du FEW: quels objectifs, quelles possibilités?", in Iliescu, Maria *et al.* (eds). *Actes du XXV*[e] *Congrès International de Linguistique Romane (Innsbruck, 3-8 septembre 2007)*. Tübingen, Niemeyer.

Renders, Pascale (in progress). "Modélisation d'un discours étymologique. Prolégomènes à l'informatisation du FEW (*Französisches Etymologisches Wörterbuch*)" [thesis, Université de Liège / Université Nancy 2].

Ringenbach, Jean-Loup (2003). "Bibliographie des sources de Frédéric Godefroy", in Duval F. (ed.). *Frédéric Godefroy. Actes du X*[e] *colloque international sur le moyen français organisé à Metz du 12 au 14 juin 2002 par le Centre "Michel Baude, littérature et spiritualité" et par l'ATILF, UMR 7118*. Paris, École des Chartes: 191-206.

—. (forthcoming). "La Bibliographie du Dictionnaire de Godefroy", in Iliescu, Maria *et al.* (eds). *Actes du XXV*[e] *Congrès International de*

Linguistique Romane (Innsbruck, 3-8 septembre 2007). Tübingen, Niemeyer.

Rothwell, William *et al.* (2005[2]) *Anglo-Norman Dictionary.* London, Maney Publishing for the Modern Humanities Research Association [http://www.anglo-norman.net (1977–1992[1])].

Souvay, Gilles (2007). "LGeRM: un outil d'aide à la lemmatisation du moyen français", in Trotter, David (ed.). *Actes du XXIVe Congrès International de Linguistique et de Philologie Romanes.* Tübingen, Niemeyer, vol. 1: 457-466.

Steinfeld, Nadine (forthcoming). "Étymologie-origine, étymologie-histoire et déonomastiques : le cas de poubelle (avec une annonce de la création de la Base des Mots-fantômes)", in Iliescu, Maria *et al.* (eds). *Actes du XXVe Congrès International de Linguistique Romane (Innsbruck, 3-8 septembre 2007).* Tübingen, Niemeyer.

Steinfeld, Nadine / Andronache, Marta (forthcoming). "Quoi de neuf du côté de la lexicographie étymologique? La méthode utilisée dans le cadre du projet TLF-Étym pour distinguer les emprunts au latin de l'Antiquité de ceux faits au latin médiéval", in Pierrel, Jean-Marie *et al.* (eds). *Actes du Colloque international "Lexicographie et informatique: bilan et perspectives" (Nancy, 23-25 janvier 2008).*

Tobler-Lommatzsch = Tobler, Adolf/ Lommatzsch, Erhard / Christmann, Hans Helmut (1925–2002). *Altfranzösisches Wörterbuch*, 11 vols. Berlin / Wiesbaden / Stuttgart, Weidmann-Steiner.

Wunderli, Peter (1982). *Du mot au texte: Actes du IIIe Colloque international sur le moyen français (Düsseldorf, 17-19 septembre 1980).* Tübingen, Narr.

PART II

SYNCHRONIC PERSPECTIVE ON OLD AND MODERN LEXICOGRAPHY

ON THE ORIGINS OF MODERN BILINGUAL LEXICOGRAPHY: INTERACTIONS BETWEEN PORTUGUESE AND OTHER EUROPEAN LANGUAGES[1]

TELMO VERDELHO

1. From its origins and throughout history, Portuguese lexicography has followed the general pattern of other European languages, although with some delay and within more modest dimensions, which are indicators both of linguistic marginality as well as of limited demographic relevance.

As in most modern languages, Portuguese dictionaries have an inter-linguistic origin; they evolved through a process of interaction, first with Latin and later *vis-à-vis* neighbouring contemporary languages.

In the history of lexicographical relations, among all European languages Portuguese had the privilege of being the first one to associate itself with remote Eastern languages. Portuguese was a pioneer since it took the Latin alphabet to China and Japan, thus becoming a protagonist in the earliest transeuropean lexicographical exchanges.

In 1588, the Italian Jesuit missionaries Michele Ruggieri (1543-1607) and Matteo Ricci (1552-1610) compiled the first Portuguese-Chinese dictionary in Macao. Portuguese nomenclature is based – with only minor changes since its conception – on Jerónimo Cardoso's *Dictionarium ex Lusitanico in Latinum sermonem*, the first printed dictionary of Portuguese, published in Lisbon by João Álvares in 1562-1563.[2]

The first interlexicographical meeting between the Portuguese and Japanese languages took place in the mid-sixteenth century and in the following forty years it developed in a number of handwritten texts. It was

---

[1] I am grateful to Maria Sofia Pimentel Biscaia for her kindly and precious support in revising the English translation of the text.

[2] John W. Witek (ed.), *Dicionário português-chinês*, s.l., Biblioteca Nacional de Lisboa, Instituto Português do Oriente, Ricci Institute, University of San Francisco, 2001 (edition and facsimilar reproduction of the ms. belonging to Archivum Romanum Societatis Iesu, Japonica et Sinica). Cf. Barreto 2002.

not until 1595 that the first printed edition came to light in Nagasaki with the publication of a version of the Calepino, containing both Portuguese and Japanese translations using the Latin nomenclature.[3] Less than a decade later, in 1603-1604, an important Japanese-Portuguese bilingual dictionary was published in Nagasaki, containing about 32,000 Japanese entries transcribed by Jesuit priests and friars in the Latin alphabet with their Portuguese equivalents.[4]

As a language used by missionaries, Portuguese appeared both in India and Brazil since the sixteenth century, its history being defined by a series of unique and highly-sophisticated lexicographical meetings. This pioneering exploration of other languages employed and perfected a long-established scholarly tradition whose origins could be traced back to Greek and Latin metalinguistics.

It is likely that the "lexicography of the missionaries" had neither a material influence nor a profound impact on the advancement of modern Portuguese lexicography, even in the case of bilingual dictionaries. Rather, it was in the context of grammatical knowledge and discursive arts applied to the institutionalised teaching of Latin that the lexicographical meeting of Portuguese with other modern European languages emerged and was put into practice.

2. The lexicographical works which originated from the interaction of Portuguese with other European languages, particularly French and English, not only have specific linguistic and historical relevance for diachronic studies, but also contribute to the history of language and culture. In addition, such volumes are essential for an accurate understanding of the relations maintained by Portugal with foreign states, and, most especially, of the development of both Portuguese lexicon and lexicography.

The history of Portuguese bilingual lexicography in Europe has yet to be considered in a systematic way. Although there do exist some partial

---

[3] *Dictionarium Latino Lusitanicum ac Iaponicum ex Anbrosii Calepini volumine depromptum: i quo omissis nominibus propriis tam locorum quam hominum, ac quibusdam aliis minus usitatis, omnes vocabulorum significationes, elegantioresque dicendi modi apponuntur: in usum et gratiam Iaponicae iuuentutis, quae Latino idiomati operam nauat, necnon Europeorum, qui Iaponicum sermonem addiscunt.* In Amacusa in collegio Iaponico Societatis Iesu. Cum facultate Superiorum. Anno M.D.XCV.

[4] *Vocabulario da lingoa de Iapam com a declaração em Portugues, feito por alguns padres e irmãos da Companhia de Iesu*, Nagasaki, Colégio Typography, 1603-1604 (cf. Verdelho 1998).

and rare studies in this field, we are, nevertheless, unable at this stage to offer a well-documented and informed account of the situation, one describing the relatively abundant output of those four centuries, corresponding to the production of several hundred texts, and which reached its peak in the second half of the eighteenth century. This article will attempt to provide a general and comprehensive overview of the origins and early developments of Portuguese bilingual lexicography up until the nineteenth century. Due to the thematic constraints of the volume, this article will not consider Latin-Portuguese lexicography, as its general features are sufficiently known so as to justify its exclusion in this instance, even though studies on this subject have so far been limited.

This article will attempt to trace the above-mentioned production through an examination of known and accessible texts – especially those in printed form – which register direct meetings between Portuguese and other languages.

3. Meetings between Portuguese and other European languages flourished from the end of the sixteenth century (1598) with Berlaimont's plurilingual vade-mecum entitled *Colloquia et Dictionariolum octo Linguarum, Latinae, Gallicae, Belgicae, Teutonicae, Italicae, Anglicae, et Portugallicae. Liber omnibus linguarum studiosis domi ac fori apprime necessarius.*[5]

Its lexical corpus is relatively elementary in nature, consisting of about 1100 entries according to the alphabetic order of one of the other languages. Its universal usage is basically limited to essential communication of travellers in strange lands and to commercial discourse. Portuguese is included in only twenty editions published between 1598 and 1692. In the editions which I had access to, Portuguese words and sentences also tended to overlap with correlative languages, namely with Spanish.[6]

4. Although the authentic plurilingual knowledge of Berlaimont's glossary cannot be ignored, it is of little significance. The actual origins of the first genuine linguistic meeting between Portuguese and another European language occurred, predictably, in the Iberian Peninsula. It is in the context of an essentially Latin lexicography, based upon a trilingual corpus of Latin, Portuguese and Spanish, that the seventeenth-century

[5] Cf. Gallina 1959: 73-91.

[6] Riccardo Rizza (ed.), *Colloquia et dictionariolum octo linguarum Latinæ, Gallicæ, Belgicæ, Teutonicæ, Hispanicæ, Italicæ, Anglicæ, Portugallicæ*, Viareggio-Lucca, Mauro Baroni Editore, 1996 (repr. of Venezia, Tip. Juliana, 1656).

works of Amaro Roboredo (*Raizes da lingua latina mostradas em hum tratado, e diccionario: isto he, hum compendio do Calepino com a composição, e derivação das palavras, com a ortografia, quantidade e frase dellas*, Lisbon, Pedro Craesbeeck, 1621, cf. Verdelho 1999) and Bento Pereira (*Prosodia in Vocabularium Trilingue, Latinum, Lusitanicum, & Hispanicum digesta, in qua dictionum significatio, et sylabarum quantitas expenditur*, Eborae, Apud Emmanuelem Carualho Academiae Typographum, 1634, cf. Verdelho 1992) were created. However, these works, which can be defined as Castilian lexicographical annotations, on the whole remain unsystematic, thin, fragmented and almost dissimulated. Their entries appear to be integrated within a Latin system which does not take into consideration either the Castilian or Portuguese alphabetical layout. Amaro Roboredo, in the introductory *Advertencia*, offers the following explanation:

> faltando a castelhana, sabe que a mesma palavra sem nenhuma differença, he Portuguesa e Castelhana, ao menos quanto aas letras, e significação, posto que a pronunciação seja diversa [in the absence of a Castilian word, it is assumed that that word, without any dissimilarity, is both Portuguese and Castilian as far as spelling and signification are concerned, even though the pronunciation might be different].

This same criterion, which is based exclusively on a certain disparity between the languages, appears to have been adopted by Bento Pereira as well.

There is no data relating to the reception, usefulness, or repercussions of these lexicographical records. In fact, Amaro Roboredo's dictionary was published in only one edition, while Pereira's *Prosodia* became a bilingual dictionary with the 1697 edition, thus omitting all data pertaining to the Castilian language. It is clear at this stage that such comparisons between the two peninsular languages deserve a more in-depth and attentive study.

In 1721, Bluteau published, as an appendix to the eighth volume of his monumental *Vocabulario*, a *Diccionario castelhano y portuguez* (189 pages, *magno in quarto*), in which corresponding terms are listed in simple alphabetical order for both languages. The Portuguese-Spanish volume contains a basic vocabulary of around 1200 words, while the Spanish-Portuguese volume is notably richer, with a total of some 22,000 entries. As with previous dictionaries, the wordlists are ordered according to the corresponding term in the other language, while a more systematic layout is achieved through the alphabetisation of both the Spanish and Portuguese entries. In the case of analogous forms between Castilian and Portuguese in the Spanish-Portuguese dictionary (of which there are more than 11,000) the entry is simply replaced with the Latin particle *id.*

The lexicographical content presents the standard equivalent and paratactic sequence of equivalent forms for each language but it is optimised by the addition of elements of semantic value, and which typically lie outside the framework of bilingual intercommunication.[7]

5. In terms of pre-modern bilingual lexicography, besides its relationship with Spanish, the contact between Portuguese and other European languages can be said to have initiated in London in 1701, and in Amsterdam in 1714. In London was published a bilingual dictionary entitled *A Complete Account of the Portuguese Language, Being a Copious Dictionary of English with Portuguese, and Portuguese with English.* This dictionary was signed with the enigmatic initials A.J., maybe referring to Alexander Justice; however, further research on this matter would be required to confirm a positive identification of its author.[8]

The first section of the dictionary, entitled *Vocabularium Anglo-Lusitanicum*, is 195 pages long, while the second, *Vocabularium Lusitano-Anglicum*, contains 181 unnumbered pages. It has not been possible so far to verify the origins of the English wordlist, although it may have been copied from John Bullokar's dictionary, *An English Expositor, or, Compleat dictionary: teaching the interpretation of the hardest words, and most useful terms of art, used in our language, first set forth by J. B.*,

---

[7] The *Diccionario castelhano y portuguez* includes about 2000 proper nouns and toponyms (cities, islands, kingdoms, rivers, mountains, etc.), as well as over 500 annotations of hyperonimic classifiers and terms relating to specialised fields, with the following order of frequency for a total of up to nine occurrences: *Ciudad* 'city' (975), *Termino* 'term' (287), *Villa* 'town' (212), *Region* 'region' (210), *Yerva* 'herb' (202), *Rio* 'river' (129), *Pueblos* 'peoples' (105), *Medico* 'physician' (104), *Isla* 'island' (94), *Ave* 'bird' (68), *Reyno* 'kingdom' (60), *Arbol* 'tree' (54), *Monte* 'hill' (45), *Provincia* 'province' (43), *Anatomico* 'anatomical' (34), *Animal* 'animal' (32), *Cavallo* 'horse' (29), *Piedra* 'stone' (28), *Mar* 'sea' (25), *Pece* 'fish' (25), *Pescado* 'fish for human consumption' (24), *Titulo* 'title' (23), *Astronomico* 'astronomical' (20), *Moneda* 'currency' (20), *Canto* 'singing' (19), *India* 'India' (19), *Lugar* 'place' (17), *Planta* 'plant' (17), *Fruto* 'fruit' (16), *Figura* 'picture' (15), *Flor* 'flower' (15), *Nautico* 'nautical' (15), *trigo* 'wheat' (14), *casa* 'house' (13), *Islas* 'isles' (13), *Palabra* 'word' (13), *tierra* 'land' (12), *Medida* 'measure' (11), *Navio* 'vessel' (11), *Color* 'colour' (10), *dentes* 'teeth' (10), *Dignidad* 'dignity' [noble title] (10), *Musica* 'music' (10), *pequena* 'small' (10), *Aguas* 'waters' (9), *Chimico* 'chemical' (9), *Constelacion* 'constellation' (9), *Cousa* 'thing' (9), *Moço* 'lad' (9) (cf. Salas Quesada 2003).

[8] Cf. Torre 1996.

originally published in 1616, and continually re-edited throughout the seventeenth century up until 1688. It is possible however that other English-Latin dictionaries were also used as reference sources for selecting entries in the first section, most notably, those compiled by John Rider (1562-1632) and Elisha Coles (1624-1680) and repeatedly reedited in the second half of the seventeenth century. The Portuguese wordlist pertaining to the second section (*Lusitano-Anglicum*) is transcribed in its entirety from Bento Pereira's *Tesouro da lingua portuguesa* (Lisboa, Craesbecck, 1647) and is part of a Portuguese alphabetisation of 24,000 entries.[9] The same wordlist was later used in *Tesóuro dos Vocábulos das dûas Línguas Portuguéza, e Bélgica*, published in Amsterdam in 1714 by Abraham Alewyn and Joannes Collé.

It is clear from their place of publication (England and The Netherlands) that both dictionaries were intended for English and Flemish speakers; it can only be assumed that their Portuguese readership had limited access to these works owing to the fact that not only were they never re-edited, but they also failed to establish any concrete lexicographical tradition. As far as the Portuguese language is concerned, the most interesting feature of these lexicographical milestones remains the significant Portuguese wordlist contained within the articles of the English-Portuguese dictionary.

6. Effectively the first interlinguistic contact with the languages of central Europe took place in seventeenth-century Portugal with the organisation of grammars. The Barbosa Machado's *Biblioteca Lusitana* (vol. III, pp. 343-344) refers to two manuscripts, the *Arte de Grammatica Italiana* and the *Arte de Grammatica Francesa*, edited by Manuel Pires de Almeida (1597-1655) in or around the 1640s, which unfortunately are now lost.

The book *Arte da lingoa francesa para facilmente, e brevemente aprender a leer, escrever, & fallar essa Lingoa*, a small volume (86 [2] pages, 14 cm) written by João da Costa and published in Lisbon in 1679, marks the beginning of the interlinguistic relationship between Portuguese and European languages. This relationship would develop further in the early decades and throughout the eighteenth century with the publication of other teaching handbooks for French, Italian, Flemish, English and German, in which the lexical information was gradually enlarged.

In terms of its interaction with other European languages, the lexical component represented an important precursor to the bilingual dictionary,

---

[9] The text has been digitally registered as part of the project Corpus Lexicográfico do Português and can be accessed at http://clp.dlc.ua.pt.

as a necessary appendix in the grammar books designed for the teaching of Portuguese abroad or for the teaching of foreign languages in Portugal.

Among those earlier handbooks with sections devoted to vocabulary, the most important is the *Grammatica Anglo-Lusitanica ... With a Vocabulary of Useful Words in English and Portugueze*, published anonymously in Lisbon in 1705. As the place of publication suggests, this volume was produced for Portuguese readers, and it was certainly for this public that such basic dictionary was highlighted in the title. The dictionary *A compleat account of the Portugueze language* had been published in London four years earlier, but remained largely inaccessible to those living in Portugal who wished to study English.

The French and Italian grammar handbooks written by Luís Caetano de Lima (1671-1757) can be said to be of equal importance in terms of their lexical contribution. The *Grammatica franceza, ou arte para aprender o francez por meio da lingua portugueza* was first published in 1710 and then republished in 1733, followed in 1734 by the *Grammatica italiana e Arte para aprender a Lingua Italiana por meyo da Lingua Portugueza*, both of which were issued in several editions.

These grammars followed a relatively systematic layout and included significant lexical data. Their copious wordlists contain both prosodic and morphological information, as well as abundant listings of grammatical paradigms such as irregular verbs, nouns, adverbs, and connectors in both languages. Aside from a para-lexicographical corpus of the type used in most foreign language and even vernacular grammar handbooks, there are also a small number of vocabularies taking the form of small dictionaries, which list the lexicon used in oral and written communication. One example of such a vocabulary is the afore-mentioned *Grammatica italiana e Arte para aprender a Lingua Italiana por meyo da Lingua Portugueza*, published in Lisbon in 1734 by the Theatine Luís Caetano de Lima and republished in 1756 and 1784 without significant alterations.

In the 1756 edition, specific lexical data occupies some 140 pages and is divided into two sections: Italian-Portuguese and Portuguese-Italian. The former coincides with chapter XXXII (pp. 273-351) and is entitled *De alguns Nomes e Verbos, que encerrão alguma difficuldade mais particular; e das observaçoens que sobre elle fazem os Academicos da Crusca, ou algum author dos de melhor nota, póstos por ordem Alfabetica*. It presents around 900 entries arranged in a dictionary way, listing the Italian word followed by its Portuguese equivalent and also including some synonyms. Certain Italian expressions – which are also translated into Portuguese – have been added to many of the definitions. The first entry is *Acconciare*, accompanied by the following definition:

> Concertar, preparar, pôr em bom estado. *Acconciarsi la testa*. Concertar o cabello, toucar-se. *Acconciarse* sómente. Concertar-se, vestir-se, compor-se. *Acconciarsi insieme*. Ajustar-se entre si, compôr-se, reconciliar-se. *S'aconciò cò Fiorentini*. Ajustou-se com os Florentinos (p. 273).

Of equal interest are the definitions offered for the following entries: *biasimare, brusco, caldo, Crusca*,[10] as well as *Schiudere, Spavento, Scrocare, Vago*.[11]

The lexicographical data concerning Portuguese to Italian is added in the final section as an appendix, which is not included in the 34 chapters of the grammar's initial index. It occupies pages 351 to 412 and is contained under the title: *Compendio de varios nomes proprios, e termos particulares de artes e sciencias, divididos por classes de materias*. This final section is methodically organised and takes the form of a small dictionary compiled along didactic lines, with some 2000 words arranged according to semantic domains. The model for this kind of vocabulary was clearly well-established, as similar works are known to have been used for the teaching of Latin in medieval monastic schools. These "pocket dictionaries" (a little scholarly handbook of word meanings) were to appear in large numbers all over Europe from the sixteenth century onwards. In 1551 one of these small lexicographical handbooks introduced the biblionym *dictionarium* into Portuguese typography, the *Hieronymi Cardosi Dictionarium Iuventuti studiosae admodum frugiferum*.

The vocabularies of Caetano de Lima were sufficiently sophisticated and methodical lexically speaking, even enough to place them on a par with the basic dictionaries of today, which are organised resorting to linguistic statistics. For example, the *Vocabulário do Português Fundamental*, published in 1984, contains 2217 entries and, from a semantic point of view, its wordlist corresponds to a similarly elementary level. The diachronic contrast between these two bilingual dictionaries provides significant information regarding the history of both languages, daily life and, more generally speaking, cultural memory.

---

[10] «Farello. Nome que tomou a famosa Academia da Crusca, para mostrar que com o seu trabalho separa a farinha mimosa dos farellos, isto he, as palavras boas das más» (p. 285).

[11] «Errante. *Le stelle vaghe*. As estrellas, os astros errantes. Significa tambem desejoso. *Queste cose mi fanno vago di saper chi tu sii*. Estas cousas me fazem vir a curiosidade de saber quem tu és. Tambem se diz daquillo que dá gosto, que agrada. *Di questo sogliono le donne essere più vaghe*. Disto se costumaõ pagar, ou aggradar mais as mulheres. Algumas vezes quer dizer gentil, engraçado. *La sua vaga bellezza*. A sua engraçada formosura» (p. 344).

The numerous reprints of Caetano de Lima's handbook on Italian are a clear indicator of the significant presence of the language in eighteenth-century Portugal. This growing interest in Italian saw the publication at the end of the century of an extensive bilingual dictionary (to be discussed later) and this influence was to continue into the nineteenth century with the wide circulation of António Michele's[12] *Thesouro da Lingua Italiana* (1803).

Prior to the diffusion of dictionaries, another important work to be considered is Carlos Folqman's *Grammatica hollandeza, ou Methodo compendioso para aprender a bem fallar, e escrever a lingua Hollandeza.* As with others, the lexicographical component in this volume, along with the grammatical information, is also to be used in the teaching of Flemish, which is enriched, as the title suggests, with 'abundant nomenclature, a variety of dialogues, and a collection of selected proverbs in both languages' («huma nomenclatura copiosa, varios Dialogos, e huma collecçaõ dos mais selectos Proverbios de ambas as linguas»). Compared to its predecessors, this is a smaller dictionary, listing around 1000 different words which like the others refer ostensibly to aspects of daily life and bourgeois society. In Folqman's wordlist, the entries are listed in Dutch alone and, as a result, their Portuguese equivalents do not conform to an established nomenclature, demonstrating both the originality and colloquial fluency of the author. This work also provides us with interesting information regarding the history of Portuguese language, such as, for example, the thematic section with the curious title of *Qualidades Infames* (p. 92), which includes the words *Matador, traydor, Feiticeiro, Ladraõ, Puta, Putanheiro, Ladraõ de estrada, Prêzo, Agarrador, quadrilheiro, Forca, Carrasco.*

The interlinguistic and pre-dictionaristic context had a plurilinguistic expression in foreign language teaching handbooks such as in a booklet published by Álvares da Silva in 1764: *Collecção da palavras familiares portuguezas, francezas, latinas e britanicas: com huma breve instrucção para perceber e ainda fallar o idioma frances.* This volume takes the form of a small teaching handbook in which Latin and Portuguese are presented alongside English and French, the two modern languages most in demand across Europe, and destined to be established as the core subjects in interlinguistic studies. The handbook opens a general dictionary of 45 pages consisting mainly of nouns and organised into semantic or thematic fields which follow the established pattern of previous vocabularies of its kind. In addition, ten pages of verbs are also included following a

[12] An interesting personality, he was appointed to the chair of *Língua Italiana, Francesa e Inglesa* in Lisbon.

Brevissima instrucçaõ para perceber com brevidade o Idioma Frances (pp. 46-100). The word entry is Portuguese, followed by French, Latin and English, while for the verb wordlist the sequence is French, Portuguese, Latin, English. The volume contains some 1800 words, including verbs. Contrary to what the title appears to propose, the entries included are, for the most part, unsuitable for everyday language demands.

It is not known what the reception for this book was, but it undoubtedly was used for teaching purposes, thus positively demonstrating the growing rate of the teaching itself of the most sought-after languages. From this moment on, the supply of handbooks for the study of languages increased considerably and bilingual dictionaries also began to appear, voluminous at first, then gradually reduced to "pocket size" dimensions. The number of reprints increased.

With regard to the lexical interaction between Portuguese and German, the first vocabularies are to be found in two grammar handbooks printed in 1778 and 1785 respectively: Jung's *Portugiesische Grammatike*, published anonymously in Frankfurt, and Abraham Meldola's *Nova Grammatica Portugueza*, published in Hamburg. Once again, the entries are organised into thematic groups of quite considerable size. The former volume contains 1870 entries organised into 41 semantic groups. The latter offers a wider context for bilingual comparison: besides an anthology of literary texts with translation, it presents a Portuguese-German dictionary made up of 37 thematic groups, which form a total of 2708 entries.[13]

7. In the second half of the eighteenth century, Lisbon became the centre of a growing user and commercial demand for bilingual dictionaries and it was this period that saw the publication of the first comparative dictionaries of Portuguese and other European languages, some forty years before the first monolingual vocabularies were to appear. Meanwhile, the great Lisbon earthquake of 1755 nearly halted production of three other dictionaries, amongst which was the first French-Portuguese dictionary edited by P. José Marques. This is confirmed in the introduction (*Avis au public*) to the dictionary published by the same author in 1758:

> Nous donnames il y a quatre ans [1754?] au public ce Dictionnaire François, & Portugais, mais l'incendie du Tremblement de Terre du

[13] On the value of this linguistic "corpus" as precious evidence for the historical memory see Clara 1989 and 1997.

> premier Novembre de 1755 en aiant consumé toute l'impression, ainsi que tout ce que nous avions de librairie...[14]

The earthquake also played a part in delaying production of the first Portuguese-French dictionary, edited by the same J. Marques; the original had been approved by censors for publication in 1748, but it did not actually appear until 1764.

Despite the repercussions of the earthquake, the industry was to recover surprisingly fast, to the extent that the last decades of the eighteenth century do in fact represent the most fertile period in the history of Portuguese lexicography. Although relative to the literacy levels and actual book consumption of the time, the fifty dictionaries produced in these years can be said to constitute something of a boom. Apart from a number of smaller works, this period also saw the publication of three large dictionaries, dedicated to French, English and Italian respectively. The language of Camões finally had the lexicographical instruments necessary to interact and communicate with the rest of Europe.

These dictionaries were compiled using the Latin method established by the vocabularies of the humanist tradition, consequently setting Latin as the lingua franca amongst the speakers of Europe's numerous vernacular tongues. It should also be added that, by the end of the eighteenth century, the majority of European languages already had their own monolingual dictionaries, compiled around a set of stable and theoretically well-established vocabulary.

Once the preserve of academic and cultural circles, dictionaries came to represent a fundamental element of civilisation; they gradually acquired a level of sophistication which was testament to the unique collaboration of lexicographers and publishers who sought to improve not only the typographic layout, but also their overall functionality as works destined for public consumption. Dictionaries became a much sought-after consumer product and assumed a great value on the book market.

---

[14] Amongst those which suffered setbacks as a result of the earthquake were a Portuguese dictionary compiled by José Caetano (1690-?) as a supplement to Bluteau's *Vocabulário* which had previously been published in part (I. Silva, *Dicionário Bibliográfico*, t. IV, p. 282), and a Portuguese-Latin dictionary, mentioned by Joaquim José da Costa e Sá in the *Aviso ao Editor* of the 1794 Portuguese-French and Latin dictionary: «O Diccionario Portuguez e Latino do Padre *Carlos Folqman*, impresso em Lisboa por Miguel Manescal da Costa no anno de 1755. Esta Obra he Muito rara, por se ter queimado quasi toda a Impressão no incendio, e terremoto, succedido no mesmo anno».

Having established links with the rest of Europe, Portuguese lexicographers were able to use the new resources at their disposal in order to develop a considerably sophisticated interlinguistic lexicography.

During this period of rapid and progressive expansion of the Portuguese vocabulary, its first and most intimate links were with French. As yet we do not have a precise understanding of the way in which French-Portuguese dictionaries developed, nor how they were distributed or expanded; the result of this being that precise information regarding their authors, augmenters and revisers, as well as their reception and authority in Portuguese speaking territories is somewhat limited. We do possess, however, at this point, enough knowledge to reconstruct and build upon this picture.

Although some editions were published anonymously, the basic list of authors includes the following "pioneers": José Marques, Manuel de Sousa (1737?-?), Joaquim José da Costa e Sá (1740-1803), and Miguel Tibério Pedegache Brandão Ivo (1730?-1794). Amongst those whose contribution, while less significant, is still worthy of mention are: Vicente Pedro Nolasco da Cunha (c. 1773-1844), Vicente de Bastos Teixeira, Manuel Joaquim Henriques de Paiva (1752-1829), Pedro Mariz de Sousa Sarmento (c. 1742/1745-1822).

The lexicographical interaction between Portuguese and French was largely defined by the latter (i.e. French-Portuguese sequence), which would suggest that French was not only widely read, but that bilingual dictionaries were needed to meet the demand for a growing French readership abroad. The Portuguese public was in fact a passive receiver, and without an active need to speak French the demand for Portuguese-French dictionaries was considerably less.

Up until the beginning of the nineteenth century, four French-Portuguese dictionaries with some differences among them had been published in Lisbon; three of these are large dictionaries with rather extensive nomenclatures and a vast textual accumulation. They can be identified by author as the following: José Marques (1754; 1758-1764; 1775-1776); Manuel de Sousa and Joaquim José da Costa e Sá (1784-1786); Manuel de Sousa, Joaquim José da Costa e Sá and Vicente Pedro Nolasco da Cunha (1811).

These three French-Portuguese dictionaries are large-format, densely-filled works, in small print, containing a wealth of textual data. Named amongst their sources are the most esteemed French authors and lexicographers: the *Académie Française*, Trevoux, Furetiere, Tachard, Richelet, Danet, Boyer, to mention a few. In addition to constituting an interesting insight into the lexicographical and cultural exchange between

Portugal and France, as well as the rest of Europe, these dictionaries represent valuable instruments in the diffusion of Portuguese vocabulary by testifying abundantly on documented neologisms and offering a more complete diachronic perspective of the period 1750-1811.

Of this group of publications, one is worthy of particular mention: the *Nouveau Dictionnaire François-Portugais, composé par le Capitaine Emmanuel de Sousa, & mis en ordre, rédigé, revû, corrigé, augmenté, & enrichi de tous les termes techniques, & propres des sciences, des arts, des métiers de geographie; &c. sur la dernière édition de celui de M. l'Abbé François Alberti, & des Tables de l'Encyclopédie par Joachim Joseph da Costa & Sa* (1784-1786). Compared to previous French-Portuguese dictionaries this represents a highly innovative work, both for the breadth of vocabulary and the quality of its content. 1200 pages long and produced in small, dense print, this dictionary includes not only an extensive French nomenclature, but also a carefully organised section on Portuguese rich in synonyms, sayings and proverbs which fulfil what is promised in its preface:

> He superior este Diccionario, pois nelle se encerra hum copiosissimo Thesouro da Linguagem Portugueza dos Sabios da Idade aurea da nossa lingua; e nelle se encontrarão por sua ordem, methodicamente, e em seu justo lugar as denominações, ou significações primigenias de todos os Termos, e Vocabulos, com as Synonymas; as suas accepções translatas, ou figuradas; as Locuções, Frases, e Proverbios; &c. tudo sobre maneira digerido, e ordenado, que facilmente se poderáõ achar ao primeiro golpe de vista. / Houve hum vigilantissimo cuidado de se lhe accrescentarem todos os termos technicos, e facultativos das Sciencias, e das Artes; &c. Os Anatomicos, Botanicos, Physicos, Jurisconsultos, Theologos; &c. acharáõ nelle se não tudo, ao menos quasi tudo, o que respeita as suas Faculdades [This is a superior Dictionary, as it contains a very rich Thesaurus of Portuguese from the Golden Age of our language and it methodically reports the denominations, or primigenial meanings, of all the terms and words as well as the synonyms, figurative meanings, locutions, sentences and proverbs, all presented in an ordered way so as to be easily found at first glance. It also carefully registers a significant number of technical and specific terms from the sciences and the arts; anatomists, botanists, physicists, jurists, theologians, etc. can find most of the words related to their field of studies] (de Sousa, da Costa e Sá 1784-1786, *Aviso dos Editores*).

The print run of these dictionaries was limited and the fact that they were most likely never reissued is as much a result of the high costs they incurred as their limited functionality. This, however, was not the case with another French-Portuguese dictionary, which was the first of its kind intended for common use to be published in Portugal. The dictionary appeared at a time of great political as well as cultural upheaval, defined by the gradual "migration" of the Portuguese language to Brazil.

8. The end of the eighteenth century saw a gradual shift in Portuguese lexicography towards Luso-Brazilian, most particularly in its bilingual production, and it was in this period that the first French-Portuguese dictionary of common use became available. This dictionary, published some years prior to 1778, takes the format of an octavo pocketbook, and according to its authors was re-issued in many reprints of which at least six appeared before 1800. Here is a description from the fourth edition, which appeared in 1778 and was the first to cite the name of its author: *Novo Diccionario Francez-Portuguez, composto sobre os melhores diccionarios, illustrado com os termos facultativos das sciencias, e artes liberais e mecanicas ... por Miguel Tiberio Pedegache Brandão Ivo.*

Competition amongst the dictionary's various co-authors may explain the absence of their names from the other editions, as well as changes to the work's title; this is the title of the fifth edition: *Novo Diccionario Francez e Portugues, composto segundo os mais célebres diccionarios e enriquecido de muitos termos de medicina, de anatomia, de cirurgia, de farmacia, de quimicia* (sic), *de historia natural, de botanica, de mathematica, de marinha, e de todas as outras artes e sciencias, notavelmente corrigido, emendado, e addicionado com hum sem numero de termos, e locuçoes, e algumas frazes em ambos os idiomas*. Alterations to many of its entries and definitions also defined the changing face of the dictionary over the years, but the emphasis on the numerical order of each new edition would seem to imply that the overall structure and nature of the work remain essentially unchanged. The identity of the author Miguel Tibério Pedegache Brandão Ivo (1730?-1794) is confirmed in the introduction *Ao leitor* of the fourth edition and in Inocêncio Silva's *Dicionário bibliográfico* (vol. 6, p. 250). A revision, or collaboration between authors, is also documented. It is ascribed to Manuel Joaquim Henriques de Paiva (1755-1829), who is considered to be one of the leading interpreters of the intercommunication between Portugal and Brazil at the beginning of the nineteenth century.

From a lexicographical point of view, this dictionary is of great interest to scholars, particularly for the modern timbre of its format. Its French wordlist was carefully selected from a database of around 34,000 entries, which meant it could meet the particular demands of the growing French readership in Portugal. The rapid diffusion of this work can be taken as the first indication of a growing democratisation of the dictionary in the Portuguese language, in which the contribution of Brazil was becoming ever more prevalent. From the beginning of the nineteenth century the diffusion of the dictionary for general use would continue with the introduction of numerous "pocket" dictionaries. These volumes, which soon became the staple of an increasingly competitive market, were almost entirely produced in France, were constantly updated and became ever more compact and portable.

As far as lexicographical relations between the two languages are concerned, the non-uniform development of French-Portuguese dictionaries intended to meet the demands of a growing bilingual readership does not preclude what can be identified as an evident spirit of reciprocity amongst their compilers. The Portuguese-French version, despite the understandable lack of demand, had been elaborated almost simultaneously with the French-Portuguese one.

9. The first Portuguese-French dictionary was published in Lisbon in 1764 (although there are printing licences dated 1748), and is considered as the second volume in a set, of which the first volume would be the French-Portuguese dictionary printed in 1758 and released as a *Supplement* in 1764. On the opening page it presents a lengthy title which provides, besides other information, notes on the main sources: *Novo Diccionario das línguas portugueza, e franceza, com os termos latinos, tirado dos melhores Authores, e do Vocabulario Portuguez, e Latino do P. D. Rafael Bluteau, dos Diccionarios da Academia Francez, Universal de Trevoux, de Furetiere, de Tachard, de Richelet, de Danet, de Boyer, &c. Com os nomes proprios das Naçoens, dos Reinos, das Provincias, das Cidades, das Comarcas, dos Rios do Mundo, &c.*

The corpus in Portuguese, including nomenclature and definitions, is taken from Bluteau's *Vocabulario* with no detectable criteria or lexicographical justification. The definitions do not conform to a homogeneous structure; it presents peculiarly longer texts to illustrate what can be termed "exotic" words, but it omits many forms from daily and basic use. Despite its limited functionality, it was the only one of its kind and sold out in the space of a few years.

Portuguese-French lexicography was injected with new life by Joaquim José da Costa e Sá, one of the most dedicated Portuguese lexicographers of all time. In 1794 he published the *Diccionario portuguez-francez-e-latino*, which became the essential reference tome for all monolingual Portuguese dictionaries. In its introduction, *Aviso dos editores* (Viúva de Bertrand e Filhos), the author makes particular reference to José Marques' dictionary, which was the only one in existence at that time; in a note he observes that:

> [a] obra precisava para a sua melhor perfeição de outra ordem mais methodica, e que requeria se enriquecesse de maior número de Termos, e de Frases [To be refined [that] work needed a more methodic order and a larger number of terms and sentences].

This observation describes the aim of those two monumental volumes, whose 1229 pages were compiled with care and contained a wealth of valuable lexicographical data. This dictionary constitutes a milestone in the history of Portuguese lexicography, and its importance would most certainly merit a dedicated monographic study. Never reissued, it survived as a monumental work on its own. There was an abbreviated version (Sá 1808) which seems to have been intended as a practical monolingual Portuguese dictionary. This work included brief additional notes on French equivalents.

Portuguese-French dictionaries were not in frequent demand in the first half of the nineteenth century; as a result, only schematic pocket dictionaries of very limited dimensions and basic lexical information were printed.

After Costa e Sá's work, the Portuguese-French dictionary most worthy of note is one compiled by Inácio Roquete and published in Paris in 1841 under the title: *Nouveau dictionnaire portugais-français ... composé sur les plus récents et les meilleurs dictionnaires des deux langues*. The dictionary, which appeared in some ten editions before 1882, is accompanied by an introductory text which contains much metalinguistic and metalexicographical data of academic interest.

10. Following the isolated publication of the short-lived 'copious dictionary' («copioso dicionário») in 1701, contact between English and Portuguese was not renewed until 1773 with the appearance of a new work compiled by António Vieira Transtagano, entitled: *A Dictionary of the Portuguese and English Languages, in two parts, Portuguese and English: and English and Portuguese.*

This dictionary constitutes a fundamental work in the history of Portuguese lexicography; appearing in numerous editions and revised several times, both to extend and to condense its size, it enjoyed notable success, and undeniably represents one of the most significant elements in the Luso-Britannic relation. The preface offers the reader an interesting insight into aspects of the dictionary's production as well as the intentions of its author. Vieira declares that his work is entirely new and mentions with a certain disdain the 1701 dictionary, referring to it as: «a thing known as a Portuguese and English Vocabulary published many years ago». Doubts have been raised as to the veracity of this statement, although it has not been possible so far to satisfactorily confirm the author's account.

From a Portuguese standpoint, the most interesting product of this lexicographical development would appear to be the process of interaction between the two languages. In its relationship with English, Portuguese was able to access a vast lexicon whose differing approach to linguistic creativity encouraged the employment of diverse skills in the composition of new words.

11. Portuguese bilingual lexicography of the eighteenth century was further improved by a startlingly original Italian-Portuguese dictionary, 'edited' («coordenado»), as the author describes, by Joaquim José da Costa e Sá: *Diccionario Italiano e Portuguez. Extrahido dos melhores lexicógrafos, como de Antonini, de Veneroni, de Facciolati, de Franciosini, do Dicionário de Crusca e da Universidade de Turin* (published in two volumes in 1773 and 1774 respectively).

This dictionary, which represents an exceptional event in the history of linguistic interaction between these two languages, has yet to be subjected to any significant philological study or even critical review. It represents a monumental work, comprising two volumes *in-folio* of a total of 1650 pages, with some 70,000 Italian entries expounded in several thousand sentences and matched by a remarkably developed textual collection of Portuguese equivalents.

We have, up until this point, been unable to confirm to what extent this dictionary makes use of the nomenclatures contained in other Italian dictionaries, nor how useful its data might be for the study of Italian language and lexicography. What it does offer is a long series of semasiological data identifying the various meanings and nuances a word may possess, such as, for example, *cavalo*, which presents a collection of more than fifty varieties:

CAVALLO. s.m. Cavallo, animal de quatro pés muito conhecido.
Cavallo bajo. Cavallo baio, de cor baia.
Cavallo di bagaglio /// Cavallo de carga, de albarda.
Cavallo da somma.
Cavallo da basto.
Cavallo corsiero. Cavallo corredor.
Cavallo da posta. Cavallo da posta, ligeiro, que vai de andadura, ou de furtapasso.
Cavallo castrato. Cavallo capado, castrado.
Cavallo salvatico. Cavallo silvestre.
Cavallo bolso. Cavallo asmatico, cançado, que lhe custa a respirar.
Cavallo calcitroso // Cavallo, que atira couces.

Cavallo frisone. /// Cavallo frizão, Cavallo malhado.
Cavallo pomellato.
Cavallo pomato.
Cavallo ginetto. /// Cavallo ginete, quartão, Cavallo pequeno.
Cavallo ambiante.
Cavallo chinea.
Cavallo griccioloso. Cavallo, que deita o cavalleiro ao chão.
Cavallo domato. Cavallo manso.
Cavallo indomito. Cavallo indomito.
Cavallo intero. // Cavallo inteiro, não castrado, garanhão, cavallo de lançamento.
Cavallo stallone.
Cavallo roano. Cavallo alazão, ruivo.
Cavallo sauro. Cavallo alazão.
Cavallo leardo rotato. Cavallo ruço rodado.
Cavallo morello. Cavallo morzelo.
Cavallo ombroso. Cavallo tímido, medroso, timorato.
Cavallo senza freno. Cavallo desenfreado. [...]
(Costa e Sá, *Diccionario Italiano e Portuguez*, vol. I, p. 269).

Semasiologic sequences of this type, as well as other onomasiologic enumerations have their origins in the medieval and humanist pre-lexicographical tradition and could certainly be found in Italian dictionaries from this time.

From a Portuguese perspective, there are no doubts as to the reliability of this source; the author is clearly committed to the progress of his mother-tongue via an active exchange with Italian vocabulary; the result of this interaction being that many new words were adopted and personalised by the Portuguese language, significantly expanding its lexical horizons in the process. The author defends his position in the introduction:

> Muitas vezes me vi obrigado, especialmente nos Nomes abstractos, de que tanto abunda a lingua Italiana, a dar-lhes terminação Portugueza; não deixando com tudo de definir a sua significação por hum circumloquio mais estenso. Eu me imagino que as pessoas razoaveis, e doutas me desculparáõ a temeridade de innovar alguns Vocabulos; o que só pertence aos sogeitos de mais fundamental conhecimento na nossa Lingua. Eu confesso porém, que muitos dos que usei se achão nos Escritos, que ha tres annos a esta parte se tem divulgado, os quaes são mui authorizados para qualificarem proprios do Lusitanismo os taes Vocabulos. O certo he, que nas Linguas vivas a Regra infallível da sua pureza he o uso, e o costume das mesmas // Nações, á qual se encostão os Homen doutos, e polidos, cuja authoridade he bastante para provar de classicos, e proprios os Termos, ou Frases, que se adoptão. Esta razão só poderia livrar-me de todo o cuidado nesta parte; mas tambem me lembro, que como a lingua Portugueza he

irmã, e mui semelhante da Italiana, não lhe fiz injuria de tomar della o que faltava na nossa, o que succedeo com bastante raridade [Many times, most especially in the case of abstract nouns, which are numerous in Italian, I was called upon to provide them with a Portuguese term, prior to defining their meaning with a more extensive periphrasis. I believe that reasonable and learned persons will surely forgive the audacity I have displayed in creating these terms, a matter which usually falls to the experts of our language. I must add that I found the majority of the words contained in the writings to have spread in the last three years, qualifying them as authorities for the defining of these terms as Lusitanisms. As a rule, the purity of a given language is determined by its use and national customs, to which those scholars who are the authorities in proving the value of the terms or sentences adopted do refer. This is one of the reasons why I felt free to use these new terms; the other being that Portuguese is to be considered a sister of Italian for the strong similarities it exhibits, and so in a few cases it has simply taken from Italian what it was lacking].

Thanks to this dictionary, words of the Italian superstratum such as *gigantesco* and *sonata* were integrated in the Portuguese language. However, the most creative element of the dictionary refers to the synonymic study of language and to the abundant derivational innovation within the Portuguese lexicographical universe. The author took special care to provide a wide range of equivalences for each Italian headword therefore proffering the Portuguese section with a plentiful vocabulary.

Opening the dictionary at random, we find, for example, the forms *piacèvole* and *piacevolezza* with the following equivalents:

PIACÈVOLE. adi. m. Agradavel, cortez, affavel, civil, que se accommoda ao genio dos outros, tratavel, humano, benigno, brando, plácido, manso.
Piacèvole. Agradavel, grato, que causa gosto, engraçado, festivo, divertido, lindo, galante, aceito.
Ragionamento piacèvole. Discurso galante, e engraçado.
Luogo piacèvole. Lugar agradavel, divertido.

PIACEVOLEZZA. s.f. Affabilidade, cortezia, humanidade, brandura, facilidade, gentileza, doçura, que tem as acções, ou as palavras de alguem.
Piacevolezza. Prazer, gosto, appetite, jucundidade.
Piacevolezza. Zombaria, cousa dita, ou feita para divertir, galanteo, galanteria, brinco, gracejo.
Piacevolezza. Mansidão, brandura.
Senza piacevolezza. Defengraçado.

And also:

PIAGGIAMENTO. s. m. Adulação, lisonja, complacencia, affago, carinho; a acção de adular.

PIAGGIARE. v. a. Costear o mar, navegar por junto de huma costa. *Piaggiare.* no fig. Adular, lisonjear, comprazer, obsequiar, assentir, condescender, ir com a vontade de alguem, favorecer com a doçura das palavras a opinião de alguem para vir cautamente, e quasi com engano muito de mansinho ao fim do seu pensamento.

This is probably the bilingual dictionary offering the greatest number of synonyms in Portuguese.

Although Luso-Italian bilingual lexicography was improved and developed by various lexicographers throughout the nineteenth and twentieth centuries, it never matched the dimensions of this pioneering text.

12. As previously stated, the last decades of the eighteenth century represent a golden era in Portuguese lexicography, illuminated by the advances of Pedro José da Fonseca (1737?-1816), António de Morais Silva (1755-1824), António Vieira Transtagano (?), Joaquim José da Costa e Sá (1740-1803). The Portuguese language also owes a great debt to the work of lesser-known figures who, nevertheless, made significant contributions of their own, most particularly in specialised fields within the sphere of literary lexicography and in regaining its historical memory.

Generally speaking, it would be possible to say that interlinguistic lexicography played an important role in this fertile period of linguistic development which witnessed not only an emphasis on the history of Portuguese language, but also the inauguration of Portuguese lexicography. Broadly speaking, we are able to describe what we consider to be the three defining characteristics of this period.

First and foremost there is the progressive expansion of Portuguese to Brazil, a development which irrevocably changed the face of the linguistic landscape. Of the many consequences of this migration perhaps the most important one was the influence of the Brazilian dictionary market on the whole of future lexicographical production.

The second observation is that this period marked the beginning of a process aimed at the wider distribution of dictionaries, a phenomenon related with the increase of schooling. The outcome was that these texts became more user-friendly and functional, as well as shorter, more compact, and more readable; with this, however, also came reduced accuracy and an excessive simplifying of information.

Finally, in the last decades of the eighteenth century we can observe a general process of linguistic change, most evident in the Portuguese lexical corpus, and resulting from the proliferation of neologisms. There is at this time an increasing flow of technical terms and a growth of prefixes and suffixes in all languages, no doubt a preponderant synergetic factor in interlexicography. It was around this time that many dictionaries started to vaunt the vast quantity of their technical and scientific terminologies, perhaps unaware that it would become increasingly difficult to circumscribe. Moreover, dictionaries of this time generally contained an excess of material, as lexicographers sought to include the numerous neologisms created by the derivative processes generated by the very productive linguistic mechanisms of derivation with groups (or "constellations") of suffixes. In sixteenth-century dictionaries we find, for example, only three or four words formed by the suffix *-ismo*; at the end of eighteenth century the terms ending in *-ismo* might be over fifty, while in contemporary dictionaries the number of occurrences run into thousands. This unstoppable trend is very likely associated to multilingual interaction facilitated and intensified by multilingual dictionaries.

APPENDIX

Portuguese bilingual dictionaries (up to the beginning of nineteenth century)

Alewyn, Abraham / Collé, Joannes, *Tesóuro dos Vocábulos Das dûas Línguas Portuguéza, e Bélgica; Em que circunstanteménte se demõstrão as sinificaçoës das Palávras Poruguézas segúndo a abundáncia da Belgica siéncia da Linguágem; Hüa óbra, geralménte, Péra tódos os amadóres das ámbas Línguas, e Principalménte Péra ós ensinadóres e discípúlos das mésmas grandeménte proveitósa. Por Mtre. Abrahamo Alewyn, e João Collé.* Amsterdam, Pieter Vandevanden Berge, 1714.

Bluteau, Rafael, *Diccionario Castellano, y Portuguez para facilitar a los curiosos la noticia de la lengua Latina, con el uso del Vocabulario Portuguez, y Latino, printed in Lisboa por orden del Rey de Portugal D. Juan V.* Lisboa Occidental, Imprenta de Pascoal da Sylva, Impressor de Su Magestad, 10 vols, 1712-1728, repr. Rio de Janeiro, 1841. [With a foreword by Raphael Bluteau, *Prosopopeia del idioma Portuguez, a su hermana la lengua Castellana; y a este discurso se sigue una Tabla de palabras Portuguezas, mas remotas del idioma Castellano*, published as an appendix to the eighth volume of *Vocabulário* (1721)].

Colloquia et dictionariolum octo linguarum Latinæ, Gallicæ, Belgicæ, Teutonicæ, Hispanicæ, Italicæ, Anglicæ, Portugallicæ, edited by Riccardo Rizza et alii. Viareggio-Lucca, Mauro Baroni Editore, 1996 [Repr. of Venezia, Tip. Juliana, 1656].

Costa, João da, *Arte da lingoa francesa para facilmente, e brevemente aprender a leer, escrever, & fallar essa Lingoa. Offerecida a Sra. D^a. Violante Manrique de Mendonça.* Lisboa, Miguel Des Landes, 1679.

Dictionarium Latino Lusitanicum ac Iaponicum ex Ambrosii Calepini volumine depromptum: in quo omissis nominibus propriis tam locorum quam hominum, ac quibusdam aliis minus usitatis, omnes vocabulorum significationes, elegantioresque dicendi modi apponuntur: in usum et gratiam Iaponicae iuuentutis, quae Latino idiomati operam nauat, necnon Europeorum, qui Iaponicum sermonem addiscunt. Amacusa, Collegio Iaponico Societatis Iesu, 1595.

Folqman, Carlos, *Grammatica hollandeza, ou Methodo compendioso para aprender a bem fallar, e escrever a lingua Hollandeza segundo o estylo mais moderno, principalmente de W. Sewel. Com huma nomenclatura copiosa, varios Dialogos, e huma collecçaõ dos mais selectos Proverbios de ambas as linguas*. Lisboa, Herd. de Antonio Pedroso Galram, 1742 [2nd ed. Amsterdam, J. Kok, 1765; 3rd ed. Lisboa, Imp. Regia, 1804].

Grammatica Anglo-Lusitanica: Or a short and Compendious System of an English and Portugueze Grammar, Containing All the most Useful and Necessary Rules of Syntax, and Construction of the Portugueze Tongue. Together with some Useful Dialogues and Colloquies, agreable to common Conversation. With a Vocabulary of Useful Words in English and Portugueze. Designed for, and fitted to all Capacities, and more especially such whose Chance or Business may lead them into any part of the World where that Language is used or esteemed. Lisboa, Miguel Manescal, Impressor do Santo Officio, 1705.

Ivo, Miguel Tibério Pedegache Brandão, *Novo Diccionario francez-portuguez, composto sobre os melhores diccionarios, illustrado com os termos facultativos das sciencias, e artes liberais, e mecanicas, dedicado ao Illust.mo e Excellent.mo Senhor Marquez de Anjeja, dos Conselhos da Rainha N. Senhora, e de Guerra, Gentil-homem da sua Cammara, Tenente General dos seus Exercitos, Ministro adjunto ao despacho do seu Gabinete, Presidente do Erario Regio, Intendente Geral da Marinha, Commendador da Ordem de Christo, e Sant-Iago, &c., &c., &c.. Por Miguel Tiberio Pedegache Brandão Ivo. Quarta edição Examinada, revista e addicionada*. Lisboa, Na Regia Officina Typografica, 1778 [Com licença da Real Meza Censoria].

Ivo, Miguel Tibério Pedegache Brandão, *Novo Diccionario Francez e Portugues, composto segundo os mais célebres diccionarios e enriquecido de muitos termos de medicina, de anatomia, de cirurgia, de farmacia, de quimicia (sic), de historia natural, de botanica, de mathematica, de marinha, e de todas as outras artes e sciencias, notavelmente corrigido, emendado, e addicionado com hum sem numero de termos, e locuçoes, e algumas frazes em ambos os idiomas*. Lisboa, Filipe da Silva e Azevedo, 1786 5th ed.

J. (Justice ?), A.(Alexander ?), *A compleat account of the Portugueze language, being a copious dictionary of English with Portugueze, and Portugueze with English. With an Easie And Unerring Method of its Pronunciation*. London, R. Janeway, 1701 [Repr. Menston, The Scholar Press Limited, 1970].

[Junck (Jung ou Junk), Johann Andreas von], *Portugiesische Grammatik. Nebst einigen Nachrichten von der portugiesischen Litteratur, und von Büchern die über Portugall geschrieben sind*. Frankfurt, Carl Gottlieb Strauss, 1778.

Lima, Luís Caetano de, *Grammatica franceza, ou arte para aprender o francez por meio da lingua portugueza.* Lisboa, Off. Real Deslandense, 1710 [multiple reeditions].

Lima, Luís Caetano de, *Grammatica italiana e arte para apprender a lingua italiana por meyo da lingua portugueza. Oferecida À Serenissima Princeza Nossa Senhora.* Lisboa, José da Costa Coiombra, 1756 [1st ed. Lisboa, Off. da Congregação do Oratorio, 1734].

Marques, José, *Nouveau dictionnaire des langues françoise et portugaise: Tiré des Meilleurs Auteurs & des Dictionnaires de l'Academie, de Trevoux, de Furetiere, de Tachard, de Richelet, de Danet, de Boyer, &c. Avec les Noms des Nations, des Royaumes, des Provinces, des Villes, des Contrées, des Riviéres du Monde, & les Noms Propres d'Hommes, & de Femmes, &c.*, Seconde edition revue, corrigée, & augmentée d'un supplément, Avec permission, & privilége du Roy, Tome premier. Lisbonne, chez Jean Joseph Bertrand, Libraire au Seigneur Jesus da Boa Morte (Joseph da Costa Coimbra's typography), 1758, p. IV + 677. Addition of a 183 page long *Supplément*, printed in Offi. Patr. de Francisco Luiz Ameno. At the end of the *Supplément* there is this note (p. 183): "Le Tome second, qui s'intitule Diccionario novo Portuguez e Francez com os termos latinos, par le même Auteur; est fini d'imprimer, & se vend de même que celui ci chez Jean Joseph Bertrand ao Senhor Jesus da Boa-Morte, où l'on trouvera les Grammaires Françoise & Italienne du P. D. Louis Caetano de Lima C. Reg. & beaucoup de livres curieux tant en François, que Latin, Italien, &c." [The first edition dated back to 1754, but it was destroyed in the fire of the 1755 earthquake. Second volume, 1764].

Marques, José, *Nouveau Dictionnaire des langues française et portugaise... avec les noms des nations, des royaumes, des provinces ... par le prêtre Joseph Marques*, Troisieme Edition revûe, corrigée, augmentée, & d'un *Supplément*, Tome premier. Lisbonne, Imprimerie Royale, 1775.

Marques, José, *Supplement au Nouveau dictionnaire des langues françoise et portugaise du Pretre Joseph Marques, tiré des Dictionnaires de meilleurs Auteurs*, Troisieme Edition, revue, corrigé, & augmentée par ***. Lisbonne, Imprimerie Royale, 1776.

Marques, José, *Novo Diccionario das línguas portugueza, e franceza, com os termos latinos, tirado dos melhores Authores, e do Vocabulario Portuguez, e Latino do P. D. Rafael Bluteau, dos Diccionarios da Academia Francez, Universal de Trevoux, de Furetiere, de Tachard, de Richelet, de Danet, de Boyer, &c. Com os nomes proprios das Naçoens, dos Reinos, das Provincias, das Cidades, das Comarcas, dos*

Rios do Mundo, &c..., Pelo Padre Joseph Marques, Capellaõ Regente do Coro, e Mestre da Musica da Igreja de Nossa Senhora do Loreto, Primeira ediçaõ, Tomo segundo. Lisboa, Off. Patriarcal de Francisco Luiz Ameno, MDCCLXIV, Com as licenças necessar. e Privilegio Real, p. IV + 763 [The printing licences refer to 1748].

Meldola, Abraham, *Nova Grammatica Portugueza: 1 Ortographia. 2 Etymologia. 3 Syntaxe. 4 Prosodia com Supplemento. 5 Lavores da Lingoa. 6 Miscellanea.* Hamburgo, M.C. Bock, Printing costs financed by the author, 1785.

Pereira, Bento, *Prosodia in Vocabularium Trilingue, Latinum, Lusitanicum, & Hispanicum digesta, in qua dictionum significatio, et sylabarum quantitas expenditur.* Eborae, Apud Emmanuelem Carualho Academiae Typographum, 1634.

Pereira, Bento, *Tesouro da lingua portuguesa.* Lisboa, Craesbecck, 1647.

Ricci, Matteo / Ruggieri, Michele, *Dicionário português-chinês.* s.l., Michele John W. Witek ed.; Biblioteca Nacional de Lisboa, Instituto Português do Oriente, Ricci Institute, University of San Francisco, 2001 [Facsimile edition and reproduction of ms. (ca. 1588) kept in the "Archivum Romanum Societatis Iesu, Japonica et Sinica"].

Roboredo, Amaro, *Raizes da lingua latina mostradas em hum tratado, e diccionario: isto he, hum compendio do Calepino com a composição, e derivação das palavras, com a ortografia, quantidade e frase dellas.* Lisboa, Pedro Craesbeeck, 1621.

Roquete, José Inácio, *Nouveau dictionnaire portugais-français composé sur les plus recents et les meilleurs dictionnaires de deux langues.* Paris, Guillard, 1841, p. XVI + 1238.

Sá, Joaquim José da Costa e, *Diccionario Italiano e Portuguez. Extrahido dos melhores lexicógrafos, como de Antonini, de Veneroni, de Facciolati, de Franciosini, do Dicionário de Crusca e do da Universidade de Turim. E dividido em duas partes; na primeira se comprehendem as palavras, as frases mais elegantes e diffíceis; os modos de fallar; os provérbios e os termos facultativos de todas as artes e sciencias; na segunda parte se contém os nomes proprios dos homens illustres; das principaes cidades, villas, castellos, montes, rios, etc. Que o dedica e consagra ao illustrissimo e excellentissimo Senhor Sebastião José de Carvalho e Mello, Conde de Oeyras, Marquez de Pombal, do Conselho de Estado de sua Magestade Fidelissima, seu Plenipotenciario, e Lugar-Tenente na Fundação da Universidade de Coimbra; e seu Ministro, e Secretario de Estado dos Negocios do Reino. Alcaide Mor de Lamego, e Commendador das Tres Minas, &c. &c. &c.,* Tomo primeiro. Lisboa, Regia Officina Typografica,

MDCCLXXIII, "Com licença da Real Meza Censoria", "Vende-se na loge de João José Bertrand, ao pé da Igreja dos Martyres ás portas de Santa Catharina" [First Part. First Volume A-L; fol. XIV + 828]; MDCCLXXIV [First Part, Second Volume M-Z; fol. IV + 804; the last four pages consist of: "Taboa em que se explicão as notas e os breves de que se usou neste diccionario"; "Catalogo dos verbos irregulares dispostos por ordem alfabetica"; "Catalogo chronologico das obras que o author deste diccionario tem impresso" e "Obras do mesmo author que estão no Prélo". Among them there is a *Diccionario Italiano e Portuguez, que contém os Nomes dos Homens Illustres, das Cidades famosas, etc., com as Fabulas dos Poetas*. Part. II, Tom. III].

Sá, Joaquim José da Costa e, *Diccionario portuguez-francez-e-latino novamente compilado, que á augustíssima senhora D. Carlota Joaquina, Princeza do Brasil, offerece, e consagra Joaquim José da Costa e Sá, Professor Régio de Lingua Latina, e Sócio da Academia Real das Sciencias de Lisboa.* Lisboa, Simão Thaddeo Ferreira, MDCCLXXXXIV, Vende-se na loja da Viuva Bertrand, e Filhos aos Martyres, p. VIII + 674, 555.

Sá, Joaquim José da Costa e, *Diccionario abreviado das linguas portugueza, e franceza, ou compendio do grande diccionario portuguez, francez, e latino, composto por Joaquim José da Costa e SÁ, Professor Regio de Lingua Latina, e Socio da Academia Real das Sciencias de Lisboa: accrescentado, e enriquecido com os Termos proprios, e technicos de todas as Sciencias, e Artes, extrahidos dos Classicos Antigos, e Modernos de melhor nota, que se achaõ universalmente recebidos*. Lisboa, Typografia Rollandiana, 1808. Com Licença da Meza do Dezembargo do Paço. Vende-se na Loja da Viuva Bertrand e Filhos, Mercadores de Livros, junto à Igreja dos Martyres, N. 45, pp. 2-926.

Silva, Bartolomeu Álvares da, *Collecção de palavras familiares, portuguezas, francezas, latinas e britanicas, com huma breve instrucção para perceber e ainda fallar o idioma frances*. Coimbra, Real Officina da Universidade, 1764.

Sousa, Manuel de / Sá, José Joaquim da Costa e, *Nouveau dictionnaire françois-portugais, composé par le capitaine Emmanuel de Sousa, & mis en ordre, rédigé, revû, corrigé, augmenté, & enrichi de tous les tremes techniques, & propresdes sciences, des arts, des métiers, de géographie; &c. sur la derniére édition de celui de M. l'Abbé Alberti, & des tables de l'Encyclopédie par Joachim Joseph da Costa & Sá, Professeur de Belles-Lettres & associé de l'Académie Royale des Sciences de Lisbonne; dedié à Son Altesse Royale Monseigneur Le*

Prince de Bresil, tome premier A-K. Lisbonne, chez Borel, Borel, & Compagnie... Imprimerie de Simon Thaddée Ferreira, 1784; tome second L-Z, 1786.

Sousa, Manuel de / Sá, José Joaquim da Costa e / Cunha, Vicente Pedro Nolasco da Cunha, *Dictionnaire françois-portugais. Composé Par le Capitaine Emmanuel de Sousa; Mis en Ordre & Augmenté Par Joachim Joseph da Costa & Sá, seconde edition, revue, corrigeé & augmenteé de tous les mots adoptés dans la langue Françoise, depuis plusieurs anneés; des synonymes de la meme langue, & enrichie de nouveaux termes de botanique & de ceux de la noivelle nomenclature chimique; & le tout soigneusement recueilli des meilleurs dictionnaires qui on paru jusqu'a ce jour & principalement de celui de l'Academie Françoise edition de 1802. Par le Docteur Vincent Pierre Nolasco da Cunha*, 2 vols. Lisbonne, chez Borel, Borel, & Compagnie... Imprimerie de Simon Thaddée Ferreira, 1811.

Vieira Transtagano, Antonio, *A Dictionary of the Portuguese and English Languages, in two parts, Portuguese and English: and English and Portuguese Wherein I. The words are explained in their different Meanings, by Examples from the best Portuguese and English Writers. II. The Etymology of the Portuguese generally indicated from Latin, Arabic, and other Languages. Throughout the Whole are interspersed a great number of Phrases and Proverbs*. Londres, J. Nourse. Two unnumbered volumes. Multiple reeditions: 1782, 1794, 1805, 1813, 1827, 1837, 1860-1861.

Vocabulario da lingoa de Iapam com a declaração em Portugues, feito por alguns padres e irmãos da Companhia de Iesu, Nagasaki, tipografia do Colégio, 1603-1604.

References

Almeida, Átila (1988). *Dicionários parentes e aderentes, uma bibliografia de dicionários, enciclopédias, glossários, vocabulários e livros afins em que entra a língua Portuguesa*. João Pessoa, FUNAPE / Nova Stela.

Almeida, Horácio de (1983). *Catálogo de dicionários portugueses e brasileiros*. Rio de Janeiro, Companhia Brasileira de Artes Gráficas.

Almeida, Justino Mendes de (1959). "Lexicógrafos portugueses da língua latina. 1 O primeiro lexicógrafo português da língua latina: Jerónimo Cardoso", in *Evphrosyne* 2, 1959: 139-152.

—. (1963). "Lexicógrafos portugueses da língua latina. 2 Agostinho Barbosa: o segundo lexicógrafo português da língua latina", in *Revista de Guimarães* 75, 1/4: 31-40.

—. (1967). "Lexicógrafos portugueses da língua latina. 3 A *Prosódia* de Bento Pereira", "4 O *Diccionario Lusitanico-latino* de Frei Pedro de Poyares", in *Revista de Guimarães* 77, 1/2: 5-12, 12-17.

—. (1969a). "Lexicógrafos da língua latina em Portugal. 5 *A Porta de línguas (Ianva lingvarum)*, de Amaro de Roboredo", "6 *Amalthea sive hortus onomasticus*, do P. Fr. Tomás da Luz", "7 O Vocabulario portuguez e latino de D. Rafael Bluteau", "8 O Aparato critico para a correção do diccionario intitulado *Prosodia in vocabularium bilingue digesta*, de António Pereira de Figueiredo", "9 O *Diccionario portuguez, e latino* do Padre Carlos Folqman", in *Revista de Guimarães* 79, 1/2: 5-7, 7-13, 13-27, 27-36, 36-40.

—. (1969b). "Lexicógrafos da língua latina em Portugal. 10 O *Breve diccionario da latinidade pura e impura* de António Pereira de Figueiredo", "11 Os *Dicionários* de Pedro José da Fonseca", "12 O *Magnum lexicon*, de Frei Manuel de Pina Cabral", "13 O *Diccionario portuguez-francez-e-latino novamente compilado* por Joaquim José da Costa e Sá", in *Revista de Guimarães* 79, 3/4: 193-198, 198-210, 210-216, 216-226.

—. (1972). "Lexicógrafos da língua latina em Portugal. 14 O *diccionario latino, e portuguez*, por Damião de Froes Perim (Fr. João de S. Pedro)", "15 Nomenclatura port., e latina", in *Revista de Guimarães* 82, 3/4: 151-162, 163-168.

Barreto, Luís Filipe (2002). "Ricci, Matteo e Ruggieri, Michele, *Dicionário português-chinês* (Michele John W. Witek, ed., 2001)", in *Bulletin of Portuguese / Japanese Studies* 5: 117-128.

Bibliografia Filológica Portuguesa (Dicionários, Gramaticas, Ortografias. etc.). Lisbon, Centro de Estudos Filológicos [1544 files were published between 1935 and 1950].

Cardoso, Simão (1994). *Historiografia gramatical: 1500-1920: língua portuguesa: autores portugueses.* Porto, Fac. Letras.

Clara, Fernando (1989). *A Europa da diferença.* Master thesis, University of Lisbon (UNL).

—. (1997). "Gramáticas da diferença (Imagens de Portugal nas primeiras gramáticas portuguesas para alemães)", in Lüdtke, Helmut / Schmidt-Radefeldt, Jürgen (eds). *Linguistica contrastiva. Deutsch versus Portugiesische – Spanisch – Französisch.* Tübingen, Narr: 285-302.

Ettinger, Stefan (1991). "Die zweisprachige Lexikographie mit Portugiesisch", in Hausmann, Franz Joseph / Reichmann, Oskar /

Wiegand, Herbert Ernst / Zgusta, Ladislav (eds). *Wörterbücher-Dictionaries-Dictionnaires: Ein internationales Handbuch zur Lexikographie*, 3 vols. Berlin / New York, de Gruyter, 1989-1991, II: 3020-3030.

Gallina, Annamaria (1959). *Contributi alla storia della lessicografia italo-spagnola dei secoli XVI e XVII*, Firenze, Olschki.

Machado, Diogo Barbosa (1965-1967). *Bibliotheca Lusitana : historica, critica, e cronológica na qual se comprehende a noticia dos authores portuguezes, e das obras, que compuserão desde o tempo da promulgação da Ley da Graça até o tempo prezente*, 4 vols. Coimbra, Atlântida [facsimile of the first edition of 1741-1759].

INIC, CLUL (1984). *Português fundamental: Vocabulario e Gramática*, vol. 1.1, *Vocabulário.* Lisbon, Instituto Nacional de Investigação Científica.

Salas Quesada, Pilar (2003). "Los comienzos de la lexicografía bilingüe con el portugués y el español. El Dicionário castelhano-portuguéz de Raphael Bluteau", in *Res Diachronicae. Anuario de la Asociación de Jóvenes Investigadores de Historiografía e Historia de la Lengua Española* 2: 343-351.

Silva, Inocêncio Francisco da (1858-1958). *Dicionário bibliográfico português*, 23 vols. Lisbon, Imprensa Nacional [ed. facsimile: Lisbon, Imprensa Nacional, 1973].

Silvestre, João Paulo Martins Silvestre (2004). *Rafael Bluteau e o Vocabulario Portuguêz e Latino: Teoria metalexicográfica, fontes e recepção.* Aveiro, Ph.D diss.

Torre, Manuel Gomes da (1996). "Who Wrote *A Compleat Account of the Portugueze Language*?", in *Revista de Estudos Anglo-Portugueses* 5: 33-47.

Verdelho, Telmo (1990). "Os dicionários bilingues até ao fim do séc. XVIII fonte privilegiada da lexicografia portuguesa", in *Actas do Colóquio de Lexicologia e Lexicografia (26-27 Junho 1990).* Lisbon, Universidade Nova: 248-256.

—. (1992). "Aspectos da obra lexicográfica de Bento Pereira", in *XX*[e] *Congrès International de Linguistique et Philologie Romanes*, vol. 4, Section 6, Zurich: 777-785.

—. (1994). "Lexicografia", in Holtus, Günter / Metzeltin, Michael / Schmitt, Christian (eds). *Lexikon der Romanistischen Linguistik*, vol. 6, 2. Tübingen, Max Niemeyer: 673-692.

—. (1995). *As origens da gramaticografia e da lexicografia latino-portuguesas.* Aveiro, Instituto Nacional de Investigação Científica.

—. (1998). "O Vocabulario da lingoa de Iapam (1603), uma fonte inexplorada da lexicografia portuguesa", in Ruffino, Giovani (ed.). *Atti del XXI Congresso Internazionale di Linguistica e Filologia Romanza, (Palermo, 18-24 settembre 1995)*, 6 vols, III *Lessicologia e semantica delle lingue romanze*. Tübingen, Niemeyer.

—. (1999-2000). "O Calepino em Portugal e a obra lexicográfica de Amaro Reboredo", in *Revista Portuguesa de Filologia* 23: 125-149.

Verdelho, Telmo / João, Paulo Silvestre (eds) (2007). *Dicionarística portuguesa: inventariação e estudo do patrimómio lexicográfico*. Aveiro, Universidade de Aveiro.

Woll, Dieter (1990). "Portugiesische Lexikographie", in Hausmann, Franz Josef / Reichmann, Oskar / Wiegand, Herbert Ernst / Zgusta, Ladislav (eds). *Worterbucher-Dictionaries-Dictionnaires: Ein internationales Handbuch zur Lexikographie*, 3 vols. Berlin / New York, de Gruyter, 1989-1991, II: 1723-1735.

A FEW POINTS ON ITALIAN LEXICOGRAPHY IN THE NINETEENTH CENTURY[1]

MARIAROSA BRICCHI

1 The Century of Dictionaries

> Non più si disputa sul Vocabolario della Crusca, ma si ristampa; e o quello emendano accrescono migliorano, o in altre guise altri ne fanno [No more do people dispute on the *Vocabolario della Crusca*, but they reprint it; and they correct, enlarge, ameliorate it, or make new ones in different ways][2] (*Tramater* 1829-1840: v).

So reads, in 1829, the Preface to *Tramater*, one of the many dictionaries created in the nineteenth century Italy on the *Crusca* model. This statement reveals an early awareness of the fact that the spread of dictionaries was such a broad phenomenon as to become a distinctive character of nineteenth century lexicography. Nevertheless it also offers information that is essentially incorrect since the disputes concerning the *Vocabolario della Crusca* and dictionaries in general were very lively throughout the century. Evidence for this appears ten years later, in a long essay by Cesare Cantù, *Di due recenti vocabolari italiani e di varii altri punti intorno alla lingua*, in which the *Crusca veronese* by Antonio Cesari (1806-11) and the debate which followed were said to be the starting point for a growing interest in lexicographical matters:

> D'allora, come in ogni altro studio, così in questo crebbe l'ardore; l'eloquenza salata e piccante di Vincenzo Monti lo rese quasi di moda, ed una vera furia di libri e libercoli dietro materie appartenenti alla lingua uscirono questi ultimi anni [From then on, the ardour increased in this

---

[1] Most of this paper was written during my semester (Spring 2008) as a Fellow at the Italian Academy for Advanced Studies in America at Columbia University, New York. I am grateful to its Director, David Freedberg, and the whole staff for providing me with an ideal working environment. My warmest thanks also to Irina Oryshkevich for her friendly help in revising my English.

[2] Here and onwards, the translations are mine.

> matter as in every other one; the tasty and spicy eloquence of Vincenzo Monti turned it into fashion, and a real fury of books and booklets on linguistic matters were printed in the last few years] (Cantù 1836: 295).[3]

These debates involved long-term questions regarding the methods used in creating dictionaries (including major points, such as the language of usage vs. the language of writers, the very meaning of the term *usage*, the inclusion or exclusion of archaic words and scientific terminology, etc.). They also dealt with three additional, more recent seminal points: the very existence of an Italian language, which was both the object and the instrument of lexicographers but at the same time a virtual presence, the reality of which was debatable; the ability of a dictionary to serve as a tool for language learning; the opportunity to diversify and specialise dictionaries with regard to the audience they addressed, a process unknown in previous centuries.

The following analysis will focus on these three main points, which should be considered to constitute not only a distinctive character but the very foundations of nineteenth century innovations in lexicography, and should also be set in relation to the highly peculiar situation of language and nationhood in Italy. At the end, a list of selected dictionaries organised by typologies will be provided.

2 Italian Existed, Exists and Is Evolving?

The *Préface* to the first edition (1694) of the *Dictionnaire de l'Académie Françoise* states that the dictionary was created and made its appearance «dans le siecle les plus florissant de la Langue Françoise». It continues along these lines:

> On dira peut-estre qu'on ne peut jamais s'asseurer qu'une Langue vivante soit pervenuë à sa derniere perfection; Mais ce n'a pas esté le sentiment de Ciceron, qui après avoir fait de longues reflexions sur cette matiere, n'a pas fait difficulté d'avancer que de son temps la Langue Latine estoit arrivée à un degré d'excellence où l'on ne pouvoit rien adjouster. Nous voyons qu'il ne s'est pas trompé, et peut-estre n'aura-t-on pas moins de raison de penser la mesme chose en faveur de la Langue Françoise, si l'on veut bien considerer la Gravité et la Variété de ses nombres, la juste cadence de ses Perio-

[3] The reference to the abundance of dictionaries relies on a long bibliographical note at the end of the first part of the essay (Cantù 1836: 350-352) where about forty dictionaries published between 1819 and 1834 are listed. The Monti text which is referred to is *Proposta di alcune correzioni ed aggiunte al Vocabolario della Crusca*, Dall'Imperial Regia Stamperia, Milano 1817-1826.

des, la douceur de sa Poësie [...], et sour tout cette Construction directe, qui sans s'eslogner de l'ordre naturel des pensées, ne laisse pas de rencontrer toutes les delicatesses que l'art est capable d'y apporter. C'est dans cet estat où la Langue Françoise se trouve aujourd'huy qu'a esté composé ce Dictionnaire (*Dictionnaire de l'Académie Françoise*, *Préface*: XIV).

In Italy, where the first edition of the *Vocabolario della Crusca* had been published eighty years earlier, endless linguistic questions not only remained alive for centuries, but there was a need – expecially in the *Ottocento* – to face a problem that reversed the proud *Académie*'s proposition. For while French not only existed, but began to be recorded at the peak of its excellence, there was no consensus on the fact that Italian – already described in quite a few dictionaries and the medium for so much distinguished literature – even existed.

In the fifth draft of his unfinished treatise *Della lingua italiana*, which dates to the early Forties but was published posthumously, Manzoni devoted his first chapter to demonstrate that an Italian language did not exist, either in spoken form (due to the co-existence of different dialects) or in written form (due to the inability of the literary language to fulfil all communication needs). His text assumes the form of a dialogue between a fictional character, who is indifferent to the *questione della lingua*, and the author, who tries to involve him in his research. The exchange is uneven, because the character utters merely a few brief sentences, while the author delivers a long argument, which hints at the other person's presence only here and there (through rhetorical questions, exclamations, etc.). In order to prove that the Italian language does not exist, Manzoni organises his arguments in stages, using a series of examples.

Supponete ancora, che si trovino insieme un inglese, un tedesco, uno spagnolo, ognuno dei quali ignori la lingua degli altri due, e tutti sappiano passabilmente il francese. Potranno, con questo mezzo, discorrere tra di loro alla lunga, per degli anni a un bisogno, chiedere e dar notizie, raccontare, discutere [...]. E noi diremo che s'intendono; ma diremo forse che possiedano una lingua in comune? [Suppose that an English, a German, a Spanish are together, each of them ignorant of the others' language, but all of them knowing French rather fluently. They will be able, with French, to talk for a long time, even for years if necessary, to ask for and give news, to tell, to discuss [...]. And we will say they understand one another; but shall we say that they have a language in common?] (Manzoni 1974: 539).[4]

[4] All the quotations of this essay come from the fifth draft of Manzoni (1974).

Thus, the fact that people are able to understand one another is no evidence of the existence of a shared language.

> Che voglio io con questi esempi? Una cosa sola; e son certo d'averla ottenuta: far dire a voi medesimo, che il fatto generalissimo d'un intendersi, non è la prova del possedere una lingua in comune; che, se ogni lingua è un mezzo d'intendersi, non ogni mezzo d'intendersi è una lingua; che si può intendersi più o meno, in gradi e in modi molto differenti, e non aver però in comune quel pieno, quel sicuro [...] quello special mezzo d'intendersi, che si chiama lingua [What do I wish to reach with these examples? Only one thing; and I am sure I have succeeded: I wish to make you assert that the general fact of understanding one another is no evidence of possessing a common language; that, if any language is a tool to understand one another, not any understanding tool is a language; that it is possible to understand one another at different levels without sharing that full, sure […] peculiar understanding tool which is called a language] (Manzoni 1974: 539).

Dialect is a good example: were somebody with a native knowledge of Milanese dialect to switch to Italian, he would be less fluent and precise. Thus, what is missing is «un mezzo di dir tutti nella stessa maniera ciò che diciamo tutti, ma in non so quante maniere» [an instrument for everybody to say in the very same way what everybody says in many different ways] (Manzoni 1974: 542).

Manzoni's linguistic labour had commenced two decades earlier in response to a literary problem, that is, the quest for a language to use in his novel. He faced the question from the outset through a comparison to French culture with which he was so familiar. After choosing the Florentine dialect spoken by the educated class as the language for *I promessi sposi* (much as the language of Paris became the literary language of France centuries earlier), Manzoni did not give up meditating on the problem, but delved into it more deeply, and thirty years later ended up being designated the official researcher and champion of the continuously re-born linguistic debate by the *Ministro della Pubblica Istruzione* of the new Italian nation. At the request of the Minister, Emilio Broglio, Manzoni wrote a report entitled *Dell'unità della lingua e dei mezzi di diffonderla* (1868), the main novelty of which was that the problem was no longer claimed to be a literary but a social and political one. In short, the question was which variety of Italian should become the (spoken and written) standard language of Italy, capable of covering all the needs of shared, common life? Furthermore, what were the appropriate means to spread its knowledge? The starting point, however, had not changed; Manzoni was still certain that the Italian language did not exist. Indeed the old writer maintained it was not true that

> ci sia in Italia una lingua comune di fatto [...]. Che ci sia una quantità indefinita di locuzioni comuni a tutta l'Italia [...] è un fatto che a nessuno potrebbe neppure venire in mente di negare. Ma nessuno vorrà affermare che una quantità qualunque di locuzioni basti a costituire una lingua [... a true common language existed in Italy [...]. That there are a large number of expressions which are common in the whole Italy [...] is a fact that nobody would ever think to deny. But nobody will feel like asserting that a number of expressions is enough to make a language] (Manzoni 1990: 611-12).

Manzoni, in fact, came to understand through his personal experience as a novelist that just as there was no shared language for speakers who sought a more than basic exchange, so there was no modern written language endowed with a uniform and regulated vocabulary. Novel this was not. But it was new to claim that the lack of a common modern language corresponded to the lack of a language in general. A further point to be stressed regarding Manzoni's theory is that, from the Forties on, he kept on suggesting that written language should emerge not from other written texts, but from living speech. It was this sort of writing, nourished by continuous interchange with educated oral Italian, that did not exist.

Predictably, most reactions to Manzoni's report focussed on the country's linguistic condition. The assumption of the lack of a common language was often only partially understood, and was always the target of strong attack. The report of the second session of the commission established by Broglio, based in Florence and directed by Raffaello Lambruschini, must be mentioned first. Among other points, its report stated that «v'è una lingua italiana da conoscere, da rispettare e da studiare, *non da inventare* [An Italian language is there to know, to respect, to study, *not to invent*] (my emphasis)» (Lambruschini 1868).[5]

In addition, Niccolò Tommaseo, a partisan for a mixture of the living language and one inherited from literary tradition, was appointed to express his views at an official event, a meeting of the *Accademia della Crusca* held in September 1868, a few months after the March publication of Manzoni's *Dell'unità della lingua*. In this indirect yet clear response to Manzoni, Tommaseo could not accept the statement that Italian did not exist. His view likewise diverged from that of his counterpart with regard to the importance of common locutions in Tuscan and other dialects. His argument began to reverse one of Manzoni's points, namely, that locutions

---

[5] The report by Lambruschini, dated April 18, 1868, was published in May (see Lambruschini 1868).

shared by Florentine and other dialects, rather than being insufficient in granting a common background, existed in large and very significant quantities:

> Fatto è che, prendendo qualsiasi degli odierni dialetti italiani, se ne potrebbe comporre un discorso tutto di vocaboli e locuzioni prette toscane, variata soltanto la forma grammaticale; e che, prendendo un dialetto toscano, o, per più determinare, il fiorentino, potrebbesi un intero discorso tesserne di parole e di modi a tale o tale altro dialetto d'Italia non solamente intelligibili ma più o meno usitati [It is a fact that, taking any one among Italian dialects, it would be possible to compose a speech all made up with Tuscan words and expressions, switching only the grammatical form; it is also a fact that from a Tuscan dialect or, to be more precise, the Florentine dialect, it would be possible to forge a whole speech with words and expressions that are not only understandable but more or less in use in any other Italian dialect] (Tommaseo 1868: 48).

This was enough to dissolve the debate:

> la disposizione dei più a bene intendersi, è, ancora meglio che necessità prudentemente avvertita, fatto irrecusabilmente avverato [The attitude showed by most people to understand one another is, rather than a necessity felt out of prudence, a fact which has already doubtlessly happened] (Tommaseo 1868: 51).

The problem also needed to be faced from a historical point of view. In an article published in the review *Nuova antologia*, Gino Capponi initiated a dialogue with Manzoni from this perspective. Rather than accept the argument for the language's non-existence, Capponi, following the secular history of Italian, emphasised its fragmentation into genres and registers. He wrote about the separation of poetry (which had had a consistent language for centuries) and literary prose, which had frozen into an imitation of the ancients.[6] Hence came the divide between speech and writing, the former evolving over time, the latter secluded within literary circles:

> Laonde a chi scrive manca una scuola molto essenziale quando egli non abbia la mente già instrutta di quelle forme per cui si esprimono parlando le cose che egli vuole scrivere. La quale mancanza che fu in Italia dai tempi antichi e si protrasse poi nei moderni, ha dato spesso ai nostri libri

---

[6] «Fu a noi tristo privilegio che la lingua o si dovesse o si credesse dovere attingere dal trecento» [It was our sad privilege to be forced – or to believe to be forced – to take our language from the Trecento] (Capponi 1869: 668).

> certa aridità solenne la quale ebbe nome di stile accademico [Thus those who write miss an essential school, unless they already keep in their minds the forms through which what they wish to write about is expressed in speech. This lack, which was there in Italy from the ancient times and continues in modern ones, often gave our books a certain solemn emptiness which was named academic style] (Capponi 1869: 670).

According to Capponi, the ideal tongue in which literature and life were not separated by a great gulf could only emerge from the interaction of speech and writing, of the language of people and the language of writers. He had expressed the very same idea some forty years earlier in a lecture delivered at the *Accademia della Crusca*:

> Ma dalle cose fin qui piuttosto accennate che dette, io deduco questi due canoni. Che la lingua scritta non può divenir mai abbastanza popolare, quando essa non si accosti a una lingua parlata. Che questa lingua parlata per divenire illustre, cioè degna di passar nella lingua scritta, ha bisogno d'essere usata da' chiari uomini [but, from what has been so far more alluded to than said, I infer the two following points. Our written language can never become popular enough, if it does not get near to the spoken language. This spoken language, in order to become illustrious – that is worth to be written – needs to be used by illustrious men] (Capponi 1829: 459).

What was missing, Capponi stressed, was not the language in general, but one that could be used for plain prose communication. This, moreover, was due to the fact that back in the *Cinquecento*

> questa lingua per certi rispetti più accuratamente scritta, fu meno parlata; e la parola meno di prima fu espressione di forti pensieri ed autorevoli e accetti a molti: vennero fuori i letterati, sparve il cittadino; scriveva per il pubblico chi nella vita non era avvezzo a parlare ad altri che alla sua combriccola: quindi l'eloquenza cercò appropriarsi all'uso delle accademie le quali erano una sorta di sparse chiesuole [this language, more accurately written, was less spoken; and, less than before, it was used to express strong, authoritative widely-shared thoughts: literary people were born, the citizen disappeared; he would write for the public who, in everyday life used to talk to none but his crew: thus eloquence started belonging to Academies, which were sort of spread little churches] (Capponi 1869: 679).

What was missing was the "language of the citizen". That was, after all, the language which a novelist needed for his work – the language which Manzoni dramatically lacked. Dissenting from Manzoni, however, Capponi did not identify the language of the citizen with language *tout court*.

More aggressive was Pietro Fanfani, who wrote an article, *Nobiltà ed eccellenza della lingua italiana*, in which he reacted to Manzoni's report with a passionate apology for the vast literary tradition of Italian. Usage, according to Fanfani, was what had been settled by people and regulated, purified, and elevated by writers:

> Le lingue, è vero, son trovato del popolo, ma può una lingua esser detta tale nel suo più nobil significato, se prima gli scrittori non la formino, dandole forma certa, e facendola vitale? A me par di no [Languages indeed are made by people, but can a language be considered a language in its most noble significance if it has not been shaped and made alive by writers? I do not think so] (Fanfani 1872: p. 252).

Italian did exist and was made great by its literary tradition: Fanfani's basically purist position found unacceptable what appeared to be a misrecognition of the language's past glory in Manzoni's theory:

> per carità non si faccia all'Italia la vergogna di dire che la lingua fin'ora non c'è stata, e che per opera della Commissione ci sarà e si muoverà; chè *la lingua italiana*, benedetto Dio, *c'è stata, c'è, e si muove* [for God's sake, let us not insult Italy asserting that the language was not there so far, and that it will exist and it will be moving thanks to the commission: *the Italian language* – Goodness Gracious – *was there, is there, and is moving*]. (Fanfani 1872: 272) (my emphasis).

Thus a distinctive character of nineteenth century lexicography was the floating state of its very object. It is true that these linguistic speculations revealed a new vital force that led to flourishing debates as well as to a veritable explosion of dictionaries. Yet this abundance was not blessed with harmony, even with regard to the seminal point as to whether the language of so many dictionaries did or did not exist. Far from being a side issue, this question was bound to have a huge impact on the process of conceiving and shaping dictionaries.

3 Dictionaries as an Engine of National Linguistic Consciousness

The different positions on the existence or the absence of a shared language, the persisting presence of the past's literary tradition, the social and cultural weight of local identities as represented – from a linguistic point of view – by dialects, all this should be read in the context of a very peculiar political situation. Italy was not a nation until 1861. Linguistic debates, therefore, focussed on the search for a national language without a nation. When the nation eventually came into existence, it soon appeared evident that political unity did not provide the dense, shared cultural network which had been missing for centuries. On the other hand, it was this situation which shaped and sharpened the intellectuals' sensitivity toward the relation between language and national identity – a relation of such importance in the *Ottocento* that it, in fact, became one of the key features of the lexicographical debate. Just as it appears, for instance, in the very title of Fanfani's book of 1872 – a compilation of earlier essays – *Lingua e nazione,* the parallel between the two terms was a *tópos* that the intellectuals of the time agreed to emphasise. Fanfani himself stressed the adhesive role that a language played in a divided country:

> E poi, non è la lingua carissimo vincolo nazionale in questa Italia così divisa? non è ella ciò per che siamo italiani? [And then is not the language our dearest national link in this divided Italy? Is it not the reason why we are Italians?] (Fanfani 1872: 4).

The book's title suggested a link of coordination, while the above note on the role of a common language in a divided country provided the terms for a relation of substitution (the common language – which according to Fanfani did exist – replaced the non-existing political unity). Fanfani went one step further in his *Introduction*, where he established a real identification between the two objects:

> Lingua e Nazione sono una cosa medesima [Language and nation are one thing] (Fanfani 1872).

Gino Capponi too was considering the identification between language and nation, but he actually reversed Fanfani's assumptions: for the latter language united what was divided, while for the former a united nation was a precondition for a shared language:

> Se (come fu detto) lo stile è l'uomo, la lingua può dirsi che sia la nazione: quindi all'esservi una lingua bisognava che ci fosse una Italia [If (as it was said) style is man, language can be considered nation: thus, in order to have a language, one Italy was needed] (Capponi 1869: 680).

In his report *Dell'unità della lingua*, Manzoni basically suggested that the conditions for the unification of language should be created by national institutions. In short, he expected the Government to elect Tuscan as the official language of Italy, and to promote its diffusion through a series of means – including a dictionary. On the other hand, some of his contemporaries at the end of the Sixties and the beginning of the Seventies

– that is, about ten years after the unification of Italy – were able to foresee the limits of central political action and drew attention to national cultural density as a condition for linguistic unification. Thereupon new pairings, such as language and society (or language and thought, language and culture, language and intellectual life), replaced the previous pair, language and nation. Capponi, for instance, noted:

> Più grave è fatto il nostro debito ora in tempi di sorti mutate, di sorti maggiori ma più difficili da portare; noi siamo venuti ad esse non preparati, e s'io dovessi quanto alle future condizioni della lingua fare un prognostico, direi senz'altro: la lingua in Italia sarà quello che sapranno essere gli Italiani [Our duty is heavier now, when our fate has changed into a greater but more difficult one; we came to it unprepared and, should I make a prevision on the future conditions of our language, I would definitely say: language will be in Italy what Italians will be] (Capponi 1869: 682).

Luigi Settembrini too showed an interest in the social aspect of the linguistic issue, and set a relation between language and thought that ran parallel to Capponi's relation between language and people. It was significant that both authors insisted on reversing the terms of the question as settled by Fanfani. To Capponi, Italians would create the Italian language (and not viceversa); to Settembrini,

> il pensiero fa la lingua, non la lingua fa il pensiero [thought makes language, language does not make thought] (Settembrini 1868).

Capponi and Settembrini seemed to anticipate some points of what is now the best known response to Manzoni's report and to its main practical result, the publication of the Giorgini-Broglio dictionary of usage: Graziadio Isaia Ascoli's *Proemio*, or introduction, to the first issue of a new scientific journal, *Archivio glottologico italiano* (Ascoli 1873). A historical linguist, Ascoli was the first to become involved in the debate not as a literary figure, but as a trained scholar. Relying on his historical background, Ascoli was easily able to show that Italy had never had a common language because it had never enjoyed the social and cultural conditions which made such a situation possible in other countries. A common language was the product of the labor of shared brains. Thus Italy did not possess a language because it did not possess a dense, consistent, lively intellectual life.

Tommaseo likewise emphasised a similar concept in his lecture *Intorno all'unità della lingua italiana*, noting that the common language would develop and flourish alongside the moral and civil growth of the country. Thus the secular linguistic debates would end only when moral and civil education had reached an equilibrium. This position was based on an assumption that seemed to anticipate the theories of Antonio Gramsci:

> Ogni questione letteraria da ultimo riesce a una questione morale e civile [Every literary question ends up into a moral and civil question] (Tommaseo 1868: 79).

4 Should a Dictionary Teach the Language or Guide its Use?

> Uno [...] de' mezzi più efficaci [...] per propagare una lingua è, come tutti sanno, un vocabolario [One of the most effective tools to spread a language is, as everybody knows, a dictionary] (Manzoni 1990a: 583).

> Col Dizionario non s'impara a comporre un periodo, come non s'impara a far versi contando le sillabe [With a dictionary one does not learn to forge a sentence as one does not learn to make verses by counting the syllables] (Tommaseo 1868: 74).

Needless to say, these two statements must be read in context, but it is clear that each of them is the synthesis and an extremist expression of a viewpoint that hardly finds conciliation with the other, and that involves deeply rooted ideas on the very meaning of dictionaries, their target audience and their aims.

Manzoni's *Dell'unità della lingua* suggested as a means for spreading the language a dictionary that did not rely on literary quotations but, for the very first time in Italy, on examples drawn from the spoken (Florentine) language. It is worth noting that despite the stress Manzoni laid on the social significance of his task,[7] what he did, in fact, was to extend to a nationwide scale his personal approach as a writer who had long been seeking a language for his novel, had eventually found it, and had tried to master it through his work on dictionaries. Here lays a contradiction in Manzoni's theory, for it focused on social communication needs but suggested, if not the language, at least the selective process and training skills typical of a literary figure.

Another point worth noting is the fact that within an analytical, detailed argument such as Manzoni's, the individuation of the dictionary

---

[7] «Il signor Ministro ha sostituita la questione sociale e nazionale a un fascio di questioni letterarie» [Our Minister has replaced a group of literary matters with a social and national matter] (Manzoni 1990: 622).

as the main tool for spreading knowledge of the language was not demonstrated but simply taken for granted, offered as an assumption, while the most subtle arguments were reserved for descriptions of the forthcoming dictionary's features. Far from being easily accepted, this assumption raised new debates.

Tommaseo, as the passage shows, came up with a problem – a huge one indeed – that was absent from Manzoni's perspective, namely, the insufficiency of the lexicon alone for disseminating knowledge of a language, and the vital role played by syntax:

> voci e modi, ciascuno da sè, fanno lo scheletro della lingua: ma nel congegno è l'armonia della vita [words and expressions, taken separately, make the skeleton of a language: but the harmony of life lies in the machinery] (Tommaseo 1868: 72-3).

A dictionary was thus an imperfect tool. This was even more true of a dictionary such as the one suggested by Manzoni, which lacked literary examples, since the function of the examples was, according to Tommaseo, to provide pulp for the lexicon, which was nothing more than a bony framework. Nor Tommaseo found the French example appropriate, since

> non fu il Dizionario che fece ai Francesi l'unità della lingua; fu la lingua formata che rendette possibile un dizionario [it was not the dictionary which gave France the unity of language; it was the already organised language which made a dictionary possible] (Tommaseo 1868: 73).

A respectful though polemical position toward Manzoni's indifference to syntax was also taken up by Capponi, who noted in his essay in *Nuova Antologia*:

> Ma se a dire lingua si dice qualcosa fuori d'una semplice nomenclatura, e se invece si tenga essere l'espressione di tutto il pensare d'un popolo colto, certo è che gli usi di questa lingua sono diversi quanto diverse le relazioni cui deve servire; e che in ciascuna, oltre all'essere diseguale il numero delle parole che si adoperano, varia è anche la scelta di queste parole: al che si aggiunga (e ciò è capitale) che oltre alle parole, le frasi e il giro e i collocamenti di esse e la contestura del periodo ed in certi suoi elementi la forma di tutto il discorso che sempre ha del proprio e del distinto in ogni nazione, tutte queste cose insieme fanno la lingua di quella nazione [But if by language one means something more than a mere list of words, rather the expression of the whole thought of the educated people, it is certain that the usages of this language are as different as different are the relations it should be used for; and in each, besides being uneven the number of

words which are used, also the selection of these words is different: it is also to be added – and this is vital – that together with words, sentences, their construction, their position, the shape of the paragraph and in some elements of it the form of the speech, which is always peculiar to each nation, all these points together should make the tongue of a nation] (Capponi 1869: 668-69).

As Capponi did not forget to point out, the dictionary recommended by Manzoni was a most useful means for the unification of language. But it was certainly not a definitive one or one without limitations.

The reactions of Tommaseo and Capponi must also be read in relation to the position of the *Accademia della Crusca*, of which both scholars were members. The official position of the *Accademia* towards the reports of Manzoni and Lambruschini and particularly towards the dictionary proposed by Manzoni – a very different one indeed from the dictionary being prepared by the *Crusca* – was expressed by its *Arciconsolo*, or President, Marco Tabarrini. This was a position definitely differing from Manzoni's with regard to the conception and role of the dictionary in Italy. In his *Rapporto generale sui lavori dell'Accademia nell'anno corrente 1868*, Tabarrini updated his audience on the progress of the fifth edition of the *Vocabolario della Crusca*, focussing mainly on its innovative features (an independent *Glossary* devoted to archaic words; extended control and re-organisation of examples, etc.)[8]. These novelties were the best evidence of the *Crusca*'s contribution to the linguistic debate – a contribution that did not mean taking an active part in the controversies, rather producing "the" dictionary of the national language, based on its written usage and the quotations of its best authors, instead of "one" dictionary among many:

La Crusca apparecchia all'Italia il vocabolario della lingua nazionale, lasciando poi libero ognuno di scrivere ostrogoto o celtico come più gli talenta [The *Crusca* is preparing for Italy the dictionary of national language, then anybody is free to write Ostrogoth or Celtic if he feels like it] (Tabarrini 1868: 16).

Through its dictionary, aimed at the needs of both speakers and writers, *Crusca* maintained the unity of the language for centuries, and thus preserved the essence of its mission. This was a mission that could be stated by reversing the goal that Manzoni assigned to the dictionary:

quello che deve essere un Vocabolario [è] scorta sicura a bene usare della lingua, non ad insegnarla a chi non la sa [what a dictionary must be is a

[8] On these subjects see Parodi 1985.

sure guidance towards the good use of language, not an instrument to teach it to those who do not know it] (Tabarrini 1868: 23).

Still, according to Tabarrini, it was important that the role of a dictionary not be overestimated:

> Del resto si persuadano gl'Italiani che non saranno mai i Vocabolari che suppliranno alla vacuità di pensiero che si deplora in molti dei nostri scrittori di pura forma. Grandi scempiataggini si sono scritte e si scrivono in fiorentino, e in italiano illustre e curiale, nè il Vocabolario ci porrà rimedio [Let the Italians be persuaded that it will not be dictionaries to counteract the emptiness in thought about which we complain in many writers who are interested in the mere form. Silly things have been written in Florentine and in illustrious, curial Italian, and not even the dictionary will help against this] (Tabarrini 1868: 27).

Finally, a hint – once again a veiled polemic directed at Manzoni – of the possibility of a dictionary not limited to words, but with some access to the syntactic pulp of the language:

> assai gioverebbe il ritemprare la lingua alla sua fonte viva; ed a questo può soccorrere anche un Vocabolario, il quale dia non solo le parole comuni per esprimere i pensieri così alla grossa, ma insegni altresì i modi e le frasi più efficaci per coglierne le sfumature, per riprodurne le finezze, per dare insomma alle scritture un che di proprio, di semplice, di schietto [it would be helpful to recover the language bringing it back to its living source; for this also a dictionary may help which does not record only the ordinary words to express thoughts roughly, but shows also the forms and sentences which are most effective to grasp nuances, to reproduce subtleties, to provide writing with something peculiar, simple, true] (Tabarrini 1868: 27).

Thus a vital point in the dictionary debate was the very goal of the work: was it to teach and spread the language, or to guide its proper and precise use?

The impossibility of reconciling these positions provided the premises that generated another controversial matter, that is, the variety of users of a dictionary, and the different needs of such a composite readership.

5 A Fragmentation of Dictionaries

Manzoni defended the opportunity to keep the historical dictionary separate from the dictionary of usage. In *Dell'unità della lingua* he stated that a dictionary could have two very different aims: on the one hand to produce an instrument to understand writers of any time, on the other to represent, as much as possible, the current usage of a living language. This could simply mean that it is one of a lexicographer's responsibilities to label words in order to provide information about their broad or restricted usage, their register, their geographical flavour. Such a task was being performed, on different levels, by both of the great dictionaries of post-unity Italy: the fifth edition of *Crusca* and Tommaseo-Bellini. Manzoni, however, went further: the two goals were so different that each of them

> basta per un lavoro separato, anzi lo richiede tale, non c'essendo un perché d'unire e d'intralciare materialmente delle cose che, per ragione, sono distinte. Un vocabolario destinato a propagare in una nazione intera l'uso d'una lingua, deve servire a un numero molto maggiore di persone, che non siano quelle che mirino all'altro intento. A questo, del rimanente, potrà provvedere un vocabolario apposito [should be the object of a separate work, and requires it, given that there is no reason why different things are mixed up. A dictionary aimed at spreading the language usage in a whole nation will serve a much larger number of people that one oriented towards the other aim. Which will be provided by a dedicated dictionary] (Manzoni 1990: 616).

According to Manzoni, the lasting confusion between the two aims of dictionaries was due to the influence of dictionaries of dead languages – which can but collect an immovable thesaurus. The result, Manzoni pointed out in the *Minuta autografa* of his report (which was more articulate than the final text on this point), is that

> per insegnare quale deva essere il vocabolario della lingua italiana, si siano presi gli esempi e gli argomenti da lingue morte: effetto naturale del non volerne una viva [in order to show what the dictionary for Italian language should be, examples and models from dead languages were taken: the obvious effect of not wanting a living language] (Manzoni 1990: 634).

The same difference was also stressed by Fanfani, who, in his essay *L'uso del popolo e l'uso degli scrittori*, accused the *Crusca* of disseminating dictionaries in which

> le cose più comuni e più usuali, [...] le più belle, le più universali, le più efficaci parole e modi del popolo non si registrano, sol perché non si trovano scritte da coloro che agli Accademici della Crusca saltò il ticchio di citare per testi di lingua [the most common things, the most ordinary, the most beautiful, the most universal, the most effective words and expressions of people's tongue are not recorded, only because they were

not written by those whom the *Accademici della Crusca* decided to choose as language models] (Fanfani 1872: 66).

In France, Fanfani wrote, they had separated the dictionary of the *Académie*, a faithful and true portrait of the language of usage, and the historical dictionaries. Nevertheless, considering how demanding it would be for the *Crusca* to produce two separate works, Fanfani came to the conclusion that it would be correct to record the real language, as used by writers, without forgetting the contribution of the Tuscan dialects. That is to say, he went back to advocating contamination and distanced himself from Manzoni's theories about the need to keep the two types of dictionaries separate.

The uniqueness of the dictionary as a product, and the uniqueness of its target audience were important features in Italian lexicography from its very inception; the *Crusca* dictionary and its offspring, emulators or competitors, were to record the written language and to address those who wrote the same language. From the first edition of the *Crusca* (1612), the ideal readership was labelled with the term *studiosi*.[9] The very same word appeared, two centuries later, in the *Preface* to Tramater (1829-1840).[10] In early Italian the term *studiosi*, literally 'scholars', conveyed also the meaning of 'those who love, are fond of, cultivate'. One must assume that both meanings still overlapped in the nineteenth century. The fact remains that dictionaries addressed only educated, literary people.

The renewed polemical attention in the *Ottocento* made it clear that there was no consent on dictionaries' target (speakers or writers?) even in the public sphere, or any agreement on the organisation of its material (historical or based on the language of everyday usage?). Furthermore, Minister Broglio's attempt to put an authoritative intellectual such as Manzoni in charge of the inquiry turned out to be ineffective because it did not alleviate the debate, but made it harsher. Among other consequences of such strongly dissenting lines, was a diversification and specialisation of dictionaries that began in the second half of the *Ottocento* but had previously been unknown.

---

[9] «Vedendo noi, per manifesti argomenti, salire ogni giorno in più stima la nostra lingua, e col numero degli *studiosi* di quella [...] crescere insieme la vaghezza di conoscer le sue bellezze [As we see very clearly that every day our language is growing in consideration, and increasing the number of *scholars* of it, the wish to know its beauties is also growing]» (*Vocabolario della Crusca* 1612, *Introduzione*) (my emphasis).

[10] «In questo libro adunque intendiamo che trovino gli *studiosi*... [in this book *scholars* can expect to find...]» (*Tramater* 1829-1840, *Prefazione*) (my emphasis).

This was indeed a novelty, which dictionaries themselves recorded when they offered entries for the terms *dizionario* and *vocabolario*. In the two first editions of *Crusca* (1612 and 1623) there was no entry for *dizionario*, which appeared only in the third edition:

> Libro ove sian raccolte, e esposte varie dizioni [A book where different words are recorded and explained] (*Vocabolario della Crusca*, 1691).[11]

The *Crusca* definition with minor changes passed on to later dictionaries, up until the great early nineteenth century lexicons, such as D'Alberti (1797-1805) and Tramater (1829-1840). A different position was assumed by Tommaseo who, in his *Dizionario dei sinonimi* (1830), did not limit himself to consider a dictionary as a collection of words, but drew a (theoretical) distinction between collections of dead and living words:

> Nella lingua italiana è impossibile, per ora, dividere in due opere il vocabolario e il glossario [according to Tommaseo, a collection of archaic words], perché in fatto di linguaggio e di civiltà, gli italiani non sanno ancora nettamente distinguere il vivo dal morto, e locuzioni e cose che a taluni paiono morte sono più vive e vitali della recenti [In Italian it is at the moment impossible to divide into two books the dictionary and the glossary, because as far as language and civilisation are concerned, the Italians cannot yet separate what is dead from what is alive, and what seems dead to somebody can be livelier and more vital than recent ones] (Tommaseo, *Dizionario dei sinonimi*).

Eventually, the great *Dizionario della lingua italiana* Tommaseo-Bellini (1861-1879) recorded the phenomenon of the fragmentation of dictionaries, which had by then become a significant feature, by asserting that there were many dictionaries and by listing some of their genres, for instance «Vocabolario domestico» or «Vocabolario d'arti e mestieri».

In this way the theoretical distinction between historical dictionaries and dictionaries aimed at everyday usage encouraged the birth of one new genre, the so-called dictionaries of usage. This group of lexicographical works included, besides the *Novo vocabolario* directed by Giorgini and Broglio and the direct result of Manzoni's report, a series of other works, some of which were very successful, such as those by Policarpo Petrocchi

---

[11] *Vocabolario*, in the first and second editions, re-directed the reader to *vocabolo*: «E da vocabolo vocabolario, che è una raccolta di vocaboli come è questo libro» [and from *vocabolo*, vocabolario, which is a collection of words like this book] (*Vocabolario della Crusca* 1612 and 1623).

or by Fanfani. Dictionaries of usage, which represented «the great novelty of post-unity Italy»,[12] addressed for the first time not scholars but the common reader. Furthermore they often differentiated their offerings based on the categories of their various readerships. This occurred, for instance, in the many dictionaries published by Petrocchi, who explained the fragmentation in his foreword to the *Piccolo Dizionario Universale*, of 1894:

> Col presente, compio la serie de' miei dizionari manuali. Una lingua essendo un materiale immenso, la scelta delle parole e delle frasi in tali libri varia secondo le persone cui sono diretti. Quello *Universale* [...] più che altro destinato a letterati e persone colte in genere, è il più ricco di voci e di esempi; l'altro *Scolastico* [...] fatto specialmente per le scuole classiche, oltre si capisce alla parte arcaica necessaria allo studio dei testi, à l'esemplificazione e abbondante, e le etimologie. Questo che servirà alle scuole elementari e agli uffici, tascabile, in brevi proporzioni, non à etimologie ... [With the present one I close the series of my handbook-dictionaries. Since a language is an enormous material, the choice of words and expressions varies according to the readers it wants to reach. The *Universale* [...], mainly addressed to literary and educated people, is the richest in entries and examples; the *Scolastico* [...], mainly addressed to Grammar schools, besides the archaic stuff which is necessary to approach the classical texts, offers a huge body of examples and etymologies. This one, which addresses primary schools and offices, in pocket size, short, has no etymologies....] (Petrocchi 1894, *Prefazione*: III).

Within the typical variety of dictionaries meant to reach different groups of readers should also be recorded an earlier phenomenon: the dictionaries of dialect, which flourished in Italy from the first decades of the *Ottocento* and which were usually conceived as a bridge from dialect to Italian (that is, Florentine dialect). Some of them listed this goal among others, and considered it their task both to enable native dialect speakers to master Italian and to provide people who did not know it with an access to the dialect (more so if the dialect in question had a literary tradition worth knowing and preserving).

A typical example of this attitude was the *Vocabolario milanese-italiano* by Francesco Cherubini. The foreword to the second edition of Cherubini's work (1839-56) reads:

[12] Serianni 1990: 72. For a map of dictionaries in the nineteenth century see also Serianni 1989. Among others surveys on lexicography see Della Valle 1993; and the classic Migliorini 1960.

> In questo Vocabolario [...] è mio intendimento ajutar a voltare l'idioma nostro vernacolo nella lingua scritta della nazione; dar modo ai non Milanesi di capire noi medesimi se favelliamo con essi [...]; serbare col comprendimento delle voci e dei modi nostrali anche quello delle belle opere poetiche dettate da ingegni esimj nel nostro volgare [...]; suggerirne [oggetti] definiti ai cultori della lingua nazionale moltissimi altri pei quali, se io male non osservai, non esiste finora alcun rappresentativo nei Vocabolarj di essa [In this dictionary [...] it is my aim to help turning our vernacular into the written language of the nation; provide those who are not from Milan with a tool to understand us if we talk to them; to preserve, through the understanding of our words and expressions, the understanding of the beautiful poetry written by great brains in our vernacular [...]; to suggest to the scholars of the national language many objects which, if I am not mistaken, are not included, so far, in its dictionaries] (Cherubini 1814: V).

Here were several different objectives that involved a bi-directional exchange between the Milanese dialect and national language. The first point was to help translate dialect into Italian, but what followed was actually oriented the other way, since Cherubini spoke about helping non-Milanese people understand the spoken and written literary dialect (which had produced such a distinguished literature over the centuries); and about suggesting words that did exist in Milanese and seemed to be missing from national dictionaries. In short, there were divergent goals as well as a dual target audience: those who knew the Milanese dialect and those who did not.

Giuseppe Boerio, in a *Discorso preliminare* to the second edition of his *Vocabolario del dialetto veneziano* (1856), likewise recalled the former glories of Venetian vernacular literature and emphasised the role of dictionaries of dialect in enriching the national language. Every city should indeed provide its dictionary

> per poter indi compararli tra loro, estrarne i migliori e i più comuni termini, arricchire la lingua de'dotti ed accrescere il gran Vocabolario della Crusca [in order to make it possible to compare [the various dictionaries], to pick up from them the best and more common words, to enrich the educated people's language and to enlarge the great *Vocabolario della Crusca*] (Boerio 1829: 9).

Other dictionaries were presented simply as practical Italian-learning tools, and addressed to a non-literary, dialect-speaking public. This was clearly stated in the introductions to various works. An early example can be found in Claudio Ferrari, the author of a *Vocabolario bolognese co' sinonimi italiani e franzesi* published in 1820:

> Uno dei mezzo più acconci per agevolare l'acquisto della lingua italiana e per utilizzarla a poco a poco anche nei luoghi, dove si parlano i dialetti meno puri, che cioè più da essa si allontanano [...] è stato sempre riputato, oltre l'assidua lettura degli ottimi libri, anche il vocabolario, direm così casalingo di ogni dialetto co' vocaboli dirincontro della lingua comune scritta [One of the most effective means to help learning the Italian language and practicing it step by step even in places where the less pure dialects are spoken, i.e. those which are most remote from it [...] has always been considered, besides reading good books, also the dictionary of any dialect which offers for each word the common written language match word] (Ferrari 1820: I).[13]

The choice of public (only those who do not master the written language) and the instrumental role of dialect, used as a bridge to the Italian language, are clear and stressed: the dictionary is aimed at

> far imparare ai men pratici i vocaboli della lingua italica scritta *e non a rovescio* [teaching those who are less experienced the Italian words, and *not the reverse*] (my emphasis) (Ferrari 1820: II-III).

In his lecture *Intorno all'unità della lingua italiana*, some fifty years later, Tommaseo (1868) was still thinking of dialects as an intermediate stage towards a language, and suggesting that everyday practical words should be deleted from the *Crusca* dictionary and collected in as many dictionaries as there were important dialects («in tanti Dizionarii quanti sono i principali dialetti», Tommaseo 1868: 73). By then, the general idea that «tanti Dizionari», aimed at the different targets and varied needs of the audience, already existed and should exist was widely accepted.

[13] Among other similar statements, see that of Michele Ponza, in the foreword to his *Vocabolario piemontese-italiano e italiano-piemontese* of 1843: «Egli è fuor d'ogni dubbio, che fra le cagioni per cui la lingua italiana [...] non fiorisce, ma è per così dire strappazzata [...], vuolsi annoverare la mancanza di Vocabolarj di dialetto» [It is doubtless that among the reasons why the Italian language [...] does not flourish, but is abused [...] should be counted the lack of dictionaries of dialect].

References

Dictionaries

Hereafter some of the most important modern Italian dictionaries are listed by typology. Only typologies which are referred to in this essay are considered.

Crusca and other historical dictionaries (in chronological order)

Vocabolario degli Accademici della Crusca (1729-1738). Firenze, Manni. [fourth impression].

D'Alberti di Villanuova, Francesco (1797-1805). *Dizionario universale critico, enciclopedico della lingua italiana.* Lucca, Domenico Marescandoli.

Crusca veronese = *Vocabolario degli Accademici della Crusca. Oltre le giunte fatteci finora, cresciuto d'assai migliaja di voci e modi de'classici, le più trovate da' Veronesi* (1806-1811). Verona, Stamperia di Dionigi Ramanzini.

Costa, Paolo / Cardinali, Francesco (1819-1828). *Dizionario della lingua italiana*, 7 vols. Bologna, Masi.

Tramater = *Vocabolario universale italiano compilato a cura della Società tipografica Tramater e C.* (1829-1840). Napoli, Dai Torchi del Tramater.

Manuzzi, Giuseppe (1833-1840). *Vocabolario della lingua italiana già compilato dagli Accademici della Crusca ed ora novamente corretto ed accresciuto*. Firenze, Passigli.

Gherardini, Giovanni (1852-1857). *Supplimento a' vocabolarj italiani*, 6 vols. Milano, Bernardoni.

Tommaseo-Bellini = *Dizionario della lingua italiana nuovamente compilato dai signori Nicolò* [sic] *Tommaseo e cav. Professore Bernardo Bellini, con oltre 100.000 giunte ai precedenti dizionari raccolte da Nicolò Tommaseo, Gius. Campi, Gius. Meini, Pietro Fanfani e da molti altri distinti filologi e scienziati* (1861-1879). Torino, Pomba. [quoted from reimpression Torino, UTET 1929].

Vocabolario degli Accademici della Crusca (1863-1923). Firenze, Cellini. [fifth impression]. [with *Glossario* (1867). Firenze, Cellini, *A-B*].

Dictionaries of usage

Giorgini-Broglio = *Novo vocabolario della lingua italiana secondo l'uso di Firenze, ordinato dal Ministero della Pubblica Istruzione, compilato sotto la presidenza del comm. Emilio Broglio dai Signori Bianciardi*

Stanislao, Dazzi Pietro, Fanfani Pietro, Gelli Agenore, Giorgini Giovan Battista, Gotti Aurelio, Meini Giuseppe, Ricci Mauro (1870-1897). Firenze, Cellini.

Petrocchi, Policarpo (1887-1891). *Nòvo dizionario universale della lingua italiana*. Milano, Treves.

Petrocchi, Policarpo (1894). *Piccolo dizionario universale*. Firenze, Vallardi.

Rigutini-Fanfani = *Vocabolario italiano della lingua parlata compilato da Giuseppe Rigutini e Pietro Fanfani* (1875). Firenze, Tipografia Cenniniana.

Dictionaries of dialect

Boerio, Giuseppe (1829). *Dizionario del dialetto veneziano*. Venezia, Santini.

Cherubini, Francesco (1814). *Vocabolario milanese-italiano*. Milano, Stamperia Reale.

Ferrari, Claudio (1820). *Vocabolario bolognese co'sinonimi italiani e franzesi*. Bologna, Tipografia Nobili.

Mortillaro, Vincenzo (1838-1844). *Nuovo dizionario siciliano-italiano compilato da una Società di persone di lettere*. Palermo, Tipografia del Giornale letterario.

Sant'Albino, Vittorio di (1859). *Gran dizionario piemontese-italiano*. Torino, Società Unione Tipografico-editrice.

Ponza, Michele (1843). *Vocabolario piemontese-italiano e italiano-piemontese*. Torino, Tipografia di Gio. Battista Paravia.

Puoti, Basilio (1841). *Vocabolario domestico napoletano e toscano*. Napoli, Libreria e tipografia Simoniana.

Dictionaries of synonyms

Fanfani, Pietro (1879). *Novo vocabolario dei sinonimi ad uso delle scuole*, prefated by Costantino Arlìa. Milano, Carrara.

Rabbi, Carlo Costanzo (1732). *Sinonimi ed aggiunti italiani. Con in fine un trattato de' sinonimi, degli aggiunti e delle similitudini*. Bologna, Costantino Pisarri.

Romani, Giovanni (1825-1827). *Dizionario generale de' sinonimi italiani*, Milano, Silvestri.

Tommaseo, Niccolò (1830). *Dizionario dei sinonimi*. Firenze, Pezzati.

Zecchini, Stefano Pietro (1848). *Dizionario dei sinonimi della lingua italiana*. Torino, Pomba.

Primary sources

Ascoli, Graziadio Isaia (1873). "Proemio", in *Archivio glottologico italiano* 1: V-XLI.

Cantù, Cesare (1836). "Di due recenti vocabolari", in *Ricoglitore italiano e straniero* March: 289-352; April: 433-487; May: 577-606.

Capponi, Gino (1829). "Se sia alcuna specie di vero nella opinione di quelli che vogliono doversi ammettere in Italia una lingua illustre distinta dal dialetto della Toscana. Lezione detta nell'Adunanza del dì 31 Luglio 1827", in *Atti dell'Imperiale e Reale Accademia della Crusca*, vol. 3. Firenze, Tipografia all'Insegna di Dante: 455-462.

—. (1869). "Fatti relativi alla storia della nostra lingua", in *Nuova Antologia* August: 665-682.

Fanfani, Pietro (1872). *Lingua e nazione. Avvertenze a chi vuol scrivere italiano*. Milano, Carrara.

Lambruschini, Alessandro (1868). "Relazione", *Nuova Antologia* 8, May: 99-108.

Manzoni, Alessandro (1974). *Della lingua italiana*, in Manzoni, Alessandro. *Tutte le opere*, edited by Alberto Chiari, Fausto Ghisalberti, vol. 5, *Scritti linguistici e letterari*, Tomo primo, *Della lingua italiana*, edited by Luigi Poma, Angelo Stella. Milano, Mondadori: 533-721.

—. (1990). *Dell'unità della lingua e dei mezzi di diffonderla*, in Manzoni, Alessandro. *Tutte le opere*, edited by Alberto Chiari, Fausto Ghisalberti, vol. 5, *Scritti linguistici e letterari*, Tomo secondo, *Scritti linguistici*, edited by Angelo Stella, Luca Danzi. Mondadori, Milano.

Settembrini, Luigi (1868). "Della lingua italiana", in *Universo illustrato* May 10th.

Tabarrini, Marco (1868). "Rapporto generale sui lavori dell'Accademia nell'anno corrente", in *Adunanza solenne della R. Accademia della Crusca tenuta il 13 settembre del 1868*. Firenze, Cellini e C. alla Galileiana: 9-35.

Tommaseo, Niccolò (1868). "Intorno all'unità della lingua italiana", in *Adunanza solenne della R. Accademia della Crusca tenuta il 13 settembre del 1868*. Firenze, Cellini e C. alla Galileiana.

Secundary sources

Bricchi, Mariarosa (2000). *La roca trombazza. Lessico arcaico e letterario nella prosa narrativa dell'Ottocento italiano*. Alessandria, Edizioni dell'Orso.

Della Valle, Valeria (1993). “La lessicografia”, in Serianni, Luca / Trifone, Pietro (eds). *Storia della lingua italiana*, vol. 1. *I luoghi della codificazione*. Torino, Einaudi: 29-91.

Migliorini, Bruno (1960). *Storia della lingua italiana*. Firenze, Sansoni. [Engl. transl. *The Italian Language* abridged, recast and revised by T. Gwinfor Griffith. London / Boston, Faber & Faber 1966].

Parodi, Severina (1985). “L’utopia del vocabolario nell’unificazione linguistica dell’Italia”, in *La Crusca nella tradizione letteraria e linguistica italiana. Atti del Congresso Internazionale per il IV centenario dell’Accademia della Crusca (Firenze, 29 settembre-2 ottobre 1983)*. Firenze, Accademia della Crusca: 387-393.

Serianni, Luca (1989). *Storia della lingua italiana. Il primo Ottocento*. Bologna, il Mulino.

—. (1990). *Storia della lingua italiana. Il secondo Ottocento*. Bologna, il Mulino.

MODERN GERMAN DICTIONARIES AND THEIR IMPACT ON LINGUISTIC RESEARCH

ANNETTE KLOSA

The German dictionary landscape changes increasingly. Aside from printed dictionaries, there are CD-ROM publications, and over the past couple of years, new lexicographic reference works for German have been offered on the Internet. In this paper we will look at this diversity while, at the same time, we will get an impression of how results of linguistic research and corpus linguistic achievements stimulate lexicographic work in Germany today. Finally, we will address the question of how dictionaries can offer suggestions for linguistic research arising from their lexicographic practice.

We will focus primarily on online dictionaries because it is here in particular that corpus linguistic achievements as well as results of linguistic research are utilised. Most of the online dictionaries discussed here are monolingual, but we will also have a brief look at one bilingual dictionary on the Internet. CD-ROMs will be ignored here, because those published in Germany are in most cases merely digitalised versions of printed dictionaries, which offer easier ways of information retrieval but do not necessarily apply new lexicographic or linguistic methods.

To begin with, we will compare two recently published dictionaries of German as a second language in printed form, which are the state of the art in German printed dictionaries.

1 Printed Monolingual Dictionaries for German as a Second Language

Two of the major dictionary publishers in Germany, the Langenscheidt group[1] and the Duden publishing house,[2] offer pocket dictionaries for German as a second language addressed primarily to students at the

[1] See http://www.langenscheidt.de.
[2] See http://www.duden.de.

beginning and intermediate levels. Both dictionaries are interesting because they show new features as regards content and layout.

Let us first look at the layout. Here, as in other German dictionaries published recently, we find that a second colour helps in marking either all the headwords (as in *Langenscheidt Taschenwörterbuch Deutsch als Fremdsprache*; see fig. 1) or specific headwords (as in *Duden Wörterbuch Deutsch als Fremdsprache* where the blue colour selects entries belonging to the certificate vocabulary of German [see fig. 2]).

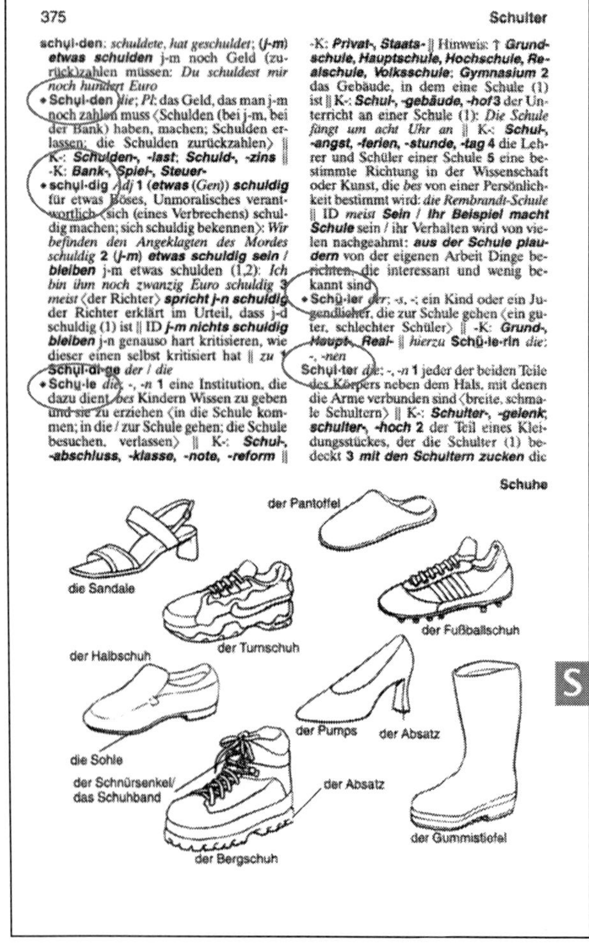

375 Schulter

schul·den: *schuldete, hat geschuldet*; **(*j-m*) *etwas schulden*** j-m noch Geld (zurück)zahlen müssen: *Du schuldest mir noch hundert Euro*

• **Schul·den** *die*; *Pl*: das Geld, das man j-m noch zahlen muss ⟨Schulden (bei j-m, bei der Bank) haben, machen; Schulden erlassen; die Schulden zurückzahlen⟩ ‖ K-: ***Schulden-, -last***; ***Schuld-, -zins*** ‖ -K: ***Bank-, Spiel-, Steuer-***

• **schul·dig** *Adj* **1 (*etwas* (*Gen*)) *schuldig*** für etwas Böses, Unmoralisches verantwortlich ⟨sich (eines Verbrechens) schuldig machen; sich schuldig bekennen⟩: *Wir befinden den Angeklagten des Mordes schuldig* **2 (*j-m*) *etwas schuldig sein / bleiben*** j-m etwas schulden (1,2): *Ich bin ihm noch zwanzig Euro schuldig* **3** *meist* ⟨der Richter⟩ ***spricht j-n schuldig*** der Richter erklärt im Urteil, dass j-d schuldig (1) ist ‖ ID ***j-m nichts schuldig bleiben*** j-n genauso hart kritisieren, wie dieser einen selbst kritisiert hat ‖ *zu* **1 Schul·di·ge** *der / die*

• **Schu·le** *die*; -, *-n* **1** eine Institution, die dazu dient, *bes* Kindern Wissen zu geben und sie zu erziehen ⟨in die Schule kommen; in die / zur Schule gehen; die Schule besuchen, verlassen⟩ ‖ K-: ***Schul-, -abschluss, -klasse, -note, -reform*** ‖ -K: ***Privat-, Staats-*** ‖ Hinweis: ↑ ***Grundschule, Hauptschule, Hochschule, Realschule, Volksschule***; ***Gymnasium*** **2** das Gebäude, in dem eine Schule (1) ist ‖ K-: ***Schul-, -gebäude, -hof*** **3** der Unterricht an einer Schule (1): *Die Schule fängt um acht Uhr an* ‖ K-: ***Schul-, -angst, -ferien, -stunde, -tag*** **4** die Lehrer und Schüler einer Schule **5** eine bestimmte Richtung in der Wissenschaft oder Kunst, die *bes* von einer Persönlichkeit bestimmt wird: *die Rembrandt-Schule* ‖ ID *meist* ***Sein / Ihr Beispiel macht Schule*** sein / ihr Verhalten wird von vielen nachgeahmt; ***aus der Schule plaudern*** von der eigenen Arbeit Dinge berichten, die interessant und wenig bekannt sind

• **Schü·ler** *der*; *-s*, *-*; ein Kind oder ein Jugendlicher, die zur Schule gehen ⟨ein guter, schlechter Schüler⟩ ‖ -K: ***Grund-, Haupt-, Real-*** ‖ *hierzu* **Schü·le·rin** *die*; *-*, *-nen*

Schul·ter *die*; -, *-n* **1** jeder der beiden Teile des Körpers neben dem Hals, mit denen die Arme verbunden sind ⟨breite, schmale Schultern⟩ ‖ K-: ***Schulter-, -gelenk***; ***schulter-, -hoch*** **2** der Teil eines Kleidungsstückes, der die Schulter (1) bedeckt **3 *mit den Schultern zucken*** die

Fig. 1. Blue entries in *Langenscheidt Taschenwörterbuch Deutsch als Fremdsprache*

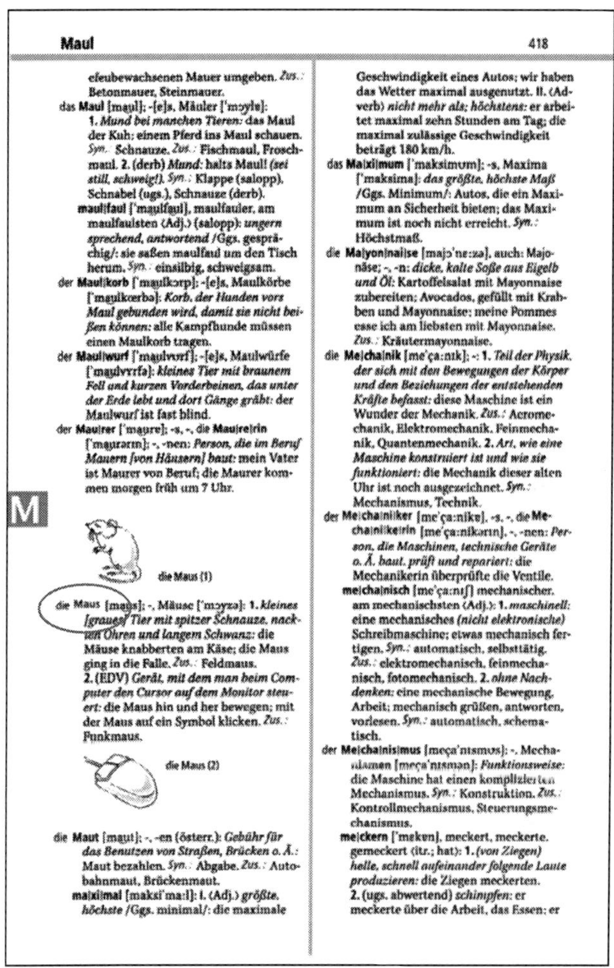
Maul 418

efeubewachsenen Mauer umgeben. *Zus.:* Betonmauer, Steinmauer.

das **Maul** [maul]; -[e]s, Mäuler ['mɔylɐ]: 1. *Mund bei manchen Tieren:* das Maul der Kuh; einem Pferd ins Maul schauen. *Syn.:* Schnauze. *Zus.:* Fischmaul, Froschmaul. 2. (derb) *Mund:* halts Maul! *(sei still, schweig!). Syn.:* Klappe (salopp), Schnabel (ugs.), Schnauze (derb).

maul|faul ['maulfaul], maulfauler, am maulfaulsten ⟨Adj.⟩ (salopp): *ungern sprechend, antwortend* /Ggs. gesprächig/: sie saßen maulfaul um den Tisch herum. *Syn.:* einsilbig, schweigsam.

der **Maul|korb** ['maulkɔrp]; -[e]s, Maulkörbe ['maulkœrbə]: *Korb, der Hunden vors Maul gebunden wird, damit sie nicht beißen können:* alle Kampfhunde müssen einen Maulkorb tragen.

der **Maul|wurf** ['maulvʊrf]; -[e]s, Maulwürfe ['maulvʏrfə]: *kleines Tier mit braunem Fell und kurzen Vorderbeinen, das unter der Erde lebt und dort Gänge gräbt:* der Maulwurf ist fast blind.

der **Mau|rer** ['maurɐ]; -s, -, die **Mau|re|rin** ['maurərɪn]; -, -nen: *Person, die im Beruf Mauern [von Häusern] baut:* mein Vater ist Maurer von Beruf; die Maurer kommen morgen früh um 7 Uhr.

M

die Maus (1)

die **Maus** [maus]; -, Mäuse ['mɔyzə]: 1. *kleines [graues] Tier mit spitzer Schnauze, nackten Ohren und langem Schwanz:* die Mäuse knabberten am Käse; die Maus ging in die Falle. *Zus.:* Feldmaus. 2. (EDV) *Gerät, mit dem man beim Computer den Cursor auf dem Monitor steuert:* die Maus hin und her bewegen; mit der Maus auf ein Symbol klicken. *Zus.:* Funkmaus.

die Maus (2)

die **Maut** [maut]; -, -en (österr.): *Gebühr für das Benutzen von Straßen, Brücken o. Ä.:* Maut bezahlen. *Syn.:* Abgabe. *Zus.:* Autobahnmaut, Brückenmaut.

ma|xi|mal [maksi'ma:l]: I. ⟨Adj.⟩ *größte, höchste* /Ggs. minimal/: die maximale Geschwindigkeit eines Autos; wir haben das Wetter maximal ausgenutzt. II. ⟨Adverb⟩ *nicht mehr als; höchstens:* er arbeitet maximal zehn Stunden am Tag; die maximal zulässige Geschwindigkeit beträgt 180 km/h.

das **Ma|xi|mum** ['maksimʊm]; -s, Maxima ['maksima]: *das größte, höchste Maß* /Ggs. Minimum/: Autos, die ein Maximum an Sicherheit bieten; das Maximum ist noch nicht erreicht. *Syn.:* Höchstmaß.

die **Ma|yon|nai|se** [majɔ'nɛ:zə], auch: Majonäse; -, -n: *dicke, kalte Soße aus Eigelb und Öl:* Kartoffelsalat mit Mayonnaise zubereiten; Avocados, gefüllt mit Krabben und Mayonnaise; meine Pommes esse ich am liebsten mit Mayonnaise. *Zus.:* Kräutermayonnaise.

die **Me|cha|nik** [me'ça:nɪk]; -: 1. *Teil der Physik, der sich mit den Bewegungen der Körper und den Beziehungen der entstehenden Kräfte befasst:* diese Maschine ist ein Wunder der Mechanik. *Zus.:* Aeromechanik, Elektromechanik, Feinmechanik, Quantenmechanik. 2. *Art, wie eine Maschine konstruiert ist und wie sie funktioniert:* die Mechanik dieser alten Uhr ist noch ausgezeichnet. *Syn.:* Mechanismus, Technik.

der **Me|cha|ni|ker** [me'ça:nikɐ], -s, -, die **Me|cha|ni|ke|rin** [me'ça:nikərɪn], -, -nen: *Person, die Maschinen, technische Geräte o. Ä. baut, prüft und repariert:* die Mechanikerin überprüfte die Ventile.

me|cha|nisch [me'ça:nɪʃ] mechanischer, am mechanischsten ⟨Adj.⟩: 1. *maschinell:* eine mechanisches *(nicht elektronische)* Schreibmaschine; etwas mechanisch fertigen. *Syn.:* automatisch, selbsttätig. *Zus.:* elektromechanisch, feinmechanisch, fotomechanisch. 2. *ohne Nachdenken:* eine mechanische Bewegung, Arbeit; mechanisch grüßen, antworten, vorlesen. *Syn.:* automatisch, schematisch.

der **Me|cha|nis|mus** [meça'nɪsmʊs]; -, Mechanismen [meça'nɪsmən]: *Funktionsweise:* die Maschine hat einen komplizierten Mechanismus. *Syn.:* Konstruktion. *Zus.:* Kontrollmechanismus, Steuerungsmechanismus.

me|ckern ['mɛkɐn], meckert, meckerte, gemeckert ⟨itr.; hat⟩: 1. *(von Ziegen) helle, schnell aufeinander folgende Laute produzieren:* die Ziegen meckerten. 2. (ugs. abwertend) *schimpfen:* er meckerte über die Arbeit, das Essen; er

Fig. 2. Blue entries in *Duden Wörterbuch Deutsch als Fremdsprache*

The use of colours in structuring dictionary entries is a fairly new feature in German dictionaries, which may have been introduced by the publishers more as an incentive to buy the dictionary rather than as a feature chosen for metalexicographic considerations.[3] Another layout feature in both dictionaries is the illustrations. While there are pictorial

[3] See Klosa 2004: 271–273.

dictionaries for German,[4] there is no fixed tradition of illustrating monolingual dictionaries of German.[5] As in the examples, it is mainly in learners' dictionaries that we find illustrations, for instance when homonyms are to be explained (as in fig. 2 the illustrations accompanying the entry **Maus**, where the animal *mouse* and the computer tool *mouse* are depicted). There are also illustrations of lexical fields (as for the entry **Schuhe** in fig. 1, where different types of shoes and their parts are depicted). Whether learners will take advantage of illustrations in understanding a word's meaning or in enlarging their vocabulary is an interesting question, which could stimulate lexicographic research.

A new layout feature, not only in learners' dictionaries for German, but in an increasing number of monolingual and bilingual printed German dictionaries, are small boxes integrated into the text. Those boxes are used in *Duden Wörterbuch Deutsch als Fremdsprache* to explain more about life in Germany (see fig. 3 with the entry **Frühstück**, explaining how breakfast is served in Germany).

Frühstück	
Zum Frühstück essen viele Deutsche, Schweizer und Österreicher Brot. Wer es gern süß mag, streicht Marmelade oder Honig darauf. Wer lieber herzhaft isst,	belegt das Brot mit Wurst oder Käse. Sehr beliebt sind auch Cornflakes oder Müsli. Dazu trinken die Erwachsenen Kaffee oder Tee, die Kinder Milch.

Fig. 3. Box entry for **Frühstück** in *Duden Wörterbuch Deutsch als Fremdsprache*

Box entries are also used to give grammatical explanations (see fig. 4, where questions of gender of German river names are discussed for the entry **Fluss**). These boxes are complemented by some of the dictionary's outer texts, such as texts on how to communicate in a coffee shop or restaurant. Boxes like the ones shown here not only are a new layout feature but also represent a new type of dictionary entry, which has not yet been metalexicographically explored. It would, for example, be interesting to investigate how box entries are integrated into the dictionary's mediostructure.

---

[4] As, for example: *Duden – Das Bildwörterbuch. Die Gegenstände und ihre Benennung*. Mannheim / Leipzig / Wien / Zürich, Dudenverlag 2005 (6th edition).

[5] The relatively new *Wahrig Illustriertes Wörterbuch der deutschen Sprache* edited by Renate Wahrig-Burfeind (Gütersloh / München, Wissen Media Verlag 2004) is based on the *Illustrated Oxford Dictionary* (Dorling Kindersley 1998).

Fluss	
Die Namen der Flüsse sind im Deutschen meist weiblich: »die Oder«, »die Elbe«, »die Spree«, »die Mosel«, »die Donau«. Nur einige Flussnamen, die	noch aus vorgermanischer Zeit stammen, sind männlich: »der Rhein«, »der Neckar«, »der Main«, »der Inn«.

Fig. 4. Box entry with grammatical information for **Fluss** in *Duden Wörterbuch Deutsch als Fremdsprache*

Nevertheless, both dictionaries presented here are traditional learners' dictionaries inasmuch as they compile the list of entries mainly from other dictionaries or other word lists and are not based primarily on corpus data. Collocations and examples are not extracted according to their statistic relevance in huge electronic text corpora, but mainly according to their assumed relevance for learners.[6] In this respect, German learners' lexicography is behind the English learners' lexicography. Corpus-based dictionaries have been published in English for over twenty years.[7]

The entries themselves in both *Duden Wörterbuch Deutsch als Fremdsprache* and *Langenscheidt Taschenwörterbuch Deutsch als Fremdsprache* follow the traditional archetype (headword – grammar – definition – examples, and so forth), but new box entries and illustrations introduce at least additional ways of looking up words or finding information in the dictionary. A new feature for the definitions is that both dictionaries try to define with lemmatised words only.

2 Bilingual Dictionaries: An Online German-Italian Dictionary (*ELDIT*)

In this paragraph we will look at an online bilingual learners' dictionary: the *Dizionario Elettronico per apprendenti Italo-Tedeschi* (*ELDIT*)[8], which is published by the European Academy in Bolzano. This is a very interesting project where the potential of an Internet presentation is being largely explored. The *ELDIT* online-dictionary addresses students of German with Italian as first language and students of Italian with German as first language. It covers a basic vocabulary with approximately

[6] See Klosa 2004: 284–286.

[7] The first corpus based dictionary of English, the Collins Cobuild English Language Dictionary, was published by John Sinclair in 1987. See also Sinclair (1987) for an account on this dictionary project.

[8] See http://dev.eurac.edu:8081/MakeEldit1/Eldit.html.

3500 entries. *ELDIT* is designed for use in text production and aims at increasing and reinforcing users' vocabulary. It is only published online. Due to its data structure and forms of presentation, it cannot be published in print. As a data basis, *ELDIT* mostly uses secondary sources (i.e. other dictionaries) in addition to its own electronic text corpus. It offers information that has been written by lexicographers based on these sources, an enhancement with automatically extracted information from the text corpus is planned.

The information given covers the full range expected to be in a learners' dictionary: orthography, morphology, pronunciation, meaning, equivalents in Italian and German respectively, collocations, phraseology, paradigmatic partners, and so on. The metalanguage chosen is always the first language of the user, and linguistic terminology is avoided as far as possible. Abbreviations and symbols have been dropped so that all information is as explicit as possible. Thus, *ELDIT* meets its users at their level, namely: at the beginning of learning a second language.

ELDIT explores the entire range of providing information on the Internet: written explanations, audio files (for information on pronunciation), graphs (for information on lexical fields), animated graphics (for information on verbs and their syntactic behaviour), videos (in the tutorial on how to use *ELDIT*), and illustrations. The entries are connected to each other through extensive linking: from the entry **Haus** for example, we can click on **Gebäude**, from there we can select **Bau,** and so on (see fig. 5).

Another feature of *ELDIT* is animated graphics used for example in the entry **geben** to illustrate the syntactic behaviour of this verb (see fig. 6). *ELDIT* offers several ways of access to the data: you can either search for a word form or a word paradigm, you can click through the complete word list, or you can follow the links between different dictionary entries. It does not yet offer other ways of access used in English online-dictionaries, such as, going from illustrations to entries.[9]

[9] The *American Heritage Dictionary of the English Language*, for example, includes in its online presentation the possibility to find entries in the dictionary via an illustration index.

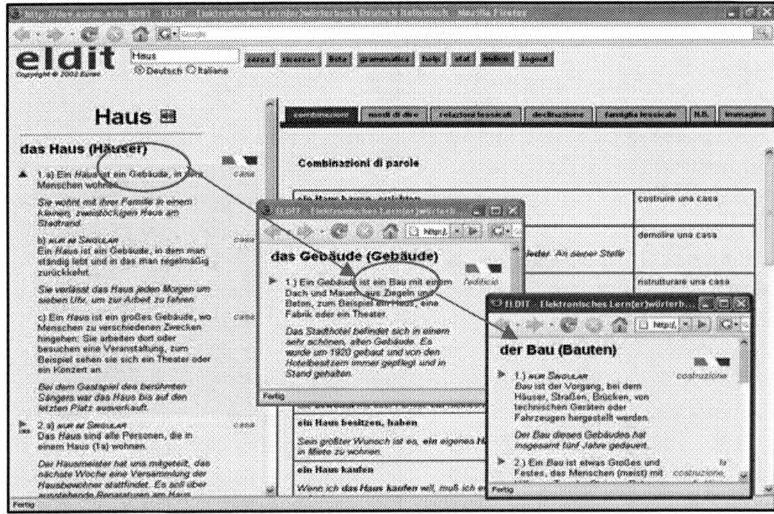

Fig. 5. Linking between the entries in *ELDIT*

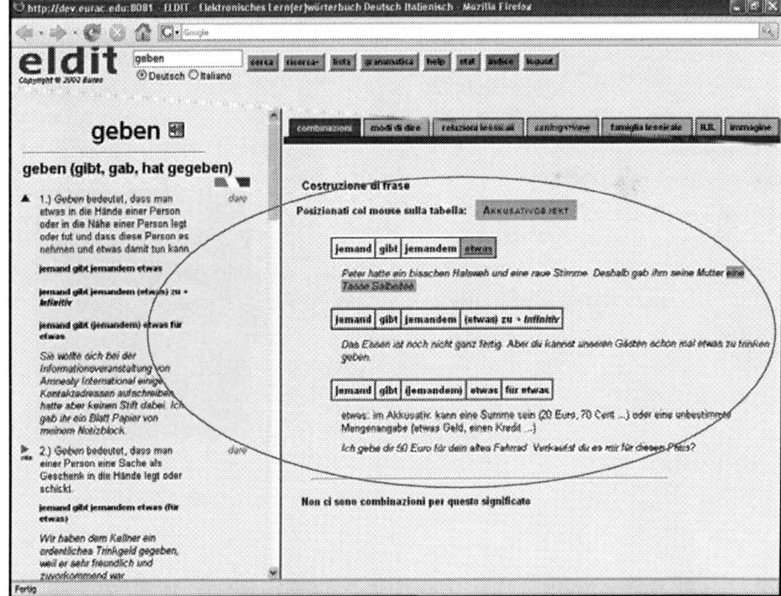

Fig. 6. Animated graphics for the verb entry **geben** in *ELDIT*

3 Monolingual Dictionaries on the Internet

3.1 Dictionaries of New Words

To begin with monolingual dictionaries on the Internet, we will look at two monolingual dictionaries concentrating on new words. For a lexicographic description of new words the Internet definitely seems to be the appropriate medium since it allows up to date publishing. But dictionaries of neologisms are also interesting because here corpus linguistic methods may be especially beneficial. Two completely different German dictionaries on new words are online: the *Neologismenwörterbuch* compiled at the *Institut für Deutsche Sprache* in Mannheim, and the dictionary *Wortwarte* developed by Lothar Lemnitzer from the University of Tübingen.

The *Neologismenwörterbuch* is a traditional dictionary, although it deals with new words. It gathers its information from an electronic text corpus and a collection of printed citations (mainly from newspapers). It does not yet extensively use corpus linguistic methods to find candidates for new words but instead relies on the lexicographers' ability to decide on questions such as: when was the word used for the first time? Is it used only in specific sociolects or dialects or is it a word that the majority of German speakers would recognise as belonging to the common vocabulary and would describe as new?

The dictionary entries themselves (see fig. 7 and fig. 8 for the entry **Direktbank**) offer information on the often varying orthography (*Direktbank* is written in one word or with hyphen), on word formation (*Direktbank* is a compound of *direkt* and *Bank*), on meaning (*Direktbank* denotes a bank where you execute your banking business by telephone or via computer), and so forth. They also record the time that the lemma has been in use (*Direktbank* has been in use since the late nineties of the last century), and they give, where necessary, additional encyclopaedic information.

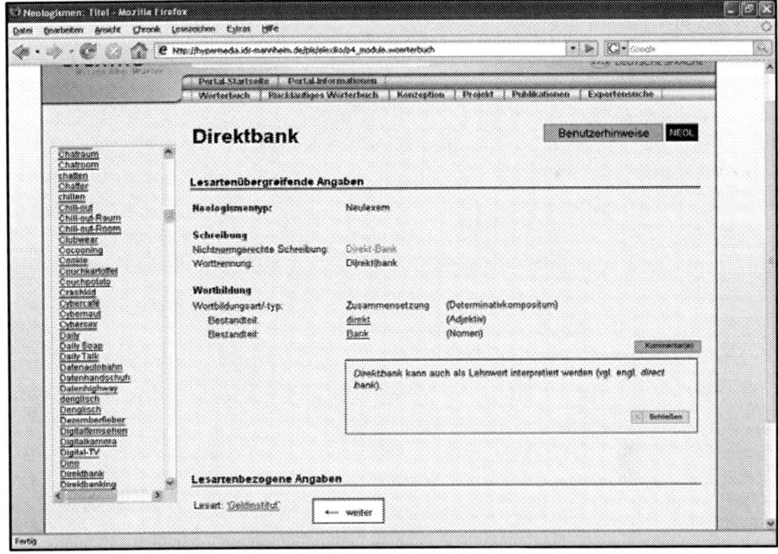

Fig. 7. First screen of the entry **Direktbank** in *Neologismenwörterbuch*

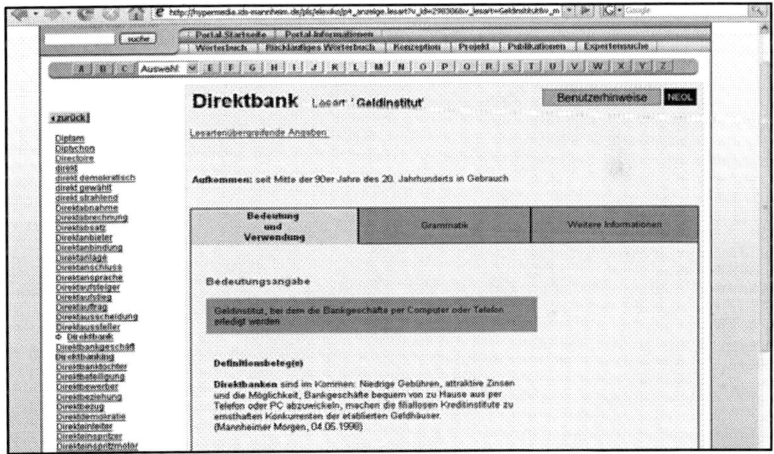

Fig. 8. Second screen of the entry **Direktbank** in *Neologismenwörterbuch*

The *Neologismenwörterbuch* is the first dictionary of new words ever published in German, whereas in English, French, and Russian, there is a long tradition of new word dictionaries.[10] An advantage of the *Neologismenwörterbuch* is that it offers several possibilities of information query. For example, users can quickly search through the whole dictionary and find all words that originate at the end of the last century or find all nouns that are abbreviated. Extending these possibilities of information retrieval is one of the project's future aims. Another aim is to benefit more from corpuslinguistic methods in finding new words and especially in finding new word meanings, the latter certainly being the trickier task when you deal with neologisms.

How does the *Wortwarte* [word look-out] find new words, and how are they described? The corpus used in this project is a collection of German Internet newspapers. It is searched almost daily with corpus tools developed in the project *German reference corpus* at the University of Tübingen, together with the *Institut für Deutsche Sprache*, and other partners. The outcome is a list of words which in a second step is matched with the word list of the German reference corpus. All words already included in that list cannot be candidates for new words and are deleted.

The rest contains, for example, misspelled words as well as new words. These are the ones which are scanned in a third step by the project's lexicographer to separate out occasionalisms. Between 10 to 50 words are finally left over almost every day and are published in a list online. Every day's list is filed in an archive sorted either alphabetically by thematic relevance (see fig. 9 with thematic groups) or by date. These archives are an especially useful tool for every linguist interested in the German lexicon and its development.

The entries in the word list itself (see fig. 10 with an example from October 2007) contain the headword with grammatical information (part of speech, gender, etc.) as well as one citation with the headword in the middle of the context. Each entry is assigned to a thematic area and links to Google or Wikipedia enable the user to find more citations or encyclopaedic information.

[10] For new word dictionaries of English, French and Russian see Herberg / Kinne 1998: 43-44.

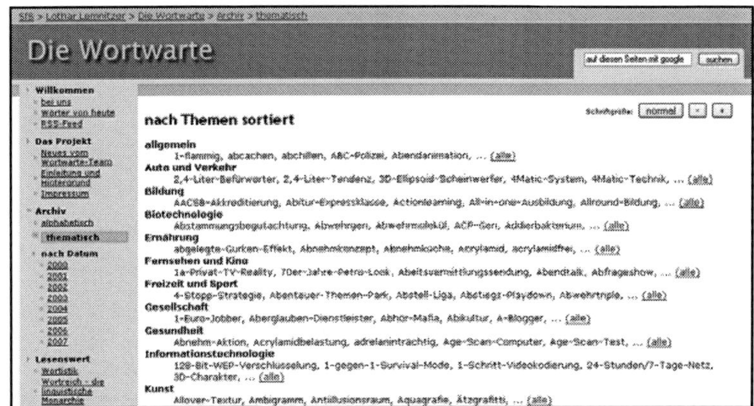

Fig. 9. Thematic groups of new words in *Wortwarte*

Fig. 10. Entries in *Wortwarte*

Should the *Wortwarte* be called a dictionary? The *Wortwarte*-site itself does not use the term *dictionary* but describes itself as a "collection of new words". It does contain typical elements of dictionaries (headwords, grammatical information, citations) but does offer data-recall facilities, which (at least) printed dictionaries cannot provide. There is no team of lexicographers, but only one person, who checks the automatically compiled wordlists. Unlike other dictionaries, the corpus is not fixed, nor is it supported by secondary sources. However, the major difference, especially in comparison to the *Neologismenwörterbuch*, is that the *Wortwarte* does not really evaluate the data collected automatically. It is left to the user to decide, whether the words listed as "new" are in fact new. The *Neologismenwörterbuch*, on the other hand, offers more reliable information.

We will look at some other automatically compiled Internet sites with lexical information on German. In doing so, we will pursue the question of whether we should call these sites "dictionaries". At the same time, we will analyze in which way those pages may stimulate linguistic research.

3.2 Two Online-Information Systems on the German Language: *Wortschatz Deutsch* and *Digitales Wörterbuch der deutschen Sprache*

Since 1998 a group of computer scientists at the University of Leipzig have been developing the project *Wortschatz Deutsch* [German vocabulary]. Its aim has been to explore automatic language processing and to publish the results on the Internet. Today, among other things, the project offers words of the day, a link to an international word database, and a German dictionary. This dictionary also contains English equivalents of about 100,000 words and phrases and can be used as a bilingual German-English dictionary. We will focus here on the information given for German, which is compiled automatically. The data is extracted from an electronic corpus of "public sources" on the Internet (unfortunately there is no further information on the sources). The project states that almost six billion tokens with information on frequency, grammar, subject group, and examples are accumulated. It is supposedly the most extensive data collection on the German language online.

When opening the dictionary site, the only way to look up a lexeme is to type in a word form. For example, the plural form *Wörterbücher* [dictionaries], is not ascribed to its basic form so that the hit list for this search only contains the plural form, and when opening the entry for *Wörterbücher*, it only contains information on the plural (see fig. 11).

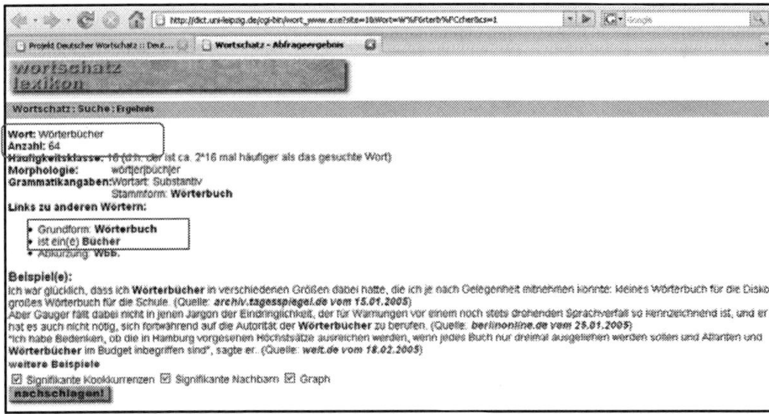

Fig. 11. Entry *Wörterbücher* in *Wortschatz Deutsch*

This may frustrate users due to the fact that they will most likely be looking up words in their basic forms. However, the entry *Wörterbücher* does contain a link to *Wörterbuch* under the rubric *Grundform* [principal form]. We will look closely at the entry *Wörterbuch* and reflect on how the information given might be useful for users, but also for linguists (see fig. 12).

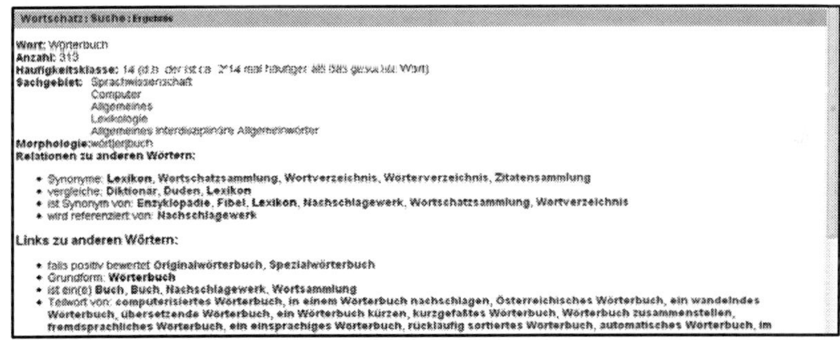

Fig. 12. Entry *Wörterbuch* in *Wortschatz Deutsch*

Under the rubric *Relationen zu anderen Wörtern* [relations to other words], we find a list of synonyms for *Wörterbuch*, like *Lexikon*, *Wortverzeichnis*, and others. We also learn that *Wörterbuch* should be compared to *Diktionär*, *Duden*, and *Lexikon* and that *Wörterbuch* is a synonym of *Enzyklopädie*, *Fibel*, *Lexikon*, etc. There also seems to be a connection between *Wörterbuch* and *Nachschlagewerk* (reference book).

What exactly a dictionary is and the ways it differs from an encyclopaedia or a reference book, cannot be evinced when consulting lists of this kind. What we do learn is that all these words seem to be related to each other in a certain way, by forming a lexical field. Automatically compiled information like this always needs to be evaluated carefully by the user and may well be inaccurate, as another look at the entry for *Wörterbuch* shows. Here the word *Zitatensammlung* [collection of citations] is given as a synonym of *Wörterbuch*, which is certainly not the case.

Perhaps a close look at the citations from the corpus will help us to find out what a dictionary is. *Wortschatz Deutsch* always offers three automatically chosen text clippings from its corpus under the rubric *Beispiele* [examples]. In our instance (see fig. 13), we find three clips that unfortunately do not tell very much about what a dictionary is, how we can use it, what it looks like, and so on. To choose the best citations for a dictionary entry is one of the most complex and, therefore, hardest jobs for any lexicographer. An automatic selection cannot replace a careful and considered human choice, but it may possibly supplement it in an online dictionary.

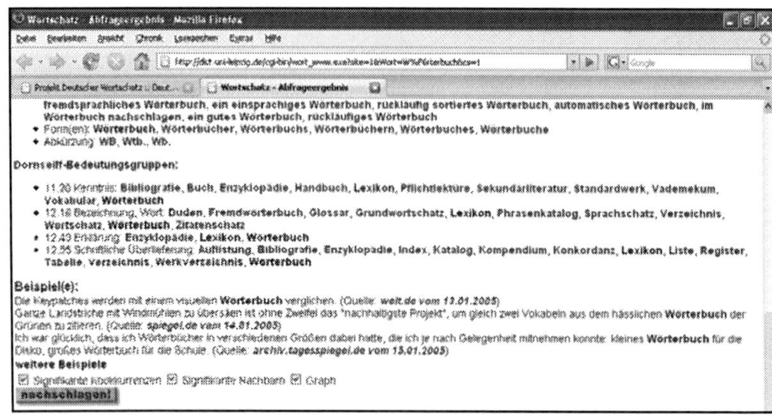

Fig. 13. Examples for *Wörterbuch* in *Wortschatz Deutsch*

Wortschatz Deutsch offers very interesting information when a linguist is interested in one of the following subjects: word formation (since it gives information on words in which the headword is contained), cognitive linguistics (since it illustrates with its graphs the other words evoked by the headword), in a word's potential of co-occurring with other words. *Wortschatz Deutsch* may also be used by teachers of German as a second language when they prepare tutorials on vocabulary.

The same is true for the second online information system on the German language: *Das Digitale Wörterbuch der deutschen Sprache des 20. Jahrhunderts* (*DWDS*) [Digital Dictionary of the German Language in the 20th Century]. This site is maintained at the Academy of Science in Berlin and aims at the development of a digital dictionary system on the basis of very large and well-balanced corpora. When opening the site, we find three different digital sources: the corpora, a retrodigitalised monolingual dictionary of German (first published in the 1960s and 1970s in the German Democratic Republic) and the "Wortinformation" [information on a word]. We will focus on the last source, because it combines automatically compiled word information with lexicographic information.

When typing a word in the search box, here again *Wörterbuch*, a screen divided into four different parts opens (see fig. 14). We can read the entry *Wörterbuch* from the retro-digitalised German dictionary *Wörterbuch der deutschen Gegenwartssprache* mentioned before. In addition we find a few keywords in context lines with *Wörterbuch* on which we can click to read citations from the *DWDS*-corpus. These citations are chosen automatically (with the same disadvantages already mentioned for *Wortschatz Deutsch*). An advantage of the *DWDS*-clippings is that they come from a corpus the composition of which was planned carefully. As users, we are able to understand the corpus composition, because it is described extensively on the site.

As in *Wortschatz Deutsch* we also find a graphic representation of collocations for *Wörterbuch*. These graphs are also compiled automatically. Comparing the graphs from *Wortschatz Lexikon* and *DWDS* (see fig. 15), it is quite interesting to notice how different they appear. None of the collocations given for *Wörterbuch* in the *DWDS* are found in the other graph and vice versa. This shows how much influence the corpus composition has on the results and how carefully we have to evaluate such data.

The *DWDS* also gives automatically compiled information on paradigmatic relations of a headword (see fig. 14). Here again, the range of synonyms is not really convincing (for example, *Sachwörterbuch* is a synonym of *Enzyklopädie* and not of *Wörterbuch*). On the other hand, the information under the rubric *Untergeordnete Begriffe* [subordinate terms] lists quite correctly a couple of compounds with *Wörterbuch* as the basic word. Of course, this list could easily be extended with more compounds, but the given compounds are probably some of the most frequent ones in German.

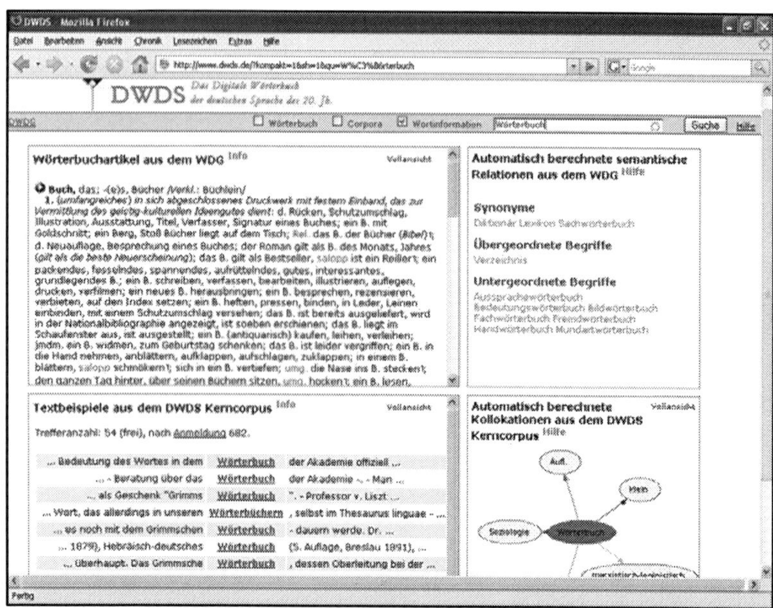

Fig. 14. Information on *Wörterbuch* in *DWDS*

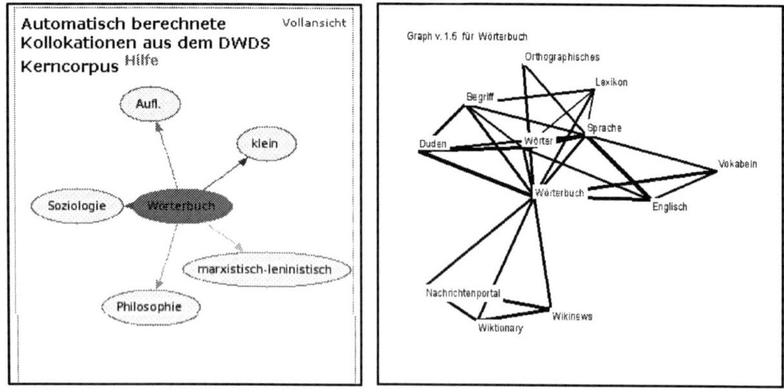

Fig. 15. Graphs for *Wörterbuch* from *DWDS* (left) and *Wortschatz Deutsch* (right)

Let us draw a conclusion: we have looked at three online information systems on the German language (*Wortwarte, Wortschatz Deutsch* and *DWDS*), which probably should not be called online dictionaries. This is true as long as we define *dictionary* as a reference work compiled by human beings. It is not true when we focus our definition on the fact that a dictionary is a reference work giving information on a specific language. In that case the Internet sites shown are indeed dictionaries. The difference lies more in what kind of information we find and the way in which we look something up.

Metalexicography should turn to questions like that and reconsider how to define *dictionary*. The sites discussed here also pose new questions concerning their macrostructure, mediostructure, and microstructure. On neither of the sites do we find a word list as the main element of a dictionary's macrostructure. As we have seen, the entries differ widely in their microstructure. There are elements of mediostructure in *DWDS* when, for example, collocates in the graph function as links to their entry. On the other hand, citations in *DWDS*, for example, are not linked with the retrodigitalised dictionary entry they accompany. Last but not least, language information systems as the ones shown pose new questions on how the user is guided through the pages, on the way he or she looks up something, and on how he or she evaluates the results. In answering questions like that, metalexicography has to work together, for example, with scientists testing the usability of Internet sites.

3.3 A New Online Dictionary on the German Language: *elexiko*

Questions like the ones mentioned above also are relevant in regards to the German online dictionary we will look at more closely, the *elexiko*-dictionary.[11]

> *elexiko* is a relatively new lexicological-lexicographic project based at the Institut für Deutsche Sprache. This project compiles a reference work that explains and documents contemporary German; it was specifically designed for online publication. The primary and exclusive basis for lexicographic interpretation is an extensive German corpus. If one refers to *elexiko* as an Internet dictionary, it is purely for practical reasons. *elexiko* is (far) more than a dictionary in its traditional sense although, of course, it contains descriptions of the meaning and use of a lexeme just as any traditional dictionary. It is both, a hypertext dictionary and a lexical data information system. While corpus-based lexicography has been carried out for English for almost 20 years, for German, there is no dictionary that has been developed exclusively on the basis of a comprehensive corpus. Furthermore, no large-scale German dictionary has been designed for the

[11] See www.elexiko.de, Klosa (2005), Klosa / Schnörch / Storjohann (2006) and Storjohann (2005 b).

Internet. Hence, *elexiko* is a landmark in German lexicography (Klosa *et al.* 2006: 1).

Filling *elexiko* in modules is (besides the corpus-based approach) one of the two main lexicographic methods for this dictionary. *Elexiko* is compiled not following alphabetical order, but by describing either a complete word class, an entire word family, or a semantic field systematically and separately. Modules may also be defined according to levels of frequency and distribution of lexemes in the *elexiko*-corpus.

Along with publishing the list of headwords (taken exclusively from the *elexiko*-corpus) on the Internet, the dictionary was filled with sense-independent information for each headword generated automatically or semi-automatically from the underlying corpus. This concerns 300,000 single-word entries comprising details on spelling, spelling variation, and syllabication. In a second step, the first 250 headwords, which were defined as "Demonstrationswortschatz" [demonstration module], have been fully lexicographically described. The *Demonstrationswortschatz* primarily explains lexemes forming a semantic field around the core headword *Mobilität* [mobility], and lexemes that are morphologically derived from *mobil* (e.g., *hochmobil* [highly mobile], *immobilisieren* [to immobilise], and *Mobilitätszentrum* [center for mobility]). *Elexiko* is now working on a module called *Lexikon zum öffentlichen Sprachgebrauch* [Dictionary on Public Discourse]. It contains approximately 2,800 entries selected mainly by their (high) frequency in the *elexiko*-corpus.

Lexicographically fully described entries entail sense-independent information on morphology and word formation (*Lesartenübergreifende Angaben*) as well as a number of senses and their relationship. They also offer a large scope of sense-related information (*Lesartenbezogene Angaben*) in detail, meaning definition, collocations, syntagmatic patterns, sense-related terms, pragmatics, and grammar. With this wide spectrum of lexical information, *elexiko* exceeds other existing German dictionaries, as will be shown in detail below.

The list of headwords and lexicographically fully described headwords on the *elexiko*-site is offered to users along with specific search features. Someone consulting *elexiko* not only finds single headwords, but also groups of lexemes with the same semantic, syntactic, or morphological characteristics.

For the process of writing and presenting *elexiko* on the Internet, the project uses numerous technologies and software tools, such as the corpus query and processing tool COSMAS II[12] developed at the *Institut für*

[12] For COSMAS II see http://www.ids-mannheim.de/cosmas2/.

Deutsche Sprache and its incorporated collocation program *Statistische Kollokationsanalyse and Clustering.*[13] Those are used for numerous corpus-guided investigations within the practical working procedure. All lexical entries are structured XML-instances following a highly granular lexicographic data model (*Document Type Definition*) with over 400 tagging elements. This *DTD* has been developed specifically for the intended microstructure of the dictionary.[14]

3.3.1 Sense Disambiguation

Words may have a number of senses. While writing a dictionary entry, it is often difficult to differentiate between those word senses and put them in a coherent order. Due to this fact *elexiko* consistently uses the linguistic inventory of concept shifting, such as metaphorisation, generalisation, and so on, to differentiate between senses. Unlike other dictionaries, where senses are arranged in a diachronic way, meaning the oldest sense is given first and other, often metaphoric senses, are given subsequently, in *elexiko* the senses are listed in a frequency-based hierarchy. The most frequent sense in the *elexiko*-corpus comes first. Thus senses belonging to each other such as the literal and the metaphoric sense are sometimes torn apart. At the same time, there may be word senses that are not related to the others at all.

Accordingly, in the *elexiko*-entries users find an explanation on how the senses are arranged and connected (see fig. 16). On the first screen opening after typing in the search word, we find a list of all senses, which are not numbered but labelled with words; here *das Bedienen* [serving], *Personal* [personell], and so on. Under the rubric *Zum Zusammenhang der Lesarten* [On the Relationship between the Senses] their relationship is explained: the word sense 'Personal' is a metonymy of the word sense 'das Bedienen'.

---

[13] For the collocation programme *Statistische Kollokationsanalyse and Clustering* see: http://www.ids-mannheim.de/kl/projekte/methoden/ka.html.

[14] See Müller-Spitzer 2005 and 2006.

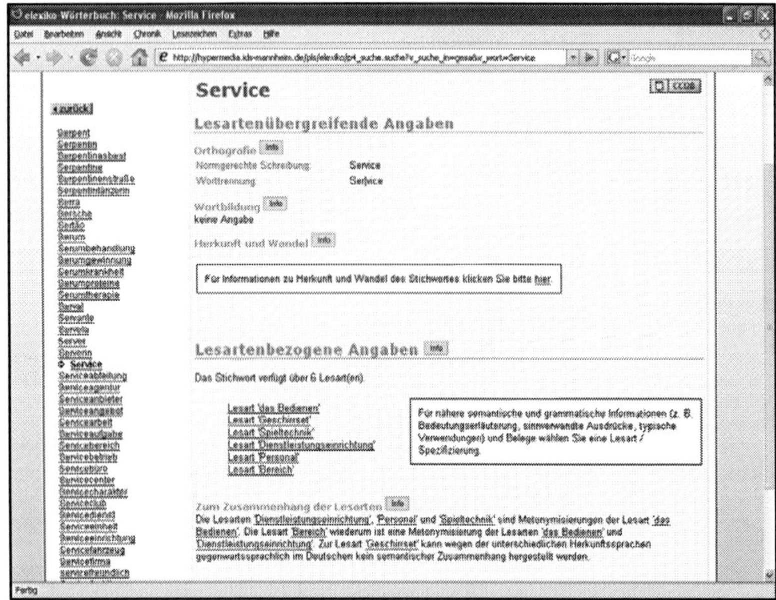

Fig. 16. Entry *Service* in *elexiko* with an explanation on the relationship between senses

3.3.2 Lexical Relations

When clicking on one of the senses from the list shown in the first screenshot, the user opens the complete range of sense-related information (*Lesartenbezogene Angaben*) in *elexiko*. When the *elexiko*-lexicographers planned the dictionary, they tried to consider results of linguistic and metalexicographic research concerning, for example, meaning definition, collocations, pragmatics, or grammar. We will look at one example – lexical relations[15]:

> Contextual lexical relations such as sense relations have traditionally played an essential role in disambiguating word senses in lexicography, as they offer insights into the meaning and use of a word. However, the description of paradigmatic relations in dictionaries is often restricted to a few types such as synonymy and antonymy. The limited description of various types of relations and the method of presenting these relations in existing German dictionaries are often problematic (Storjohann 2005: 1).

[15] See Storjohann 2005b for the following.

Since *elexiko* aims at describing the meaning and use of a word, the lexicographers decided on including paradigmatic partners of each headword, not only to list synonyms but also to show how words are connected with each other. *Elexiko,* therefore, offers a new way of presenting sense relations in «a differentiated system of paradigmatic relations including synonymy, various subtypes of incompatibility (such as antonymy, complementarity, converseness, reversiveness, etc.), and vertical structures (such as hyponymy and meronymy)» (Storjohann 2005: 1) (see fig. 17). In *elexiko* antonymy is a special case of incompatibility that is restricted to semantically gradable adjectives.

> Complementarity, converseness, and reversiveness are also specific sense relations of opposition and subtypes of incompatibility. Within vertical patterns, lexical relations are separated into hyponymy / hyperonymy and meronymy / holonymy. [...] Synonymy in particular is not further subclassified in *elexiko*, but it is used to refer to all types of semantic identity, ranging from absolute sameness and propositional identity to more vague categories such as near-synonymy (Storjohann 2005: 4).

horizontal structures		**vertical structures**
incompatibility	antonymy	hyperonymy
	complementarity	hyponymy
	converseness	holonymy
	reversiveness	meronymy
synonymy		

Fig. 17. Classification or paradigmatic relations in *elexiko* (Storjohann 2005: 3)

For example, the entry *Glück* 'Freude' [happiness] lists as synonyms *Freude* [joy], *Heil* [good fortune], *Wohl* [welfare], as complementary partner words *Elend* [misery], *Leid* [sorrow], *Schmerz* [grief], *Unglück* [distress], and so forth (see fig. 18). Incompatible partner words that occur statistically relevant in the *elexiko*-corpus are, for example, *Erfolg* [success], *Freiheit* [freedom], *Liebe* [love], *Zufriedenheit* [contentment]. Each of the partner words is illustrated in *elexiko* by a citation, and each one is a hyperlink that users can follow if they want to learn more about it.

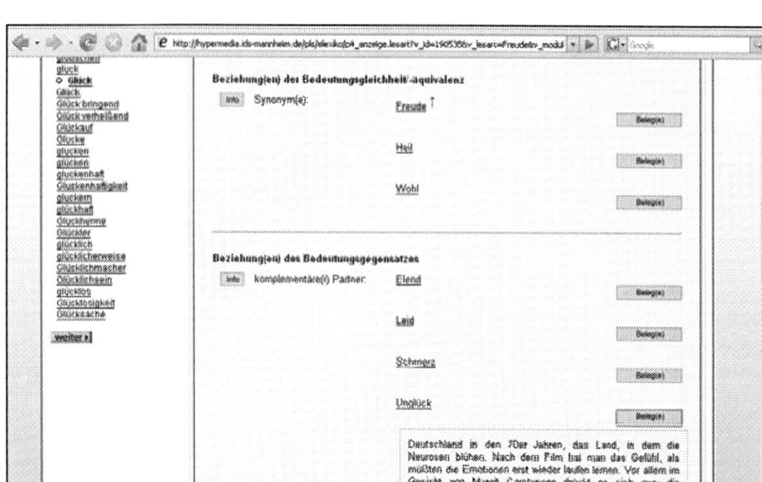

Fig. 18. Paradigmatic partners for **Glück** 'Freude' in *elexiko*

In order to gather lexical information like that, the statistically significant co-selections of a word are analyzed with the data processing tool *COSMAS II*. Among the results of this analysis lexicographers will often find words related in a semantic way to the headword. This is why analyzing collocations automatically is the first step the *elexiko*-lexicographers take on their way to identifying paradigmatic relation – without relying on intuition or personal linguistic competence. The second step is evaluating the results gathered automatically: they classify the sense relations found and search for citations from the corpus texts which exemplify the sense relation concerned. Since in some cases the corpus-tools cannot provide a comprehensive description of the sense relational patterns, the corpus is checked in a third, supplementary procedure, particularly so as to extend or complete paradigmatic descriptions. The difference to the fully automatically compiled information on paradigmatic relations as shown above for *Wortschatz Deutsch*, for example, is obvious.

4 Conclusion

German lexicography is, as we have seen, diverse in regards to publication, methods and contents. While printed dictionaries and CD-ROMs tend to be rather traditional, in online dictionaries we find new methods and contents: huge electronic text corpora are exhausted either automatically or by lexicographers. On the Internet, information other than text (graphs, videos, and so forth) adds new ways of using a dictionary. Electronic dictionaries also offer extensive possibilities of information retrieval. On the other hand, some online information systems on the German language are to a large extent compiled automatically and demand the user's careful evaluation of the data.

While a lot of corpuslinguistic achievements and linguistic research results are already considered in academic dictionary projects, this does not quite hold true for German dictionaries from publishers. On the other hand, the impact of German lexicography on linguistic research is still very limited: metalexicography should deal more with online information systems on any language. Linguists should analyze the information offered here when they research the German lexicon.

References

Dictionaries

The American Heritage Dictionary of the English Language (2000). [fourth Edition] [http://www.bartleby.com/61/].

Burfeind, Renate (2004). *Illustriertes Wörterbuch der deutschen Sprache.* Gütersloh / München, Wissen Media Verlag.

Duden – Das Bildwörterbuch. Die Gegenstände und ihre Benennung (2005). Mannheim / Leipzig / Wien / Zürich, Dudenverlag. [sixth, revised and enlarged edition].

Duden Wörterbuch Deutsch als Fremdsprache. Deutsch für die Grund- und Mittelstufe (2003). Mannheim / Leipzig / Wien / Zürich, Dudenverlag.

Elektronisches Lernerwörterbuch Deutsch-Italienisch / Dizionario Elettronico per Apprendenti Italo-Tedeschi (*ELDIT*, Eurac Resarch Bozen). [http://dev.eurac.edu:8081/MakeEldit1/Eldit.htm].

Illustrated Oxford Dictionary (1998). London / New York / Munich / Melbourne / Delhi, Dorling Kindersley Publishing / Oxford University Press.

Langenscheidt Taschenwörterbuch Deutsch als Fremdsprache, Das einsprachige Lernerwörterbuch für Einsteiger (2003). Berlin / München / Wien / Zürich / New York, Langenscheidt. [Dieter Götz / Hans Wellmann (eds), in collaboration with Langenscheidt-Redaktion].

Neologismenwörterbuch (Institut für Deutsche Sprache Mannheim). [http://www.owid.de/Neologismen/index.html] [see also Herberg, Dieter / Kinne, Michael / Steffens, Doris. *Neuer Wortschatz*, Neologismen der 90er Jahre im Deutschen, with the collaboration of Elke Tellenbach and Doris al-Wadi. Berlin / New York, 2004].

Sinclair, John (1987). *The Collins Cobuild English Language Dictionary*. London, Harper Collins.

Wortwarte [http://www.wortwarte.de or http://www.sfs.uni-tuebingen.de/~lothar/nw/] [published by Lothar Lemnitzer, Tübingen University].

Wortschatz Deutsch. Leipzig University [http://wortschatz.uni-leipzig.de].

Das Digitale Wörterbuch der deutschen Sprache des 20. Jahrhunderts (DWDS). Berlin, Brandenburgische Akademie der Wissenschaften. [http://www.dwds.de].

elexiko – Wissen über Wörter. (Institut für Deutsche Sprache, Mannheim). [http://www.elexiko.de].

Secondary sources

Herberg, Dieter / Kinne, Michael (1998). *Neologismen*. Heidelberg, Julius Groos Verlag [Studienbibliographien Sprachwissenschaft 23].

Klosa, Annette (2004). "Langenscheidt Taschenwörterbuch Deutsch als Fremdsprache und Duden Wörterbuch Deutsch als Fremdsprache. Ein kritischer Vergleich", in *Lexicographica* 20: 271–304.

—. (2005). "elexiko. Ein Onlinewörter>buch< zum Gegenwartsdeutschen", in *Sprachreport* 3: 6-9.

Klosa, Annette / Schnörch, Ulrich / Storjohann, Petra (2006). "ELEXIKO – A lexical and lexicological, corpus-based hypertext information system at the Institut für Deusche Sprache, Mannheim", in Corino, Elisa / Marello, Carla / Onesti, Cristina (eds). *Proceedings of the 12th EURALEX International Congress / Atti del XII Congresso Internazionale di Lessicografia, EURALEX 2006 (Turin, Italy, 6th–9th September 2006)*, 2 vols. Alessandria, Edizioni dell'Orso, I: 425–430.

Müller-Spitzer, Carolin (2005). "Die Modellierung lexikografischer Daten und ihre Rolle im lexikografischen Prozess", in Haß, Ulrike (ed.). *Grundfragen der elektronischen Lexikographie. elexiko – das Online-Informationssystem zum deutschen Wortschatz*. Berlin / New York, de Gruyter: 20–54 [Schriften des Instituts für Deutsche Sprache 12].

—. (2006). *Das Konzept der Inhaltsstruktur. Ein Ausschnitt aus einer neuen Konzeption für die Modellierung lexikografischer Daten*. Mannheim, Institut für Deutsche Sprache [OPAL – Online publizierte Arbeiten zur Linguistik 2].

Sinclair, John (ed) (1987). *Looking Up. An account of the COBUILD Project in lexical computing and the development of the Collins COBUILD English language Dictionary*. London, Harper Collins.

Storjohann, Petra (2005a). "Corpus-driven vs. corpus-based approach to the study of relational patters", in *Proceedings from the Corpus Linguistics Conference Series* 1, 1, Birmingham [Corpus Linguistics 2005, ISSN 1747-9398, http://www.corpus.bham.ac.uk/PCLC/].

—. (2005b). "elexiko – A Corpus-Based Monolingual German Dictionary", in *Hermes. Journal of Linguistics* 34: 55–82.

PART III

THE PERSPECTIVE OF INFORMATION TECHNOLOGY ON LEXICOGRAPHY

ENCODING THE LANGUAGE OF LANDSCAPE: XML AND DATABASES AT THE SERVICE OF ANGLO-SAXON LEXICOGRAPHY[1]

PETER A. STOKES AND ELENA PIERAZZO

LangScape is a new electronic resource being developed at the Centre for Computing in Humanities at King's College, London, which provides both opportunities and challenges to the lexicographer.[2] The primary output is a web-driven database of all known Anglo-Saxon boundary-clauses.[3] The Anglo-Saxons left a substantial corpus of close to 2000 charters purporting to be drawn up before the Norman Conquest of 1066, and many of these charters consist of grants of land by a king or other powerful figure to an individual or institution. Many of these documents in turn contain boundary-clauses, namely descriptions in Old English (and sometimes Latin) of the boundaries of the land-units in question. Roughly

---

[1] Any coauthored paper normally involves close collaboration and this is no exception. Nevertheless, we shall attempt to delineate our respective contributions. Peter A. Stokes was primarily responsible for the following sections: 'The Corpus', 'Technical Framework: The LangScape Database', 'Linguistic Analysis', 'The Process of Markup', 'Semiautomatic Markup', and 'The Output'. Elena Pierazzo was primarily responsible for 'Modelling Humanities Data in a Digital Framework', 'Technical Framework: XML Encoding' (incorporating 'The TEI P5 Schema' and 'The LangScape Encoding Model'), and 'Conclusions'.

[2] Much of the material in these opening paragraphs is paraphrased from the project website, http://www.langscape.org.uk. The people involved in the project are listed at http://www.langscape.org.uk/content/about/project_team.html, but we wish to mention here those who made more substantial contributions: Joy Jenkyns (senior researcher), Peter Stokes (research associate), John Bradley and Gerhard Brey (database design and supervision), Elliot Hall (database and search development), Elena Pierazzo (XML analysis and development), and Paul Vetch (web interface development).

[3] Boundary-clauses are also known as charter bounds or simply bounds.

a thousand of these boundary-clauses survive, either in contemporary documents or (more commonly) in medieval or later copies.[4]

Anglo-Saxon boundary-clauses allow us to see something of the English landscape and its place-names as they stood a thousand or more years ago. They can teach us much about Anglo-Saxon England: about social issues such as settlement and ownership, about ecological and environmental concerns, about the early-medieval representation of landscape and place, and even about where we might find archaeological remains. From a linguistic point of view, they provide an extremely rich source of localisable and datable material, and thus detailed analysis of the clauses can provide a great deal of primary evidence for the study of dialect, vocabulary, language-change and orthography.

The core data of the resource is the texts of every boundary-clause surviving in copies from before 1600, along with texts of later copies where appropriate. The aim is that these texts can be searched by their metadata, by lemmas, or by forms as they appear in the manuscripts. The results are also integrated with *Global Information Systems* (*GIS*), and so a researcher can plot the geographical distribution of a particular lemma or form with hitherto unprecedented ease. The resource will also be linked directly with other related resources: certainly the *Revised Electronic Sawyer* and potentially also the *English Place-Names* database and the *Prosopography of Anglo-Saxon England* database.[5]

The primary audience in the first phase is specialist users, particularly those interested in Old English philology and name-studies. However, central to the project's goals is access for as wide a range of people as possible. Applications therefore range from providing simple access to texts which have previously been scattered across a wide range of editions through to complex data manipulation and analysis for academic research. However, such a resource requires very detailed and extensive markup as every word in the corpus must be tagged with information (in particular its lemma) to allow such complex searching. This markup is by no means straightforward given the material's wide geographical and chronological range, spanning periods during which English changed significantly, and when orthography and scribal practices were by no means consistent. In this paper we therefore hope to present some of the challenges that we

[4] The most authoritative statement of the corpus of Anglo-Saxon charters and the manuscripts in which they survive is Sawyer 1968, the most recent version of which is *The Electronic Sawyer* (http://www.esawyer.org.uk).

[5] The respective projects can be found at http://www.esawyer.org.uk; http://www.nottingham.ac.uk/english/ins/epntest/intro.html; and http://www.pase.ac.uk.

faced in producing this resource, and to present the novel solution we developed to overcome them. We hope that this solution might be transferable to other similar projects, in part if not *in toto*, but we also hope to highlight the complexity of a task of this size lest those planning their own work underestimate the substantial time, thought and effort that it requires.

The Corpus

The corpus consists of 1048 surviving boundary-clauses in 825 charter-texts; including copies from different manuscripts, the database contains some 1881 distinct texts. Most of these texts are quite short, often only a few lines in a modern printed edition, although some are much longer. They tend to be very formulaic, usually listing a sequence of geographical features such as trees, hills, rivers, and ditches or dikes, leading the reader «first from A to B, then from B to C, then from C to D, ... and so back to A».

Although it would be interesting to specify the languages in these texts, this is more problematic than one might first imagine. A crude count suggests that 892 boundary-clauses are extant in their earliest surviving form in English, 132 in Latin, and the remaining seven in some mixture of the two languages. However, precision is difficult for several reasons. The periodisation of English, and the definition of Old versus Middle English in particular, has been the subject of much recent academic debate (Swan / Treharne 2000). This debate is particularly relevant here, since many boundary-clauses survive in copies made in the twelfth century, a time when the written language shows particularly rapid change as a result of Norman influence. Some boundary-clauses survive in their Old English form, that is, they were composed and copied before the Norman Conquest of 1066 and show no direct influence from French nor substantial breakdown in inflectional endings, although these often contain Scandinavian or Celtic place-name elements. Other boundary-clauses are clearly in Middle English and show a good deal of influence from Anglo-Norman French, even with occasional French words mixed in with the English or Latin (or both).[6] Many boundary-clauses were composed in Old English, but then copied by scribes who updated some of the orthography or language to their own Middle English, and others show clear signs of

[6] For examples see especially the bounds from Malmesbury, where a sequence like *et sic per la forches usque sandweye* [and thus by the crossways to sand way] (Kelly 2005: 261–62) is typical.

being first written in Old English, but then translated into Latin.[7] Most of the texts usually described as being in Latin show directional terms in that language but have boundary-points in English,[8] and still others are outright forgeries, claiming to be Anglo-Saxon but clearly composed after the Old English period.[9] Given all these complexities, we have made no attempt to differentiate between the different linguistic periods and have simply distinguished between Latin and English.[10]

Many of the texts survive in more than one copy. These copies vary in date from before the Norman Conquest right through to the seventeenth century and beyond, and an explicit aim of the project is to include as many surviving copies as possible from before A.D. 1600. However, it is not feasible to manually collate the texts in any strict sense of the term, although the potential remains for full collation in future and this could perhaps be automated once lemmatisation is complete. Until such time as this may happen, we have chosen a "top" or primary text which most users are expected to work with, but the so-called "duplicate" texts will still be fully available. This "top" text is the one which has been deemed the most authoritative, usually (but not necessarily) because it is the oldest. If the text has been published in a modern edition then the editor's judgment is followed here, and if not then the text used was normally that given first in the latest version given on the *Electronic Sawyer* website. In very rare cases the researchers decided to use a different manuscript than that given on the site but this was only done in exceptional circumstances and no systematic attempt was made to evaluate the authoritativeness of different manuscripts, not least because this work is already being done by editors of the British Academy's series of Anglo-Saxon Charters.

As well as variation between manuscripts, another type of variation is that of the printed editions. Almost all of the texts have been edited and published before, but many of these editions are outdated and are sometimes quite unreliable. Indeed, the *LangScape* resource began with electronic copies of these editions which had been compiled for the *Dictionary of Old English* and which were kindly supplied to us by

---

[7] The most striking example of both phenomena is the trilingual (Old English, Middle English and Latin) texts in the so-called *Liber de Hyda*; see Miller 2001. For wider discussion see also Lowe 1999.

[8] For examples see Kelly 2005, *passim*.

[9] For one noteworthy example see Sawyer 1968, no. 68: a charter from Peterborough described as «one of the most elaborate post-Conquest forgeries produced in England» (Fleming 1985: 255, n. 4).

[10] For a similar approach to much the same problem, see the *English Manuscripts 1060-1220* website (http://www.le.ac.uk/ee/em1060to1220).

members of that project.[11] Although extremely useful, this electronic corpus was only a starting-point, as every text has been corrected against or newly transcribed from the original manuscripts. We have also chosen a small number of recently published editions and have checked our texts against these as well, marking up any variation between our readings and the editions'. This is partly as a way of checking our own work, partly to correct the editions, but partly also to build users' confidence in the authority of our material.

Modelling Humanities Data in a Digital Framework

To scholars contemplating digital research projects today, many possibilities for data modelling and exploitation are available. The choice among these depends on many factors, including the breadth of the project, the nature of the data, and the goals of the project. In general, however, two options are available:[12] a relational database or an XML-encoded archive. Although database-technology has a relatively long tradition (long, at least, in computing terms), the XML encoding language is only ten years old, being the first (and, to date, the last) release of the language issued in 1999.[13] In spite of its relative youth, XML has experienced an immediate success in digital humanities as it was chosen early on by the TEI (Text Encoding Initiative) Consortium[14] as the language of its well-known encoding model. The authoritativeness of the TEI, combined with XML's simple syntax and flexible vocabulary, has made the latter probably the single most important technology in humanities computing. Indeed, XML is sometimes chosen for a project without any attempt by researchers to evaluate other data models. In particular, XML is now taking over territories traditionally held by relational databases, the latter almost now being considered "old-school".

[11] The dictionary and corpus are both found at the *DOE* website (http://www.doe.utoronto.ca). The authors wish to thank Antonette diPaolo Healey of the *Dictionary of Old English* for the corpus and for her continuing assistance thereafter.

[12] Excluding – on purpose – any design involving the usage or the development of proprietary formats.

[13] It should, of course, be noted that XML is based largely on SGML which has a much longer history. This Standard Generalised Markup Language became an ISO standard in 1986 (ISO 8879 1986) but the first versions were released during the Seventies, and development started in the Sixties.

[14] The Text Encoding Initiative (TEI) Consortium is responsible for the most important encoding model in the digital humanities community. For more details see § *The TEI P5 Schema*, below.

The truth is that both technologies have different strengths and weaknesses, that they are suitable for different kinds of data, and that, when starting a new digitalisation project, they each have to be carefully weighed against the other in order to choose the best option and not waste precious project time (and money) by a wrong choice. There has been some convergence of the two more recently, as some applications claim to manage XML repositories as if they were databases. Unfortunately, however, the authors' experience to date suggests that these facilities are not practical in a large-scale project as the verbosity of XML (especially given the richly and deeply annotated datasets typical of humanities computing) leads invariably to poor performance.

A relational database is better suited as a model for highly structured data than XML is. Such structured data includes bibliographic material, photographic archives, dictionaries, and prosopographies: in short, any case where relationships among different kinds of data are rigidly predictable. For example, a book is always owned by a library, and never the contrary, so the relationship between books and libraries is structured and thus suited to a relational database. An XML data model, thanks to its flexibility, is more suitable for semistructured data such as text, where the structure, and the order of components within a structure, cannot be readily predicted. An example here is an authorial correction which might be contained within a paragraph, but conversely such a correction may contain a paragraph. The relationship here is not fixed or predictable, and so XML is a more appropriate technology.

A close analysis of the *LangScape* data has indicated that it is both highly structured and semistructured at the same time. It is highly structured because the connections between lemmas, forms and translations are rigidly controlled and are almost always easily predictable; furthermore the relationships between them are of a one-to-many kind (e.g. one lemma has many forms) or even of a many-to-many kind (for instance, in case of uncertainty, several different forms could be connected to several different lemmas and *vice versa*). These kinds of relations are clumsily performed by an encoding language such as XML, since XML works best when describing a one-to-one kind of relationship, and this might suggest that a relational database would be a better model. However, the *LangScape* dataset is also semistructured. The texts in the dataset come from manuscripts, and manuscripts contain features such as additions, deletions, corrections, errors, abbreviations, and spacing, any of which may occur anywhere in the text. They may also occur at any level of granularity: in other words, they may be at the level of a paragraph, a sentence, a word, or even a character. In order to preserve this semistructured data, then, XML might seem the better model.

Such a situation has lead to a solution of mixed technologies: data and metadata are stored in a relational database, but the textual components of the database contain XML markup. In this way the advantages of both technologies can be exploited, minimizing their respective weaknesses. However, this solution, ideal from a project design point of view, has complicated the storage, management and delivery of data a good deal, as the mixing of two technologies has almost duplicated the technical issues involved.

Technical Framework: The *LangScape* Database

Now that the theoretical background to the project has been considered, the following sections of this paper present the practical implementation, beginning with the database. As noted above, all of the data for the project are stored in a relational database, and this data includes texts encoded in XML. A simplified diagram of the database architecture is presented below.

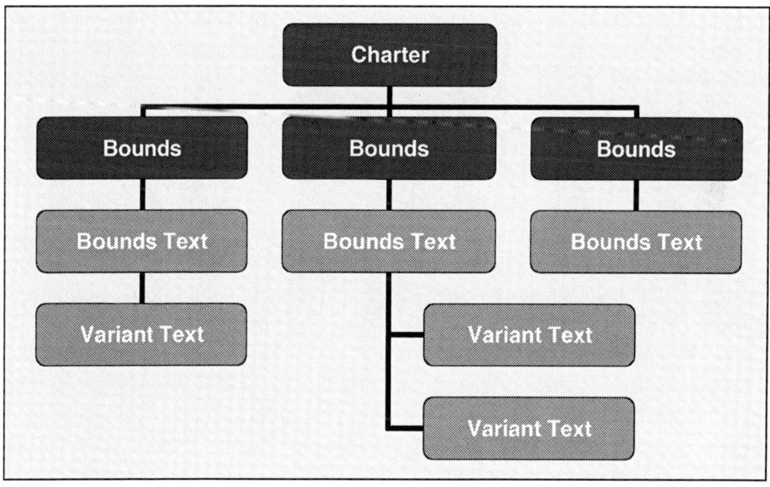

Fig. 1. Simplified structure of the *LangScape* Database

The top table (*Charter*) contains metadata for each charter. The information corresponds directly to that in Peter Sawyer's *Anglo-Saxon Charters* (Sawyer 1968), with each record in the table representing an entry in Sawyer's list. The metadata was drawn from Sawyer's work in the first instance but has been checked and updated as far as possible and in close collaboration with researchers on the *Revised Electronic Sawyer* and the annual British Academy Anglo-Saxon Charters Symposia.

Each charter in the *LangScape* database can have one or more boundary clauses associated with it. The database therefore incorporates a second table (*Bounds*) containing metadata relating to the estate or piece of land which the boundary clause describes.

Each record of metadata at the estate level corresponds to a single boundary clause. This metadata is the text itself which is encoded in XML and which was stored in a separate table during development (*Bounds Text*). The XML encoding initially followed a non-standard schema so that the project researchers could mark up the text quickly and easily, with the necessary detail and granularity, but could still leave the text readable by people. The markup was then converted into a TEI-compliant schema, for which see § *Technical Framework: XML Encoding.*

Any boundary clause may survive in more than one manuscript copy. If such further copies do indeed survive, then information about them is stored in an additional table (*Variant Texts*). This table contains a small amount of metadata in order to identify the copy, and it also contains a transcription of that copy using the same conventions and schema as in the *Bounds Texts*. This markup was then also converted into TEI-compliant XML but without the detailed lexicographical information for each word.[15] Such a lack of detail is due only to time constraints and we hope to provide the additional information in a future phase of the project. Of course more tables than just these four are required, but in practice the remaining tables in the database are essentially all "authority lists", namely lists of data such as repositories, archives, place-names, counties, and the like, which are used for data entry and searching.

Several plug-ins have been developed in order to extract data from the database into an XML environment and back; other plug-ins allow the researchers to export data to external applications in order to query and manage the information for research purposes; these plugins are considered in more detail shortly.[16] The database has thus been used not

[15] For further details of this lexicographical markup see § *Linguistic Encoding*.

[16] See § Semiautomatic Markup.

only to store and prepare a resource for the final outcome, but it has also been used for ongoing research during development.

Technical Framework: XML Encoding

The TEI P5 Schema

As has been noted above, the textual data are stored in the database but are encoded using a customised TEI model and will be available as a sharable downloadable resource once the encoding is completed.

The advantages of XML are now well understood in the community of digital humanities. The possibility of detailed description of semi-structured data such as texts; the ability to re-arrange, manipulate, and organise data in potentially infinite ways; the availability of tools and experience from a large and growing community; all these make XML an almost necessary choice in any digital humanities project.

Such advantages are magnified by the adoption of an encoding standard, namely the Text Encoding Initiative. Since its institution in 1987, the TEI has been a mandatory point of reference for any digital research project in the humanities. The *TEI Guidelines* (TEI Consortium 2007) not only offer an explanation on how to use the encoding schema, but also provide a theory of the text in a digital framework. These two points make unavoidable reading for anybody contemplating a text-encoding project, even if the researchers decide not to not adopt the TEI encoding schema – a decision that cannot be taken without providing good reasons to the scholarly community.

The last version of the TEI schema offers the possibility of a flexible standard that is open to local implementation in a more formalised way than has been offered previously.[17] The new version is distributed through powerful software named *Roma* that allows one to easily build project-based customisations of the schema and to bind together an encoding model, project guidelines, and a data sample.

The TEI Consortium recognised from the beginning that they could not incorporate every possible textual feature in the core schema, nor could they foresee all future scholarly needs. Instead, customizing the TEI schema is a common practice and is encouraged by the Consortium, at least within certain boundaries. Not all customisations are the same: the *Guidelines* provide detailed rules on how to customise a schema while

[17] This version is known as *P5* and is edited by Lou Burnard and Syd Bauman. For full details see TEI Consortium 2007.

remaining compatible with the TEI core, and to extend it in a standardised documented way (TEI Consortium 2007, Section 23).

Customisation is not to be taken lightly, however, as any local extension to some extent must break full compliance with the core schema, a fact that might prevent encoded files being shared fully with the scholarly community. Nevertheless, in the case of *LangScape*, the data was peculiar enough to justify three different kinds of extension.

The TEI schema was integrated with the *XInclude* schema, a W3C standard that allows external files to be included within the main document (W3C 2006b). This facility has been used in each XML document to include a portion of the metadata set that encodes and describes all special non-standard characters used to transcribe the text. In this way we created a sort of lookup of characters shared by all the documents, facilitating the management of these documents both in the encoding process and the delivery.

Several new elements have been introduced and grouped in a *LangScape* local extension. These elements include `<formulaic>` and `<bound>` to encode structure, non-structural elements such as `<estate>` to mark estate names, and new attributes like `@trans` to host translation of lemmas. Most of these elements have been added to make the encoding more intuitive and easier to apply for scholars and they can thus be described as the "syntactic sugar" of the encoding. In some cases new elements cannot be added or modified without breaking compatibility with the core TEI encoding model. For example, the `<w>` element in TEI encodes words (see § *Linguistic Encoding*), but, unlike in TEI, the *LangScape* model allows these elements to be enclosed within `<choice>` elements in order to encode alternative interpretations. Another example is the newly-created `<altLemma>` element which is not in the TEI model at all and which encodes alternative undecided lemmas and translations for words. These new elements mean that the *LangScape* schema can be formally described as a TEI extension.[18]

A further extension, largely modeled on XInclude, was created in order to allow integration of material from several CCH projects sharing the same source material, namely Anglo Saxon charters, and sharing the same encoding schema, namely TEI; we called the extension "CCH", denoting its specificity. The usage of these newly introduced elements has been demonstrated in a pilot project by Arianna Ciula and Elena Pierazzo which

[18] For discussion of different kinds of TEI conformance, see TEI Consortium 2007, Section 23.3.

can integrate data from the *Anglo-Saxon Charters* Project[19] and the *LangScape* Project. This pilot was presented as a poster at the TEI Meeting of 2007. As *LangScape* does not encode texts of the whole charter but just the boundary-clause, the pilot demonstrated the feasibility of drawing the remainder of the texts from other TEI-encoded XML documents in an automated, user-driven way, which maintained compliance[20] through an enriched TEI schema.

The TEI specifications state that any new inclusion or extension must be identified by one or more "namespaces" (W3C 2006), a feature of XML that indicates that a given element or an attribute belongs to a specific schema. Such belonging is immediately recognisable by the namespace prefix which is followed by a colon and which is appended to the name of the new element or attribute. XInclude elements are therefore identified by a *xi:* prefix, *LangScape* elements and attributes by a *lngs:* prefix, and CCH elements by a *cch:* prefix.[21] As one example, then, the `<formulaic>` element which has been added as part of the *LangScape* namespace, for which see point (2) above, is designated with its namespace as `<lngs:formulaic>`.

The *LangScape* Encoding Model

The TEI schema is inevitably abstract as it is designed to fit the largest possible variety of texts and research purposes. It is therefore necessary to adapt it to fit the specific needs of each project, essentially by choosing for a given situation an appropriate subset of tags from the different possibilities offered by the abstract schema. This preliminary operation leads to the creation of a so-called "encoding model" which is basically a list of the elements that have been actually used in the encoding, reflecting the project's needs.

Three main requirements drove the creation of the *LangScape* encoding model:

1. Linguistic annotation, in terms of lemmatisation, language and translation.
2. Preservation of selected features of the manuscripts.
3. Recording of editorial interventions.

These three requirements will now be treated in turn.

[19] For which see the project website at http://www.esawyer.org.uk.

[20] Or *validity*, in technical terms.

[21] All extensions have been document via an ODD XML file, as per TEI specifications (TEI Consortium 2007, Section 23.3.5).

Linguistic Encoding

The linguistic encoding is centered on the `<w>` element. In TEI's abstract terms, this element encodes «a grammatical (not necessarily orthographic) word» (TEI Consortium 2007, Section 17.1). In *LangScape* terms, however, it represents a complex phenomenology which includes compounds, composed words, constituent parts, and uncertain and undecided cases. In the process from common to proper noun, syntagmatic designations gradually become words on their own and it is therefore important, for lexicographic purposes, to recognise the end result, the starting point, and the intermediate stage.

The encoding model used for the project tries to reflect faithfully the complexities of scholarly analysis. The following discussion will therefore present some of that model, introducing examples and explanations to show how data are modelled according to specific research needs, both from an analytic and a processing point of view.

The most straightforward case is represented by the encoding of a single word, for instance the manuscript form *more* 'marsh':

```
<w lemma="mor" lngs:trans="marsh" part="N">more</w>
```

The `<w>` element here carries four attributes:

1. `@lemma`: contains a pointer to the Glossary where each lemma is defined and annotated.
2. `@lngs:trans`: a *LangScape* extension of the TEI schema, this contains a suggested translation of the lemma to aid those users not familiar with the language (for further details see § *Semiautomatic Markup*).
3. `@part`: tells which part of the word is described, with *N* meaning 'full word', *I* standing for 'initial part of a word', *M* for 'a medial part of a word' and *F* for 'final part of a word'; *N* is the default value and is normally omitted in the encoding.

A much more complex example is given by the compound form *suþintuna*. This form appears in the phrase *suþintuna gemæru* and can therefore be translated within its context as 'Sodington's (boundary)'. Within the word three component parts can be recognised: *suþ* 'south', *in* 'in' and *tuna* 'settlement'.

The encoding model for compound forms like this provides an upper level `<w>` element encoding the lemma and translation for the whole compound and three different nested <w> elements, each of them encoding lemma and translation of the constituent elements.

```
<w lemma="Sodington" lngs:trans="Sodington's" part="N"
                          rend="dst">
   <w lemma="suþ" lngs:trans="south" part="I">suþ</w>
   <w lemma="in" lngs:trans="in" part="M">in</w>
   <w lemma="tun" lngs:trans="settlement"
part="F">tuna</w>
</w>
```

The attribute rend="dst" marks that the compound has to be displayed as a single word. Such a detailed encoding enables users to search for components at any level while still allowing fine control over display independently of context, such separation of content and display being a key design-feature of XML. This facility will be a great help to researchers involved in etymological and lexical studies.

In some cases, such as when letters are shared by component parts, to split a compound word into its components is not a trivial matter. In the form *stretones*, for instance, we recognise two components, *stret* and *tones*, to be translated as *street* and *farm's* respectively. The problem here is that the letter *t* in the compound is shared by the two components. However, XML does not allow elements to overlap, so an encoding such as <w1>stre<w2>t</w1>ones</w2> is expressly forbidden. Instead, our encoding reflects the shared letter by duplicating it in an element created expressly for this purpose: <lngs:shared>. It is then up to the processing tools to visualise the entire compound form correctly when required (*stretones*, with just one letter *t*), and also to present the two parts each with its own *t* (so *stret* and *tones*, but not *stret* and *ones* or *stre* and *tones*). This is achieved at the level of encoding by the following markup:

```
<w lemma="Stretton" lngs:trans="Stretton's" part="N"
rend="dst">
       <w lemma="stræt" lngs:trans="street" part="I">
              stre<lngs:shared>t</lngs:shared></w>
       <w lemma="tun" lngs:trans="farm's" part="F">
              <lngs:shared>t</lngs:shared>ones</w>
</w>
```

Such shared letters are found not only within compound words (for which we are able to provide a single top-level lemma and translation), but also between distinct words for which no single top-level lemma can be provided but which (for whatever reason) have been written as a single element.[22] In this case the splitting and the encoding of a shared component has been done within a <seg> ('segment') element rather that within an upper level <w> element as in the *stretones* example. In *sandune*, for instance, the *d* of the second element *dune* 'hill' has been incorporated into the preceding *d* of the first element *sand* 'sand'. The *sandune* compound has not been treated as a composed word, but as a segment and therefore encoded as follows:

```
<seg>
      <w lemma="sand" lngs:trans="sand" part="I">
                      san<lngs:shared>d</lngs:shared></w>
      <w lemma="dun" lngs:trans="hill" part="F>
                      <lngs:shared>d</lngs:shared>une</w>
</seg>
```

In addition to problems of compounding and word-separation, other difficulties are also encoded in the *LangScape* model. One such example is where no single lemma (and thus no single translation) could be chosen, and so all reasonable alternatives have been encoded. In a charter, for instance, the word *grindeles* could be linked to at least three different lemmas, all of them acceptable in the context: *grindel* 'grind-stone', **grendel* 'gravelly-place' or *Grendel*, a personal name. In cases like this, the lemmas and translations are not recorded within a <w> element but instead in a series of <lngs:altLemma> elements, all of which are wrapped within a <choice>. The <lngs:altLemma> element has the same attributes as the <w> element but with one addition: a @degree attribute which is used to rank the choices in order of researchers' preference. This attribute is used to help the queries and to order alphabetically the results in a concordance of the text: specifically, in any situation where a single lemma must be chosen to produce meaningful output, then the one with the highest degree is used automatically. The word *grindles*, then, would be marked up as follows:

[22] It should be noted that the compound may also result from the scribe's own pronunciation or even lack of linguistic competence. At that time no standard orthography was established, and writing-practice substantially reflected a mixture of rendered pronunciation and Latin graphic habits.

```
<w type="multiple">grindeles
  <choice>
       <lngs:altLemma lemma="grindel"
       trans="grindstone's"
       degree="0.35"/>
       <lngs:altLemma lemma="*grendel" trans="gravelly-
       place's" degree="0.33"/>
       <lngs:altLemma lemma="Grendel(persn)"
       trans="Grendel's"   degree="0.32"/>
  </choice>
</w>
```

Among these cases of difficult interpretation, the most complex is perhaps the one in which the alternatives have different textual granularity, in other words, when a given segment can either be a single word or a compound of two or more words. For example, the word *ærning* could stand either for *ærning* 'running' or for two separate words, *ærn* 'building' and *-ing* 'place'. In such circumstances, it is the `<w>` element itself that needs to be encoded within a `<choice>` element and to carry the `@lngs:degree` attribute.

```
<w type="alternate">
      <choice>
             <w lngs:degree="0.6" lemma="ærning"
             lngs:trans="running/racing">ærning</w>
             <w lngs:degree="0.4">
                    <w lemma="ærn"
                    lngs:trans="building"
                    part="I">ærn</w>
                    <w lemma="-ing" lngs:trans="place"
                    part="F">ing</w>
             </w>
      </choice>
</w>
```

Transcriptional Encoding

One of the more interesting things about this resource is that the encoding never forgets the nature of the source material: namely, that all the texts have been checked against the surviving manuscripts. This is in contrast to most linguistic resources which are normally based on a copy-text or edited text; here, linguistic markup is mixed with transcriptional markup. Therefore features are recorded and are available to the user in combination with the linguistic and toponymic information. These features include:

- unclear readings
- scribal deletions
- scribal additions
- scribal errors
- damages and gaps in the support
- abbreviations and expansions
- *scriptio continua* and editorial spacing.

Editorial Encoding

In addition to transcriptional markup, editorial markup is also necessary. For instance, obvious scribal errors have been followed by editorial correction, as in this example where the manuscript reading *om* has been corrected by the editors to *on*:

```
<w lemma="on" lngs:trans="to">o<choice>
   <sic>m</sic>
   <corr>n</corr>
   </choice>
</w>
```

Missing text (usually because of physical damage to the support) is supplied, where possible, by the editors:

```
<w lemma="Beadugyþ"
    lngs:trans="Beadugyth's">beadg<gap
    extent="3"/>
    <supplied reason="illegible">iðe</supplied>
</w>
```

As discussed earlier in this paper, many of the texts have been collated with a selection of recent and accessible printed editions (such as the British Academy editions of Anglo-Saxon Charters, and Della Hooke's editions of charter bounds) and any conflicts in reading have been recorded in the markup. In the example below, the printed edition reads *ac* (with an *a*) but in the researchers' opinion the manuscript in fact reads *æc* (with an *æ*); the printed edition is here referenced via the abbreviation *ChartAbing*:

```
<app>
    <lem>
            <w lemma="ac" lngs:trans="oaks">æc</w>
    </lem>
    <rdg wit="ChartAbing">ac</rdg>
</app>
```

XML at Work: Different Outputs and Checking Facilities

The encoding model described in this paper allows users to select different views of the same material according to their preferences and interests. Specifically, the website offers a semidiplomatic transcription, an edited transcription and a glossed transcription, the last displaying lemmas and translation for each word or word component. Indeed, this is what makes XML so special: the possibility of encoding and annotating any kind of feature of a text according to scholarly needs. It is then up to the processing tools to select the encoding layers that are needed for a specific visualisation task. In the *LangScape* system, the database uses the linguistic encoding for searches, concordances and the like, while readable versions of the text are produced using scripts written in a language called XSLT, which can select any combination of layers according to the kind of visualisation chosen by users. For the user, then, the detailed encoding is a strength as it allows choice while hiding the complexity underneath.

For the project researchers who must add this encoding, however, the situation is rather different. They must be exposed to the encoding in its entirety, but the resulting text is extremely densely encoded and in some cases almost unreadable by a human. The possibility given by XML to annotate texts at any depth comes with a price: specifically, an editor may loose control of the text because of the density of encoding, and this must always be considered possible in any XML-based project (Eggert 2005: 425–27). To avoid this risk a number of XSLT scripts have been integrated into the editorial work from the very beginning of the encoding process. These scripts are designed to produce provisional human-readable output for checking purposes, with different scripts designed for different types of checking. For example, one key requirement of the editing process is to check for consistency, and an XML-based approach provides enormous potential to ensure that scholarly rigor is applied by allowing project members to isolate and check the context of XML-encoded materials in a potentially infinite number of ways. This is particularly important because people often underestimate the amount of time required for checking data in digital humanities projects, but robust checking facilities allied to a flexible yet well-structured encoding model can both save time and improve the results of the scholarly process.

Generally speaking, any element that has been included in the encoding model is meant to mark a significant feature of the text and therefore needs to be checked for consistency. More specifically, for any encoding-based project some elements are meant to carry the scholarly "added value" of the project and the checking facilities should necessarily focus on them. For instance, in transcriptions of primary sources, these elements of "added value" might be deletions, interlinear insertions, and abbreviations; for bibliographical resources the main focus could be on authors, titles, and dates; for historical documents, on names of people and places together with dates and events, and so on. In addition to these, structural elements and key attributes may also be usefully double checked, together with all those elements that will be used to create a particular output. Thus one could look for consistent use of divisions, headings, identifiers, page and line breaks, consistent representation of lemmas and translations, and the correct display of elements intended to be italicised, bold, or linked to other resources.

Metadata: Source Description

The previous section has considered the encoding model, namely the way in which the text is marked up according to the project's extension of the TEI standard. This markup is relevant to texts, but the *LangScape* resource also includes metadata about those texts. These metadata are stored in several tables in the relational database, but they are also exported (but not edited) together with the textual content of the database in the XML model. This inclusion of at least a subset of the metadata in the XML is necessary to completely identify the text if it should come to "live" outside the database. Although it may not be used in practice, the system must allow for the possibility of scholars downloading the encoded text of a particular boundary-clause. The problem is that if they do so then their downloaded text becomes independent of the *LangScape* resource and its metadata. Some information must therefore be appended to the start of the text to allow subsequent identification. Among the metadata, the most important is the so-called "Sawyer Number". This is a number which originated in Peter Sawyer's annotated list of Anglo-Saxon charters, a standard list which unambiguously identifies charter-texts, which is widely used by Anglo-Saxonists, and which incorporates subsequent additions approved by the British Academy.[23] This unambiguous and standard designator allows the *LangScape* material to be connected with a full batch of web resources relating to Anglo-Saxon charters, each of which aims to analyse the material from different points of view and to make this available to scholars and the web community in general.[24]

LangScape metadata have quite a complex structure with many dependencies, and for this reason it has been judged more efficient to keep them within the relational database and simply export a subset of them as required before uploading files onto the website. XML has been used as the main editorial framework for the transcribed texts, but on the other hand for metadata it is simply a means of exporting in order to build standalone documents and to display essential details about the visualised text. Although this is partly for reasons of efficiency and structure, as discussed above,[25] there is another reason why only essential fields from the database have been exported into XML. This is because, at the time of writing, there is no international agreement on which information is to be included in descriptions of charters, and therefore the existing XML standards do not offer any model for encoding.

There is an international project devoted to encoding guidelines for charters: it is called the *CEI* (*Charters Encoding Initiative*),[26] and its results, once available, will have a significant impact on this situation. However, it has not yet produced any stable proposal that can be safely used in a research project.

Developing an *ad hoc* model for encoding metadata was not a reasonable option, since any such model would not be compatible with any existing systems. We therefore decided to slightly adapt the TEI module for describing manuscripts (TEI Consortium 2007, Section 10) in such a way that, within the standard `<teiHeader>` element, the `<msDesc>` element has been filled automatically from the relational database. For each boundary-clause, therefore, the following information is also included:

– a text identifier: a unique internal code generated specially for each text
– the Sawyer number
– the library and shelf-mark of the manuscript, and the folio or page-numbers of the relevant material.

---

[23] The original source is Sawyer 1968, and for updates see the *Electronic Sawyer* given in n. 4.
[24] For some such projects see n. 5.
[25] See § *Modelling Humanities Data in a Digital Framework*.
[26] See the project website at http://www.cei.uni-muenchen.de/index.htm.

– the name of the estate being described

Linguistic Analysis

Aside from correcting transcripts against the original manuscripts, the main task of the project has been linguistic analysis. This analysis consisted primarily of lemmatisation and translation but also involved some semantic analysis.

As has been specified in the discussion of the encoding-model above, one function of the markup is to provide brief translations of each form into modern English. Each form therefore needs a short, context-specific translation to produce a rough word-by-word translation of the text. This rough translation should provide sufficient assistance for users with minimal Old English to read the text and to appreciate the relationship between form, translation, and lemma. Doing this also means that the time and effort required for fluent prose translations could instead be spent on the word-by-word analysis of the text, a task which was more useful and a much higher priority of the project. Indeed, one of the project's chief aims is to set down a solid lexicographical base to allow the reassessment of individual terms both within their immediate textual contexts but crucially also comparatively across the corpus. Thus this translation acts as a starting point, precisely anchoring lemma and translation to each individual word of Old English text so that users can better understand how published translations are arrived at and can refine their own translations with the aid of dictionaries and glossaries. To further emphasise this point, these translations are presented in a manner deliberately unlike connected prose, as shown in

Table 1, thereby stressing that it is *not* a full translation in any sense, and that the user would have to exercise her or his own judgment in interpreting the text.

Form	**Fram**	**suð**	**geate**	**west**	**andlanges**	**wealles**	**oð**	**norð**	**lanan**
Lemma	*fram*	*suþ*	*geat*	*west*	*andlang*	*weall*	*oþ*	*norþ*	*lane*
Translation	From	south	gate	west	along	(the) wall	as far as	north	lane

Table 1. Example of text with lemmas and translations

As well as translations of forms, the lemmas themselves can also be given relatively full translations, and these lemma-translation pairs then used to generate a glossary for the user. In addition to translation, though, the concept of adding information to each lemma can easily be extended by reversing the direction of mapping and allowing users to find all forms and occurrences of a given lemma. Taking this idea further, if each lemma is categorised semantically then the database can easily map from a category back to all matching lemmas and thence to all forms in the corpus and all occurrences of each form. Although such semantic searching is limited at this stage, the capacity is in place, and the hope is to extend it substantially by importing the classification already used in the *Thesaurus of Old English* which is now also online,[27] and this, if successful, would allow very sophisticated semantic analysis of our corpus indeed.

The Process of Markup

The discussion so far has presented the encoding-model and, as discussed above, the base texts were stored in a relational database with some simple *ad hoc* tagging to reflect some details of the manuscript and its reading. The problem, therefore, was how best to extract these texts and add tagging for lemmatisation without disturbing the original markup. Fully automatic markup was not possible for several reasons. First, the non-standard database and initial markup precluded any "out-of-the-box" system, although it would have been relatively straightforward to transform our material into TEI-compliant markup, as we later did. More significantly, though, relatively little material is available for automatic processing of Old English. Quite a lot has been done for Latin, but most of this is for Classical Latin,[28] whereas the Latin (and even the Old English) of boundary-clauses is quite different and much more problematic. Furthermore, although the meanings of words in boundary clauses can be precise, they are often ambiguous in practice, particularly when taken out of context and placed in a glossary-database like the one used for this project. This ambiguity is particularly because orthography in Old English, and even in Latin as written by the Anglo-Saxons, is quite inconsistent and dependant on the dialects, training, and personal idiosyncrasies of the scribes, and such difficulties are compounded by later copying, particularly when the copyists are not familiar with the original language. Thus the manuscript-form *mere* could signify a pool (whence modern *mere*), but it could also represent *(ge)mære*, a boundary. Similar but even harder to disambiguate in late material is Old English *ham*, a homestead, alongside *hamm*, an enclosure or water-meadow, where often only clues

[27] http://libra.englang.arts.gla.ac.uk/oethesaurus.

[28] For one particularly well-known set of tools for Classical Latin (and Greek) see the *Perseus* Project (http://www.perseus.tufts.edu).

from the linguistic and semantic context indicate the more likely lemma. In some cases, too, it is unclear whether a given form functions as a common noun or as a personal name. All of these difficulties meant that fully automated markup using existing material was not a viable option.

Instead of fully automated markup, the quantity of material necessitated, and the formulaic nature of the material allowed, that a semiautomated system could be used. Regarding the formulaic nature of the text, it has already been observed that boundary-clauses are often (though by no means always) of the form "from A to B, from B to C...". In addition to this, we know from Zipf's Law that a relatively small number of forms accounts for a relatively large percentage of the corpus, and similarly that a large number of forms occur only once or twice in any large body of texts (Zipf 1949). Specifically, the *LangScape* corpus contains over thirteen thousand distinct forms, but only thirty of these forms account for nearly a third of the whole material, whereas over seven thousand different forms occur only once each. Furthermore, the frequently-occurring forms are very often straightforward and without any of the difficulties discussed above. To identify every one of the approximately seven thousand *hapax legomena*, all out of context, would be an enormous task with little benefit, particularly as so many of these forms are problematic, as just discussed. Instead, a system to automatically mark up only the more frequent (and usually more straightforward) forms yielded much greater and more rapid returns. Thus a semiautomatic system was developed to deal with the frequent and straightforward cases quickly, thereby freeing the researchers to concentrate on the more difficult material which could not reasonably be marked up by a computer.

The (rather idealised) principle behind the semiautomatic system was straightforward:

- A list of all forms in the corpus would be generated.
- A list of lemmas would be compiled to account for the forms.
- A table of correspondences would be produced, linking form to lemma.
- A very short translation would be provided for each form.
- This table of correspondences would be used to mark up the text with an automatic "best guess" of the most likely lemma and translation (or, in ambiguous cases, lemmas and translations) for each form.
- Project researchers would then read through all of the texts, manually emending and tailoring the markup and adding editorial comments as required.

This was the principle, and it was implemented with a series of custom-built or modified tools centred around a database of lemmas, translations and forms, and a script for the markup. However, this simple principle conceals a multitude of complexity and editorial decision-making, and so it is worth exploring in detail exactly how these steps were implemented.

Semiautomatic Markup

The first step was to extract all the forms from the corpus in an organised way. This initial list of forms was generated using a textual analysis program called *TextSTAT* which is produced by the department of Dutch Linguistics at the Free University of Berlin (*Niederländische Sprachwissenschaft an der Freien Universität Berlin*).[29] This programme is designed to read in a body of texts, to produce a list of all forms in the corpus, and to search for occurrences of such forms in the texts (see fig. 2). It therefore provided almost exactly the functionality we needed, and it also performed well in testing and seemed well designed and easy to use. Just as importantly, it is open-source and written relatively clearly in the *Python* programming language using modular design.[30] Because this language is relatively straightforward but powerful, and because it comes with modules that allow it to communicate directly with relational databases, we were able to write additional modules allowing *TextSTAT* to query our relational database directly and to process our custom markup itself. Once *TextSTAT* had generated the list of forms, we exported the list to a plain text file and then imported that into a simple relational database to facilitate the mapping from forms to lemmas in step two.

This next step was to generate the list of lemmas. As noted above, Old English lacked a standardised orthography, which indeed existed in several different dialects, and lexicographers have not always agreed on the most appropriate spelling for their lemmas. Indeed, toponymists typically prefer the East Anglian forms while lexicographers normally use the West Saxon ones. To complicate matters further, the two most recent and authoritative sources for Old English and place-name vocabulary are still incomplete, with the *Dictionary of Old English* containing only the entries *A-F*, and the *Vocabulary of English Placenames* from *A* to *Cockpit*.[31] Researchers at the *Dictionary of Old English* were kind enough to provide us with their

---

[29] *TextSTAT* is copyright (c) 2002–2004 Matthias Hüning <mhuening@zedat.fu-berlin.de> and can be found at http://www.niederlandistik.fu-berlin.de/textstat/software-en.html.

[30] *Python* is a registered trademark of the Python Software Foundation (http://www.python.org/about/legal/).

[31] While we were writing the final version of this paper, researchers at *The Dictionary of Old English* announced the release of entries for *G*: see diPaulo Healey 2008.

anticipated lemmas for the entire alphabet but they emphasised that those for letters after *F* were very much subject to revision, and the list would not have helped users trying to find particular words as they would not themselves know what the lemmas were. Finally, some words, most notably personal names and river names, have their own specialist dictionaries, and in some specific cases we wished to collapse forms which were distinguished in dictionaries but which could not be distinguished in the limited context of boundary-clauses. With all these complications, it is inevitable that different users will expect given lemmas to be spelled in different ways and will therefore have difficulty finding the ones they want. As one of the more difficult examples for users, the word for a 'ploughing' is spelled *yrð* in some dictionaries and *erð* in others; thus someone expecting the former spelling would look under *Y* and may never think to check under *E* (Clark Hall 1960; Smith 1956).[32]

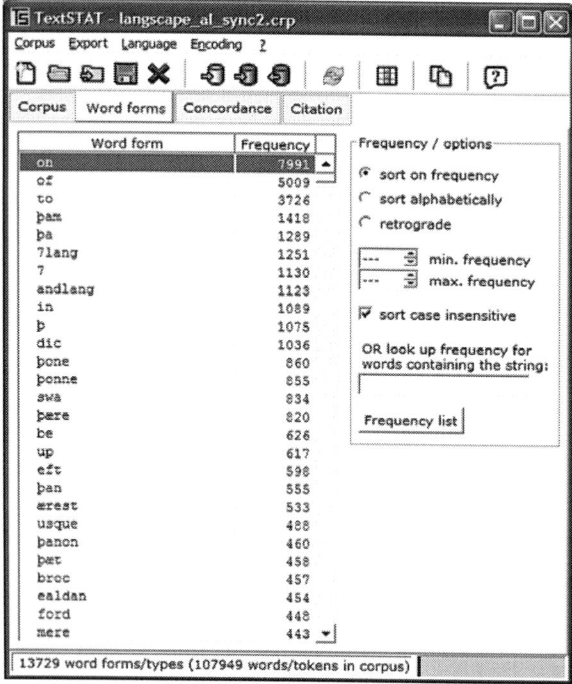

Fig. 2. TextSTAT and the list of forms

[32] Clark Hall also listed *earð* as an alternative to *yrð*, and under *ierð* gives cross-references to both *eorð(e)* ('ground' or 'soil') and *yrð* (Clark Hall 1960).

To overcome this difficulty we recorded the spellings of lemmas from six major dictionaries (listed in Table 2), and also created further lists for proper nouns and for words in Latin. One lemma, usually but not always from this list, has also been chosen as the "official" *LangScape* one, and this form is used as the default whenever a single lemma is required. Users' searches can then be run against all six Old English spellings, as well as those for Latin words, proper nouns, and the "official" *LangScape* lemma, and this should enable them to find the word they want, whichever system they are following.

Abbreviation	Source
DOE	Cameron *et al.* 2003
CHM	Clark Hall / Meritt 1960
SmithEl	Smith 1956
PNNotts	[Unpublished Database of English Place-Names][33]
VEPN	Parsons *et al.* 1997–
Gelling	Gelling / Cole 2003
Proper	[Proper nouns]
Latin	[Latin words]

Table 2. Sources for lists of lemmas

Although this inclusion of different lemmas simplifies matters for the user, it introduced a great deal more complexity for the researchers. Equating lemmas from different dictionaries was by no means straightforward, as lexicographers have not always agreed about when identical forms with different meanings should be given different lemmas, whether different forms constitute different words or alternatives of the same word, and so on. Even choosing the "default" *LangScape* lemma involved a significant amount of editorial thought and discretion which should not be underestimated. Indeed, this "simple" table of equivalent lemmas from the major dictionaries was itself a significant product of research and could in principle be used in other related onomastic resources.

Alongside the compiling of these lists and equating of lemmas, we also needed to map the lemmas to the word-forms in the corpus. This was greatly assisted by pre-existing mappings of forms to lemmas which were extracted from the *Dictionary of Old English* CD-ROM and the

[33] We wish to thank David Parsons of the Centre for Name Studies, University of Nottingham, for kindly providing us with this resource.

Nottingham Database; these were imported into our *Glossary* database as a starting-point, and a data-input form was created for the researchers to map forms to the "official" *LangScape* lemma, and to map the lemmas from the different dictionaries to each other. This process was significantly assisted by the *TextSTAT* software since it allowed the researchers to quickly and easily see the relevant forms in their contexts, thereby helping to identify the appropriate lemma. Researchers also found useful the ability to alphabetise the data either by form or by lemma in the data-entry form of the glossary database. When the data was ordered by form, as shown in

Fig. 3, then different similarly spelled forms of the same lemma tended to appear together, and this meant that the single lemma could be added quickly and easily to an entire group of words. Similarly, ordering the list by lemma allowed researchers to check the consistency of their mappings, and indeed of their translations. In practice, then, the mapping of forms to lemmas and translations was accompanied by a process of refining both the lemmas themselves and the mapping between the lists of lemmas from different dictionaries.

Since this mapping was only ever intended to be an intermediate stage in the semiautomatic markup, and since project members would be checking all the marked-up texts, it followed that the mappings did not need to be complete or perfectly accurate. Thus words occurring fewer than five times, if not readily identifiable, could be left to be done manually and in context. Very often the researchers needed to provide two or more possible translations for a single form in the database, even when the lemma was known with certainty, but in many cases these possibilities could be narrowed down manually when the entire text was checked at a later stage. Sometimes two or more lemmas were possible, in which case the translation field was used as a temporary holding-point to store the possibilities. For example, as noted above, the manuscript-form *mere* could represent either *mere* 'pool', or *(ge)mære* 'boundary'. Since the former is more likely, the lemma would automatically be inserted as *mere*. However, the automatic translation would be 'pool *gemære+*'. The researchers could then manually delete *gemære+* when the automatic "best guess" was correct, but if the word should have been *boundary* then the *gemære+* served as a reminder to correct the lemma as well as the translation.

Microsoft Access - [LSConcordance2]

File Edit View Insert Format Records Tools Window Help

Freq.	Form		Lemma		Meaning	DOE/CHM	
1	gemyþun	☐	(ge)	myþe	confluences		
1	gemæ	☐					
1	gemæ[]re	☐	(ge)	mære	boundary		
3	gemænan	☐	(ge)	mæne	common		
6	gemæne	☐	(ge)	mæne	common		
1	gemænen	☐	(ge)	mæne	common		
29	gemær	☐	(ge)	mære	boundary		
194	gemæra	☐	(ge)	mære	boundaries		
22	gemæran	☐	(ge)	mære	boundaries		
346	gemære	☐	(ge)	mære	boundary bou		
1	gemæreres	☐	(ge)	mære	(the) boundar		
84	gemæres	☐	(ge)	mære	(the) boundar		
1	gemærie	☐	(ge)	mære	boundary		
184	gemæro	☐	(ge)	mære	boundaries		
5	gemæron	☐	(ge)	mære	boundaries		
1	gemærsode	☑	(ge)	mærsian	marked out	(ge)	mærs
92	gemæru	☑	(ge)	mære	boundaries	(ge)	mære
9	gemærum	☐	(ge)	mære	boundaries		
1	gemæræ	☐	(ge)	mære	boundary		

Record: 5045 of 13659

Form View

Fig. 3. Input-form for mapping lemmas and meanings to forms[34]

The next stage was to use the mapping to mark up the text automatically. This markup has been implemented with a combination of different programming languages. As noted above, the texts were initially stored in a relational database; a button was therefore added to the data-entry form displaying the texts, and by clicking on this button the researcher could automatically save the text in an external file, add XML tags to every word in the file with the appropriate lemma and gloss, transform any existing markup from the project-specific custom scheme to a fully TEI-compliant one, and finally load the resulting form into the

[34] Although it is not apparent from the screen-shot, it should be noted that the *Lemma* and *DOE/CHM* fields are not free-text but only allow the user to select from a predetermined list (authority-list) of lemmas. Furthermore, the fields containing lemmas from the different dictionaries are redundant in many cases, insofar as all forms with a given lemma should be mapped to the same dictionary-forms. Thus, in the example shown, all forms of *gemære* should be mapped to the same DOE/CHM lemma *gemære*, and thus the mapping to the DOE/CHM lemma needs only be entered into the database once. The ticks in the third column of the form indicate the rows which contain mapping for the relevant lemmas.

<oXygen/> XML Editor for the researchers to check and edit as required.[35] This automatic markup was performed via a "live" connection to the glossary-database: that is, the list of lemmas and translations was read for every text, and thus any changes which the researchers may have made to the glossary database were reflected immediately in any future automatic markup.[36]

The advantages of this system were numerous, but the most significant was the way in which it could immediately implement any changes made by the researchers. Because each text was marked up individually, and because the automatic process connected directly to the glossary database, the project researchers could alter any information in that database and have the changes reflected in all subsequent markup. Thus, if the researchers found that a particular choice of translation was not the most effective, for example, that translation could be changed quickly and easily through the glossary-database with immediate effect. One alternative approach would have been to mark up the entire corpus in a single process, but this meant that any changes to the glossary required the entire corpus to be marked up anew, and any work on the texts to that point would have been lost. Similarly, attempts were made to export the mappings from the glossary-database into a standalone XML file, but this made it much more difficult for the researchers to alter any mappings or translations, thus increasing the likelihood that the tools would not be properly used and that inconsistencies would be introduced as a result.

---

[35] <oXygen/> is a registered trademark of SyncRO Soft Ltd. in the United States and other countries (http://www.oxygenxml.com). The <oXygen/> XML Editor is hereafter referred to as *Oxygen*.

[36] The relational database was implemented using the MySQL database server but with Microsoft Access as a graphical user interface. The form therefore used Visual Basic to save the file and launch a perl script, and the perl script performed the actual markup, communicating with the glossary-database via ODBC. MySQL is a registered trademark of MySQL AB in the United States, the European Union and other countries (http://www.mysql.com/company/legal/trademark.html). Microsoft Access is a registered trademark of Microsoft Corporation in the United States and other countries (http://www.microsoft.com/library/toolbar/3.0/trademarks/en-us.mspx).

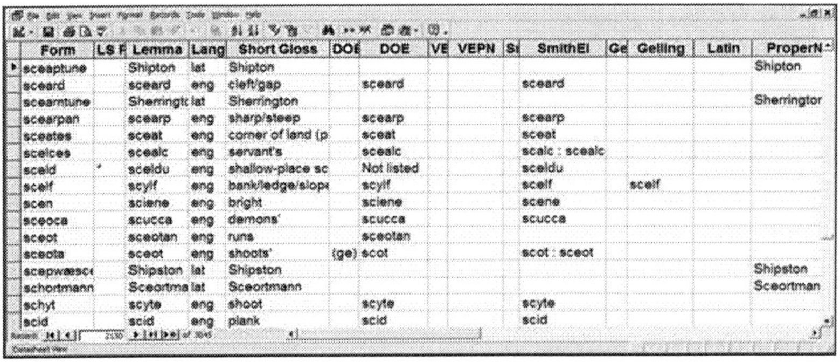

Form	LS F	Lemma	Lang	Short Gloss	DOE	DOE	VE	VEPN	S	SmithEl	Ge	Gelling	Latin	ProperN
sceaptune		Shipton	lat	Shipton										Shipton
sceard		sceard	eng	cleft/gap		sceard				sceard				
sceamtune		Sherringt	lat	Sherrington										Sherringtor
scearpan		scearp	eng	sharp/steep		scearp				scearp				
sceates		sceat	eng	corner of land (p		sceat				sceat				
scelces		scealc	eng	servant's		scealc				scalc ; scealc				
sceld	*	sceldu	eng	shallow-place sc		Not listed				sceldu				
scelf		scylf	eng	bank/ledge/slop		scylf				scelf		scelf		
scen		sciene	eng	bright		sciene				scene				
sceoca		scucca	eng	demons'		scucca				scucca				
sceot		sceotan	eng	runs		sceotan								
sceota		sceot	eng	shoots'	(ge)	scot				scot ; sceot				
scepwaesc		Shipston	lat	Shipston										Shipston
schortmann		Sceortma	lat	Sceortmann										Sceortman
schyt		scyte	eng	shoot		scyte				scyte				
scid		scid	eng	plank		scid				scid				

Fig. 4. Mapping forms to lemmas and translation

Once the automatic process had been run on a given text, the researcher was then presented with a fully marked-up, TEI-compliant XML file. This was then edited using *Oxygen*. The researcher could then view the marked up text and read through the automatically-applied markup, all the time viewing it with the aid of published discussions of the texts and correcting, annotating, and adjusting the markup as required. One requirement at this point was to make the markup itself as unobtrusive as possible, thereby allowing the researchers to focus on the scholarly content instead of the mechanical process of tagging. This was achieved in part by some basic scripts which could transform the XML into a more human-readable HTML; this could then be displayed in a web browser and so checked relatively easily. In addition, though, we quickly found that the same small set of corrections needed to be applied over and over again. These were usually because the automatic stage of markup was not perfect, not only in terms of the lemma and translation it chose, as discussed above, but also because it could not account for every possible combination of *ad hoc* markup when translating into the TEI-compliant schema. Rather than spending a lot of time trying to perfect the automatic stage, it was deemed more efficient to create additional tools which would allow the researchers to make these corrections quickly and easily on a case-by-case basis. Fortunately *Oxygen* is designed in such a way that it can be extended by writing custom plugins. Particularly useful was the so-called "selection" form of plugin: if a researcher working on an XML file selected a portion of text, then this portion of text could be passed to a plugin and reformatted automatically. For example, if the researcher decided that a given lemma was inappropriate, then she would highlight the lemma in question and run the *Change Lemma* plugin. The plugin would then open a connection to the glossary-database, read in the list of lemmas and translations, select the lemma which is closest to the one highlighted by the researcher, and allow the researcher to choose a different lemma (or cancel the operation). This new lemma would then be substituted back into the XML, assuming that the researcher did not cancel the operation.[37] Such a procedure helped to combine the benefits of XML markup and database authority-lists. By using the plugin to change lemmas and translations, the researcher could be certain of consistency with the rest of the markup. Similarly, but even more importantly, by connecting directly to the glossary-database, any changes in lemmas would be reflected immediately in the plugin, and thus researchers could refine the glossary as they went and could have such refinements reflected in further markup even in the same text, much as they have in the markup-script discussed in the previous section. Of course the possibility remained that a lemma could be altered in the glossary database which had been used in a previous XML file, as the plugin made no attempt to scan through lemmas already in the XML, nor to look through files which had been manually checked earlier. However, this difficulty has been easily accommodated by running a check on all files which have been marked up to date, and it can be further confirmed by a batch check of all files once the markup is complete.

In addition to this more complex plugin, several others were provided to aid in correcting the markup. Most of these had the same underlying structure, namely that a string matching one pattern was transformed into one of a different pattern. For example, words which were compound in the initial database sometimes needed to be split into two separate entities. Since these plugins were so similar to one another, it was possible to pre-build most of the functionality and to extract the remainder into a template, meaning that new plugins could be developed in just a few minutes.

[37] *Oxygen* is written entirely in Java, and so plugins need simply to implement the appropriate interface and include the appropriate jar files. For further details see SyncRO Soft Ltd. The link to the glossary database was implemented using the JDBC-ODBC bridge, thereby allowing the database to be in any ODBC-compliant system such as the MySQL database server, Microsoft Access, or many others. Java and JDBC are registered trademarks of Sun Microsystems, Inc., in the United States and other countries (http://www.sun.com/suntrademarks/index.jsp).

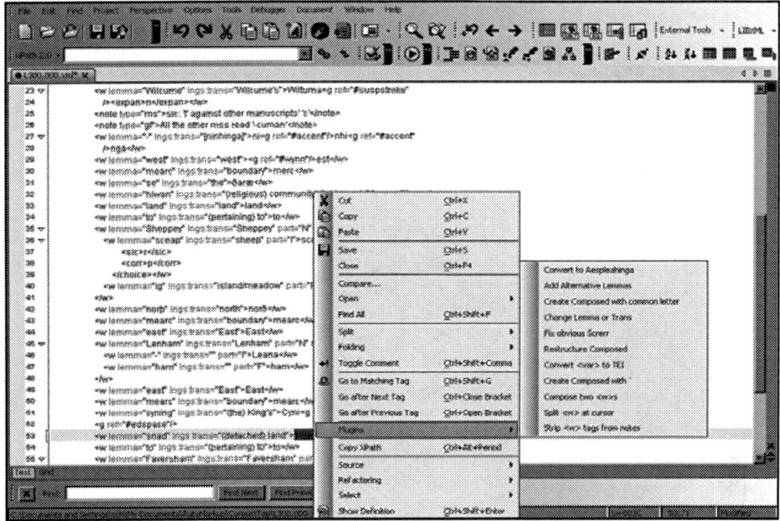

Fig. 5. *Oxygen* plugins

The Output

The main outcome of the project is a website offering several entry-points to the corpus, including static precompiled indices as well as search and browsing facilities. These entry-points can lead to different forms of output: a "keyword in context" or "KWIC" display which shows each occurrence of the given word (or words) in its context (or their contexts), a GIS display which shows on a map of England the location of each estate whose bounds match the search-terms or include particular form(s) or lemma(s), and a full-text display which shows the full text of a boundary-clause with varying levels of editorial notes and translations.

This final web-based resource is driven partially by the database and partially by the XML-based framework. In general, all searches are driven by the database, and all displays of full text come from the XML. This is consistent with the theoretical discussion at the start of this paper: as noted there, databases are good for structured data and structured searches, and XML is good for semistructured data such as text. However, this interaction between database and XML is unusual and has required some novel solutions to some difficult problems. A full discussion of these is beyond the scope of this paper, but a brief summary can be presented. To enable complex database-searches on words encoded in XML, the XML files are uploaded into the database in a one-off process and are connected to the tables of lemmas. This is done automatically, with one word per database-record, using a data-flow model. Searches for lemmas are done from the database using the standard query-language known as SQL. When matching lemmas or forms are found, there are two different types of text-based output which may be required (not including the graphical GIS output mentioned above). In some cases, the user may want only the word in its immediate context: this is the so-called "KWIC" display. In this case, since the full text is not required, it is unnecessary and extremely inefficient to go to the full, encoded XML files for every text. Instead, fragments of XML are stored in the database and these are used for such display. On the other hand, if the user wishes to see the full boundary-clause matching his or her searches then the full XML file, complete with the metadata, can be used. The full file and the fragments both use essentially the same encoding model, and this means that the KWIC display can be formatted like the full text: this is important not only for consistency but also to alert the user to any doubts or editorial interventions in the material which is being examined.

This searching can be further enhanced by extended use of the glossary database. As discussed above, this database was intended primarily to map from forms to lemmas as an aid in markup, but it can also be used in the other direction to find all forms or occurrences of a given lemma.[38] The tables were thus designed in such a way that they could be imported back into the final relational database containing all the texts. A user could then search for a lemma as it appears in Smith's *Elements*, for example, or could even search for the Modern English translation of a lemma, and could then discover not only how that lemma is spelled in the other sources but could also find all the forms in the corpus, view a KWIC display of these forms, and even view a map of the locations of all the estates whose boundary-clause contains the relevant form or lemma. The structure of the database would then be something like that shown in fig. 6.

---

[38] For this database and the principle of mapping from lemmas to forms see § *Linguistic Analysis*.

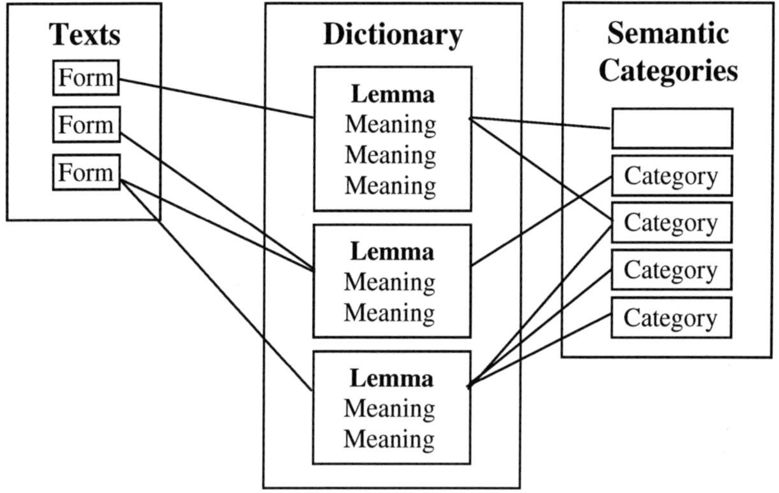

Fig. 6. Structure of semantic database

Conclusions

In addition to the *LangScape* resource itself, another useful outcome of the project is the many good lessons that have been learnt by all the people involved and that might fruitfully be shared with the scholarly community.

The design and development of a project such *LangScape* demonstrates that a resource in digital humanities is not a simple combination of computing techniques and humanities data. Instead the mixture of the two components is deeply interlaced: from the very beginning data must be analysed and modelled with an awareness of the computational techniques and instruments to be used. Conversely, these techniques and instruments cannot be developed without a thorough understanding of the complexities and unconventional structure that inevitably come with data in the humanities. Underestimating the complexity of computing in digital humanities projects can easily lead to a situation in which the technical development is felt to be extraneous to the research aims of the project, an unnecessary complication to the scholar's "real" work. The result of such a situation is usually one of underdeveloped resources, missed deadlines, and missed budgets, and the outcome very often satisfies the researchers' needs barely, if at all.

On the other hand, if the computing and humanities researchers work closely together and are careful to understand and accommodate each others' needs, then the result can be a much happier one. In the *LangScape* project, for example, we feel we were able to take advantage at a very high level of computing techniques at all stages. The emphasis on the structural model of the dataset followed naturally from the automatic processing which was required, but it also forced us to look at the data from unexpected points of view. The automation of different stages in data elaboration freed up precious project time, and facilities for checking helped to monitor and control the editorial process, allowing more rapid error-checking and better consistency of data.

These achievements required the cooperation of many people, and indeed the *LangScape* could not have been considered were not many different competencies available. These competencies ranged across much of computing and the humanities, including lexicography and database-management, encoding models and palaeography, geography and Java, onomastics and XML, and much more besides. The availability of such a large and multiskilled team represented one of the main strengths of the project but was also one of its problematic points. Research projects in digital humanities are necessarily team-based projects as it is impossible to think of a single scholar possessing all the necessary skills, but the coordination of so many people and the consequent need to compromise viewpoints and requirements is often very difficult in practice. Nevertheless, in a world where "interdisciplinarity" and "multidisciplinarity" are often cited as goals but are increasingly now seen as overworked and under-realised ideals, projects such as *LangScape* offer exciting opportunities for collaboration in ways that were unimaginable until recently. Such projects are not to be undertaken lightly, but, if they are properly planned, if the pitfalls are understood in advance, and if the required skills and experience are available, then the results are most certainly worth the effort.[39]

References

Cameron, Angus / Amos, Ashley Crandell / diPaolo Healey, Antonette (eds.) (2003). *The Dictionary of Old English in Electronic Form: A–F*. Toronto, Pontifical Institute of Medieval Studies Department of Publications.

[39] The authors wish to thank Joy Jenkyns for her extensive comments on early versions of this paper. Any errors or inconsistencies that remain are, of course, entirely those of the authors.

Clark Hall, John R. (1960). *A Concise Anglo-Saxon Dictionary*, with a supplement by Herbert D. Meritt. Cambridge, Cambridge University Press [fourth ed.].

diPaulo Healey, Antonette (2008). "Dictionary of Old English: A-G Online" [http://www.mun.ca/Ansaxdat/] [posting to ANSAX-NET mailing list on 9th January].

Eggert, Paul (2005). "Text-encoding, Theories of the Text, and the 'Work-Site'", in *Literary and Linguistic Computing* 4: 425-435.

Fleming, R. (1985). "Monastic Lands and England's Defence in the Viking Age", in *English Historical Review* 100: 247-265.

Hüning, Matthias (n.d.). *TextSTAT Simple Text Analysis Tool.* [http://www.niederlandistik.fu-berlin.de/textstat/software-en.html] [computer software; accessed 9th November 2007].

Kelly, Susan (2005). *Charters of Malmesbury Abbey.* Oxford, Oxford University Press [Anglo-Saxon Charters 11].

Lowe, Kathryn A. (1999). "Latin Versions of Old English Wills", in *Journal of Legal History* 20: 1–23.

Gelling, Margaret / Cole, Ann (2003). *Landscape of Place-Names.* Stamford, Shaun Tyas [reprinted with corrections].

Miller, Sean (2001). *Charters of the New Minster, Winchester.* Oxford, Oxford University Press [Anglo-Saxon Charters].

Parsons, David / Styles, Tania *et al.* (1997–). *Vocabulary of English Place-Names*, 3 vols. Nottingham, Centre for English Name-Studies.

Sawyer, Peter H. (1968). *Anglo-Saxon Charters: An Annotated List and Bibliography.* London, Royal Historical Society [Royal Historical Society Guides and Handbooks 8].

Smith, Albert H. (1956). *English Place-name Elements*, 2 vols. Cambridge, Cambridge University Press.

Swan, Mary / Treharne, Elaine (eds.) (2000). *Rewriting Old English in the Twelfth Century.* Cambridge, Cambridge University Press.

SyncRO Soft Ltd. *How to Develop an <oXygen/> Plugin.* [http://www.oxygenxml.com/doc/HowToDevelopOxygenPlugins.pdf] [accessed 15th June 2006].

TEI Consortium (eds) (2007). *TEI P5: Guidelines for Electronic Text Encoding and Interchange.* [http://www.tei-c.org/Guidelines/P5/] [1.0. Last modified 28th October 2007; accessed 25th January 2008].

World Wide Web Consortium (W3C) (2006). *Namespaces in XML 1.0.* [http://www.w3.org/TR/REC-xml-names/, second edition 16th August] [accessed 25th January 2008].

World Wide Web Consortium (W3C) (2006b). *XML Inclusions (XInclude).* [http://www.w3.org/TR/xinclude/] [second edition 15th November] [accessed 25th January 2008].

Zipf, George K. (1949). *Human Behaviour and the Principle of Least Effort: An Introduction to Human Ecology.* New York, Haffner Publishing Company.

Web Sites

Charters Encoding Initiative (CEI) (2004). http://www.cei.uni-muenchen.de/index.htm [accessed 25th January 2008].

Dictionary of Old English (2007–). http://www.doe.utoronto.ca [accessed 27th January 2008].

Electronic Sawyer: Online Catalogue of Anglo-Saxon Charters (2007). http://www.esawyer.org.uk [accessed 15th February 2008].

A Key to English Place-Names (n.d.). http://www.nottingham.ac.uk/english/ins/epntest/intro.html [accessed 15th February 2008].

Language of Landscape: Reading the Anglo-Saxon Countryside (2008). http://www.langscape.org.uk [accessed 12th January 2008].

Perseus Digital Library (2005). http://www.perseus.tufts.edu [accessed 4th February 2008].

Production and Use of English Manuscripts 1060 to 1220 (2005). http://www.le.ac.uk/ee/em1060to1220 [accessed 22th January 2008].

Prosopography of Anglo-Saxon England (PASE) (2005). http://www.pase.ac.uk [accessed 18th January 2008].

Thesaurus of Old English (TOE Online) (2005). http://libra.englang.arts.gla.ac.uk/oethesaurus [accessed 29th January 2008].

ACCADEMIA DELLA CRUSCA'S ONLINE DICTIONARIES*

MARCO BIFFI

0 Introduction

Lessicografia della Crusca in rete [Crusca's online dictionaries] is the title given to the five online editions of *Vocabolario degli Accademici della Crusca*. This project, funded by the Italian Government,[1] was launched in 2001 and ended in 2006, when the database and the search engine for consultation became available on the *Accademia*'s website (www.accademiadellacrusca.it), linked from the section "Virtual library" (the electronic version of *Vocabolario* is also available on www.lessico-grafia.it).

Lessicografia della Crusca in rete is both a digital library and an electronic vocabulary. The text of the first four editions (1612, 1623, 1691, 1729-1738) was entirely transcribed and annotated with markers, and the whole text of all five editions (including the fifth one, published from 1863 to 1923 and left unfinished up to letter *O*, headword *ozono*) was also acquired as digital image. As a digital library, *Lessicografia della Crusca in rete* gives the opportunity to show the digital images of all the 22 volumes of the five editions of *Vocabolario* (one volume for the 1612 edition, one for the 1623 edition, three for the 1691 edition, six for the 1729-1738 edition, eleven for the fifth and last edition), for a total of over

* *Accademia della Crusca* is institutionally in charge of promoting and circulating the Italian language in collaboration with similar institutions in foreign countries and some organisations of both the Italian Government and the European Union that work towards plurilinguism in Europe. During the Conference *Lexicography in Italy and in Europe* the talk, devoted to an instrument *Accademia* has developed to enhance both *Vocabolario* and the Italian linguistic heritage, was given in Italian. This written version in English is motivated by the reasons of coherence within the volume.

[1] With a grant ("Otto per Mille") from *Presidenza del Consiglio dei Ministri.*

20,000 pages. The first four editions, in addition to the facsimile reproduction, are also available in full electronic transcription. All the electronic data, either in text or image format, can be searched by headwords in all the editions of *Vocabolario*; furthermore, the first four editions, thanks to both their transcription and markup, allow a precise and systematic search of the lexical (and lexicographical) database, which is very important for Italian and its history.

For the construction of the database and the search engine, *Accademia* collaborated with a team of young researchers and with several institutions: the Institute *Opera del Vocabolario Italiano – Consiglio Nazionale delle Ricerche* for the database, the MICC – Media Integration and Communication Center of the University of Florence for the software to access the digital library and for the search engine, which was named *Cruscle*.[2]

1 The *Vocabolario degli Accademici della Crusca* from Paper to Web

Vocabolario degli Accademici della Crusca is both a milestone for the history of Italian and a very innovative model for Western lexicography.

The 1612 edition was published in a very controversial cultural and linguistic climate, after a long debate regarding the most suitable model of literary language to adopt nationwide. During the first half of the sixteenth

[2] The credits (from the homepage of the website) are as follows. Project manager: Massimo Fanfani and Marco Biffi; database project: Domenico Iorio Fili, Andrea Boccellari, Massimo Fanfani, Marco Biffi; definition of the XML/TEI markup: Domenico Iorio Fili, Andrea Boccellari; text transcription and markup: Claudia Bichi, Silvia Dardi, Fiammetta Fiorelli, Rossella Gasparrini, Cecilia Palatresi; transcription and treatment of headwords in the fifth edition: Marina Bongi; transcription of Greek texts: Elena Bonaccini, Mariella Canzani, Giulio Niccoli; project direction and production of the research software: Alberto Del Bimbo (MICC – Media Integration and Communication Center). Personnel from MICC have collaborated with the team from *Crusca*: specifically, Thomas Alisi, Gianpaolo D'Amico, Niccolò Becchi, Giuseppe Becchi. Apart from the above-mentioned researchers from *Accademia della Crusca*, Giovanni Salucci has also contributed to the project for the database and the search engine. The term *Cruscle* was coined by the technicians of the MICC and was used in the first demo version in a working session at *Accademia*, but proved to be so useful and effective that it has been preserved to indicate an advanced search (*Ricerca esperta* [professional research] in the menu for the user) within the database. The project and the instruments that have been implemented are described in Alisi et alii 2006, Biffi / Fanfani 2006 e Biffi (2007: 172-77), which thus constitute a premise to this work.

century, three different theses were put forward: the model of *Tre Corone*, following especially Petrarch for poetry and Boccaccio for prose (Bembo's thesis); the thesis of an eclectic language, based on a learned *koiné*, especially that learned, aristocratic and over-regional *koiné* spoken at the Papal Court; the thesis of the model of contemporary Florentine language, favoured by those who regarded the Florentine of the fourteenth century as a dead language. In the second half of the sixteenth century, Varchi acted as a mediator in *questione della lingua* [dispute on language], suggesting the use of the learned Florentine of the sixteenth century as a reference model. In the end it was Salviati, Varchi's pupil, who suggested a way to settle the debate: adopt a Florentine of the fourteenth century that included all the works of that period and the following ones written in such a language, not only *Tre Corone*. According to Salviati, *Accademia della Crusca* created an instrument to promulgate this model of language: the *Vocabolario*, consisting of entries sorted alphabetically, with an explanation of the word, examples from "good writers", and some idiomatic or etymological information.

Such a dictionary represents on the one hand a treasure of fourteenth century language made available to writers from the seventeenth to the nineteenth century, thus becoming, with its five editions, an emblematic corpus of Italian; on the other hand, thanks to its very innovative rationale, it becomes a model for the lexicography of other European languages. In addition, if *Vocabolario* is basically normative, yet it can also be regarded as a historical dictionary, since it puts forward a set of diachronical examples that explain the several uses and meanings of words, validating their authenticity. Finally, if fourteenth century Florentine is proposed in headwords (even with the restrictions mentioned above), contemporary Florentine ("fiorentino argenteo") emerges in the entry, both in definitions and idiomatic expressions.[3]

The well-known benefits of the passage from the printed version of *Vocabolario* to the electronic version do not lie either in the higher speed of data accessing, or in their quicker and easier updating, but rather in two structural features of the lexicographical software, which are:

1) Modern dictionaries consist of entries with the same structure (headword, part of speech, definition, examples) and are thus a text that, if printed as a book, can only prioritise one of its elements, since the entries need to be placed one after the other (traditionally, in alphabetical order,

[3] The definition of *Fiorentino argenteo* is due to Arrigo Castellani (cf. Castellani 1967-1970); a first systematic description of the changes Florentine underwent can be found in Manni 1979 (then also Manni 2003: 55-60).

which is the easiest way to find a word and obtain information). Transforming the dictionary in a set of searchable entries means transforming it into a real database, restoring its original nature and making it searchable by different fields, more or less formalised, included in the structure of its entries.

2) An electronic dictionary also becomes a text of is own, whatever its original criteria, and can be consulted as a textual database, regardless the rationale of its data. It thus becomes a linguistic corpus in which one can search different word forms within the entries, as if the dictionary were a set of literary texts or treatises. But the structure can, if necessary, be restored at any moment: once the dictionary has become a real database, it can be systematically searched also within the entries even by limiting the search to one or more fields and choosing each time specific subcorpora. The importance of this very peculiar corpus obviously depends on the type of dictionary and the criteria of its compilation, but the richness of the linguistic data is an added value in itself, whatever the data.

Both features are important for the study and the analysis of *Vocabolario degli Accademici*, on account of the criteria adopted in its compilation (see above). First of all, the full text search allows one to find all the words contained in it, not only headwords (that mostly belong to fourteenth century Italian), but also words hidden in definitions, notes, observations, digressions (that belong to the Italian used by editors). This possibility was immediately recognised by scholars such as Giovanni Nencioni, who used to call it *rovesciamento* [reversing] of the dictionary.

The transformation into a database has also other important benefits, most notably the fact that unveiling the structure of the entries left implicit by the editors by marking the different fields (headword, definition, example, etc.; foreign word, idioms, etc.) enables targeted queries in each field. The advantages of accessing independently both the language of definitions (used by the editors, and so ensuing the sixteenth century) and the language of examples (fourteenth century) are noticeable. The markup of the different fields (for example definition and example) makes it possible to limit the query to one chronological variety, by discriminating the language of the sources and the one of the editors.

Accademia della Crusca experienced the potentialities of Information Technology (IT) for the first time with the first edition of *Vocabolario*, within a twenty-year project started by Giovanni Nencioni (President of *Accademia della Crusca* at the time) and Severina Parodi,[4] and coordi-

[4] Severina Parodi, a member of *Accademia della Crusca*, devoted most of her activities at the *Accademia* to the study of *Vocabolario* (among her works, see for

nated by Mirella Sessa. The starting point was in the idea that an electronic version would enable a reversing of the text, i.e. an alphabetical indexing of the whole content, so as to disclose the words (many, as scholars were aware of but could not substantiate) hidden in the definitions and the commentaries of the editors that were ignored in the wordlist strictly depending on ancient Florentine. Started in 1980, the project, after changing fortunes due to rapid transformations in the indexing techniques and data management, produced in 2001 the online version of *Vocabolario* of 1612: the software was created by *Centro di Ricerche Informatiche per i Beni Culturali della Scuola Normale Superiore di Pisa* (see www.accademiadellacrusca.it, *Biblioteca virtuale* and then *Vocabolario 1612*).[5] The electronic version of *Vocabolario* of 1612 (without images) is structured according to macro-contexts (definition with examples, definition without examples, example) and micro-contexts (subheadword with examples, subheadword without examples, cross-reference mark, commentary, locution, integration, Latin counterpart, Greek counterpart, bibliographical abbreviation, generic context). Words can thus be searched not only within the text of the entries, but also in specific contexts (both macro and micro). It appears that the macrocontexts of the examples can be separated from those of the definitions, thus making it possible to access the language the editors used in the definitions: the latter is rich in expressions and idioms belonging to the Florentine of the sixteenth and seventeenth centuries, and, more generally, words not scheduled as headwords, that elude a systematic search in the paper edition.

When the electronic version of *Vocabolario* of 1612 was about to be completed, the *Accademia* was already thinking of extending the project to all five editions. Actually, "to extend" is not the right term: with the addition of other editions, the general planning and the descriptive scheme of the entries has changed, in order to allow textual comparison between different editions. Considering either only one edition or the whole collection implies changes in the nature of the object, as well as in the research's perspectives: a database of the first four editions of *Vocabolario* becomes a tool for historical lexicography and also for history of lexicography. On the one hand, the possibility to consult the whole rich set of

---

example Parodi 1974, a collection containing the proceedings concerning the first edition).

[5] For further information, also historical, on the project, apart from the material available online, cf. Sessa 2001 (also for the bibliography); for the rationale of the project see also Sessa 1982; for a brief description of querying strategies see Biffi (2007: 170-172).

examples in the four editions means making research from the end of sixteenth century (when the first *questione della lingua* had just been solved) to the first half of nineteenth century (when the second one began, with Manzoni and *Unità d'Italia*);[6] on the other hand, the opportunity to see the evolution of a word through the four editions of one of the most prestigious and age-old vocabularies in Europe means analysing the development of the lexicographical method.

It is in this concern that two important features of *Lessicografia* have to be highlighted: 1) systematic parallel comparison of corresponding entries (i.e. entitled to the same headword) in different editions; 2) presence of text and images (on this aspect *Accademia*'s projects move away from both computerised French lexicography, more focused on electronic text and its markup rather than facsimiles, and the Spanish one, that for the historical part privileges images). In fact, the electronic search form always accesses quantitative data, specific context and its entry; but also the facsimile of the original document (see § 3.2.2), the only one able to restore the fidelity of the page in its layout, a fundamental quality for the lexicographical approach, irreparably lost because of the necessary compromises due to the passage to an electronic text. Besides, the visualisation of an entry comes with a synoptic table that shows the presence of the same headword as an entry in all the other editions and enables its access with just a click (see § 3.2.2).

2 The Database

The first step in planning the database was the overall plan of the markup system of the first four editions of *Vocabolario*, picking out those elements that had to be highlighted.

As hinted in the previous paragraph, one of the main points of the project was the need to define the language of the editors and the language of the examples. Then, a deeper analysis suggested that it was also important to define a third linguistic nucleus: the annotations added by the academicians to the examples, in order to account for them. Obviously,

[6] It is worth observing that the representativeness of the corpus is remarkable, as *Vocabolario* includes a very rich selection of examples of language use on which Italian cultural tradition was grounded between the seventeenth and nineteenth centuries. These texts are not always those that modern philology has reconstructed, but those that *Accademia della Crusca* used and that had a great influence on writers. When there arise differences with modern critical editions, this corpus allows the researcher to see the reference model the writers of the past had in mind.

they belong to the language of definitions, but are plunged into the language of the examples. A fourth category is dictated by logic and by computer needs: it is the category of headwords, that has to be isolated and stressed as peculiar linguistic context, using it as a keyword to access search and visualisation functions. A first, broad descriptive scheme is therefore composed of four macrocontexts: headword, definition, example and commentary. The scheme is simplified in comparison with that of the first electronic version of *Crusca* of 1612, for which it was significant to distinguish among the macrocontexts definitions with example from definitions without example, also stressing grammatical or etymological information (or both). Simplification became necessary for two reasons: free the computer treatment from interpretative markup and make the scheme more flexible and functional to the description of the following editions of *Vocabolario*. The problem of the interpretative schemes is very important: thrusting the rationalisation in a narrow specificity means, at last, forcing the instrument to a particular way of analysis (the one originated by the database project), taking the risk of jeopardising the results of different ones. The main choice was to arrange a scheme that could enable the most varied typologies of search, with options that allow for various interpretative searches.

Once the fundamental macrocontexts were defined it seemed relevant, in order to enrich the database's potential in relation to words that are not headwords, to note down locutions, proverbs, and colloquial expressions as well. The individuation of part of texts that correspond to locutions or colloquial expressions is not always easy, and therefore some general criteria had to be established and used with homogeneity: the category *locuzione* [locution] refers to locutions in the proper sense (with verb in the infinitive form – for instance *far la gatta morta*; for expressions with conjugated verb the marked up infinitive form can be added), idioms (always adding the infinitive form: for instance *Egli ha dato nel bue* is accompanied with a marked up note *dare nel bue*), noun phrases, verb phrases, adverb phrases and prepositional phrases; the category *parola dell'uso vivo* [colloquial expression] refers to words whose contemporaneity to the editor is testified by contextual signals, such as *oggi si dice* [today we say], *i moderni dicono* [contemporary people say] etc. or other expressions that stress a clear contrast between old and contemporary use.

As for the operation of picking out words hidden in different editions of *Vocabolario*, subheadwords have been treated with particular attention: some of them have been highlighted by the *cruscanti* (pointing them out in capital letters), others can be implicitly obtained from the context. In this case, as well as for locutions, it was necessary to establish some general criteria. Among the words that have been recorded as subheadwords there are: 1) words followed by a definition (also implicit); 2) antonyms that refer to another headword; 3) "etymons" (with or without an explanation) to which users are referred to; 4) collective plurals whose meaning differs from that of the headword; 5) synonyms (those introduced by *diciamo*, *si dice* 'we say', and the like); 6) reflexive forms of the verb (in the infinitive) if explicitly mentioned in the definition. Proper nouns, morphological variants, plurals without semantic variation and conjugated verbs to which users are referred have not been included.

Another topic that has deserved much attention is the treatment of non-Italian words: words from Latin, Greek and other languages have been marked up with subclassification of each language.

Finally, great care was taken for the sources quoted in the examples, indicated with abbreviations: it was a priority that all authors and their works had to become systematically easy to find in the four editions of *Vocabolario*. To enable a surgical analysis of all examples of any authors and any work, that in the originals are referred to with an abbreviation, it is necessary to mark up the synthetic formulas used by the academicians. Each abbreviation consists of a fixed part, that indicates author and work, and of a variable one, that indicates the specific passage: each abbreviation has been marked up keeping these two parts separate, in order to obtain a list of all the fixed abbreviations that have been used. This process, as we shall see below, made it possible to link different abbreviations of a work with a bibliographical record, starting from which we can find out all the passages; vice versa, tracing it back, we can have the explicitation of the abbreviation. Users of old dictionaries will immediately notice that the usability of the text increases a lot: one of the trickiest problems in historical lexicography is that examples are always quoted with an abbreviation, but there is no biunique mapping between abbreviation and work (more abbreviations generally correspond to one work, and they are not always explained by editors). Once all abbreviations are marked up, it is possible to get a list of the abbreviations that have actually been used; and than, linking each abbreviation to the appropriate work's title and author through a database, it is easy to produce a true and functional table of abbreviations (also comparable with the one of the editors).

Thus, in addition to the four macrocontexts (headword, definition, example and commentary), there are also several microcontexts in the markup plan: subheadword (type *A*, implicit; type *B*, made explicit by editors by using capital letters); colloquial expression; proverb; locution; Greek word; Latin word; word from another foreign language (the languages emerging from the markup are: Arabic, Castilian, Hebrew,

Etruscan, French, Provençal, Spanish, Turkish, German); bibliographical abbreviation.

According to this, the markup system shows two levels of annotations (macrocontexts level and microcontexts level), and for this reason it has to manage a nested markup (a microcontext is always included within a macrocontext). Furthermore, if macrocontexts are, according to definition, the upper level (i.e. a textual portion belongs always to only one of those), microcontexts can overlap (for instance a subheadword can be marked up as colloquial expression and locution).

The scheme and the preliminary analysis of entries in the four editions of *Vocabolario* – which although obey to some general principles, have not been planned to be rigid suggested that the best possible approach to retrieve all the requested information was a full text markup with an XML/TEI schema.[7] Such approach would allow the use of a standard markup, potentially connected with similar tools. This markup has the advantage of being both a signal of textual boundaries and of textual portions with specific features, giving the possibility, in the first case to filter the search by limiting it to the marked parts, in the second to find all words or phrases concerning a marker (mainly functional with single words, locutions and proverbs, but also with macrocontexts such as definitions and examples). Then the suitable markers have been selected among the set of TEI markers for dictionaries (a total of twenty-one elements was selected)[8] and their hierarchy has been established, defining the appropriate DTD (Document Type Definition).[9]

The marker <entry> has been chosen for entries, using attribute *hom* for disambiguating the homographs (for example, more entries have *a* as headword). The headword, that always includes original punctuation (and, when represented with two or three spelling variants, it includes conjunctions too), has been marked with <form>, defining the spelling string with <orth>; the main part of the entry has been limited with

---

[7] Cf. Sperberg-McQueen / Burnard 2002; cf. also the web site www.tei-c.org. As is well known, TEI also includes peculiar markup for dictionaries, with a rich set of markers.

[8] Apart from the twenty-one markers that have been specifically used for the organisation of the headwords in the digital edition, there are also some conventional markers for XML/TEI files according to the TEI Header and the two markers <text> and <body> which identify the body of the text.

[9] At this planning stage, especially for the definition of XML/TEI markup, collaboration with *Opera del Vocabolario Italiano*, Florentine Institute of CNR, was precious (see also n. 1).

<sense>, separating the other three macrocontexts with <def> [definition], <eg> [example] and <note> [commentary]. Other markers are: <usg> [colloquial expression], <emph> [proverb], <idiom> [locution], <ovar> [subheadword], <foreign> [non Italian words; attribute *lang* specifies each language: Greek, Latin, etc., see above]. Cited abbreviations of works have been marked up with <abbr>, limiting the fixed part with <ref>.

Some annotations became necessary for a functional browsing of the database, as well as for managing internal cross-references; in this case the starting point has been marked with <xr>, and the arrival with <hi>, so that a hypertextual link is possible during the visualisation.

The marker <add> is fundamental as well, and it is used in order to recognise all those parts that constitute an addition to the original text, inserted in the electronic version by operators. The text has been copied with great philologic accuracy and great respect for the original edition: only misprints have been corrected (*u* instead of *n*, series of three consonants or vowels, visible confusion of letters, reversal of consonants and vowels, omission of letters in presence of blank spaces, etc.) with no notifications (although all the corrections have been recorded). There are also cases in which corrections are necessary; however it would be like deleting history if no references were added, even considering that one of the main tasks of this project is to give access to research into the lexicographical history of *Crusca*. In this cases the necessary corrections have been introduced thanks to a suitable marker.

Corrections are even more necessary in those parts of the dictionary with a strong lexical specificity, or where mistakes and omissions would compromise the surfing in the electronic text. We have already hinted at some of these cases above, for example in locutions, where the phrase with infinitive verb is added when conjugated (then, in the example referred to – *Egli ha dato nel bue* – *Egli ha dato nel bue <add>dare nel bue</add>* is obtained with markers); once more, the conversational style in which some locutions appear in the entry imposes a forced rationalisation, in order to make a different search possible (for instance, for *erba giudaica detta anche pagana*, *erba pagana* was added, avoiding the loss of the locution; or, while the markup of *governare e comandare a bacchetta* as a whole would not allow to track down *comandare a bacchetta*, the addition *governare <add> a bacchetta </add> e comandare a bacchetta* allows it). Abbreviations are also fundamental for a systematic query: here as well, additions are frequent if they make the information more rational and transparent. There is a large case record for this. In many cases the title of the work is not specified, either because only the author is indicated (that however might be related to more than one text), or because two passages of the same work are quoted together (the first time) and linked with a conjunction: clearly, without making the abbreviation explicit, a search on that work would skip the second passage. All the additions have been rigorously marked with <add> (a very extensible marker, able to mark up texts in different fields, thanks to XML/TEI schema); therefore, it is always possible to foresee two levels of textual search: one excludes additions and refers to the original, printed text; the other one includes additions, giving access to an "arranged" text , which guarantees systematic results in the electronic search.

As for the delicate passage from paper to electronic format, some explanations about punctuation, apostrophes and Greek letters are necessary. Punctuation marks have been faithfully reproduced, even when different from modern criteria: abbreviation points have been indicated with the character *$*, so that during tokenisation they could be distinguishable from the full stop; according to this, the string *Bocc.* (abbreviation for *Boccaccio*) is considered as one token, while in *discoprendo. Laonde* the tokens are three: *discoprendo / . / Laonde* (the decision made since the beginning was to optimise the search of punctuation as well, together with search by word forms, in order to make syntactic analysis possible: each punctuation mark has not been eliminated during tokenisation, on the contrary it has been recognised and then indexed as well as words). The apostrophes and accents in the text have been faithfully reproduced: for example, *perche*, *perché*, *perchè* remain as three different word forms; and the accent on the final *-e* of Latin adverbs remains unchanged, as was in the use of the time. As for apostrophes, a change was necessary in order to simplify comprehension and, above all, electronic search easier (for example, *dacqua* has been changed into *d'acqua*).[10] As for Greek, UNICODE characters have been used, which makes it possible to perfectly manage the large amount of Greek words during both visualisation and search (with recent browsers it is possible to copy Greek words from the text, paste them in search fields and find their occurrences).[11]

---

[10] During tokenisation, we applied Italian rules to the apostrophe, not English rules as happens in many search engines (even in the most common ones on the web): according to Italian rules, apostrophe is part of what comes before. Then, in the string *d'acqua* we have two tokens, *d'* and *acqua*, and not only one (*d'acqua*) as would be according to English rules (see for instance *it's*, managed as a unique token).

[11] This task is now possible with Mozilla Firefox but not with Internet Explorer (version 7). The implementation of various Internet browsers will make it possible

The markup system is completed by the marker of the original printed text boundaries (<pb>), with codification of the original page number (attribute *pag*): together with other data, it provides users with a complete topographic reference (edition, volume, page), that links to the facsimile of the original.[12]

Our first task was to look for a suitable informatic way of managing the entries of the four editions of *Vocabolario*. But we also had to consider the general structure of the database, also considering the other parts of the volumes: prefaces, dedicatory epistles, tables of abbreviations, corrigenda and additions; and considering the need to allow the reader to access the whole database, but also a specific edition or a specific section.

As for the separated access to different editions, markers in each XML/TEI file header identify each volume, enabling the search into a single edition.

All the unstructured and unstructurable texts (such as dedicatory epistles and prefaces and introductions in general) have been gathered together under the label "*Apparati*" [paratext] and treated as free texts, with no specific markup, according to the XML/TEI rules; corrigenda and additions have been considered as entries, but with markers in each XML/TEI file header that enable their inclusion or exclusion from search.

The management of tables of abbreviations has been more difficult. As said before, together with tables of abbreviations provided by academicians, the markup of abbreviations in entries provides a "real" table, i.e.

---

to perfectly manage UNICODE characters so that anyone will soon be able to visualise them.

[12] In comparison with the twenty-one markers described above, three still need to be accounted for. These markers are essential to define some technical aspects: 1) <testo> is used to set specific textual boundaries (for instance the full stop that automatically follows the headword, which needs to be visualised, but must be outside the marker of the headword <orth>); 2) <ptr>, a marker within the cross-reference markup that refers to the number identifying the homograph (only for headwords with such a number); 3) markers that closely follow TEI indications although not essential to reproduce the structure of the editions of *Vocabolario*, such as <quote>, which within the category of examples <eg> specifies those which are drawn from texts (in this case, they have all been drawn from texts, so we will always find the redundant sequence *<eg><quote>...</quote></eg>*). This latter case clearly illustrates the approach that was adopted when setting up the database and the need to closely follow TEI *Guidelines*, so as to make it possible to later integrate with other tools. In the case of examples the structure of *Lessicografia* perfectly favours integration with similar marked up XML/TEI dictionaries.

with all the abbreviations that have been used, and only these. The matter was, on the one hand, to gather all these data in a functional tool; on the other, to assure an easy linking from table of abbreviations to entries and vice versa, in order to jump from a bibliographical record of a work to its quoted passages and from a single passage to bibliographical details. The table has thus been built on a real database that contains bibliographical records of every quoted work. Each record contains both data as in the original tables of abbreviations, properly rationalised into fields (*Abbreviazione della Tavola* [abbreviation in the original table], *Indicazione nella Tavola* [explanation in the original table], *Titolo* [title], *Classificazione* [classification], *Descrizione* [description])[13], and data as rationalised by operators (a special section called *Informazioni normalizzate* [standardised information] contains the fields: *Autore ricostruito* [standardised author], *Volgarizzatore ricostruito* [standardised traslator], *Titolo opera ricostruito* [standardised title], *Abbreviazioni del lemmario* [abbreviations in entries], *Cronologia* [chronology], *Note* [notes]). Thanks to this scheme the database allows to retrieve a work even if the information of the academicians is not explicit, unclear or incorrect, still remaining faithful to their "work": if users are interested in the history of lexicography, they will privilege the part of the bibliographical record with data of the original tables of abbreviations; if they are interested in language history, they will consult the corpus starting from modern attributions and work's standard titles. Each record contains a field for all the abbreviations used for that work in all the editions of *Vocabolario* and makes the software able to find out all its quoted passages (from which those abbreviations have been extracted); abbreviations contained in entries become easily linkable to the relative bibliographical record. Besides, each record contains cross-reference to the original table and page in which the work is quoted, linking up with the digital facsimile, that shows to users the work of the academicians with the greatest fidelity to their typographical arrangement.

Finally, the fifth edition of *Vocabolario* (acquired only in digital images) deserves a separate treatment. Since the beginning, the linear browsing through digital pages seemed unsatisfactory, mainly because of the size of the work (eleven volumes for more than 10,000 pages); furthermore, the separation from the other four editions would limit the historical and lexicographical value of the tool. The solution was a compromise: headwords have been marked up, in order to obtain refe-

[13] These fields describe all kinds of event found in the four editions: generally, a short author/work record and a more or less extended description follow the list of abbreviations. Besides, original tables contain a list of ancient and modern authors.

rences to volume and page and a direct link to the page that contains the searched headword. This solution also allowed to integrate the fifth edition into the database search system, with many benefits (see § 3).

As said in the *Introduction*, *Lessicografia* is, besides an electronic dictionary and a digital linguistic corpus, a peculiar bookshelf of a digital library: the net surfer can take the volume he wants from the bookshelf and start to browse through its pages, with no specific word to search, as well as Niccolò Tommaseo did during his youth when he read the *Vocabolario degli Accademici della Crusca* «come si fa d'un libro» [in the way you read a book]. Since the beginning a special "Reading room" that would receive this particular reader was expected.

One of the most difficult problems with digital libraries is to give a versatile access to volumes: the solution is generally to put together images and metadata that identify at least pages, or chapters and paragraphs. As for dictionaries, the trend is to provide at least an alphabetical access, so that the net surfer doesn't have to browse hundreds of images before he finds the entry he needs and that starts, for example, with *s*.[14] Marked up full text and digital images, for the first four editions, and marked up headwords with reference to digital pages, for the fifth edition, have provided all the metadata necessary for a functional digital reading room, that will be better explained in the following paragraph.

[14] A similar strategy was employed by *Accademia* in its *Biblioteca Digitale*, available on the web under the heading *Biblioteca virtuale* at www.accademiadellacrusca.it (or directly from www.bdcrusca.it). The digital library contains 121 volumes for a total of 111,000 images. Its first core, called *Fonti descrittive e normative dell'italiano: corpus digitale di testi dal XVI al XIX secolo* is organised in four sections: 1) grammars of Italian published from the sixteenth to the nineteenth century; 2) texts devoted to reflections on the language and to the criticism against *Crusca*; 3) non official editions of *Vocabolario*; 4) nineteenth century lexicography. The digital library clearly appears as a complementary tool to *Lessicografia*, especially in the sections that are devoted to the dictionaries that complete the lexicographical background to the various editions of *Vocabolario*. The consultation of these digital dictionaries is very easy: in fact, the initial pages of each letter of the alphabet are identified (vowel followed by consonant: AB, AC, AD, AF etc; consonant followed by vowel: BA, BE, BI, BO, BU). For more information on *Biblioteca digitale dell'Accademia della Crusca* and, more generally, on databases related to the volumes in the digital library or the materials in the archive, cf. Biffi / Fanfani 2006 e Biffi 2008.

3 Consultation: From the Reading Room to the Search Engine

On entering the *Lessicografia* homepage (fig. 1), the database modalities are positioned on the left hand as follows: *Sala di lettura* [Reading room], *Ricerca* [search], *Ricerche guidate* [assisted search].[15]

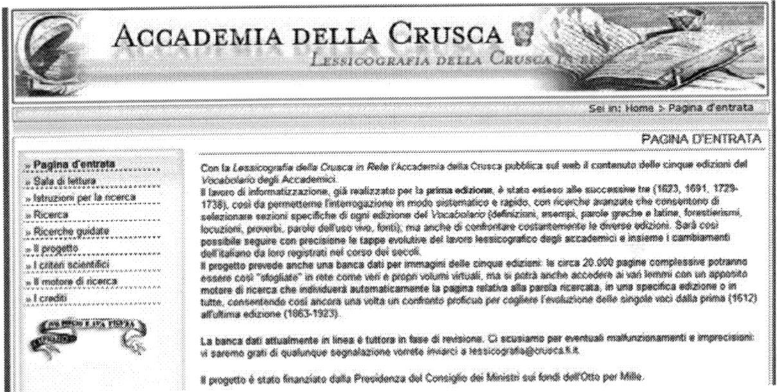

Fig. 1. Homepage of the *Lessicografia della Crusca in rete*

The three paths correspond to the expected approach of users to the provided tools: those who love to wander in between the library shelves, grab a book and look through it from cover to cover; those who look for a book, in our case a dictionary, because they have specific and precise questions in mind that need to be answered; those who approach a book without a precise idea of what they are looking for, but that are curious and open to suggestions for possible reading paths.

[15] The software technology for the access and the questioning of the databank, as we mentioned in the *Introduction*, was achieved by the MICC-Media Integration and Communication Center in collaboration with the *Accademia della Crusca* to determine the search engine computer-linguistic characteristics. The more specifically technical aspects of the reading procedures and of the databank questioning were stated in Alisi / Becchi 2006; to obtain a more detailed description we must make reference to the graduation thesis of Niccolò Becchi, *Sistema di ricerca multistrato per i vocabolari degli Accademici della Crusca*, a.a. 2004-2005, supervisors Alberto del Bimbo, Pietro Pala, Thomas Alisi.

3.1 "Reading Room"

The bibliophile will find a congenial approach in the "Reading room", which allows to access the digital version of the five editions of *Vocabolario*, both to the digital transcription and the facsimile reproduction by image (in the fifth edition, obviously, in the first case only the list of words is accessed). In both cases, after entering the room, a synoptic board will guide users in choosing edition, volume, specific section of a volume, according to the subdivision provided between paratext, entries, additions (fig. 2).

By clicking on one of the links it is possible to visualise the volume from the first page, by images (fig. 3) or in the digital version of the marked up text (fig. 4), and continue with the reading of the following pages through the available buttons.

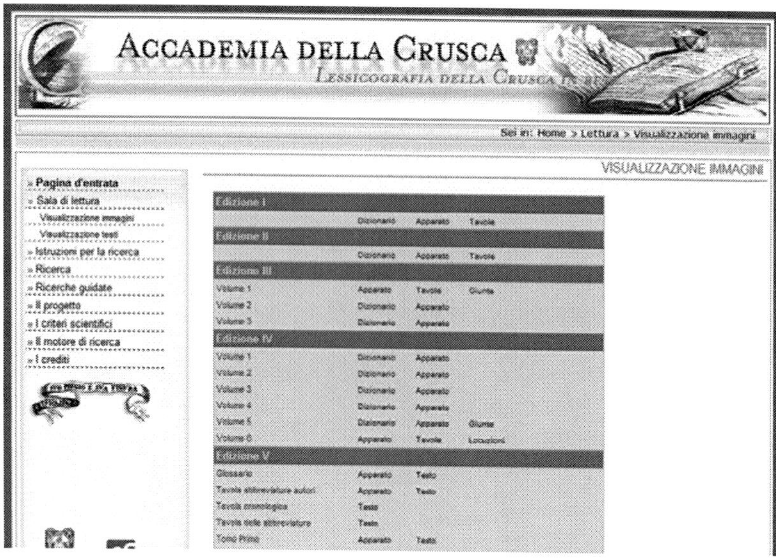

Fig. 2. Access to the "Reading Room" by images

Fig. 3. Reading by images

Fig. 4. Reading of the digital version

3.2 "Search"

There are three different levels of searching in the marked up digital text: *Ricerca libera* [free search], that addresses the need of the average users who simply wants to verify if a certain word appears or not in the *Vocabolario*; *Ricerca avanzata* [advanced search], especially devised for the researcher that wants to use all the possibilities offered by the structured marked up digitalisation of the data contained in the *Vocabolario*; *Ricerca esperta* [professional search], destined to the careful linguist that wants to exploit each small search parameter for his studies. The *Ricerca per immagini* [search by images], a fourth option shown in the menu, makes it possible to access the facsimile version of the *Vocabolario*.

3.2.1 "Search by Images"

Let us start immediately from the latter option, the easiest to use and illustrate. By choosing it, users can digit a string and decide if they want to extend the search to all or some editions: the string presence will be verified within the lists of headwords, leaving the possibility, through the specific check box, to use or not the additions inserted in the digital version.

The first result is a chart showing the quantitative data: for example, if we search *amore* we obtain three headwords (*amore*, *d'amore e d'accordo*, *per amore*), and the detailed occurrences in the singles editions are summed up for each of them, and within these, those in the single sections (D = *Dizionario*, G = *Giunte* [additions], L = *Lemmario* [wordlist]) (fig. 5).

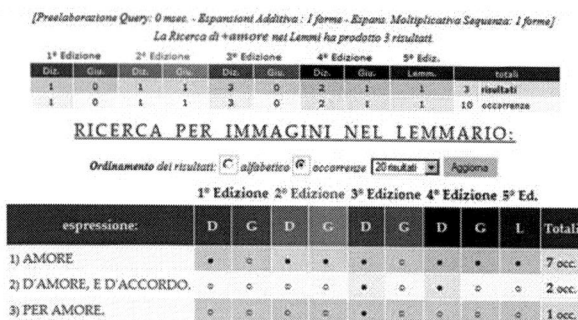

[Preelaborazione Query: 0 msec. - Espansioni Additiva : 1 forme - Espans. Moltiplicativa Sequenza: 1 forme]
La Ricerca di +amore nei Lemmi ha prodotto 3 risultati

1ª Edizione		2ª Edizione		3ª Edizione		4ª Edizione		5ª Ediz.	totali
Diz.	Giu.	Diz.	Giu.	Diz.	Giu.	Diz.	Giu.	Lemm.	
1	0	1	1	3	0	2	1	1	3 risultati
1	0	1	1	3	0	2	1	1	10 occorrenze

RICERCA PER IMMAGINI NEL LEMMARIO:

Ordinamento dei risultati: alfabetico occorrenze 20 risultati Aggiorna

	1ª Edizione		2ª Edizione		3ª Edizione		4ª Edizione		5ª Ed.	
espressione:	D	G	D	G	D	G	D	G	L	Totali
1) AMORE	•	◦	•	•	•	◦	•	•	•	7 occ.
2) D'AMORE, E D'ACCORDO.	◦	◦	◦	◦	•	◦	•	◦	◦	2 occ.
3) PER AMORE.	◦	◦	◦	◦	•	◦	◦	◦	◦	1 occ.

Fig. 5. "Search by images": result for the string *amore*

By clicking on each headword, you can move from this chart to a summary of the topographical references (fig. 6) and from here you can move to those pages that contain the entry in the chosen edition (fig. 7).

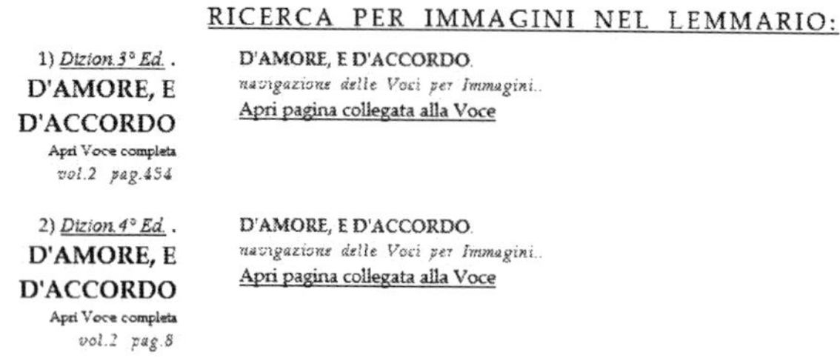

Fig. 6. "Search by images": Topographical references for *d'amore e d'accordo*

peccati, che non sono comunemente manifesti, ec. ma facciasi da lungi. Dan. Par. 16. Per giudicar da lungi mille miglia. E Inf. 8. E un'altra da lungi render cenno. Boc. Nov. 6. 10. Li quali stati alla sua predica, ed avendo udito il nuovo riparo preso da lui, e quanto da lungi fatto si fosse, ec. §. Talora in forza di preposizione, che col sesto, terzo, e quarto caso si congiunse: vale Lontano. Lat. *procul*. Cr. 2. 13. 16. Tutte le erbe ne' luoghi delle piante divelte si deono di presente gittar da lungi da loro. G. V. 7. 51. 2. Alcuna parte di loro gente a piede, e poi a cavallo da lungi all'oste valicaro il detto fosso lungo l' Arno. Boc. Vit. Dant. E così come essi stimavano questa eccedere ciascuna altra cosa di nobiltà, così vol-

DA MONTE A VALLE. Avverbialm. Da imo a som-mo, dal capo al piè. Lat. *a capite usque ad pedes.* Te-Br. 2. 36. Così come 'l sangue dell' huomo si sparg-per le sue vene, sicchè cerca tutto 'l corpo da mon-a valle, ec. E 1. 38. Egli procacciò tanto da monte e da valle, ch'egli combattè contro a Pompeo [alt-maniera dinotante Per tutti i versi, in tutti modi]

D'AMORE, E D'ACCORDO. Posto avverbialm. va-Unitamente, amichevolmente.

DA MOTTEGGIO. Lo stesso, che Da beffe. Lati-*iocose, per iocum*. All. p. 3. 153. Di quel saper, ch-non è da motteggio. E 159. Fatto parte in dadd-vero, e parte in da motteggio.

DAMUZZACCIA. Peggiorat. del diminut. di Dam-

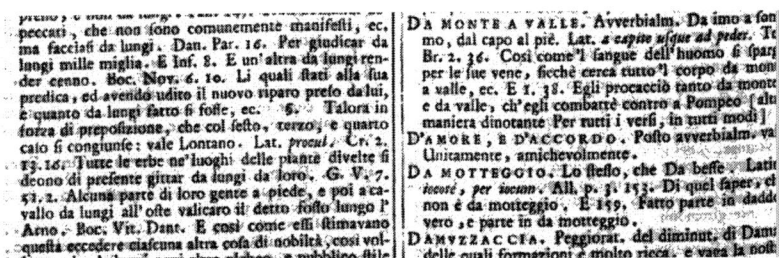

Fig. 7. "Search by images": visualisation (particular) of the entry *d'amore e d'accordo* (3rd edition)

3.2.2 "Free Search"

The "free search" in the marked up text displays again a search form similar to the one available in the search by images: here, filters are limited to single editions (considered, among other things, only for entries thus excluding "paratext" and additions); at this general level of search the consultation of the faithful edition of the text, excluding corrections, is also expected. The type of operation carried out by the computer procedure obviously changes. In this case, in fact, it is not limited to running through headwords, but results in an analytic search by word forms in the full text of the first four editions (and in the wordlist of the fifth).

By typing a word you can access to the chart of the quantitative data, and from here to the contexts' list with topographical references, then to the entry. By typing *frullone*, for example, you will obtain a first synthetic chart (fig. 8) that shows the two word forms corresponding to the string (*frullone* e *frullóne*, with original accentuation, see § 2) with all the quantitative data, the global one and those related to single editions (for the fifth edition only the occurrences in the wordlist).

	1° Edizione	2° Edizione	3° Edizione	4° Edizione	5° Ed.	
forma	Diz.	Diz.	Diz.	Diz.	Lem.	Totali
1) ☐ *frullone*	4	5	5	10	1	25 occ.
2) ☐ *frullóne*	0	0	4	0	0	4 occ.
Visualizza forme						

Fig. 8. "Free search": result for the string *frullone* (particular)

By clicking on a word form you will obtain the list of contexts: the searched word form is set inside the whole macrocontext (headword, definition, example, commentary) and next to every context the topographical reference is explained, with a link to the complete entry or to the facsimile of the page that contains the word itself (fig. 9). The list shows contexts in a order corresponding to a higher ranking, but users can choose to sort results according to the different editions, and, inside these, according to the alphabetical order of the entries.

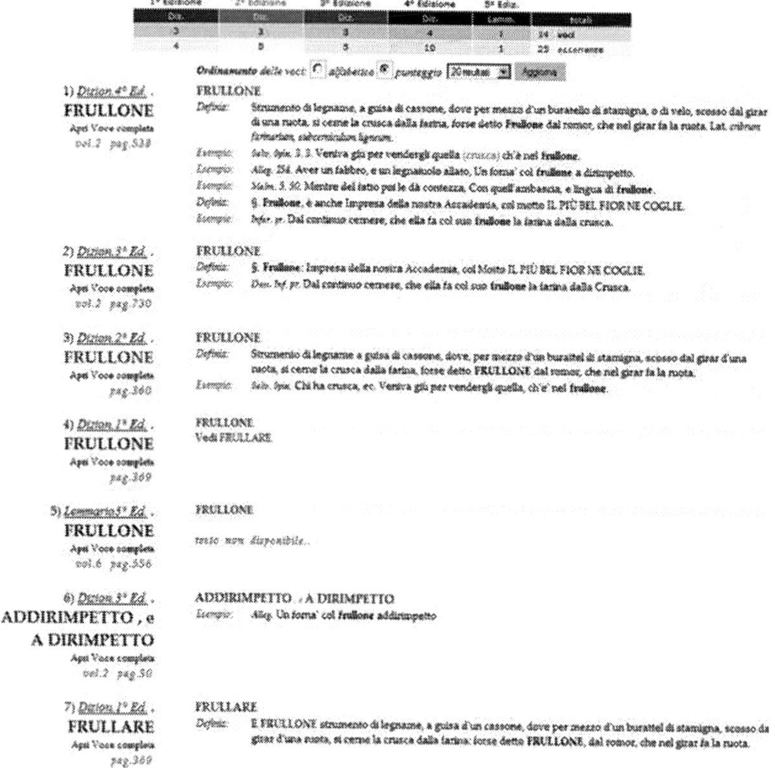

Fig. 9. Contexts of *frullone* (19 of 25)

Clicking on the link of the entry you can display the entire content and more: on the left side a chart will show the presence of that entry in the other editions – if it is the case – thus making possible to browse all the contents with a simple click (fig. 10).

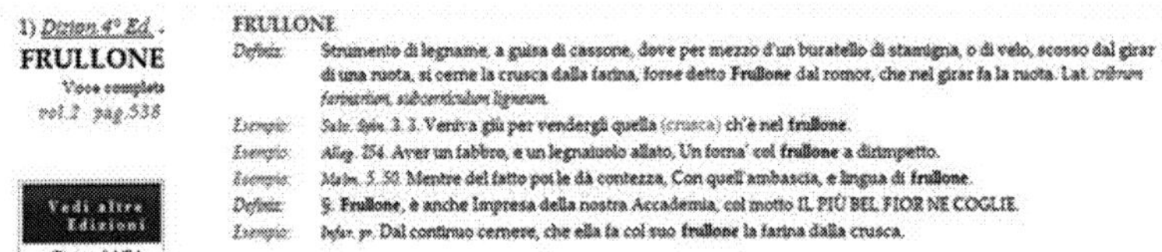

Fig. 10. Entry *frullone* in the 4th edition of the *Vocabolario*

If an entry is in an addition, the summary chart will inform the user, as it happens, for example, for the lemma *abbacinare* (fig. 11).

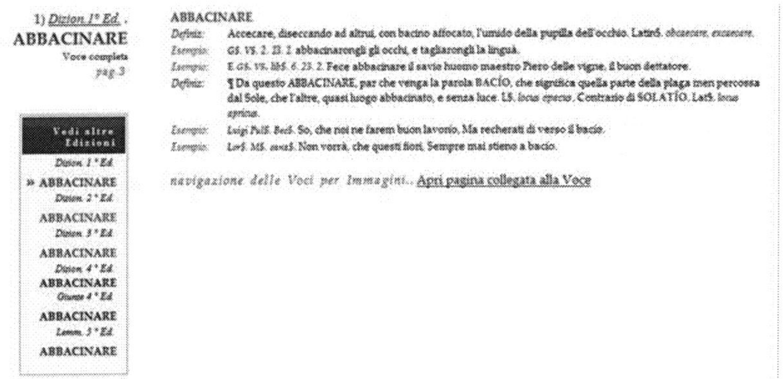

Fig. 11. Entry *abbacinare* in the 1st edition of the *Vocabolario*

Whenever some cross-references appear in one of the result display windows, being them either lists of occurrences or entire entries, a hypertextual link allows to reach the related headword. For example, while searching *stravizzo* and browsing the contexts window, in the first context, related to the headword *stravizzo* in the first edition, you only have the cross-reference “vedi MERENDA” (fig. 12): clicking on it, the entry MERENDA is opened, with the subheadword *stravizzo* (fig. 13) highlighted.

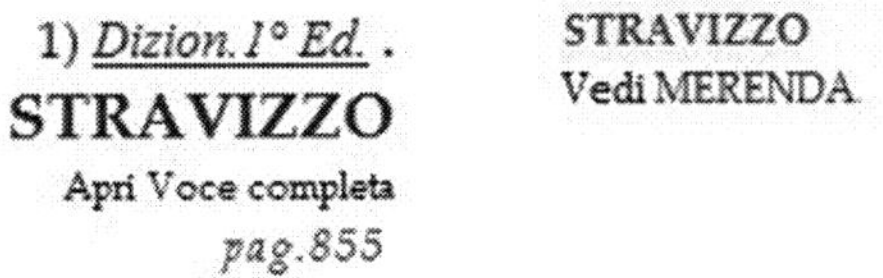

Fig. 12. Contexts of *stravizzo* in the 1st edition of the *Vocabolario*

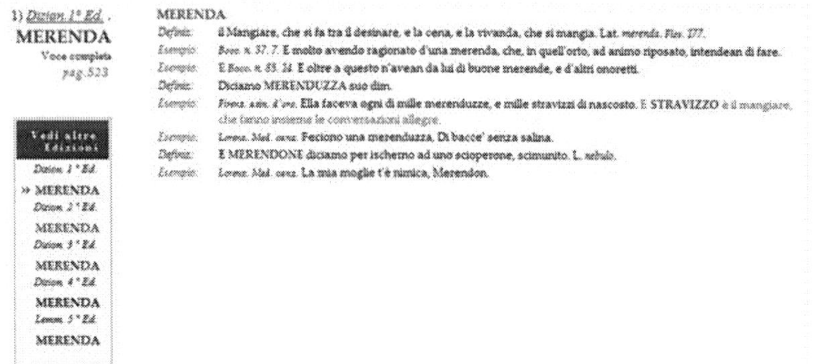

Fig. 13. Entry *merenda* in the 1st edition of the *Vocabolario*

Furthermore, in the same windows, all the fixed parts of the works' abbreviations are linked to the bibliographical database (see § 2). For the entry *merenda* (fig. 13), for example, clicking on the abbreviation *Firenz. asin. d'oro* you can get to the record with all the data concerning the quoted text, first of all in concise format (fig. 14), then in the analytical form clicking on the display button (fig. 15).

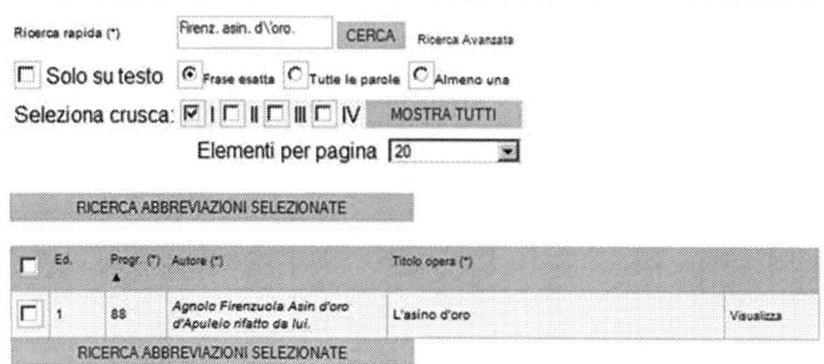

Fig. 14. Bibliographical database: short record of *Asino d'oro* translated into vernacular by Agnolo Firenzuola

As it appeared from the example of *frullone*, the word form search mode totally ignores stress marks. This choice, as well as case insensitiveness, is due to the fact that this search mode is suitable for a very general user that could loose some results (for example, the word forms *perché* or *perche*, or the Latin adverbs with *–é* if s/he doesn't have professional knowledge on history of spelling); as described later, a more analytical research is obtained by advanced query modes.

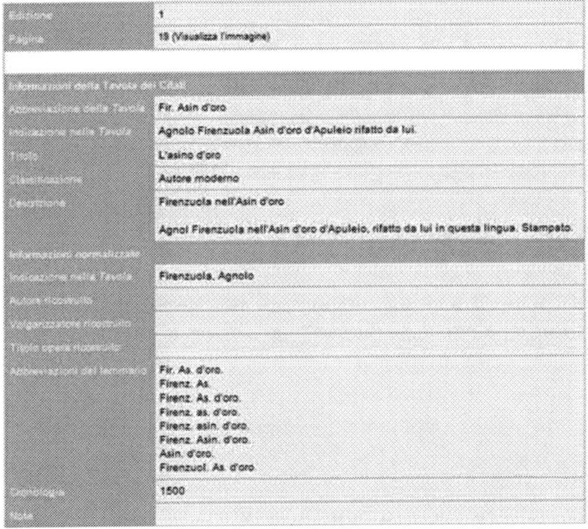

1
19 (Visualizza l'immagine)
Fir. Asin d'oro
Agnolo Firenzuola Asin d'oro d'Apuleio rifatto da lui.
L'asino d'oro
Autore moderno
Firenzuola nell'Asin d'oro
Agnol Firenzuola nell'Asin d'oro d'Apuleio, rifatto da lui in questa lingua. Stampato.
Firenzuola, Agnolo
Fir. As. d'oro.
Firenz. As.
Firenz. As. d'oro.
Firenz. as. d'oro.
Firenz. asin. d'oro.
Firenz. Asin. d'oro.
Asin. d'oro.
Firenzuol. As. d'oro.
1500

Fig. 15. Bibliographical database: analytical record of *Asino d'oro* translated into vernacular by Agnolo Firenzuola

It is worthwhile specifying that while designing the search engine of *Lessicografia* it was chosen to privilege an approach by word forms, since an automatic, or semi-automatic lemmatisation of ancient Italian was hardly possible (such procedures, based on modern dictionaries and standard languages, give good results only on contemporary written Italian texts) and a manual lemmatisation was to be excluded because of available budget. Search function features are limited while using only word forms or strings: results only contain a partial set of the morphological declension of a headword (and more: the set of its graphical-phonetic variants is partial too, due to the numerous variants in the editions of the *Vocabolario*)[16] and the lack of identification of homographs (for example,

[16] This "poverty" of the search engines by word form is particularly evident on verbs, whose declension is vast and frequently unpredictable or hard to manage (let's think of those verbs such as *andare* based on roots that differ according to modes and tenses: *andavano*, *andiamo*, *vanno*, *vado* etc.); while for what concern nouns and adjectives it is substantially easy to bypass thanks to a good use of the *jolly* characters in the final part of the string to search, as it will be shown below.

porta 'door' as noun and *porta* 'he brings' as verb). Like other similar search engines, the one designed for the *Lessicografia* provides strategies of overtaking these limits, by using some tools that, if advisably associated to a watchful and intelligent active competence of the user, allow on the one hand to recover possible gaps in the results and on the other to limit the signal to noise ratio. A first aid is given by wildcards (asterisk for any string and question mark for any character), freely usable in the search field (there are also other aids, such as the *Ignora accenti* [ignore stress marks] mentioned above).

A good example could be offered by a survey on the lucky word *colazione:* typing the string in the search box, only six results are returned, distributed between the third and forth editions.

A real problem of a search engine by word form is its inability to give back the entire morphological declension (for example, the plural) and phonetic variants (for example, the similar *colazion*, absolutely regular within the Italian phonetic frame, particularly in ancient texts). This problem could easily be solved searching the string *colazion?*: that would end up giving back the result *colazion* (1 occurrence) and also assuring the absence of the plural *colazioni.*

A wiser user, however, could suspect that other phonetic variants could exist, especially as far as vowels and dental affricate are concerned. A skilful use of the wildcards would allow to penetrate the depths of the database: by typing in *c?l??ion?* the user would have taken into account all possible variants. In fact, this search detects a longer list of word forms related to the word *colazione* (fig. 16). Some of the results obtained are "noise", but in this way also *colezione* (43 occurrences), *colezion* (six) and *colizione* (three) besides of *colazione* and *colazion* are tracked down.

The search by wildcards allows to focus the initial or final part of the words such as prefixes and suffixes. By searching, for example, for the string **udine*, the result will be a list of word forms with the suffix *-udine* (fig. 17), even though with possible noise that will force the user to evaluate the result.

The list of word forms can be either ordered alphabetically or by number of occurrences, which makes it possible to create alphabetical indexes or decreasing frequency indexes. Combining this option with wildcards, by typing * in the search box you obtain the alphabetical index and

---

However, it must be noticed that in this case the peculiar characteristics of the text, considering that the *Vocabolario* tends to show already "lemmatised" forms (that is reported to the infinitive if verbs, to singular if nouns, to masculine singular if adjectives), considerably reduce this limit, also for what concern verbs.

the decreasing frequency index of all the word forms in the four editions of the *Vocabolario*; and, thanks to the possibility of getting back to the contexts list of any word form, a complete hypertextual concordance can be obtained.

1ª Edizione	2ª Edizione	3ª Edizione	4ª Edizione	5ª Ediz.	
Diz.	Diz.	Diz.	Diz.	Lemm.	totali
1	5	5	7	3	10 forme
6	9	23	35	3	76 occorrenze

TAVOLA DELLE OCCORRENZE:

Ordinamento delle forme: alfabetico occorrenze 20 risultati Aggiorna

	1ª Edizione	2ª Edizione	3ª Edizione	4ª Edizione	5ª Ed.	
forma	Diz.	Diz.	Diz.	Diz.	Lem.	Totali
1) *colezione*	6	5	16	16	0	43 occ.
2) *calicione*	0	1	1	7	1	10 occ.
3) *colazione*	0	0	1	4	1	6 occ.
4) *colezion*	0	1	3	2	0	6 occ.
5) *calicioni*	0	1	0	2	0	3 occ.
6) *colizione*	0	0	0	3	0	3 occ.
7) *caliciòni*	0	0	2	0	0	2 occ.
8) *caldaione*	0	0	0	0	1	1 occ.
9) *caligioni*	0	1	0	0	0	1 occ.
10) *colazion*	0	0	0	1	0	1 occ.

Fig. 16. "Free search": result for the string *c?l??ion?*

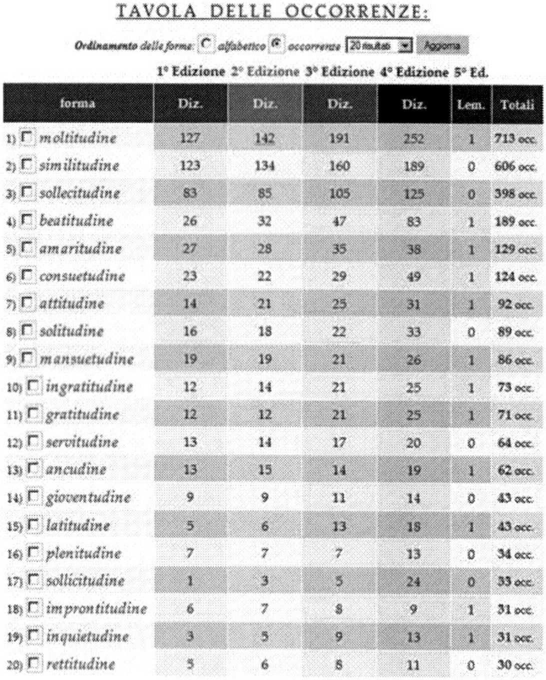

TAVOLA DELLE OCCORRENZE:

Ordinamento delle forme: alfabetico occorrenze [20 risultati] Aggiorna

forma	1° Edizione Diz.	2° Edizione Diz.	3° Edizione Diz.	4° Edizione Diz.	5° Ed. Lem.	Totali
1) *moltitudine*	127	142	191	252	1	713 occ.
2) *similitudine*	123	134	160	189	0	606 occ.
3) *sollecitudine*	83	85	105	125	0	398 occ.
4) *beatitudine*	26	32	47	83	1	189 occ.
5) *amaritudine*	27	28	35	38	1	129 occ.
6) *consuetudine*	23	22	29	49	1	124 occ.
7) *attitudine*	14	21	25	31	1	92 occ.
8) *solitudine*	16	18	22	33	0	89 occ.
9) *mansuetudine*	19	19	21	26	1	86 occ.
10) *ingratitudine*	12	14	21	25	1	73 occ.
11) *gratitudine*	12	12	21	25	1	71 occ.
12) *servitudine*	13	14	17	20	0	64 occ.
13) *ancudine*	13	15	14	19	1	62 occ.
14) *gioventudine*	9	9	11	14	0	43 occ.
15) *latitudine*	5	6	13	18	1	43 occ.
16) *plenitudine*	7	7	7	13	0	34 occ.
17) *sollicitudine*	1	3	5	24	0	33 occ.
18) *improntitudine*	6	7	8	9	1	31 occ.
19) *inquietudine*	3	5	9	13	1	31 occ.
20) *rettitudine*	5	6	8	11	0	30 occ.

Fig. 17. "Free search": result for the string **udine* (page 1 of 5)

By entering two or more word forms separated by a blank space into the search box, the engine builds a relation with the Boolean operator OR: users will therefore find all the contexts containing one of the typed word forms.

3.2.3 "Advanced Search"

With the "advanced search" the digital dictionary clearly turns into a database, thanks to the exploitation of the rich set of markers. Some differences concern general aspects of the search, as it immediately appears when opening the search box (fig. 18).

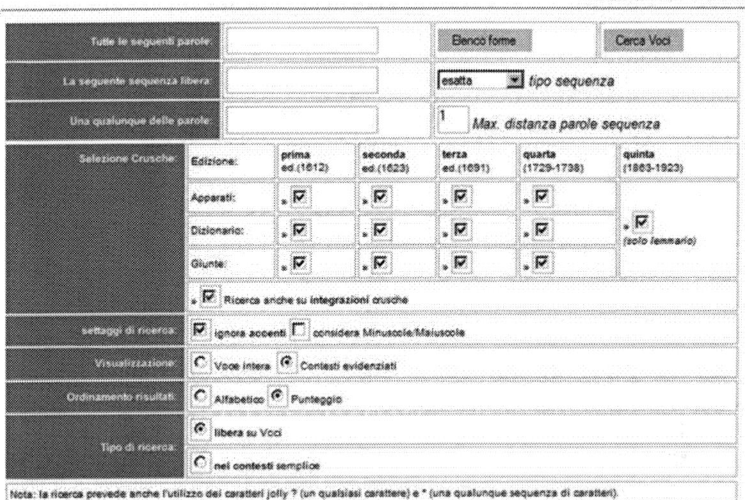

Fig. 18. The "advanced search"

The most interesting feature concerns the search for more forms together, that becomes much more flexible and refined. First of all the user can choose if looking for word forms first (and then, in case, contexts) as in the "free search", by using the button *Elenco Forme* [list of word forms]; or if tracing directly contexts by using the button *Cerca Voci* [search by entry]. This latter button also allows to search for co-occurrences, resorting to the options on the right hand side of the window.

The search option with "search by entry" are three: 1) search for contexts that contain all the typed word forms (*Tutte le seguenti parole*); 2) search for contexts that contain a specific sequence (*La seguente sequenza libera*); 3) search for contexts that contain at least one of the inserted words (*Una qualunque delle parole*).[17] In the first case, if the user types more than one word in the search box, the engine builds a relation with the Boolean operator *AND* and performs the search in the full macrocontext: therefore it will find all the contexts containing the two or more typed word forms as long as they belong to the same macrocontext (definition, example, commentary), at any distance; in the third case, in between the

[17] Clearly, using the button "list of word forms", in any of its options, the result is the list of word forms (with variants such as apostrophe or capital letter) in the chart with the summing up of the quantitative data, as happens in "free search".

searched word forms, the Boolean operator *OR* is applied. The second case is more interesting: basically it corresponds to what in the web search engines is called "search for exact wording or phrase": when typing in the string *la gatta al lardo*, the contexts containing the exact string are pointed out (spaces are considered blank spaces and not separators on which Boolean relations can be applied). And more: the drop-down menu next to the search box, besides of the option *esatta* [exact], also provides *ordinata* [ordered (wording)] and *non ordinata* [non ordered (wording)]: so the user can look for co-occurrences (in ordinate sequence or not depending on the choice) at a desired distance set up in the box below. In this way, by typing in the words *gatta* and *lardo*, with the option "ordered" and setting the distance "2", you will obtain 18 occurrences, that include examples of *gatta al lardo* and *gatta pel lardo* (fig. 19), according to a search strategy that looks more functional and effective in a corpus of ancient Italian, which can show a remarkable formal variety.[18]

Most of the other options shown in the window (fig. 18) are a refining of the "free search". The first one (*Selezione Crusche*) extends the search from entries to paratext and additions, allowing to delimit a specific subcorpus thanks to the check boxes: it is thus possible to deepen the analysis only to one or more editions, or, for example, to concentrate only on the additions; combination of filters is completely free. In the "advanced search" too, a check box allows to decide whether to widen or not the search to the electronic edition integrations added by operators (*Ricerca anche su integrazioni Crusche*). Other search options concern case-sensitivity and the function "ignore stress marks" (selected by default as in the "free search"– see § 3.2.2 – but here it can be disabled). Two displaying options also appear: one allows to display a result window with short contexts only or with the entire entries one after the other; the other (*Ordinamento risultati*) concerns displaying contexts by number of occurrences or alphabetically (but the user could anyway modify the displaying contexts directly in the result window – see § 3.2.2).

---

[18] It must be remembered that the punctuation marks have been tokenised the same way as word forms (see § 2), therefore the user can search for mixed sequences; for example, with the search in ordered sequence with distance 1 of ". *Ma*" the user will obtain the quantitative data on the adversative sentences introduced by *ma* after the full stop (7377 occurrences in 6326 entries).

1) Dizion. 4ª Ed. .
GATTO
Apri Voce completa
vol.2 pag.574-576

GATTO
Definiz: §. XVI. Andare alla gatta pel lardo: vale Andare a ricercare uno di cosa, la quale, oltre al mancargli, piaccia a lui smisuratamente, o pure avendola, ne sia avarissimo. Lat. *e flamma cibum petere.*
Esempio: *Cecch. Dissim. 3. 3.* Veggiamo, se noi troviam Simone, forse egli ci troverrà qualche riparo. S. Voi volete andare alla **gatta** pel **lardo**.
Definiz: §. XXIV. Tanto va la **gatta** al **lardo**, che ella vi lascia la zampa; e si dice del Mettersi più volte ad un rischio, che alla fine vi si rimane. Lat. *qui periculum amat, perit in illo.* Gr. [illegible]
Esempio: *Salv. Granch. 1. 2.* Tanto torna La **gatta** al **lardo**, che ella vi lascia La zampa.

2) Dizion. 4ª Ed. .
LARDO
Apri Voce completa
vol.3 pag.20

LARDO
Definiz: §. III. In proverb. Tanto torna la **gatta** al **lardo**, che ella vi lascia la zampa; e si dice del Tornare a mettersi tante volte in un pericolo, che alla fine vi si rimane. Lat. *qui periculum amat, perit in illo.*
Esempio: *Salv. Granch. 1. 2.* Tanto torna La **gatta** al **lardo**, che ella vi lascia La zampa.
Definiz: §. IV. Pure in proverb. Andare alla gatta pel lardo.

3) Dizion. 3ª Ed. .
GATTA, e GATTO
Apri Voce completa
vol.2 pag.750-751

GATTA, e GATTO
Definiz: §. Andare alla gatta pel lardo: Andare a ricercare uno di cosa, la quale, oltre al mancargli, piaccia a lui smisuratamente, o pure avendola, ne sia avarissimo.
Definiz: §. Tanto va la **gatta** al **lardo**, che ella vi lascia la zampa: e dicesi del Mettersi più volte ad un rischio, che alla fine vi si rimane.
Esempio: *Salv. Granch. Granch. 1. 2.* Tanto torna la **gatta** al **lardo**, che ella vi lascia la zampa.

4) Dizion. 3ª Ed. .
ZAMPINO
Apri Voce completa
vol.3 pag.1825

ZAMPINO
Definiz: §. Proverb. Tanto va la **gatta** al **lardo**, che vi lascia lo zampino.

5) Dizion. 4ª Ed. .
ZAMPA
Apri Voce completa
vol.5 pag.353

ZAMPA
Definiz: §. Tanto va la **gatta** al **lardo**, che vi lascia la zampa.

6) Dizion. 4ª Ed. .
SECCHIA
Apri Voce completa
vol.4 pag.446-447

SECCHIA
Definiz: (ed ha lo stesso significato, che quell'altro: Tanto va la **gatta** al **lardo**, ch'ella vi lascia la zampa.

7) Dizion. 3ª Ed. .
LARDO
Apri Voce completa
vol.3 pag.936

LARDO
Definiz: §. Tanto torna la **gatta** al **lardo**, che ella vi lascia lo *zampino*: si dice del Tornare a mettersi tante volte in un pericolo, che alla fine vi si rimane.

8) Dizion. 4ª Ed. .
ORCIO
Apri Voce completa
vol.3 pag.419

ORCIO
Definiz: §. I. Tanto va l'orcio per l'acqua, ch'egli si rompe: modo proverbiale, corrispondente al proverb. Tanto torna la **gatta** al **lardo**, ch'ella vi lascia la zampa.

9) Dizion. 1ª Ed. .
GATTA
Apri Voce completa
pag.378-379

GATTA
Definiz: ¶ Andare alla gatta pel lardo: andare a ricercare uno di cosa, la quale, oltre al mancargli, piaccia a lui smisuratamente, o pure, avendola, ne sia avarissimo.

Fig. 19. "Advanced search": contexts (14 of 18) obtained by search for *gatta lardo*, in ordered sequence with distance 2

One of the most interesting parts of the "advanced search" concerns filters on markers, that remains hidden in the first screenshot and that is shown up after moving the selection of *Tipo di ricerca* [search mode] from *libera su voci* [free search in entries] to *nei contesti semplice* [simple search in contexts] (fig. 20).

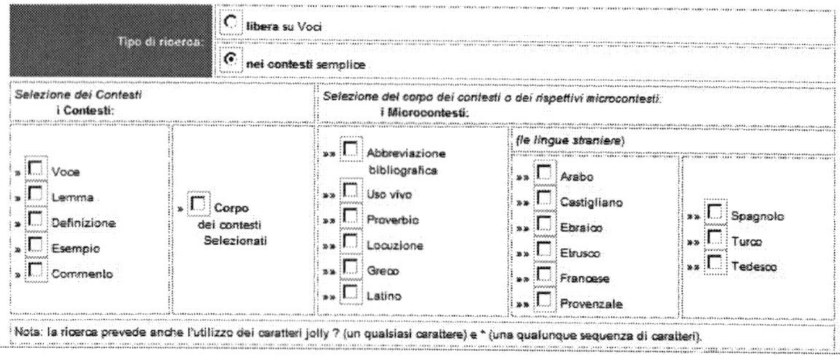

Fig. 20. Options of "advanced search" in contexts

Check boxes make it possible to select one or more macrocontexts, simply called *Contesti* [contexts] (check box *Voce* [entry] enables a search in all macrocontexts), and one or more microcontexts (check box *Corpo* [body] enables a search in the entire entry). So, for example, by activating the *Esempi* check box the search will be limited to the example contexts; by activating the *Greco* check box the search will be limited to contexts marked up as Greek; by activating both boxes search will be limited to Greek words within the examples. Users will obtain all Greek words within the examples using the wildcard while performing this kind of search (fig. 21).

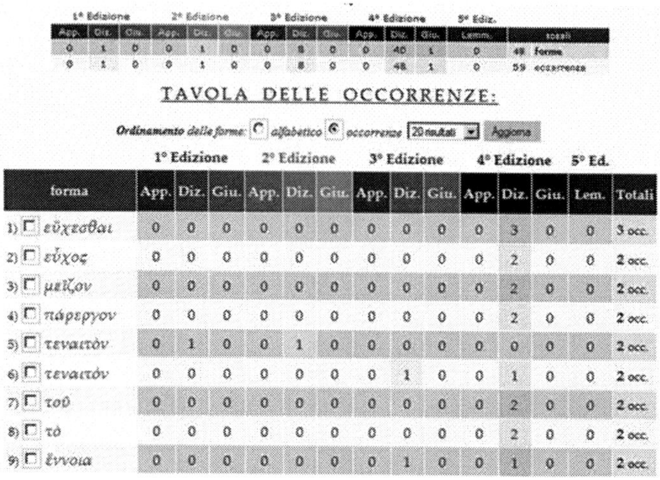

1ª Edizione			2ª Edizione			3ª Edizione			4ª Edizione			5ª Ediz.	
App.	Diz.	Giu.	App.	Diz.	Giu.	App.	Diz.	Giu.	App.	Diz.	Giu.	Lemm.	totali
0	1	0	0	1	0	0	5	0	0	40	1	0	48 forme
0	1	0	0	1	0	0	8	0	0	48	1	0	59 occorrenze

TAVOLA DELLE OCCORRENZE:

Ordinamento delle forme: alfabetico occorrenze 20 risultati Aggiorna

	1° Edizione			2° Edizione			3° Edizione			4° Edizione			5° Ed.	
forma	App.	Diz.	Giu.	App.	Diz.	Giu.	App.	Diz.	Giu.	App.	Diz.	Giu.	Lem.	Totali
1) εὔχεσθαι	0	0	0	0	0	0	0	0	0	0	3	0	0	3 occ.
2) εὖχος	0	0	0	0	0	0	0	0	0	0	2	0	0	2 occ.
3) μεῖζον	0	0	0	0	0	0	0	0	0	0	2	0	0	2 occ.
4) πάρεργον	0	0	0	0	0	0	0	0	0	0	2	0	0	2 occ.
5) τεναιτὸν	0	1	0	0	1	0	0	0	0	0	0	0	0	2 occ.
6) τεναιτόν	0	0	0	0	0	0	0	1	0	0	1	0	0	2 occ.
7) τοῦ	0	0	0	0	0	0	0	0	0	0	2	0	0	2 occ.
8) τὸ	0	0	0	0	0	0	0	0	0	0	2	0	0	2 occ.
9) ἔννοια	0	0	0	0	0	0	0	1	0	0	1	0	0	2 occ.

Fig. 21. "Advanced search" in contexts (Greek in the examples): result of the search with wildcard * (9 of 20, page 1 of 3)

Filters for macrocontexts are very useful, because they actually answer to one of the primary needs, that is to search in the subcorpus of the editors' language (definitions and commentaries) or in the examples, distinguishing the two language levels shown in the *Vocabolario* (see § 1).

Starting from quantitative results and short contexts display, the search engine works like in "free search" (link to entries and images, surfing, etc., see § 3.2.2). It must be noticed that in the "advanced search" the quantitative data charts – both the one resulting from clicking the *Elenco forme* [list of word forms] button, and the resumptive one showed on the upper side of the contexts window (see fig. 21) specify the occurrences distribution taking into account each *Vocabolario* section (dictionary, paratext, additions; only headwords for the fifth edition).

3.2.4 "Professional Search"

"Professional search" offers a peculiar access to *Lessicografia* database, allowing all search modes on the marked up text, including those in the "assisted search" menu, even with more options and a different interaction with the user. If users access the "professional search" (fig. 22), they will notice the difference with the other search windows they run into until now, and the similarity with the Google advanced search.

All these characteristics (sum of search modes, presence of more refined options, graphic similarity to a largely used search engine) have their origin in the software history of *Lessicografia*: in fact, "professional search" form, including the header *Cruscle*, is the first one introduced by the MICC computer scientists to the academy workgroup; the one which was worked on in order to develop the various procedures, and finally, the one at the origins of "simple search", "advanced search" and "assisted search". Many advanced options were firstly used by the workgroup but seemed useful to others and, therefore, were preserved. Graphics, born for fun with the nickname *Cruscle* for the software developers' own use, seemed suitable even for users, because of its resemblance to Google, with which almost all the regular web users are well acquainted. For this reason it was decided to carve out a special space for *Cruscle* the way it was born and to place it within the possible search modes.

The "professional search" provides an area, the upper and therefore the more visible one, dedicated to various search modes. As in "advanced search", but with the Google language, we can see a *Trova risultati* [find results] area, divided into four fields: 1) *che contengano tutte le seguenti parole* [that have all these words] (Boolean operator *AND*, microcontexts range); 2) *che contengano la seguente sequenza libera* [that have this free wording] (Google's "exact wording or phrase" becomes "free wording" because in *Cruscle* it is possible to find not only exact phrases, but also ordered or not ordered wording, at a distance set up by the user as described for "advanced search": see § 3.2.3); 3) *che contengano una qualunque delle seguenti parole* [one or more of these words] (Boolean operator *OR*); 4) *che non contengano le seguenti parole* [that have no of these (unwanted) words] (Boolean operator *NOT*). "Professional search", as "advanced search", allows to ask for a list of word forms with quantitative data (to trace their contexts, entries etc.) or to ask directly for the list of contexts (obviously a forced option for search for co-occurrences); and to filter the results according to the edition of the *Vocabolario* ad its parts (headwords, paratext, additions); and finally to choose if searching the database with the integrations / corrections or not. Then it is necessary to specify which *Tipo di ricerca* [kind of search]:

- *Libera su voci e apparati* [free (search) in entries and paratexts] (selected by default);
- *Nei contesti* (*semplice*) [simple (search) in contexts];
- *Nei contesti* (*combinata*) [combined (search) in contexts];
- *Dei contesti* [(search) for contexts];
- *Delle fonti* [(search) for sources];
- *Negli indici* [(search) in indexes].

If checking the specific button the user accesses specific submenus (see below).

In between the areas "find results" (yellow background) and "kind of search" (white background) there is an intermediate field (also for the background colour) that allows to activate an *Altre opzioni* [other options] submenu. Thanks to it, it is possible to specify further search engine settings and change the display of results.

All the settings provided by the "advanced search" (*ignora accenti* [ignore stress marks], *considera Minuscole / Maiuscole* [active case-sensitivity]) are still present in the "professional search", furthermore some extra features regarding the results rendering are introduced: display style choice; display by choice only microcontexts; display results by edition; what to highlight in the result window (keyword, context, microcontext, number of occurrences); display of results by alphabetical order or number of occurrences, with the addition, compared to "advanced search", of an "advanced ranking" in order to set up the display by number of occurrences and giving different importance to macrocontexts. Options concerning microcontexts are valid only choosing a search mode that implies microcontexts.

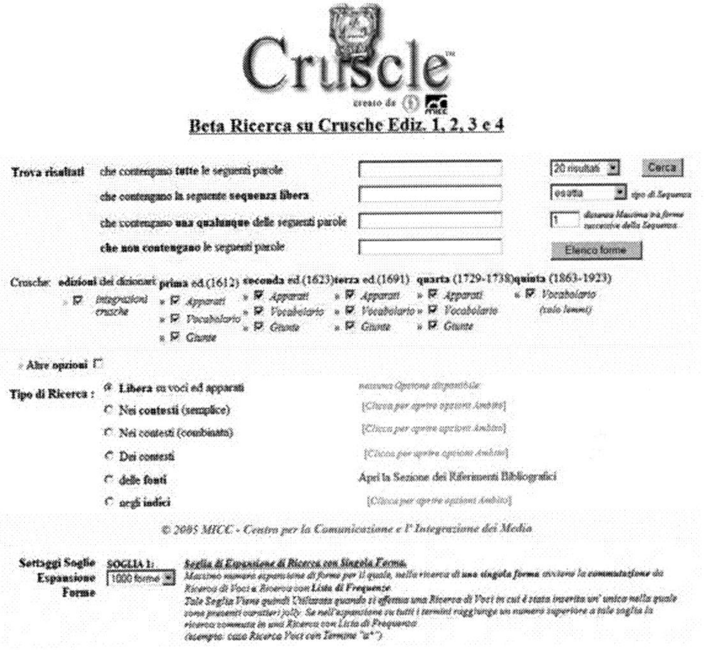

Fig. 22. The "professional search"

The "kind of search" area assembles various typologies already seen in the "advanced search" and "assisted search". "(Simple) search in contexts" works as "advanced search" (see § 3.2.3), as the user can see in submenu when selected (fig. 23).

"Combined search in contexts" allows to relate macro- and micro-contexts in all possible combinations. This kind of search can be exclusively done in "professional search" mode.

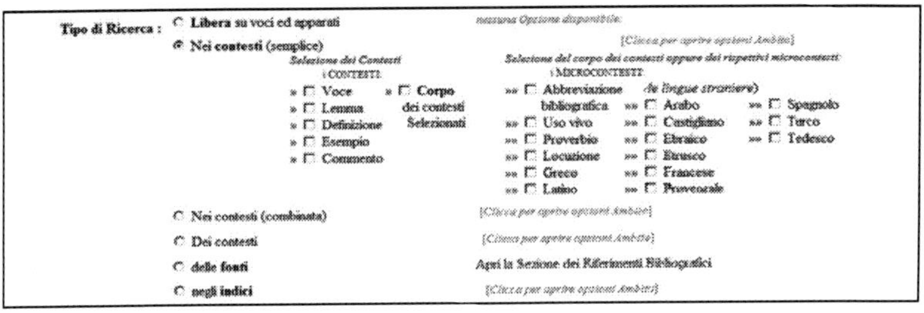

Fig. 23. "Professional search": "simple search in contexts"

"Search for contexts" (fig. 24) and "Search in indexes" (fig. 25) work as the homonymous options in "assisted search" (see respectively § 3.3.1 and 3.3.2), while "search for sources" links to the bibliographical database and corresponds to *Ricerca dei citati* [search for quoted works] in "assisted search" mode (see § 3.3.3).

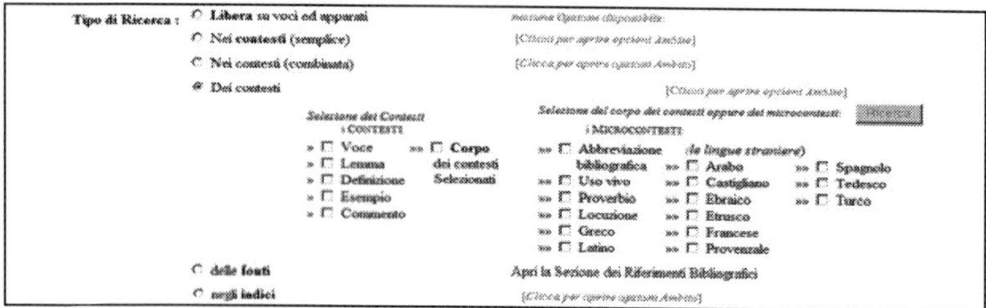

Fig. 24. "Professional search": "search for contexts"

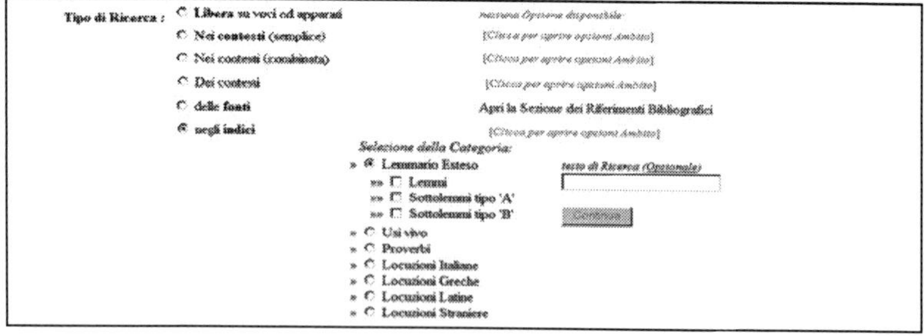

Fig. 25. "Professional search": "search by indexes"

The browsing of results is the same as in the "advanced search" mode (see § 3.2.3).

3.3 "Assisted Search"

This search mode offers three pre-established survey paths, that can be useful both for the expert researcher and the common user.

3.3.1 "Search for Contexts"

"Search for contexts" exploits the XML/TEI markers in a different perspective from those analysed until now, i.e. it does not define a portion of text, but it identifies it. It is thus possible to search for all the macro or microcontexts of a certain category (all the headwords, all the definitions, all the commentaries; or bibliographical abbreviations, locutions, proverbs, colloquial expressions, foreign words) by activating the relating check box.

As for the other search modes, users can filter the results by edition and section of the *Vocabolario*, and choose if taking or not into account the integrations / corrections. For example, by activating the "examples" and "proverbs" check boxes, all the proverbs in the examples of the first four editions are found (fig. 26).

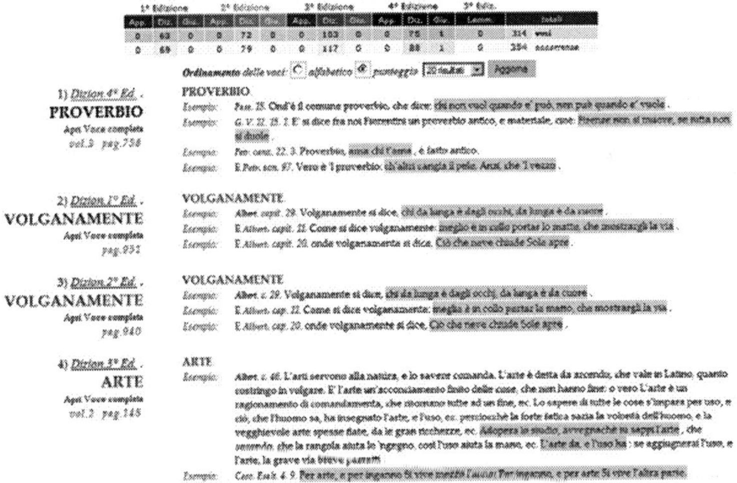

Fig. 26. "Search for contexts": result for proverbs in examples (first four entries)

3.3.2 "Search for Quoted Works"

This section manages the authors' and the quoted works' database, obtained with the normalisation of the *Tavole delle abbreviature* [tables of abbreviations] in each edition of the *Vocabolario* and with the automatic gathering of data deriving from abbreviations used in entries and integrations by operators (see § 2). The specific search window allows a free search of a word in the bibliographical database; when a *Solo su testo* [text only] check box is activated, the search is limited to the original text.

Users can choose which relation has to be used between words: an exact phrase (default setting); a co-occurence of words (*Tutte le parole* [all these words], applying the Boolean operator *AND*), an occurrence of at least one of them (*Almeno una* [at least one word], applying the Boolean operator *OR*). The *Seleziona Crusca* [choose which Crusca] field allows to filter the results on one or more specified editions (all editions are selected by default). The *Elementi per pagina* [items pro page] drop-down menu defines the number of records shown in the result page.

The *Mostra tutti* [see all] button lists the concise format of all bibliographical records: the edition of *Crusca* in which that work is quoted (*Ed.*), its ranking in the table of quoted works (*Progr.*), author, title (fig. 27); default display is alphabetical, but it can be changed by clicking on each item in the chart headline. Even in this mode users can select a specified edition.

	Ed.	Progr. (*) ▲	Autore (*)	Titolo opera (*)	
	1	1	*Agnol Pandolfini Del governo della famiglia.*	Trattato del governo della famiglia	Visualizza
	2	1	*Ammiano Marcellino.*	riferimento generico	Visualizza
	3	1	*Agnol Pandolfini. Del governo della famiglia.*	Trattato del governo della famiglia	Visualizza
	4	1	*Agnolo Pandolfini Trattato del Governo della Famiglia.*	Trattato del governo della famiglia	Visualizza
	1	2	*Luigi Alamanni. Girone Cortese poema eroico.*	Girone il Cortese	Visualizza
	2	2	*Arnobio*	riferimento generico	Visualizza
	3	2	*Luigi Alamanni. Giron Cortese. Poema Eroico*	Girone il Cortese	Visualizza
	4	2	*Luigi Alamanni Avarchide.*	Avarchide	Visualizza

Fig. 27. "Search for quoted works": complete list of records (particular of the first screenshot)

The same chart, but limited to the records that satisfy the research criteria, is obtained with a specific search. Thus, for example, by typing in *Galileo*, a list of 34 records in two pages is obtained (fig. 28).

This chart is the access point to bibliographical records (by clicking on *Visualizza* [see]) on the one hand, on the other to the passages of a work (or works) quoted in the editions of the *Vocabolario* (by activating the check boxes of the works and pressing the *Ricerca abbreviazioni selezionate* [search for selected abbreviations] button just above and below the chart). Therefore, for example, when clicking on *Visualizza* [see] next to the first record on fig. 28, the complete record of the *Discorso sulle comete* quoted in the *Tavola delle abbreviature* of the third edition will appear (fig. 29).[19]

---

[19] For a detailed description of the bibliographical record, see § 2.

Ricerca rapida (*) Galileo CERCA Ricerca Avanzata

Solo su testo · Frase esatta · Tutte le parole · Almeno una

Seleziona crusca: I II III IV MOSTRA TUTTI

Elementi per pagina 20

RICERCA ABBREVIAZIONI SELEZIONATE

	Ed.	Progr. (*) ▲	Autore (*)	Titolo opera (*)	
	3	161	*Mario Guiducci. Discorso delle Comete*	Discorso sulle comete	Visualizza
	4	195	*Mario Guiducci Discorso sopra le Comete.*	Discorso sulle comete	Visualizza
	3	217	*Galileo Galilei. Opere Diverse*	Lettera al Principe Leopoldo	Visualizza
	3	218	*Galileo Galilei. Opere Diverse*	Galileo Lettera a Madama Cristina di Lorena	Visualizza
	3	219	*Galileo Galilei. Opere Diverse*	Lettere	Visualizza
	3	220	*Galileo Galilei. Opere Diverse*	Storia e dimostrazioni intorno alle macchie solari e loro accidenti	Visualizza
	3	221	*Galileo Galilei. Opere Diverse*	Operazioni del compasso geometrico e militare	Visualizza

Fig. 28. "Search for quoted works": result of the search for *Galileo* (particular of the first screenshot)

Edizione	3
Pagina	41 (Visualizza l'immagine)
Informazioni della Tavola dei Citati	
Abbreviazione della *Tavola*	Disc. Com. M. G.
Indicazione nella *Tavola*	Mario Guiducci. Discorso delle Comete
Titolo	Discorso sulle comete
Classificazione	Autore moderno
Descrizione	Discorso delle Comete di Mario Guiducci. Discorso di Mario Guiducci nostro Accademico. Stampato fra l'Opere del Galileo.
Informazioni normalizzate	
Indicazione nella *Tavola*	Guiducci, Mario
Autore ricostruito	
Volgarizzatore ricostruito	
Titolo opera ricostruito	
Abbreviazioni del lemmario	Disc. Com. M. G. Galil. Disc. Com. M. G. Disc. Com. Mar. Guid. Disc. Com.
Cronologia	1600
Note	

Fig. 29. Record of the *Discorso sulle comete* by Galileo in the 3rd edition

The *Pagina* [page] hypertextual link opens the digital image of the *Tavola* where the work is mentioned (fig. 30).

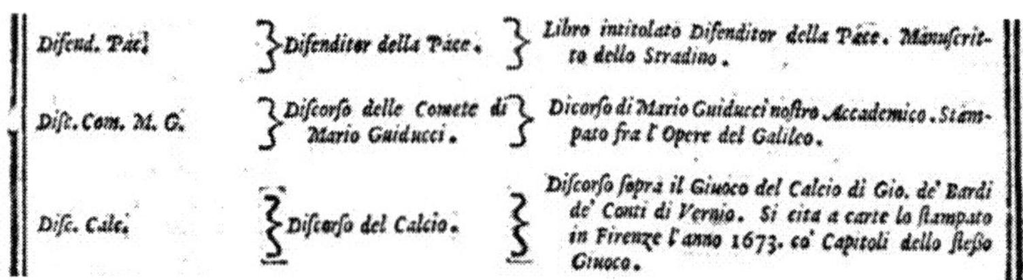

Difend. Pac.	*Difenditor della Pace.*	*Libro intitolato Difenditor della Pace. Manuſcritto dello Stradino.*
Diſc. Com. M. G.	*Diſcorſo delle Comete di Mario Guiducci.*	*Dicorſo di Mario Guiducci noſtro Accademico. Stampato fra l'Opere del Galileo.*
Diſc. Calc.	*Diſcorſo del Calcio.*	*Diſcorſo ſopra il Giuoco del Calcio di Gio. de' Bardi de' Conti di Vernio. Si cita a carte lo ſtampato in Firenze l'anno 1673. co' Capitoli dello ſteſſo Giuoco.*

Fig. 30. Digital image (particular) of the *Tavola delle abbreviature* page of the third edition containing the reference to Galileo's *Discorso sulle comete*

In the results chart, if users activate the check box on the left side of each item and click the "search for selected abbreviations" button, they will obtain a list of quoted passages from the Galilean work (fig. 31). Clearly, if the check boxes of all the items that have been pointed out are activated (a task which is made easier by the check box in the chart headline), all the Galilean quoted passages in the first four editions of the *Vocabolario* are displayed.

Beyond a free search, users can also perform an advanced search by clicking the link next to the *Cerca* [search] button. Thus they could search for keywords in specific fields, even crossing each other and limiting the search to one or more editions.

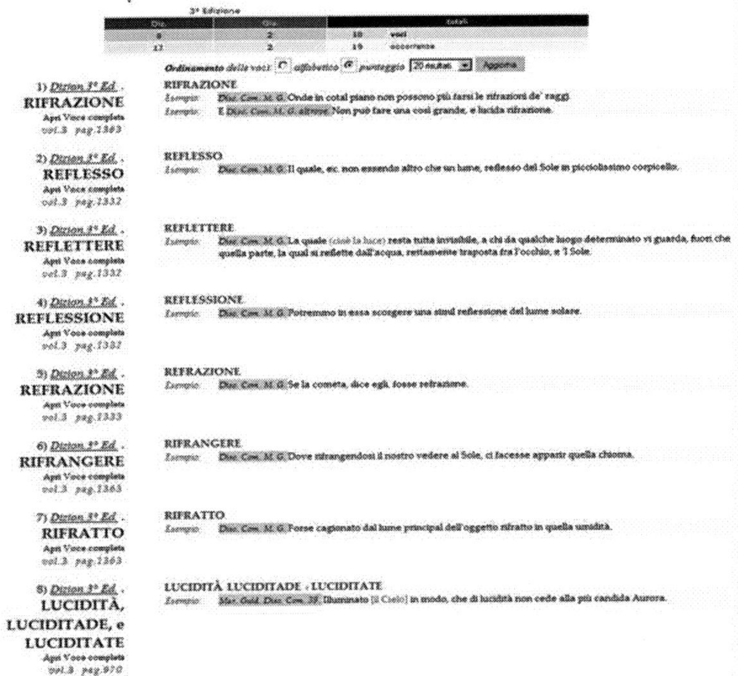

Fig. 31. "Search for quoted works": results of the *Discorso sulle comete* quoted passages in the 3rd edition of *Vocabolario* (first 8 entries of 10)

3.3.3 "Search by Indexes"

This last room of the *Vocabolario* digital library is dedicated to more traditional tools, but still appreciated by many web users: precompiled alphabetical indexes relating to the most significant topics of the database. The indexes' window allows as usual to filter the lists according to a specific edition, to more editions, to all of them (with the well-known limit to the wordlist for the fifth edition); and to take into account or not the corrections of the digital version.

Alphabetical lists of headwords, subheadwords (type A: reconstructed by operators; type B: pointed by the academicians with capital letters; see § 2), colloquial expressions, proverbs, locutions, Greek words, Latin words, other foreign words (by choosing this option the user must select one or more foreign languages) can be generated. By choosing any of the options and clicking the *Continua* [go on] button, an alphabetical keyboard is presented. The related index portion is shown clicking on a letter: results are displayed in a chart (fig. 32) with quantitative data and links to the contexts (and then entries).

So, for example, if users select type B subheadwords and chooses the *z* letter, they will obtain the complete list of subheadwords pointed out by the academicians with the capital letters and beginning with *z*; the quantitative data take care of the overall occurrencies, of the number of entries containing such subheadwords and finally of their distribution in editions and in sections of each one of them. Users can trace the contexts of all the editions or the chosen one clicking on the links in each result line (in our case either the first or the second, the only ones offering results; fig. 32).

If users have already a specific word in mind, or its beginning, they can use the *Testo di ricerca* [search for text] box. By typing in *rex* and restricting the search to Latin, they will obtain the quantitative data for the word and its distribution, with the access to contexts; by typing in *con** and restricting the search to type A subheadwords, they will obtain the usual results window with the list of subheadwords beginning with *con*.

1ª Edizione			2ª Edizione			3ª Edizione			4ª Edizione			5ª Ediz.	totali	
App.	Diz.	Giu.	App.	Diz.	Giu.	App.	Diz.	Giu.	App.	Diz.	Giu.	Lemm.		
0	11	0	0	12	0	0	0	0	0	0	0	0	15	risultati
0	12	0	0	12	0	0	0	0	0	0	0	0	24	occorrenze

TAVOLA DELLE OCCORRENZE:

Ordinamento dei risultati: ○ *alfabetico* ● *occorrenze* 20 risultati Aggiorna

	1° Edizione			2° Edizione			3° Edizione			4° Edizione			5° Ed.	
espressione:	A	D	G	A	D	G	A	D	G	A	D	G	L	Totali
1) ZAFFO	○	●	○	○	●	○	○	○	○	○	○	○	○	3 occ.
2) ZIZZOLARE	○	●	○	○	●	○	○	○	○	○	○	○	○	2 occ.
3) ZIMBELLATA	○	●	○	○	●	○	○	○	○	○	○	○	○	2 occ.
4) ZIMBELLARE	○	●	○	○	●	○	○	○	○	○	○	○	○	2 occ.
5) ZERO	○	●	○	○	●	○	○	○	○	○	○	○	○	2 occ.
6) ZEPPO	○	●	○	○	●	○	○	○	○	○	○	○	○	2 occ.
7) ZAMPETTARE	○	●	○	○	●	○	○	○	○	○	○	○	○	2 occ.
8) ZACCHERELLA	○	●	○	○	●	○	○	○	○	○	○	○	○	2 occ.
9) ZUCCONARE	○	●	○	○	○	○	○	○	○	○	○	○	○	1 occ.
10) ZINGANE	○	●	○	○	○	○	○	○	○	○	○	○	○	1 occ.
11) ZAMPILLARE	○	●	○	○	○	○	○	○	○	○	○	○	○	1 occ.
12) ZAMPATA	○	○	○	○	●	○	○	○	○	○	○	○	○	1 occ.
13) ZAMPARE	○	○	○	○	●	○	○	○	○	○	○	○	○	1 occ.
14) ZAGAGLIA	○	○	○	○	●	○	○	○	○	○	○	○	○	1 occ.
15) ZACCHERUZZA	○	○	○	○	●	○	○	○	○	○	○	○	○	1 occ.

Fig. 32. The "Search by indexes": list of type B subheadwords beginning with *z*

4 Some Quantitative Data

One of the most interesting results when analysing quantitative data concerns the size of the first four editions of the *Vocabolario*, on which there has always been disparity among scholars. Considering the numbers of volumes it seems that differences between the first and the second edition are very small (both editions come in one volume), those between the second and the third are bigger (from one to three volumes) and that there is an enormous increase in size of the fourth (six volumes). Furthermore, since the third edition gives up one of its three volumes to paratext and its layout is less thick, other scholars suggested that also the increase between the second and the third edition was not quantitatively relevant. The first, rough calculation of the real size was actually attempted while planning the *Lessicografia*, when transcription and markup work were quantified in order to estimate the costs. The empirical calculation was made counting the characters including blank spaces in each line and multiplying them by the numbers of lines in an average page, then multiplying the results by the pages of every edition. These are the results:[20]

- *Crusca* 1612: approx. 8,417,280 characters
- *Crusca* 1623: app. 9,397,400 characters (+ 12% compared to the previous)
- *Crusca* 1691: app. 14,922,453 characters (+ 59% comp. to the previous)
- *Crusca* 1729-38: app. 21,872,090 characters (+ 47% comp. to the previous)

The *Lessicografia* search engine does not allow to sum up the number of characters, but we can count those in source files with marked up text; in theory it would have been more correct to count only the text characters (maybe by "cleaning" the file automatically), but because of the target of our little survey, since we are more interested in proportions than in absolute data, it seemed adequate to consider also the expansion introduced by the markers. Thus, this count indirectly takes into account the lexicographical information added by academicians. The results obtained are:

- *Crusca* 1612: approx. 16,056,320 characters
- *Crusca* 1623: app. 17,608,704 characters (+ 10% compared to the previous)
- *Crusca* 1691: app. 28,033,024 characters (+ 59% comp. to the previous)
- *Crusca* 1729-38: app. 45,965,312 characters (+ 64% comp. to the previous).

As we can see, the data obtained are similar to the previous (even if the growth between the third and the fourth edition seems slightly higher), and this similarity strengthens the final result: if the increase from the first to the second edition has been actually moderate, from the second to the

[20] The result of this first survey was published in Sessa (2001: 4).

fourth edition of the *Vocabolario* there has been a progressive and substantial growth of lexical information/data.

The number of headwords in every edition can be verified with the *Lessicografia* tool, searching by headword macrocontexts (see § 3.3.1) and reading its results chart (including headwords of the fifth edition):

- *Crusca* 1612: 24,595 headwords
- *Crusca* 1623: 26,980 headwords (+ 2385; + 10% comp. to the previous)
- *Crusca* 1691: 36,284 headwords (+ 9304; + 34,5% comp. to the previous)
- *Crusca* 1729-38: 47,453 headwords (+ 11169; + 31% comp. to the previous)
- *Crusca* 1863-1923: 50,285 headwords (partial datum of the 11 volumes until the letter *o*).

Regarding the headwords only, while the percentage growth from the first to the second edition corresponds with the growth of size, from the second to the third and from the third to the fourth the number of headwords increases less remarkably: the average extent of entries is similar in the first and the second edition, while it is broader in the third, and even more in the fourth, with a progressive increase, as the calculation of the entries' average density confirms:

- *Crusca* 1612: on the average 652 characters per entry
- *Crusca* 1623: on the average 652 characters per entry
- *Crusca* 1691: on the average 773 characters per entry
- *Crusca* 1729-1738: on the average 968 characters per entry.

The *Vocabolario* evolution, then, shows a substantial homogeneity between the first and the second edition; an increase from the second to the third, both for number of headwords and size, but also for average length of the entries; a similar increase from the third to the fourth, where the average length of the entries grows considerably, becoming almost 50% longer than in the first and the second edition.

Another important fact, in accordance with what reported until now, is that a large part of the material is reused from the first to the fourth edition: that is easy to verify comparing the same entries from one edition to the other. Let's take the entry *senape* as an example. The first edition reports one definition and two examples, with a second definition that proposes a morphological variant (fig. 33).

1) Dizion. 1° Ed. .	**SENAPE**.	
SENAPE	*Definiz:*	Erba nota, il cui seme è minutissimo, e d'acutissimo sapore. Latin. *sinapis, sinapi*, gr. *σύνηπι σίνηπι*.
Voce completa	*Esempio:*	*Cr. 6. 110. 1.* La **Senape** si semina innanzi il verno, e dopo, e desidera terra grassa, ec.
pag. 785	*Esempio:*	*Amet. 44.* Molta della frigida ruta, e d'alta **senape** del naso nemica:
	Definiz:	oggi più comunemente si dice SENAPA.

Fig. 33. The entry *senape* in the 1st edition

The second edition offers a remarkable change: the variant *senapa* is added next to *senape* as headword, and consequently a relating example is added; first definition and examples remain unchanged; the second definition, now useless, is removed; at the end a further example is added (fig. 34).

1) *Dizion.2ª Ed.* .
SENAPE, e SENAPA
Voce completa
pag.776

SENAPE *e* **SENAPA**
Definiz: Erba nota, il cui seme è minutissimo, e d'acutissimo sapore. Lat. *sinapis, sinapi*, gr. [illegible]
Esempio: Cr. 6. 110. 1. La **Senape** si semina innanzi il verno, e dopo, e desidera terra grassa, ec.
Esempio: *Amet.* 44. Molta della frigida ruta, e d'alta **senape** del naso nemica.
Esempio: Cr. 3. 10. 2. La Senapa cessa il nocimento loro, e similmente l'aceto.
Esempio: E Cr. lib. 6. 111. 2. Contro all'asma antica, per umor viscoso, sia dia il vino, dove sia cotta **senape**, e fichi secchi.

Fig. 34. The entry *senape* in the 2nd edition

The third edition only adds an example (fig. 35).

1) *Dizion.3ª Ed.* .
SENAPE, e SENAPA
Voce completa
vol.3 pag.1502

SENAPE *e* **SENAPA**
Definiz: Erba nota, il cui seme è minutissimo, e d'acutissimo sapore. Lat. *sinapis, sinapi*. Gr. [illegible]
Esempio: Cr. 6. 100. 1. La **senape** si semina innanzi il verno, e dopo, e desidera terra grassa, ec.
Esempio: *Amet.* 44. Molta della frigida ruta, e d'alta **senape** del naso nemica.
Esempio: Cr. 3. 10. 2. La senapa cessa il nocimento loro, e similmente l'aceto.
Esempio: E Cr. 6. 111. 2. Contro all'asma antica, per umor viscoso, si dia il vino, dove sia cotta **senape**, e fichi secchi.
Esempio: *Alam. Colt.* 5. Il forte seme Della piangente senapa or si asconda.

Fig. 35. The entry *senape* in the 3rd edition

Several changes were introduced in the fourth edition (fig. 36). While the main definition is the same, most of the examples were rearranged: passages by vulgarised Crescenzio were gathered and sorted by appearance (an example was completed, and the reference of another example was corrected); the passage by *Ninfale d'Ameto* was extended; in Alamanni's quotation the exact page was defined. A locution was added at the end, with the relating definition and example.

1) *Dizion.4ª Ed.* .
SENAPE, e SENAPA
Voce completa
vol.4 pag.471

SENAPE *e* **SENAPA**
Definiz: Erba nota, il cui seme è minutissimo, e d'acutissimo sapore. Lat. *sinapis*. Gr. [illegible]
Esempio: Cr. 3. 10. 2. La senapa cessa il nocimento loro, e similmente l'aceto con sale, pepe, e origano.
Esempio: E Cr. 6. 111. 1. La **senape** si semina innanzi al verno, e dopo, e desidera terra grassa.
Esempio: E Cr. num. 2. Contro all'asma antica per umor viscoso si dia il vino, dove sia cotta **senape**, e fichi secchi.
Esempio: *Amet.* 44. In uno canto si troverebbe molta della frigida ruta, e d'alta **senape** del naso nemica, e utile a purgarsi la testa.
Esempio: *Alam. Colt.* 5. 139. Il forte seme Della piangente senapa or si asconda.
Definiz: §. Venir la senapa al naso, vale lo stesso, che Venir la muffa al naso.
v. NASO §. VII.
Esempio: *Cecch. lett.* 1. 7. Oh come vi sarebbe venuta la senapa al naso!

Fig. 36. The entry *senape* in the 4th edition

The evolution in entries is crucial in order to evaluate with more awareness the data relating to the size of the corpus, an interesting point for a database so fundamental for the study of Italian. Tools allow to calculate with accuracy the overall and partial number of occurrences in the first four editions: it is enough to perform a search using only the wildcard * without including integrations, to read the resulting data in the resumptive chart (fig. 37).

*La Ricerca di *: è stata estesa ad 231126 Forme. Tempo Totale di Ricerca in 15218 msec.*
La ricerca è stata rilevata in 231126 forme, per un totale di 11626528 occorrenze

1ª Edizione			2ª Edizione			3ª Edizione			4ª Edizione			5ª Ediz.		
App.	Diz.	Giu.	App.	Diz.	Giu.	App.	Diz.	Giu.	App.	Diz.	Giu.	Lemm.	totali	
1667	89817	1608	1639	97291	1914	1917	134902	8507	4260	180657	13751	46356	231126	forme
6718	1743988	4240	6325	1906496	3492	7146	3040677	41838	16756	4703267	94438	51147	11626528	occorrenze

Fig. 37. The occurrences resumptive chart

As we can see the overall occurrences number is 11,626,528 (with a total of 231,126 different word forms): therefore, a corpus of remarkable size, also according to the current measuring standards (a number of words between one million and 50 millions makes it a medium-big corpora).[21] Anyway, numbers have to be weighed considering that many materials of the first edition are reproduced in the following editions: the lower estimate, however, can not be lower than 4,814,461 occurrences, an amount equal to the fourth edition only (including paratext and additions); the fourth edition could represent the lower estimate even when evaluating the number of word forms (presuming, in a down estimate, that all the word forms of paratext and additions are already in the original core: additions surely contain new word forms, but these are not quantifiable according to the results chart). Also in this case, the *Lessicografia* database remains firmly in the medium-big corpora category.

The same kind of search can be made limiting the analysis of definitions (including commentaries and paratext; fig. 38) and examples only (fig. 39), in order to evaluate its representativeness with relation to the two language levels of the *Vocabolario*. There are 3,208,491 occurrences in the subcorpus referred to the language of editors (108,837 word forms) and 7,992,155 occurrences (129,993 word forms) in the examples subcorpus.

---

[21] For criteria see Chiari (2007: 45): non-representative corpus < 15,000 words; small corpus: from approx. 15,000 to 100,000 words; medium corpus: from approx. 100,000 to one million words; medium-big corpus: from approx. one million to 50 millions words; standard corpus: from approx. 50 millions to 100 millions words; big corpus: more than 100 millions words.

*La Ricerca di *: è stata estesa ad 231126 Forme. Tempo Totale di Ricerca in 13086 msec.*
La ricerca è stata rilevata in 108837 forme, per un totale di 3208491 occorrenze

1° Edizione			2° Edizione			3° Edizione			4° Edizione			5° Ediz.	totali	
App.	Diz.	Giu.	App.	Diz.	Giu.	App.	Diz.	Giu.	App.	Diz.	Giu.	Lemm.	totali	
0	44919	1181	0	46887	1361	0	62696	2830	0	90806	5530	0	108837	forme
0	490359	3474	0	521398	2824	0	833054	14592	0	1296572	46218	0	3208491	occorrenze

Fig. 38. The occurrences chart in the subcorpus referred to the language of editors

*La Ricerca di *: è stata estesa ad 231126 Forme. Tempo Totale di Ricerca in 12520 msec.*
La ricerca è stata rilevata in 129993 forme, per un totale di 7992155 occorrenze

1° Edizione			2° Edizione			3° Edizione			4° Edizione			5° Ediz.	totali	
App.	Diz.	Giu.	App.	Diz.	Giu.	App.	Diz.	Giu.	App.	Diz.	Giu.	Lemm.	totali	
0	57751	0	0	64206	0	0	90023	5728	0	113223	7906	0	129993	forme
0	1196216	0	0	1323439	0	0	2121430	23514	0	3290195	37361	0	7992155	occorrenze

Fig. 39. The occurrences chart in the subcorpus formed by examples

Extending the described considerations and criteria applied to the complete corpus, we have a lower estimate of 1,296,572 occurrences (90,806 word forms) for what concerns the subcorpus referred to the language of editors, and of 3,290,195 occurrences (113,223 word forms) for the examples; in both cases, even if close to the minimum value of the threshold, the corpora are medium-big.

Similar surveys can be easily done on all the macro and microcontexts: there is a total of 217,213 definitions (82,546 only in the fourth), 400,715 examples (155,249 in the fourth), 6443 colloquial expressions (541 in the fourth), 2658 proverbs (839 in the fourth), 35,779 locutions (15,617 in the fourth), 404,709 bibliographical abbreviations (156,605 in the fourth). If we generate frequency lists within specific microcontexts we will then count 26,076 Greek words (24,577 in the fourth), 32,614 Latin forms words (28,139 in the fourth); 31 other foreign language words (20 in the fourth).

In conclusion, it is worth observing the decreasing frequency list: finding out the most used word in a corpus has always been a curiosity. The most frequent words are the ones related to the grammatical structure (or punctuation marks, as punctuation was tokenised): full stop is the most frequent token, followed by comma; third in rank is the first alphabetical word, *e* 'and' (365,253 occurrences), followed by *di* 'of' (196,027) and *che* 'that' (188,199). Abbreviations are also very frequent: *lat.* for *latino* (123,439 occurrences, sixth in rank); *Gr.* for *greco* (53,522 occurrences, sixteenth in rank); *Bocc.* for *Boccaccio* (45,804 occurrences, twenty-fourth in rank); *Dan.* for *Dante* (30,239 occurrences, thirty-seventh in rank); *Petr.* for *Petrarca* (20,458 occurrences; fifty-third in rank). The hierarchy

Boccaccio > *Dante* > *Petrarca* is very relevant and it is also confirmed while searching in sources with a filter by author. The first non grammatical word is a verbal form with strong lexicographical value: *vale* 'it means' (16,900 occurrences, sixty-third in rank); the second, the generic word *cose* 'things' (11,926 occurrences; ninety-seventh in rank).

References

Alisi, Thomas M. / Becchi, Giuseppe *et al.* (2006). "Advanced search facilities for accessing Crusca Academy of Italian Language", in Cappellini, Vito (ed.). *Electronic Imaging & the Visual Arts EVA 2006 Florence Proceedings*. Bologna, Pitagora Editrice: 164-169.

Biffi, Marco (2006). "L'Accademia della Crusca e il Web: le biblioteche e gli archivi digitali", in *Studi Italiani* 36: 253-258.

—. (2007). "L'Accademia della Crusca e il Web: gli strumenti lessicali e lessicografici", in *Studi Italiani* 37: 169-177.

—. (2007-2008). "L'Accademia della Crusca e il Web: nuovi scaffali digitali", in *Studi Italiani* 38: 291-300.

Biffi, Marco / Fanfani, Massimo (2006). "La Lessicografia della Crusca in Rete", in Corino, Elisa / Marello, Carla / Onesti, Cristina (eds). *Atti del XII Congresso Internazionale di Lessicografia (Torino, 6-9 September 2006) / Proceedings XII Euralex International Congress (Torino, Italia, 6-9 September 2006)*, vol. I, Alessandria, Edizioni dell'Orso: 409-416.

Castellani, Arrigo (1967-1970). "Italiano e fiorentino argenteo", in *Studi linguistici italiani* 7: 3-19 [also in: Id. (1980). *Saggi di linguistica e filologia italiana e romanza (1946-1976)*, 3 vols. Roma, Salerno Editrice, vol. I: 17-35].

Chiari, Isabella (2007). *Introduzione alla linguistica computazionale*. Roma / Bari, Laterza.

Manni, Paola (1979). "Ricerche sui tratti fonetici e morfologici del fiorentino quattrocentesco", in *Studi di Grammatica Italiana* 8: 115-171.

—. (2003). *Il Trecento toscano*. Bologna, il Mulino.

Parodi, Severina (ed.) (1974). *Gli Atti del primo Vocabolario*. Firenze, Sansoni.

Sessa, Mirella (1982). "Saggio di 'rovesciamento' del primo *Vocabolario della Crusca*", in *Studi di lessicografia italiana* 4: 269-333.

—. (2001). "Il 'Rovesciamento' del primo *Vocabolario della Crusca* (1612)", in *La Crusca per voi* 22, April 2001: 3-18.

Sperberg, C. Michael / McQueen, Lou Burnard (eds) (2002). *Guidelines for Text Encoding and Interchange* [published for the TEI Consortium by the Humanities Computing Unit, University of Oxford, 2002].

THE GENERAL MULTILINGUAL DICTIONARY OF METALINGUISTIC TERMINOLOGY*

FRANCO LORENZI AND ANNA DE MEO

1. The project of a *General Multilingual Dictionary of Metalinguistic Terminology* (here referred to as *DLM*, *Dizionario generale plurilingue del Lessico Metalinguistico* for short) has developed over almost a decade, starting from the late years of the last century.[1] Intended to represent the heritage of metalinguistic thought, from a typological point of view it is a specialised dictionary of the technical vocabulary of various language sciences. There is no pre-determined language as a basis, and it can be accessed by consulting any language represented in it. Since its creation, the *DLM* has been intended as a new type of lexicographical database, in which the underlying structure of data could generate different outputs, both dictionaries and thesauri.

The *DLM* has sought to maximise research and pursue originality; it is not based on previous collections nor does it offer new definitions. In order to give scholars a comprehensive and flexible instrument, it contains the largest possible number of entries which are and were considered technical in specialised tradition, and original examples (quotations, definitions and so on) taken directly from works of linguistics and language sciences. These methodological preferences have led to a wide choice of textual sources: dictionaries, encyclopaedias, glossaries, lists and so on, and works deemed essential in the long history of linguistic thought. From a lexicographical point of view, technical collections fix the terminological heritage of disciplines and therefore represent an

* Both authors made substantial contributions to the conception and design of the paper. In particular, Lorenzi wrote the final version of §§ 1-2 and De Meo of § 3.

[1] See Vallini (2000, 2001, 2002), Vallini / Orioles (2000). Inspired by Cristina Vallini, the project has been coordinated, during the years, by Cristina Vallini, Vincenzo Orioles, Diego Poli and Domenico Silvestri, with the contribution of Italian researchers from several universities (Bologna, Catania, Cosenza, Macerata, Napoli "L'Orientale", Palermo, Perugia-Università degli Studi, Perugia-Università per Stranieri, Udine).

irreplaceable correlated tool for the various scientific paradigms. The use of original works allows the researcher to have material on which s/he can operate and reflect without passing through the filter of an editor.

The *DLM* project team decided to extract the terminology from dictionaries, collections and original works, but to use definitions and descriptions only from the latter. The *DLM* is based, therefore, on the binomial <text-author>; the relevant documentary information and the lexicon with any related quotations and, also, the coordinates of areas and scientific paradigms have been identified in any text, written in one or more language(s).

The lexicographical goal to maximise the dictionary led to the choice of using an electronic format for lexical data, because a traditional paper dictionary would certainly have hampered the collection and consultation of the material. The expanded presence of quotations drawn from original works and the multilingual character have made the *DLM* an exclusively electronic database, the only one able to handle an enormous amount of data. Among other things, quotations constitute what is called *encyclopaedic information* (Bergenholtz / Tarp 1995) and, just for its size, it makes the *DLM* unique.

2. The General Outline of the *DLM* is shown in fig. 1.[2]

As we said, the examination and indexing of the texts was carried out by the researchers involved in the project and, indeed, achieved with the help of a procedure called *lexicographical workstation*.[3]

Working with the lexicographical workstation on his computer, the researcher first inserts all documentary information about the author and the text, filling electronic records.[4] Then s/he introduces technical words, through a complex *lemma* record, which raised many lexicographical problems, well known to those working in the field.[5] At first, it was decided to make an extended lemmatisation, not limited to certain linguistic types. So N(ominal), V(erbal), ADJ(ectival) and ADV(erbial) terms were extracted and, also, terms made up of prefixes, suffixes and so

---

[2] For a more detailed description of the project *DLM* see the articles in Lorenzi (2002a) and Lorenzi *et al.* (2007).

[3] See Vallini (2002) and Di Maio (2002).

[4] The *DLM* also includes as "authors" journals or encyclopaedias in which articles appeared catalogued by researchers. This gives us an analytical framework of the contribution offered by these important instruments of scientific communication.

[5] The criteria for the examination and indexing of dictionaries and originals works were collected and described in particular by Anna De Meo; see De Meo (2002), De Meo / Lorenzi (2005).

on.[6] For example, *langue* [N; FR(ench)], *afferrare* [V IT(alian)], *phonemic* [ADJ; EN(glish)], *economically* [ADV; EN(glish)], *macro-* [X; EN(glish)], *–ema* [X; IT(alian)]. Complex terms (consisting of several words or an entire phrase) were lemmatised in the standard order of language to which they belong; for example *knowledge – lexical* was introduced as *lexical knowledge*. The category of grammatical head was used for complex expressions (for example, *phonemic composition of an utterance* [N; EN]). The language names were lemmatised. In case of homonyms explicitly introduced by the author, we have drawn up separate fields and information about <synonyms>, <translations> and <links> were reported, again proposed by the author of a text for a single term. The introduction of the field <synonyms> has made it possible to codify antonyms through a particular lexicographical symbol (><) and to establish a systematic link for acronyms. Every acronym has become a lemma in its own right (for example, *SNSD* in Bickerton 1981), so it was made explicit and, in turn, inserted as lemma (so we have, for example, *Specific-Non Specific Distinction* as lemma). Finally, a <synonym> relationship between acronym and extended expression was established, so, for example, *SNSD* has been linked to *Specific-Non Specific Distinction* and vice versa.

As we have mentioned, the researcher can insert original quotations relating to a specific lemma; s/he opens a <quotation> field in which s/he can indicate the context s/he thinks is appropriate.[7] As a general criterion we tried to offer quotations in which the user can find the widest possible range of information about entry and contexts not excessively reduced. It is important to stress that in <quotations> pictures, diagrams and formulas that are an integral part of the definitions may also appear.

For <authors>, <texts>, <lemmas> and <quotations> it is possible to introduce <markers> or <labels>, i.e. categories that formalise research areas (for example, <phonology>, <semantics> and so on) or schools of linguistic thought (for example, <structuralism>, <generative grammar> and so on). In particular, there are four specific descriptors for quotations: <definition>, <description>, <metaphor> and <similarity>. These descriptors are used for the development of the documentary network to which we will return later.

[6] They were given a dummy category *X*.

[7] The lemma is normally present in every quotation; where lacking, it is integrated using the lexicographical symbol '[ ]'.

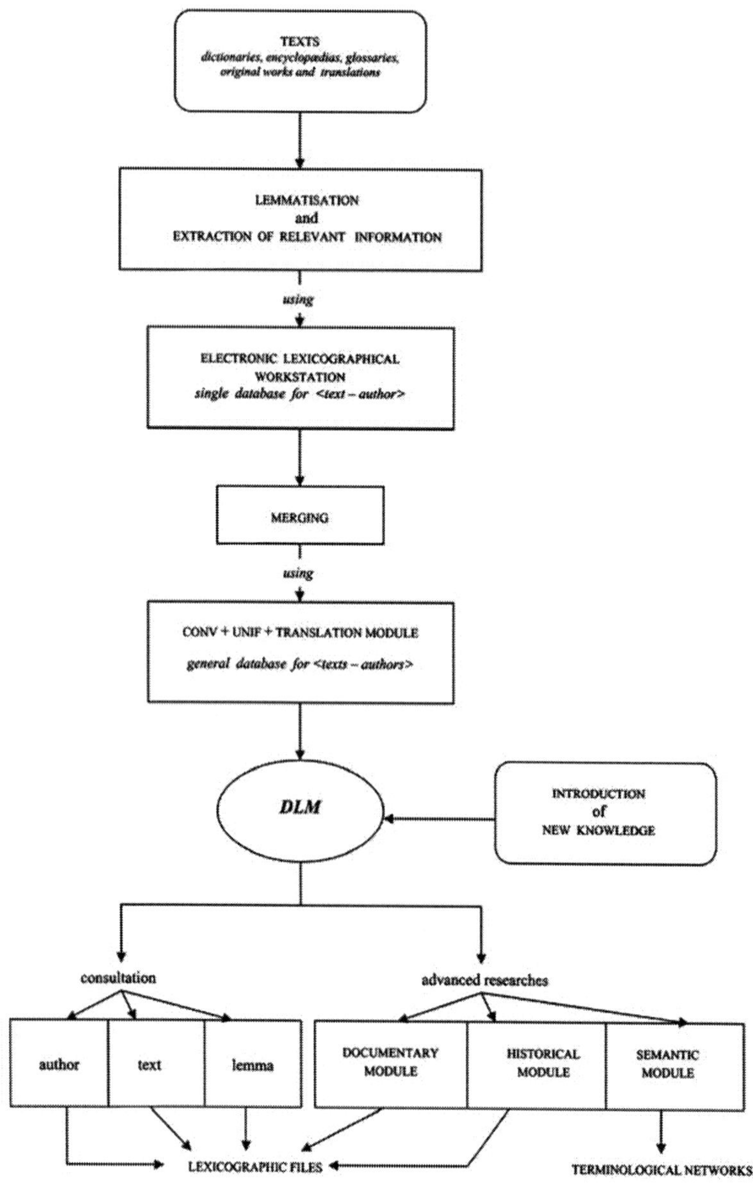

Fig. 1. General outline of the *DLM*

The last (and crucial) operation allowed by the lexicographical workstation is to include translation correspondences between works. In the event that a work has one or more translations, the researcher opens a specific window within the <quotation> field and inserts the passage that, in translation, corresponds to the original quote that s/he has already chosen. Of course, s/he encodes information about the translator and the translation and, moreover, indicates a translated lemma corresponding to the original one.[8]

The information above form the basis of the translation module in the *DLM* general database, namely procedures that allow the alignment between original works and translations. In particular, the choice of a main translation equivalent allows the generation of a new item in the general list of entry words, with related links.

As we have said, examinations and indexing made through the lexicographical workstation are integrated into the *DLM* general database.[9] There are two main steps in the process of merging: the conversion of files from the lexicographical workstation in XML format and the shifting of data to the *DLM*. For this reason two different applications have been implemented, called respectively CONV and UNIF. The received files undergo a conversion from the CONV procedure, which produces an XML file that is then shifted to the *DLM* through the UNIF procedure. Afterwards, UNIF module links up with the database and carries out the unification, making it possible to consult, print and enter the XML files produced with the CONV application. In addition, it also allows comparison of the elements already in the database with the remaining ones which must be merged.

The CONV and UNIF procedures also implement the translation module. They combine unambiguously each quotation collected by researchers with one or more corresponding translation(s), arranged by language, and add information about new translators and translated works in the database.

The examination and the indexing work for *DLM* has led to a collection of a great deal of information. Overall, over 120,000 lemma-records were included, which gave rise to more than 35,000 technical words at the end of the process of unification; there are almost 20,000 quotations. The choice of texts for examination and indexing has represented a major challenge for researchers involved in the project, putting at stake personal skills and interests next to the criteria of

[8] As we can imagine, the choice of main translation equivalents may become sensitive, because there are cases where it must be reconstructed by the researcher.

[9] See Lorenzi (2002b), Lanari (2002), Roccetti (2002), Rossi (2002).

relevance and representativeness. It is not a coincidence that in recent years we have seen a renewed and profound interest in the history of linguistic thought and in the technical vocabulary of language sciences[10] and this made it challenging to work for the *DLM*. With regard to dictionaries, it was decided to operate in extension, collecting the largest possible number of them. Thus, alongside classical vocabularies (for example, J. Marouzeau, *Lexique de la terminologie linguistique. Français, allemand, anglais, italien*, Paris, Geuthner, 1933), and encyclopaedias (such as M. Byram, *Routledge Encyclopaedia of Language Teaching and Learning*, London / New York, Routledge, 2000), sectorial indexes of terminology were reviewed (for example, E. De Felice, *La terminologia linguistica di G.I. Ascoli e della sua scuola*, Utrecht / Anvers, Spectrum, 1954, or R. Engler, *Lexique de la terminologie saussurienne*, Utrecht / Anvers, Spectrum, 1968) and also encyclopaedic dictionaries formed by complex articles (for example, *Dictionary of logic as applied to the study of language*, The Hague / Boston, Nijhoff, 1981, edited by W. Marciszewski, or *La linguistique. Guide Alphabétique*. Paris, Denoël, 1969, edited by A. Martinet).

Regarding the works, the *DLM* team decided to proceed on two levels. Starting from the western tradition, about 100 authors that may be considered fundamental were first selected: they range from classical Greeks and Latins (from Plato and Aristotle, depicted in the famous Raphael's *School of Athens*, who opened the site, to Dionysius Thrax and Marcus Terentius Varro and so on) to Medieval and Renaissance tradition, from the *Grammaire générale* to the birth of historical and comparative

---

[10] The reference is, firstly, to the great *Encyclopaedia of Language and Linguistics* (*ELL*), edited by Ron Asher and J.M.Y. Simpson, published in 1994 by Pergamon Press, and the new edition in fourteen volumes, published by Elsevier (2006) and edited by Keith Brown *et al*. In addition to *ELL*, we also mention the *History of Linguistics* edited by G.C. Lepschy (1994-1998), the series *Geschichte der Sprachwissenshaft*, edited by P. Schmitter for the publisher Narr, and the three volumes devoted to the *History of the Language Sciences*, published in *Handbücher zur Sprach-und Kommunikationswissenschaft* by de Gruyter, edited by S. Auroux, E.F.K. Koerner, H.-J. Niederehe and K. Versteegh. Of the utmost importance is the series of *ICHoLS* (*International Conferences on the History of the Language Sciences*), published by Benjamins. Other interesting terminological studies come up alongside these works, such as *Glossaries* published by Edinburgh UP and also projects like *CRGT* (*Corpus répresentatif des grammaires et des traditions linguistiques*) and *CTLF* (*Corpus des textes linguistiques fondamentaux*) (Colombat 2004a, b) that aim to achieve an electronic archive of texts considered essential in the history and development of linguistic thought.

linguistics, from the Saussurean *Cours* to structural linguistics, from generative grammar to contemporary logical grammar.

Then it was decided to work on specific areas of interest or national traditions that were, in any case, of substantial importance. Thus, for example, several texts were examined concerning cognitive linguistics, sociolinguistics, American structuralism, functional grammar, the study of pidgin and creole or Italian linguistics of the twentieth century.

Access to the *DLM* is via a homepage (http://dlm.unipg.it) with multilingual options that briefly summarises the research project (fig. 2):

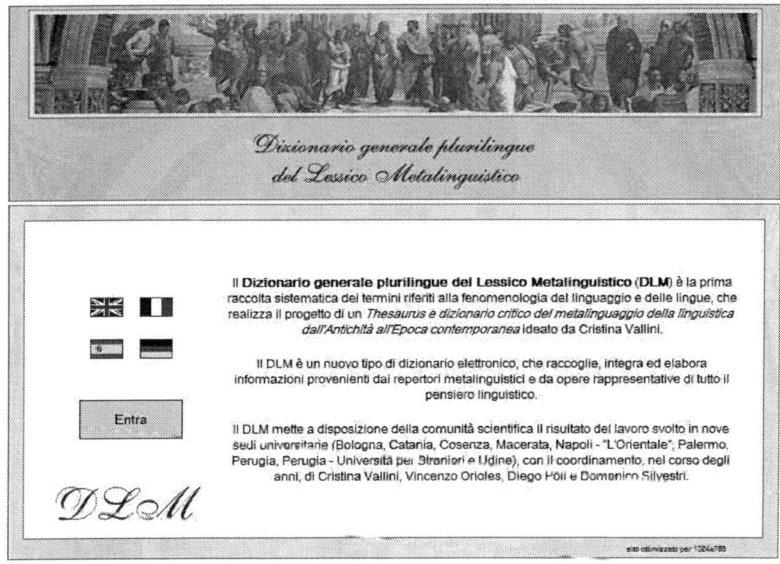

Fig. 2. *DLM* homepage

Clicking on ENTER we log on to the *DLM* through a homepage which contains the documentation on the project and from where the user can access the data (fig. 3):

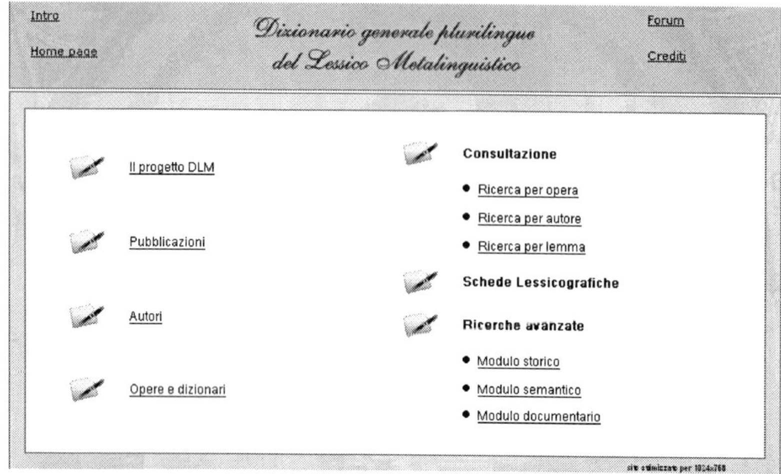

Fig. 3. Access to *DLM* documentation and data

The information consist of lists of authors, of texts from which the data are taken, in articles and technical reports (that can be downloaded in a Word or a PDF file) and bibliographical cards on volumes of the series "Lingue, Linguaggi, Metalinguaggio" (published by Il Calamo, Rome, and dedicated to the Project *DLM*) and other publications related to the project. The page provides access to the normal consultation of the dictionary and to advanced searches, i.e. documentary, historical and semantic modules, along with lexicographical entries to which we will return later.

Consultation is based on three parameters: <text>, <author>, <lemma>; the user, entering certain values, can gather the information required. Starting the search for <author>, we can make several kinds of search (<by initials>, <exact> or by a sequence of inner characters, setting the parameter <contains>), by time parameters (<period>, <date of birth>, <date of death>) or identification (<name>, <surname>), and we can freely cross the parameters.

Starting from an <author> we can see the <texts> linked to it. Starting the search from the initials of a <text> we can reach the relevant bibliographical information and the possibility to consult the lemmas in it.

In the consultation for <text>, the user sees a page in which s/he can specify several parameters to guide the search. Specific keys – such as <initials> (i.e. the tag *author-date* that can be used for a quick search), <language> (for search aimed to works written precisely in a given language) and <type> (which allows the direct consultation of a <dictionary> or original <work>) – are related to normal bibliographical indicators (<title>, <editor>, <place of publication>, <publishing house>, <year of publication>, <ISBN>). If the user clicks on the initials of a text, s/he can obtain the list of lemmas and, starting from a single entry, all information collected about it.

In the consultation of the *DLM* through the key <lemma>, the lemma-field must be filled by entering an initial or a specific sequence. Next to <lemma> the user can set <grammatical category> and <language>.[11] If the user clicks on the lemma, s/he can view the related information and then, by clicking on <vedi le citazioni> [see quotations], s/he can read a quotation. The example in fig. 4 on the next page shows the results for the lemma *mood*.

We shall briefly pass to <advanced searches>. The *documentary module* is now a work in progress. The procedures have already been tried and now the work of the researchers is focusing mainly on descriptors, which pose a problem both theoretical and methodological. As we mentioned, the markers were inserted in *DLM* in order to connect search by <authors>, <texts>, <lemmas> to currents and fields of linguistic thought, and to connect the categories <definition>, <description>, <metaphor> and <similarity> to <quotations>. The documentary network will also enable us to extract data useful for research, such as pictures, diagrams, formulas, web links, information on electronic editions of books, and so on.

After a careful study of systems of markers[12] (in particular those of the *Bibliographie Linguistique*), it was decided to start from an experimental set of linear, non-hierarchical descriptors. This solution has the advantage of flexibility, since the imposition of a rigid system, with precise levels of depth, would have made the indexing a very hard task, and the procedures for consultation unnecessarily complex. Secondly, it was decided to build sets of descriptors for different languages, but with interlinguistic matches as biunivocal as possible. The specialised lexicographical tradition of the discipline is constantly targeted in this sense, and the automatic procedure can easily follow this criterion.

---

[11] Among other possible options, the user could obtain a complete list of all the lemmas in a language, indicating only the <language> and leaving the <lemma> field blank. In addition, the search option <contains> allows us to recover those technical expressions that are a characteristic feature of the *DLM*, i.e. expressions of complementarity and opposition. The first ones contain items related by connectives like *and, e, et, und* and so on. The second ones have within them the lexicographical symbol *VS*; about this topic see Castelli (2008).

[12] See Lorenzi *et al.* (in print).

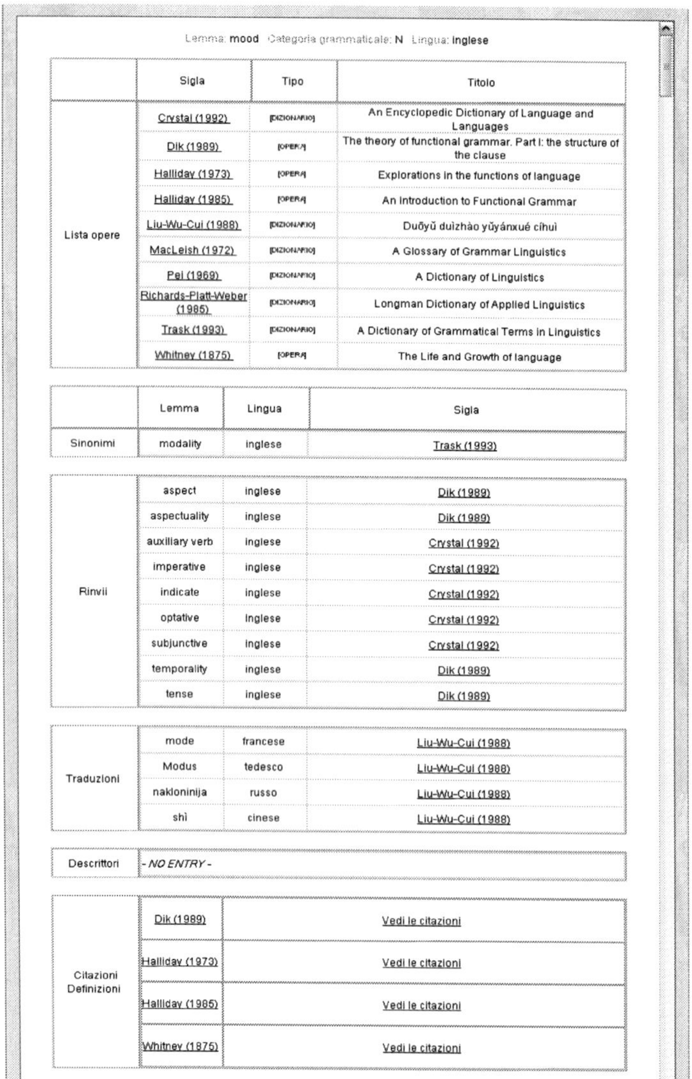

Lemma: mood Categoria grammaticale: N Lingua: inglese

	Sigla	Tipo	Titolo
Lista opere	Crystal (1992)	[DIZIONARIO]	An Encyclopedic Dictionary of Language and Languages
	Dik (1989)	[OPERA]	The theory of functional grammar. Part I: the structure of the clause
	Halliday (1973)	[OPERA]	Explorations in the functions of language
	Halliday (1985)	[OPERA]	An Introduction to Functional Grammar
	Liu-Wu-Cui (1988)	[DIZIONARIO]	Duōyǔ duìzhào yǔyánxué cíhuì
	MacLeish (1972)	[DIZIONARIO]	A Glossary of Grammar Linguistics
	Pei (1969)	[DIZIONARIO]	A Dictionary of Linguistics
	Richards-Platt-Weber (1985)	[DIZIONARIO]	Longman Dictionary of Applied Linguistics
	Trask (1993)	[DIZIONARIO]	A Dictionary of Grammatical Terms in Linguistics
	Whitney (1875)	[OPERA]	The Life and Growth of language

	Lemma	Lingua	Sigla
Sinonimi	modality	inglese	Trask (1993)

Rinvii	aspect	inglese	Dik (1989)
	aspectuality	inglese	Dik (1989)
	auxiliary verb	inglese	Crystal (1992)
	imperative	inglese	Crystal (1992)
	indicate	inglese	Crystal (1992)
	optative	inglese	Crystal (1992)
	subjunctive	inglese	Crystal (1992)
	temporality	inglese	Dik (1989)
	tense	inglese	Dik (1989)

Traduzioni	mode	francese	Liu-Wu-Cui (1988)
	Modus	tedesco	Liu-Wu-Cui (1988)
	nakloninija	russo	Liu-Wu-Cui (1988)
	shì	cinese	Liu-Wu-Cui (1988)

Descrittori	*- NO ENTRY -*

Citazioni Definizioni	Dik (1989)	Vedi le citazioni
	Halliday (1973)	Vedi le citazioni
	Halliday (1985)	Vedi le citazioni
	Whitney (1875)	Vedi le citazioni

Fig. 4. Results for the lemma *mood*

It is worth pointing out that the documentary network is of particular interest because it will allow the retrieval of selective quotations according to a first typology (which may be extended thereafter), such as indexing <metaphors>, which form a useful source of information for those dealing with the history of linguistic thought, or still pictures, diagrams and formulas, which represent iconic forms of metalanguage.

The *historical module*[13] is based on information related to <lemmas> and <texts>; it gives the *DLM* a historical projection of technical terms. In <ricerca cronologica per lemmi> [chronological search by lemmas] there are three parameters <language>, <lemma>, <year> that need to be entered for the consultation. First, we must choose the <language>, then the <lemma> and the <year>, and we can specify the starting and the final points entering the parameters <initial year> and <final year>. Figure 5 is an example of consultation of English terminology whose first element is *phonemic*, since 1930:

Lemma	1930	1935	1940	1945	1950	1955	1960	1965	1970	1975	1980	1985	1990	1995	2000
phonemic	1933		1944	1949	1951			1966				1985			
phonemic analysis						1958		1966				1985			
phonemic change						1958		1966							
phonemic component sequence			1942												
phonemic composition of an utterance					1951										
phonemic constituency				1948											
phonemic constituency of a morpheme					1951										
phonemic contour				1945											
phonemic element			1944		1951										
phonemic feature			1942		1951										
phonemic feature of a construction					1951										
phonemic form				1948	1951										
phonemic juncture				1946	1951										
phonemic loan								1966							
phonemic notation						1958						1985			

Fig. 5. Alphabetical list of English terminology with *phonemic*

The researcher can also obtain information concerning individual years or periods, reading the table above in a different order, as we can see in fig. 6:

[13] See Bonucci/Anulli (2007).

Anni	N° Lemmi	Esempio
1930	2	phonemic, phonemic structure,
1935	1	phonemic writing,
1940	5	phonemic, phonemic component sequence, phonemic element, phonemic feature ...
1945	8	phonemic, phonemic constituency, phonemic contour, phonemic form ...
1950	15	phonemic, phonemic composition of an utterance, phonemic constituency of a morpheme, phonemic element ...
1955	6	phonemic analysis, phonemic change, phonemic notation, phonemic structure ...
1960	0	
1965	15	phonemic, phonemic analysis, phonemic analysis, phonemic change ...
1970	1	phonemic transcription,

Fig. 6. Chronological list of English terminology with *phonemic*

The *DLM* project team is now working on the automatic compilation of lexicographical entries, which should support the previous procedures of consultation. If we consider the entry for *mood* shown in fig. 4. above or the outputs of historical module, we can easily see that they pose problems to consultation, because data are numerous and difficult to read on the screen. Moreover, the consultation of quotations requires further effort, since they are retrievable only for a single work at a time.

Undoubtedly, the possibility to read the outputs just as they were written in a paper dictionary would be preferable, which is why we are studying ways of generating lexicographical entries (printed or in a file), in a format similar to which the user is traditionally used to. This implies the need to move from a hypertext to a lexicographical entry through an „intelligent" procedure that simulates the work of a hypothetical human editor.

The user could request an entry containing all information related to a lemma, in an extended format. Instead of initials relating to <texts> and <quotations>, s/he will have a complete documentation, properly prepared so as to simulate the page of a specialised vocabulary.[14] As an example, the provisional lexicographical entry currently generable from the previous hypertextual entry in fig. 4 is shown in fig. 7 on the next pages. It is important to note that the orderliness of quotations is chronological (and not for <initials> of alphabetical), tracing a fundamental temporal path for the user.

The lexicographical entries give us the possibility to see, in the best possible way, how the *DLM* offers a useful tool for exploring the meaning

[14] On this issue see Lorenzi (2008), Lanari *et al.* (2006), with a first example.

and sense that technical words have had over time. For example, in future, the user will choose the information that s/he considers most interesting, excluding those s/he deems redundant.

Finally, the *semantic module*[15] is a set of procedures that allows us to connect the lemmas together to obtain a terminological thesaurus. Its structure is very complex and provides for the introduction of relations between <lemmas>, with specialised contributions in the various fields of linguistics and language sciences, and the use of selective information about <synonyms>, <translations> and <links> from dictionaries or texts. It complements the architecture of the *DLM* as lexicographical database which merges the dictionary and the thesaurus.

The semantic module links to studies aimed to develop an ontology of linguistic categories. The reference, in particular, is the project *GOLD* (*General Ontology for Linguistic Description*), led by S. Farrar and T. Langendoen (2003),[16] which promises interesting developments for the so-called „semantic web". Our starting point is the theory of sense relations, which had great development at least since the Seventies.[17] A lexical-semantic network as in *WordNet*, allow to display a knowledge base and to show explicitly conceptual relations. In the case of the *DLM*, information to build the networks comes from researchers involved in the project, who include significant links between the words, using the source consisting of the <synonyms> <translations> and <links> already stored in the *DLM*, but adding systematic relations that seem appropriate.

[15] See Lanari *et al.* (2007) and Lorenzi *et al.* (2007).

[16] See the site http://www.linguistics-ontology.org for documentation on the project and the scientific framework in which it fits. As we know, *GOLD* is based on the *Glossary* of the *Summer Institute of Linguistics*; on this issue see Bianchi – Marcaccio (2002).

[17] See Lyons (1977, 2002), Evens *et al.* (1980), Cruse (1986); for *WordNet* Fellbaum (1998).

Lemma: **MOOD** - Categoria grammaticale: **N** - Lingua: **INGLESE**

Il lemma è presente nei seguenti dizionari:

Crystal (1992) = Crystal, D., *An Encyclopedic Dictionary of Language and Languages*, USA, Blackwell, 1992.
Liu-Wu-Cui (1988) = Liu, Y. - Wu, J. - Cui, Z., *Duōyǔ duìzhào yǔyánxué cíhuì*, Běijīng, Rén mín jiāo tōng, 1988.
MacLeish (1972) = MacLeish, A., *A Glossary of Grammar Linguistics*, New York, Grosset & Dunlap, 1972.
Pei (1969) = Pei, M., *A Dictionary of Linguistics*, Totowa, New Jersey, Littlefield, Adams & Co., 1969.
Richards-Platt-Weber (1985) = Richards, J. - Platt, J. - Weber, H., *Longman Dictionary of Applied Linguistics*, Bungay, Suffolk, Longman, 1985.
Trask (1993) = Trask, R., *A Dictionary of Grammatical Terms in Linguistics*, London and New York, Routledge, 1993.

Il lemma è presente nelle seguenti opere:

Dik (1989) = Dik, S., *The theory of functional grammar. Part I: the structure of the clause*, Dordrecht, Foris Publications, 1989.
Halliday (1973) = Halliday, M., *Explorations in the functions of language*, London, Edward Arnold, 1973.
Halliday (1985) = Halliday, M., *An Introduction to Functional Grammar*, London, Edward Arnold, 1985.
Whitney (1875) = Whitney, W., *The Life and Growth of language*, London, Henry S. King e Co., 1875.
- Traduzione in italiano: D'Ovidio, F., *La vita e lo sviluppo del linguaggio*, Milano, , 1876 [tr. it. di Whitney (1875)].

Sinonimi:

modality (inglese) Trask (1993)

Rinvii:

aspect (inglese) Dik (1989)
aspectuality (inglese) Dik (1989)
auxiliary verb (inglese) Crystal (1992)
imperative (inglese) Crystal (1992)
indicate (inglese) Crystal (1992)
optative (inglese) Crystal (1992)
subjunctive (inglese) Crystal (1992)
temporality (inglese) Dik (1989)
tense (inglese) Dik (1989)

Traduzioni:

mode (francese) Liu-Wu-Cui (1988)
Modus (tedesco) Liu-Wu-Cui (1988)
nakloninija (russo) Liu-Wu-Cui (1988)
shì (cinese) Liu-Wu-Cui (1988)

CITAZIONI:

Opera: *Whitney (1875)*
Citazione a pag.220:
[...] our moods, those means of defining the contemplated relation between subject and predicate, or modifications of the copula. There are infinite shades of doubt and contingency, of hope and fear, of supplication and exaction, in our mental acts and cognitions, which all the synthetic resources of Greek moods, with added particles and adverbs, which all the analytic phraseology of English, are but rude and coarse means of signifying.

Fig. 7. Synthetic entry for the lemma *mood* (1)

Citazioni traduttive:

Lemma: modo

Categoria grammaticale: N

Lingua: italiano

Opera: Whitney (1876)

Citazione:

[...] modi, che son mezzi di definire il rapporto che si pone tra il soggetto ed il predicato, ovverosia modificazioni della copula. Vi sono sfumature infinite di dubbio e di contingenza, di speranza e di timore, di supplicazione e di esigenza, nelle azioni mentali e nelle cognizioni nostre. (pp. 267-268)

Opera: *Halliday (1973)*

Citazione a pag.41:

In the clause, the interpersonal element is represented by mood and modality: the selection by the speaker of a particular role in the speech situation, and his determination of the choice of roles for the addressee (mood) [...].

Citazioni traduttive:

Lemma: Aktionsart

Categoria grammaticale: N

Lingua: tedesco

Opera: Halliday (1975)

Citazione:

Im Satz wird das interpersonale Element durch Aktionsart und Modalität repräsentiert: die Selektion einer bestimmten Rolle in der Redesituation durch den Sprecher, seine Festlegung der Rollenwahl für den Adressaten (Aktionsart). (p.38)

Opera: *Halliday (1985)*

Citazione a pag.72:

the MOOD [...] consists of two parts: (1) the Subject, which is a nominal group, and (2) the Finite element, which is part of a verbal group.

Opera: *Halliday (1985)*

Citazione a pag.73-74:

Subject and Finite are closely linked together, and combine to form one constituent which we call the Mood [...] The Mood is the element that realizes the selection of Mood in the clause. It has sometimes been called the 'Modal' element; but the difficulty with this is that the term 'modal' is ambiguous, since it corresponds both to 'mood' and to 'modality'. The remainder of the clause we shall call the Residue.

Opera: *Halliday (1985)*

Citazione a pag.77:

[...] The Mood element has a clearly defined semantic function: it carries the burden of the clause as an interactive event. So it remains costant, as the nub of the proposition, unless some positive step is taken to change it, as in The duke has given your aunt a new teapot, hasn't he? (i) No, he hasn't. But (ii) - (a) the duchess has. - (b) he's going to. Here the proposition is first disposed of, by being rejected, in (i); this then allows for a new proposition, with change of Subject, as in (a), or change of Finite, as in (b). Each of these two constituents, the Subject and the Finite, plays its own specific and meaningful role in the propositional structure.

Fig. 7. Synthetic entry for the lemma *mood* (2)

To develop a flexible system that would allow the researcher to decide which words are to be taken into consideration, and which are the relations to be established between them, the instrument that seemed more suitable is the matrix. In a matrix, we can enter a set of lemmas and a set of relations, and specify the relations to be applied to such lemmas. Each lemma is a triple <lemma – grammatical category – language> and, in the matrix, the researchers report on the vertical axis the lemmas (i.e. the triples) in which they are interested, and then specify the relations that they deem useful to establish the terminological network, determining the properties of symmetry and inheritance. This operation provides the basis (i.e. the input) for the generation of terminological graphs which form the output of the procedure. In the experimental phase,[18] we used relations as follows:

- part-of: it denotes the link between a term *a* and another term *b*, when *b* is a meronym of *a*; in the more general case *b* is a „field of study" which is part of field of study *a*; the relation is asymmetrical: if *Phonology* is part-of *Linguistics*, then *Linguistics* is not part-of *Phonology*;
- acronym-of: asymmetrical, if V is acronym-of *verb*, then *verb* is not acronym-of V;
- synonymous-of: symmetrical, if *noun* is synonymous-of *substantive*, then *substantive* is synonymous-of *noun*;
- term-linked-to: it denotes the link between terms generically "at the same level"; symmetrical, if *sentence* is term-linked-to *clause*, then *clause* is term-linked-to *sentence*;
- term-of: it denotes the link between a term *a* and another term *b* and indicates the field of study in which *a* is used; asymmetrical, if *verb* is a term-of *grammar*, then *grammar* is not a term-of *verb*;
- kind-of: it denotes hierarchical relations and inclusiveness; asymmetrical, if *common noun* is kind-of *noun*, then *noun* is not kind-of *common noun*. This relation allows to get the inheritance of information: if *noun* is term-of *grammar* and *common noun* is kind-of *noun*, then *common noun* is term-of *grammar*.

The previous relations were taken as a prefixed set (*standard relations*), for a first consultation of terminology in *DLM*. In the site we can see some examples, like the one prepared by Bianchi *et al.* (in print) to analyse the works by R. Jakobson collected in *Essais de linguistique générale* (1963). The linguist can also operate with a free set of relations (*customised relations*), that s/he considers useful for a specific consultation of the

[18] See Lanari *et al.* (2007) and Lorenzi *et al.* (2007).

dictionary, and especially for individual texts. In this way we have a free relational table, like the one prepared by A. De Meo in the next section.

3. As we have said, the *DLM* is designed to include multilingual translations of lemmas and definitions/descriptions proposed by editors of dictionaries, authors of texts and translators of original works.[19] However, the first two events are statistically infrequent and the presence of terminology translation in one or more target languages depends mainly on the language of the text as well as on the topic and the metalinguistic awareness of the author.

Bilingual and multilingual glossaries and dictionaries usually offer one or more decontextualised equivalents, creating problems for linguists who need to use them in a technical text, since it is not always possible to randomly choose among the proposed translations of the source word. A typical example is Marouzeau's *Lexique de la terminologie linguistique* (1951), where French terms appear with translations in Italian, English and German, sometimes with more than one option for the same language. A quick glance at the lexical field of *vowel* will show terms with just one corresponding equivalent in each target language (e.g. Fr. *voyelle*: Engl. *vowel*, It. *vocale*, Ger. *Vokal*), terms without translation (e.g. Fr. *voyelle furtive* or *voyelle relâchée*), and terms with several translation options for the same target language (e.g. Fr. *voyelle d'appui*: Engl. *glide*, It. *vocale d'appoggio*, Ger. *Einschubvokal*, *Hilfsvokal*, *Stützvokal*). The editor does not provide the reader with enough information to discriminate whether multiple translations of the same French entry are a synonym set or differentiate between two or more target meanings for the same source term, as e.g. Fr. *évolution* – Engl. *evolution*, It. *evoluzione*, Ger. *Entwicklung*, *Wandel*, where actually the second German term lacks the positive connotation of the first one, since *Wandel* means 'to become different or undergo alteration', whereas *Entwicklung* means 'a gradual process in which something changes into a different and usually more complex or better form'.

Translations required by the topic are exemplified by Trask's *Dictionary of Historical and Comparative Linguistics* (2000), which „provides thorough coverage of the terminology of classical historical linguistics, including particularly Indo-European studies: UMLAUT, PALATALISATION, TRANSFERRED SENSE, *SCHWEBEABLAUT*, LENITION, *SANDHI*, *VISARGA*, LOSS OF THE CONDITIONING ENVIRONMENT and hundreds

[19] Standardised headwords taken from dictionaries of linguistics are presented without definitions, while metalinguistic terminology taken from original works or their translations is proposed with definitions and/or descriptions.

of other traditional terms are entered and explained."[20] Obviously a lexicon of historical linguistics cannot omit reference to German specialist terms, generated by scholars in the nineteenth century, and Sanskrit grammatical terms of the Indian tradition, which had enormous impact on modern linguistic scholarship and growth of the science of language in the West. Loanwords are reproduced with specific visual markers, i.e. italic and source language orthography; some terms may be easily recognised either as adapted borrowings or calques on the basis of orthographical and morphological features. Indication of source language and English equivalents (e.g. Ger. *Auslautsverhärtung* [final devoicing]) or literal translations (e.g. Ger. *Abnutzung* [abrasion]; Ger. *Rückschreibung* [back spelling]) are provided for loanwords and calques only, whereas adapted borrowings are accompanied by English synonyms, not marked as translations: e.g. *ablaut* (also *apophony*, *vowel gradation*); *umlaut* (also *vowel mutation*, *metaphony*).

Although unsystematically, foreign language equivalents can be found also in monolingual repertoires, such as G.R. Cardona's *Dizionario di Linguistica* (1988), both to explain the origin of the source term (e.g. It. *alimentante* – Eng. *feeding*; It. *diastratico* – Fr. *diastratique*) and as information supplement (e.g. It. *allocutivi* – Eng. *address forms*, Ger. *Anredeformen*, Fr. *allocutifs* or *formes de traitement*, Sp. *formas de tratamiento*).

The *DLM* collects also translations of terms occurring in original works, gathered together with their definitions and/or descriptions. Linguists may provide translations of key terminology in the context of a debate on issues already addressed by foreign scholars in other languages, as e.g. in the *Generativ grammatik på svenska* by Ö. Dahl (1971), where the Swedish linguist supports his translations of well-known standard generative terms by quoting the original English forms:

> *Transformationsregler* – I stället antar man att det finns en annan sorts regler, transformationsregler, som på olika sätt kan förändra de träd som har genererats av frasstrukturreglerna. Man brukar tala om fyra olika slags enkla transformationer:
> 1/ strykning (deletion)
> 2/ tillägg (adjunktion)
> 3/ utbyte (substitution)
> 4/ flyttning (permutation) (Dahl 1971: 5-6).

Quotations enable the *DLM* to combine the history of the words with the history of ideas, allowing the user to check every headword's value, its

---

[20] Trask (2000: VI).

potential connotations, collocations and frequency of usage, both synchronically and diachronically. An example illustrating the potentiality and peculiarities of this dictionary can be offered by the quotes accompanying some of B. Terracini's terms taken from his *Guida allo studio della linguistica storica* (1949). The Italian historical linguist offers his readers equivalents of German specialist terms and vice-versa every time he makes explicit reference to German scholars and/or schools of thought, but prefers English translations or English terms where he refers to W.D. Whitney, well-known nineteenth-century American linguist and one of the foremost Sanskrit scholars of his time. We give a few examples collected in the *DLM*:

- the German *vergleichende Sprachwissenschaft*, and its Italian equivalent *scienza comparata del linguaggio*

> „vergleichende Sprachwissenschaft", scienza comparata del linguaggio: poiché questo è il nome che prese la linguistica scientifica nella terra che le dette i natali. (Terracini 1949: 15)

- the Italian *speculazioni glottogoniche*, and its German equivalent *glottogonische Speculationen*

> (…) e tutte insieme [le identificazioni di desinenze e di elementi tematici modali o temporali, con pronomi o con le varie forme del verbo „essere"] furono designate col termine dispregiativo di "speculazioni glottogoniche" (glottogonische Speculationen) (Terracini 1949: 65)

- the Italian *scienza del linguaggio*, and its English equivalent *comparative philology*

> Whitney iniziò l'insegnamento universitario della scienza del linguaggio (comparative philology) (Terracini 1949: 78).

The *DLM* allows an immediate comparison between the choice of *scienza del linguaggio* as Italian equivalent of *comparative philology* and the definition of the last term provided in Whitney's *The Life and Growth of Language* (1875), clearly showing a misleading interpretation by Terracini:

> *Comparative philology* – Comparative philology and linguistic science, we may say, are two sides of the same study: the former deals primarily with the individual facts of a certain body of languages, classifying them, tracing out their relations, and arriving at the conclusions they suggest; the latter makes the laws and general principles of speech its main subject, and uses particular facts rather as illustrations. The one is the working phase,

the other the regulative and critical and teaching phase of the science. The one is more important as a part of special training, the other as an element of general culture (…) (Whitney 1875: 315).

In a century almost completely devoted to historical-comparative linguistics, the Yale Professor of Sanskrit and comparative philology dedicated an important part of his teaching to the theory of language and to the general principles of description and development of language, publishing two seminal books on this topic, *Language and the Study of Language* (1867) and *The Life and Growth of language* (1875), where he outlines a vision of language as a social institution and a historical product of human activity.[21] Therefore his appeal to keep separate the theoretical-methodological approach of comparative philology – the study of the particulars – and that of linguistic science – the study of the general principles – is of primary importance.

Translators will find rather challenging the section of *DLM* specifically designed to relate terms and definitions to their published translations, because it allows a reflection on the problems of translation quality and translation strategies suitable for linguistic texts. Number of target languages, quality and completeness of translations are variables depending upon available published editions of each analysed original work.

Comparing source language terms and quotations with their translations in a target language enables the highlighting of translation procedures applied by specialised translators – often linguists themselves – when they formulate an equivalence for the purpose of transferring elements of meaning from the source- to the target text, with variable qualitative results, fluctuating within a range from excellent to poor, sometimes with noticeable serious omissions, dangerous substitutions, arbitrary neutralisation of terminological differences or, on the contrary, unnecessary lexical increase.

A striking example of how metalanguage reshaping by omitting and replacing terms in a target language may affect the reception of a theory is offered by the French translation of Sapirian *drift*, an original metaphorical term denoting the gradual and largely imperceptible direction of language change:

---

[21] "[W]ith the 1875 book and Whitney's selection of topics, the way he treats them, and in particular the relative weight he accords to philosophical, historical, cultural, ethnological, social, psychological, philological, typological and grammatical considerations, the originality of his approach becomes much clearer. It is this book that would set much of the agenda for the modern 'general linguistics' that would eventually emerge in the century" (Joseph 2002: 20).

Quotation	Translated quotations
Lemma: **drift** Grammatical category: **N** Language: **English** Text: **Sapir (1921)** **Quotation page: 150** But language is not merely something that is spread out in space, as it were – a series of reflections in individual minds of one and the same timeless picture. Language moves down time in a current of its own making. It has a drift.	Lemma: **X** Grammatical category: **X** Language: **French** Text: **Sapir (1953)** **Quotation:** Mais le langage n'est pas seulement quelque chose qui s'étend dans l'espace comme une série d'images réfléchies dans les cerveaux individuels, images d'un seul et même tableau éternel. (p. 143)
Quotation page: 155 The drift of a language is constituted by the unconscious selection on the part of its speakers of those individual variations that are cumulative in some special direction.	Lemma: **évolution** Grammatical category: **N** **Quotation:** L'évolution d'un langage est constituée par une sélection inconsciente de variations individuelles, qui tendent toutes vers un certain point (…). (p. 147)

In the first excerpt, quoted from *Language* (1921), Sapir creates a visual context for the concept of *language drift*, using a verb of action (*to move down*) and a noun (*current*) to indicate the particular dynamism of language over time, almost sliding along a watercourse, dragged by a downstream movement that it doesn't control. It is relatively easy to identify that the two last source-language sentences received no translation in the French target text, an omission not arising from inattention but most certainly due to the translator's conscious decision to avoid the Sapirian metaphor, underestimating its metalinguistic value, and replacing it in further quotations with the French equivalent of *evolution*, i.e. *évolution*, as exemplified in the second excerpt.

There is no absolute correlation between difficulty of specialised terminology and quality of translation, since often limited accuracy appears attributable to limited attention paid by translators to common or recurrent terms, as in the following examples of neutralisation of source-language terminological differences, taken from L. Bloomfield's *Language* (1935) and its Italian translation (1974):

Quotation	Translated quotations
Lemma: **linguistic form** Grammatical category: **N** Language: **English** Text: **Bloomfield (1935)** **Quotation page: 138** A phonetic form which has a meaning, is a 'linguistic form'.	Lemma: **forma linguistica** Grammatical category: **N** Language: **Italian** Text: **Bloomfield (1974)** **Quotation:** Una forma fonetica dotata di significato è una 'forma linguistica'. (p.159)

Quotation	Translated quotations
Lemma: **homonym** Grammatical category: **N** Language: **English** Text: **Bloomfield (1935)** **Quotation page: 145** Different linguistic forms which have the same phonetic form (and differ, therefore, only as to meaning) are known as *homonyms*. Since we cannot with certainly define meanings, we cannot always decide whether a given phonetic form in its various uses has always the same meaning or represents a set of homonyms.	Lemma: **omonimo** Grammatical category: **N** Language: **Italian** Text: **Bloomfield (1974)** **Quotation**: Forme linguistiche diverse che hanno la stessa forma fonetica (e differiscono, quindi, solo per il significato) sono dette *omonimi.* Dato che non siamo in grado di definire con certezza i significati, non siamo sempre in grado di decidere se una data forma linguistica nei suoi vari usi abbia sempre lo stesso significato o rappresenti un insieme di omonimi. (p. 167)

The target term *forma linguistica*, a literal translation of English *linguistic form* both in the first quotation and in the opening sentence of the second one, is erroneously used as being equivalent to *phonetic form* instead of the expected *forma fonetica* in the second of the two occurrences of this term contained in the Bloomfieldian definition of *homonym*, thus creating a confusing terminological overlap and a shift of meaning in the target text.

The same effect is produced by the opposite procedure, namely multiplying target equivalents of one source term, and carelessly producing avoidable synonyms, noticeable in the English translations of the German term *lautliche Bedingung*, excerpted from Schuchardt's pamphlet *Über die Lautgesetze,* directed against the neo-grammarians (1922), and first published in 1885:

Quotation	Translated quotations
Lemma: **lautliche Bedingung** Grammatical category: **N** Language: **German** Text: **Schuchardt (1922)** **Quotation page: 59** Da es eine Reihe von Kategorien lautlicher Bedingungen gibt, wie Akzent, Silben-stellung, Beschaffenheit des unmittelbar folgenden Lautes, des unmittelbar vorausgehenden, des zweitfolgenden usw., so besteht in jedem einzelnen Falle ein Bedingungskomplex (…).	Lemma: **phonetic environment** Grammatical category: **N** Language: **English** Text: **Schuchardt (1972)** **Quotation:** Since there is a series of categories of phonetic environments such as accent, position within the syllable, nature of the directly following sound, of the directly preceding one, or of the one after the following one, etc., in every single case a complex of conditions becomes evident. (p. 53)
Quotation page: 63-64 Während die Junggrammatiker die Ausnahmslosigkeit der Lautgesetze von einer Gleichheit der lautlichen Bedingungen abhängig machen wie sie meines Erachtens überhaupt nicht besteht, halten sie die unmittelbar gegebene Verschiedenheit der Wörter dabei für gleichgültig (…) Ich halte das wenigstens in der absoluten Form wie es behauptet wird, für unrichtig (…).	Lemma: **phonetic condition** Grammatical category: **N** **Quotation:** While the neogrammarians make the unexceptionability of sound laws dependent upon equality of phonetic conditions, which in my opinion does not exist at all, at the same time they treat with indifference the immediately obvious difference between words (…) I consider this wrong, at least in the absolute form in which it is asserted. (p. 57)

The meaning of the source term *lautliche Bedingung* is not broader than that of the target term *phonetic condition*, therefore it is not necessary to create an asymmetrical relation between the two languages, introducing a second English term, *phonetic environment*, which instead has its equivalent in the German *lautliche Umgebung*.

Translators may apply opposite procedures when transferring meaning in two different target languages. The Italian and Spanish translations of the English term *drill*, collected in the *DLM* through data processing of L. Selinker's seminal paper on *Interlangue* (1972), show a translation by amplification in the first language and a translation by omission in the second one. The word *drill*, referring in its primary sense to a tool for boring holes in hard materials, has the metaphorical meaning of training or teaching by the continued repetition of an exercise, and indicates also an instructional exercise aimed at perfecting facility and skill, especially by regular practice. In the last sense, the term has acquired great popularity in the metalanguage of second language teaching, due to the well-known audio-oral method.

Quotation	Translated quotations
Lemma: **drill** Grammatical category: **N** Language: **English** Text: **Selinker (1972)** **Quotation page: 210** Since performance of *drills* in a second- language classroom is, by definition, not meaningful performance, it follows that form a learning perspective, such performance is, in the long run, of minor interest.	Lemma: **esercizio di tipo strutturale / drill** Grammatical category: **N** Language: **Italian** Text: **Selinker (1984)** **Quotation**: Poiché l'esecuzione o la produzione di esercizi di tipo strutturale o *drills,* in una classe di lingua è per definizione un tipo di produzione che non è significativa, ne consegue che dal punto di vista dell'apprendimento tale produzione è alla lunga di interesse minimo. (p. 26)
	Lemma: **ejercicio** Grammatical category: **N** Language: **Spanish** Text: **Selinker (1992)** **Quotation:** Puesto que la realización de ejercicios en una clase de lengua extranjera no es, por definición, una actuación significativa, concluiremos que desde el punto de vista del aprendizaje una actuación de este tipo tiene un interés menor. (p. 81)

Italian translation of the English technical term, metaphorical and culturally bound, proposes both a transferring of the source-language term and a descriptive equivalent (*esercizio di tipo strutturale*), while the Spanish translator uses an avoidance strategy, omitting the special term and replacing it with a generic one, *ejercicio* [exercise], obviously a careless decision in choosing the equivalent expression, causing a loss of meaning.

The editors of *DLM* place much stress on the authenticity of the translations, and they never intervene in correcting errors, leaving the users the task of detecting them and of reflecting upon the technical translation practice. In such a case the translation transfers meaning to the target reader thus contrasting with the source text, as e.g. in the case of the Bloomfieldian *bounded* and *unbounded nouns* (1935), subclasses of *common nouns*, translated in the Italian edition of *Language* (1974) as *nomi vincolati* and *nomi non vincolati*, literally 'bound nouns' and 'unbound nouns', instead of *nomi delimitati* and *nomi non delimitati*.

Quotation	Translated quotations
Lemma: **Bounded noun** Grammatical category: **N** Language: **English** Text: **Bloomfield (1935)** **Quotation page: 205** Bounded nouns in the singular number require a determiner (*the house, a house*). The class meaning is 'species of object occurring in more than one specimen, such that the specimen cannot be subdivided or merged.'	Lemma: **nome vincolato** Grammatical category: **N** Language: **Italian** Text: **Bloomfield (1974)** **Quotation**: Nomi vincolati; al singolare richiedono un determinativo (*the house, a house*). Il significato di classe è 'specie di oggetto che si trova in più di un esemplare, tale che gli esemplari non possono essere suddivisi o amalgamati'. (p. 237)

Quotation	Translated quotations
Lemma: **unbounded noun** Grammatical category: **N** Language: **English** Text: **Bloomfield (1935)** **Quotation page: 205** *Unbounded nouns* require a determiner for the definite category only (*the milk: milk*). The class-meaning is 'species of object occurring in more than one specimen, *such that the specimen can be subdivided or merged.*'	Lemma: **nome non vincolato** Grammatical category: **N** Language: **Italian** Text: **Bloomfield (1974)** **Quotation:** *Nomi non vincolati*; richiedono un determinativo solo per la categoria definita (*the milk: milk*). Il significato di classe è 'specie di oggetto che si trova in più di un esemplare, *tale che gli esemplari possono essere suddivisi o amalgamati*'. (p. 237)

In this respect it is interesting to note that the entry for *bound* in Trask's *Dictionary of Grammatical Terms in Linguistics* (1993) is a remark for non-native speakers of English, aimed at preventing misinterpretations of two similar lexical forms, such as *bound* and *bounded*:

> **bound** *adj*. The participle of **bind**, as in **binding**. See **Binding Theory**. NOTE: do not confuse the related terms **bind, bound, binding, Binding**

Theory with the entirely distinct group of terms **bounding, bounded, boundedness, bounding node, Bounding Theory.**

The *DLM* allows researchers to compare translations of contextualised terms, thus favouring a better understanding of their value and meaning on the basis of co-text and context of use, and leading to revisions and corrections of translation matches never called into question.

It also provides the opportunity to explore interlinguistic relationships, linking source and target lemmas so as to obtain a translation network with three-dimensional visualisation. The experimental translation network is an expansion of the semantic network:[22] In the matrix, the researchers report on the vertical axis the source lemma in which they are interested and its translations, and then specify the relations that they deem useful to establish the translation network, determining the properties of symmetry or asymmetry. In the experimental phase, relations are as follows:[23]

- literal-translation: the lexical choices can be contextually described as interlinguistic synonyms; symmetrical, if It. *fonema* is literal-translation of Engl. *phoneme*, Engl. *phoneme* is literal-translation of It. *fonema*;
- transference: it is the process of transferring a source language word to a target language text; asymmetric, if It. *drill* is transference of Engl. *drill*, Engl. *drill* is not transference of It. *drill*;
- transposition: it involves a change in the grammar – morphology or syntax – from source language to target language; symmetrical, if Sp. verb *fluir y transformarse* is transposition of Engl. noun *drift*, Engl. noun *drift* is transposition of Sp. verb *fluir y transformarse*;[24]
- modulation: it denotes an evident shift in the semantic surface structure, albeit retaining the same overall meaning effect in the specific context and co-text: source language and the target may appear dissimilar in terms of perspective; symmetrical, if Ger. *Strömung* is modulation of Engl. *drift*, Engl. *drift* is modulation of Ger. *Strömung*;[25]
- functional equivalence: it denotes the use of a referent in the target language text whose function is culturally similar to that of the source language referent; symmetrical, if Fr. *avoir des fissures* is functional-equivalence of Engl. *to leak*, Engl. *to leak* is functional-equivalence of Fr. *avoir des fissures*;[26]

---

[22] See § 2.
[23] See Newmark (1988), Hervey / Higgins (1992).
[24] See De Meo (2007b).
[25] Ibid.
[26] De Meo (2007a).

- paraphrase: the meaning of the source language lemma is explained in the target language; asymmetric, if It. *esercizio di tipo strutturale* is paraphrase of Engl. *drill*, Engl. *drill* is not paraphrase of It. *esercizio di tipo strutturale*;
- reduction: source language lemma is replaced with a target language lemma which does not embrace part of meaning; asymmetric, if Fr. *cas* is reduction of Engl. *case form*, Engl. *case form* is not reduction of Fr. *cas*;[27]
- expansion: the source language lemma is replaced with a target language lemma which covers the source language lemma meaning plus something else; asymmetric, if Sp. *corriente de transformación* is expansion of Engl. *drift*, Engl. *drift* is not expansion of Sp. *corriente de transformación*;[28]
- omission: source language lemma is dropped in the target language text; asymmetric.

A series of automatic procedures convert the matrix in an interactive animated 3D translation graph, and users can display 3D data from different access points: The natural ability of humans for spatial perception, orientation and spatial memories is an advantage in the process of perceiving information by means of spatial visualisation.

Transforming term networks with two levels of abstraction into trees that use the spatial depth of 3D will achieve an easy perception of their topological structure and give users intuitive control over content-oriented search paths. Below the matrix and the 3D translation graph (fig. 8 and 9) for English lemma *drift*, as used by Sapir (1933), and by his Italian (1969), French (1953), Spanish (1954), German (1961) and Dutch (1988) translators.

[27] Sapir (1921: 168) and French translation (1953: 159).
[28] De Meo (2007b).

Tabella Relazionale

Lemma	Nome relazione 1: Literal-Translation Colore (RGB): #FF0000 Simmetrica	Nome relazione 2: Transposition Colore (RGB): #00FF00 Simmetrica	Nome relazione 3: Modulation Colore (RGB): #0000FF Simmetrica	Nome relazione 4: Expansion Colore (RGB): #FF00FF Asimmetrica	Nome relazione 5: Functional-Equivalence Colore (RGB): #FFFF00 Simmetrica
évolution [N; FR]					drift [N; ENGL]
courant [N; FR]			drift [N; ENGL]		
corriente [N; SP]			drift [N; ENGL]		
fluir y transformarse		drift [N; ENGL]		drift [N; ENGL]	
mutación [N; SP]					drift [N; ENGL]
transformación [N;					drift [N; ENGL]
corriente de transfor			drift [N; ENGL]	drift [N; ENGL]	
deriva [N; IT]	drift [N; ENGL]				
deriva [N; POR]					
movimento di deriva				drift [N; ENGL]	
Strömung [N; TED]			drift [N; ENGL]		
stroming [N; OL]			drift [N; ENGL]		
driftkracht [N; OL]	drift [N; ENGL]				
drift [N; ENGL]	deriva [N; IT]	fluir y transformarse	courant [N; FR]	fluir y transformarse	évolution [N; FR]

Fig. 8. Matrix for English lemma *drift*

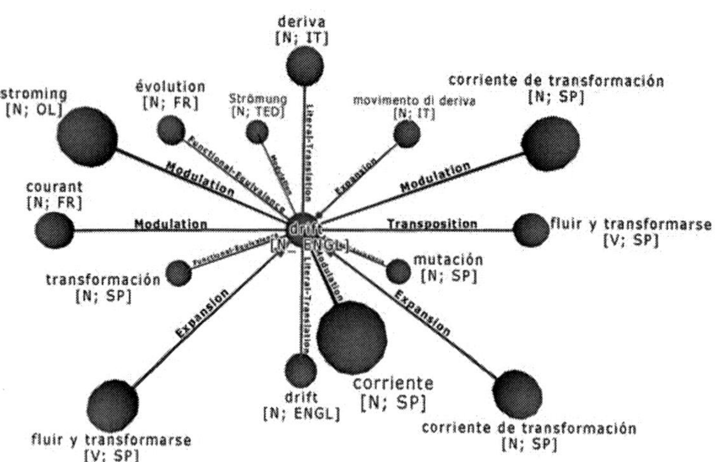

Fig. 9. 3D translation graph for English lemma *drift*

References

Auroux, Sylvain / Koerner, E.F. Konrad / Niederehe, Hans-Josef / Versteegh, Kees (eds) (2000-2006). *History of the Language Sciences / Geschichte der Sprachwissenschaften / Histoire des sciences du langage*, 3 vols. Berlin / New York, de Gruyter.

Bergenholtz, Henning / Tarp, Sven (1995). *Manual of Specialised Lexicography*. Amsterdam, Benjamins.

Bianchi, Elisa (2007). "Alla ricerca della definizione perfetta: note sulla lemmatizzazione delle opere di linguistica", in Poli (2007): 197-212.

Bianchi, Elisa / Gentili, Francesca / Marcaccio, Alejandro / Roccetti, Stefano (2006). "Analisi del metalinguaggio e reti terminologiche nel *Dizionario generale plurilingue del Lessico Metalinguistico*", in *Annali dell'Istituto Orientale di Napoli* 28: 33-61.

Bianchi, Elisa / Marcaccio, Alejandro (2002). "Lessicografia e terminologia metalinguistica in rete", in Lorenzi (2002a): 57-82.

Bickerton, Derek (1981). *Roots of Language*. Ann Arbor, Karoma.

Bloomfield, Leonard (1935). *Language*. London, George Allen & Unwin Ltd. [Italian translation by Francesco Antinucci, Giorgio Cardona (1974). *Il linguaggio*. Milano, il Saggiatore].

Bonucci, Paola / Anulli, Roberto (2007). "Per un'analisi computazionale della dimensione storica del metalinguaggio", in Poli (2007): 143-168.

Castelli Margherita (2008). "Antonimia e terminologia metalinguistica", in Facchetti (2008): 95 114.

Castelli, Margherita / Bonucci, Paola (2006). "Definizione e 'indefinibili' in linguistica cognitiva", in *Annali dell'Istituto Orientale di Napoli* 28: 63-76.

Colombat, Bernard (2004a). "CTLF – Le projet de recherche" [http://ens-web3.ens-lsh.fr/apelfrene/ctlf/article.php3?id_article=16].

—. (2004b). "CRGTL – Présentation du corpus des grammaires" [http://ens-web3.ens-lsh.fr/apelfrene/ctlf/article.php3?id_article=6].

Colombat, Bernard / Savelli, Marie (eds) (2001). *Métalangage et terminologie linguistique*. Leuven, Peeters.

Cruse, David (1986). *Lexical Semantics*. Cambridge, Cambridge University Press.

Cruse, David / Hundsnurscher, Franz / Job, Michael / Lutzeier, Peter (eds) (2002). *Lexikologie / Lexicology*, vol. 1. Berlin / New York, de Gruyter.

Dahl, Östen (1971). *Generativ grammatik på svenska*. Lund, Studentlitteratur [English translation by Terence H. Wilbur, Theo Vennemann (1972). "On Sound Laws. Against the Neogrammarians", in Wilbur, Terence H. / Vennemann, Theo (eds). *Schuchardt, the Neogrammarians and the Transformational Theory of Phonological Change*. Frankfurt am Main, Athenäum: 41-71].

De Meo, Anna (2002). "Lemmi e definizioni nel *Dizionario generale plurilingue del Lessico Metalinguistico*", in Lorenzi (2002a): 35-56.

—. (2007a). "*All grammars leak*. Usi e traduzioni di una metafora metalinguistica", in *Annali dell'Istituto Orientale di Napoli* 29: 271-299.

—. (2007b). "E se il titolo fosse infedele? Metalinguaggio dei titoli e del testo in alcune traduzioni di Sapir", in Poli (2007): 259-282.

De Meo, Anna / Lorenzi, Franco (2005). "Terminologia e lessicografia delle scienze del linguaggio: il *Dizionario generale e plurilingue del Lessico Metalinguistico*" [http://www. mediazionionline.it].

Di Maio, Francesco (2002). "Il software per il *DLM* (*Dizionario generale plurilingue del Lessico Metalinguistico*): la stazione lessicografica", in Lorenzi (2002a): 97-112.

Evens, Martha W. / Litowitz, Bonnie E. / Markowitz, Judith A. / Smith, Raul N. / Werner, Oswald (1980). *Lexical Semantic Relations: A Comparative Survey*. Edmonton, Linguistic Research Inc. [Current Inquiry into Language and Linguistics 34].

Facchetti, Giulio M. (ed.) (2008). *Mlaχ mlakas. Per Luciano Agostiniani*. Milano, Arcipelago Edizioni.

Farrar, Scott / Langendoen, Terence (2003). "A linguistic ontology for the semantic web", in *GLOT International* 7: 97-100.

Fellbaum, Christiane (ed.) (1998). *WordNet: An Electronic Lexical Database*. Cambridge, Ma., MIT Press.

Hervey, Sàndor / Higgins, Ian (1992). *Thinking Translation*. London / New York, Routledge.

Joseph, John Earl (2002). *From Whitney to Chomsky: Essays in the History of American Linguistics*. Amsterdam / Philadelphia, John Benjamins.

Lanari, David (2002). "Tra informatica e linguistica: sulla struttura del *DLM* (*Dizionario generale plurilingue del Lessico Metalinguistico*)", in Lorenzi (2002a): 113-140.

Lanari, David / Lorenzi, Franco / Rossi, Matteo (2006). "Verso la generazione automatica di voci lessicografiche nel *Dizionario generale plurilingue del Lessico Metalinguistico*", in *Annali dell'Istituto Orientale di Napoli* 28: 159-170.

Lanari, David / Roccetti, Stefano / Gentili, Francesca (2007). "Una rete semantica per la terminologia metalinguistica", in Poli (2007): 77-112.

Lepschy, Giulio C. (ed.) (1994-1998). *History of Linguistics*, 4 vols. London / New York, Longman.

—. (ed.) (1994). *Storia della linguistica*, 3 vols. Bologna, il Mulino.

Lorenzi, Franco (ed.) (2002a). *DLM – Dizionario generale plurilingue del Lessico Metalinguistico*. Roma, Il Calamo.

—. (2002b). "Il *Dizionario generale plurilingue del Lessico Metalinguistico* come banca dati multifunzionale: ideazione, risultati e prospettive", in Lorenzi (2002a): 11-34.

—. (2008). "Dizionari elettronici e documentazione lessicografica. Ipertesto e testo nel *Dizionario generale plurilingue del Lessico Metalinguistico*", in Facchetti (2008): 167-194.

Lorenzi, Franco / Peppoloni, Diana / Anulli, Roberto (2006). "L'elaborazione della rete documentaria per il *Dizionario generale plurilingue del Lessico Metalinguistico* e il sistema terminologico della *Bibliographie Linguistique*", in *Annali dell'Istituto Orientale di Napoli* 28: 171-193.

Lorenzi, Franco / Rossi, Matteo / Buttigli, Alessia (2007). "*DLM – Dizionario generale plurilingue del Lessico Metalinguistico*: stato dell'arte e prospettive di lavoro", in Poli (2007): 13-76.

Lyons, John (1977). *Semantics. I-II.* Cambridge, Cambridge University Press.

—. (2002). "Sense Relations: An Overview", in Cruse *et al.* (2002): 466-472.

Marini, Emanuela (2002). "Primi materiali per una bibliografia della lessicografia specialistica della linguistica", in Lorenzi (2002a): 83-96.

Newmark, Peter (1988). *Approaches to Translation.* Hertfordshire, Prentice Hall.

Orioles, Vincenzo (ed.) (2001). *Dal 'paradigma' alla parola. Riflessioni sul metalinguaggio della linguistica.* Roma, Il Calamo.

Poli, Diego (ed.) (2007). *Lessicologia e metalinguaggio*. Roma, Il Calamo.

Roccetti, Stefano (2002). "La procedura di unificazione lessicale nel *DLM* (*Dizionario generale plurilingue del Lessico Metalinguistico*)", in Lorenzi (2002a): 141-164.

Rossi, Matteo (2002). "Archiviazione e consultazione dei dati nel *DLM* (*Dizionario generale plurilingue del Lessico Metalinguistico*)", in Lorenzi (2002a): 165-185.

Sapir, Edward (1921). *Language: An Introduction to the Study of Speech.* New York, Harcourt, Brace and Company [French translation by Solange-Marie Guillemin (1953). *Le langage. Introduction à l'étude de la parole*. Parigi, Payot].

Schmitter, Peter (ed.) (1997-2005). *Geschichte der Sprachtheorie*, 6 vols. Tübingen, Narr.

Schuchardt, Hugo (1992). "Über die Lautgesetze. Gegen die Junggrammatiker", in Leo Spitzer (ed.). *Hugo-Schuchardt-Brevier: Ein Vademecum der allgemeinen Sprachwissenschaft*. Halle an der Saale, Niemeyer: 43-79.

Selinker, Larry (1972). "Interlanguage", in *International Review of Applied Linguistics* 10, 3: 209-231 [Italian translation by Paola Giunchi (1984). "Interlingua", in Arcaini, Enrico / Py, Bernard (eds). *Interlingua. Aspetti teorici e implicazioni didattiche. Collana di testi e documenti*. Roma, Treccani: 25-47. Spanish translation by Juana Muñoz-Liceras (1991). "La interlengua", in Muñoz-Liceras, Juana (ed.). *La adquisición de las lenguas extranjeras. Hacia un modelo de análisis de la interlingua*. Madrid, Gráficas Rogar: 79-101].

Trask, Robert Lawrence (1993). *A Dictionary of Grammatical Terms in Linguistics*. London / New York, Routledge.

—. (2000). *The Dictionary of Historical and Comparative Linguistics*. London / New York, Routledge.

Vallini, Cristina (ed.) (2000). *Le parole per le parole. I logonimi nelle lingue e nel metalinguaggio*. Roma, Il Calamo.

—. (2001). "Rivoluzioni scientifiche e ricadute terminologiche", in Orioles (2001): 73-92.

—. (2002). "Presentazione", in Lorenzi (2002a): 5-10.

—. (2007). "Aporie nella traduzione dei testi linguistici", in Poli (2007): 335-358.

Vallini, Cristina / Orioles, Vincenzo (2000). "Introduzione", in Vallini (2000): 5-7.

APPENDIX

SOME REFLECTIONS ON DICTIONARIES AND TRANSLATION

ON ITALIAN BILINGUAL AND SPECIALISED DICTIONARIES

STEFANIA NUCCORINI

Lexicographers, (bilingual) dictionaries, and translators are the "points" of a long-established, productive, but not always satisfactory, triangular relationship. The constraints, methods, expectations and results of lexicography have been analysed in depth by the professionals involved in the continuum departing from the first steps of the dictionary making process to the actual use of the resulting products. Lexicographers and dictionary users, in particular translators, have worked together on various occasions to assess the merits and the defects of dictionaries: indeed over the last fifteen years different aspects of dictionary use, from look-up and search processes to the user's degree of satisfaction (or frustration), have been monitored in large-scale surveys and in case-studies (Atkins / Varantola 1997, among others). Meta-lexicographers have contributed their usually linguistics-based comments to the discussion of moot points, analysing the nature of lexicography, as "art" and "craft", echoing Landau's (1984) sub-title, its relationship with lexicology and, more generally, with linguistics, and its status as an independent academic subject, as claimed by Sinclair as early as 1984. Much more recently, the interdisciplinary boundaries and the desirable interaction between lexicology, lexicography, terminology and translation have been highlighted by Hartmann (forthcoming).

The common aim has been to assess lexicographers' and translators' (and dictionary users' in general) different positions and to strike the balance between conflicting but often complementary, sometimes converse, views, needs and perspectives. The words *nightmare* or *desperation* are often used by lexicographers when facing difficult decisions of inclusion / exclusion or selection of information; «the linguist might well decide to leave (theoretical) problems unresolved» (Lyons 1977: 552), the lexicographer can't. *Dream* is often used by translators when confronted with missing or defective information. The "road map" for lexicographers' nightmares to be over and for translators' dreams to come true focuses in particular on bilingual dictionaries, which occupy a privileged position in this situation and which have been the object of various analyses since Marello's seminal volume of 1989. Lexicographers too have their ambitious plans and their "dreams", as Iamartino (2006) reminds us with reference to Johnson's dream to include all the words of the English language in his dictionary, but the difference often lies not in quantitative elements but in their typology and presentation – with particular reference to the "dream" of a "translator's dictionary", as Morini (2006) reconsiders it.

Towards is another key word often used in accounts of lexicographical projects, in reviews, in dictionary use reports, and in academic papers on lexicography, which testify to the latter's vitality and to the willingness to produce ever better dictionaries. On the one hand, with particular reference to bilingual learner's dictionaries as opposed to monolingual pedagogical lexicography, «the domain of bilingual dictionaries» was defined, not long ago, as «strikingly immobile» (Bogaards / Hannay, 2004: 463): on the other, there are cases of exceptionally relevant dictionary-making policies such as that represented by Dutch bilingual lexicography, as reported in a recent special issue of the *International Journal of Lexicography* (Martin, 2007).

Generally speaking, bilingual lexicography is constantly looking ahead. Italian bilingual dictionaries are no exception in this picture, though most of them are addressed to the general public and this sometimes turns them into too refined products for learners and not always satisfactory tools for professionals. The "traditional" bilingual dictionary has recently been questioned and "new" typologies have been proposed for different purposes and for different groups of "real", rather than "intended", users (for example, Béjoint 2002; Laufer / Levitsky-Aviad 2006). Electronic dictionaries certainly help to handle and present information, as highlighted, for example, by a recent Italian-Dutch dictionary (Lo Cascio 2005). Corpora, above all, and in particular comparable and parallel corpora, should be at the basis of the production of bilingual dictionaries and they should represent both cultural and commercial major investments *per se*.

Italian specialised lexicography has a rich tradition in particular in the field of dictionaries of synonyms: to my knowledge, there is no dictionary of collocations and of word combinations, which represent one of the most praised lexicographical enterprises particularly in English lexicography. These dictionaries, usually addressed to learners engaged in production activities, could also offer precious material for bilingual databases and dictionaries for translators. Bilingual specialised dictionaries are, at the moment, rather rare: however, collocations and, above all, information about the phraseology of headwords, should be included in general bilingual dictionaries, in particular when cognate and/or loan words in two languages differ in the company they keep with other words (Nuccorini 2008). Corpus-driven data would supply the necessary evidence: the term *phraseology* indeed refers to the syntagmatic patterns in which words occur and which are analysable in concordances. Patterns reveal non only linguistic but also cultural aspects. Such an approach would be particularly useful to translators and for a variety of purposes: at a minimal level it would avoid giving misleading information in dictionaries. For example the Italian and the English word *kamikaze*, though both borrowed from the same Japanese word, have developed different senses and different uses in the two languages, as made clear by the analysis of their different phraseologies (Nuccorini 2006), to the point that in most cases they could be considered as false friends. Unfortunately, they are the sole equivalents offered for each other in most bilingual dictionaries.

Conferences, journals, series, monographs, international projects and other initiatives regarding dictionaries, both existing and simply "possible"[1], are flourishing. The amount of linguists' research behind each product is impressive. Dictionary users' comments and requests are demanding and stimulating. The future of lexicography is really challenging and promising.

References

Atkins, Beryl / Varantola, Krista (1997). "Monitoring Dictionary Use", in *International Journal of Lexicography* 10, 1: 1-45.

Béjoint, Henri (2002). "Towards a bilingual dictionary for 'comprehension'", in Ferrario, Elena / Pulcini, Virginia (eds). *La lessicografia bilingue tra presente e avvenire.* Vercelli, Mercurio: 33-48.

Bogaards, Paul / Hannay, Mike (2004). "Towards a New Type of Bilingual Dictionary", in Williams, Geoffrey / Vessier, Sandra (eds.). *11th Euralex Congress Proceedings*. Lorient, UBS: 463-474.

Hartmann, Reinhard (forthcoming). "Promoting Interdisciplinary Collaboration between Lexicology, Lexicography, Terminology and Translation: towards Reference Science?". [paper presented at the International Conference on *Lexicology and Lexicography of Domain-specific Languages*. Palermo, June 21-23, 2007].

Iamartino, Giovanni (2006). "Dal lessicografo al traduttore: un sogno che si realizza?", in San Vicente, Félix (ed.). *Lessicografia bilingue e*

[1] An International Informal Colloquium on "Possible Dictionaries" was held at *Roma Tre* University on July 6-7, 2007.

traduzione: metodi, strumenti. approcci attuali. Monza, Polimetrica: 101-132.

Landau, Sidney (1984). *Dictionaries. The Art and Craft of Lexicography*. Cambridge, Cambridge University Press.

Laufer, Batia / Levitzky-Aviad, Tamar (2006). "Examining the Effectiveness of 'Bilingual Dictionary Plus' – a Dictionary for Production in a Foreign Language", in *International Journal of Lexicography* 19, 2: 135-155.

Lo Cascio, Vincenzo (2006). *Grande Dizionario Elettronico Italiano-Neerlandese, Neerlandese-Italiano*. Amstelveen, Italned.

Lyons, John (1977). *Semantics*. Cambridge, Cambridge University Press.

Marello, Carla (1989). *Dizionari Bilingui*. Bologna, Zanichelli.

Martin, Willy (ed.) (2007). "Planning Bilingual Dictionaries: the Dutch Approach", in *International Journal of Lexicography* 20, 3: 221-334.

Morini, Massimiliano (2006). "Il dizionario del traduttore. Un sogno che si realizza?", in San Vicente, Félix (ed.). *Lessicografia bilingue e traduzione: metodi, strumenti. approcci attuali*. Monza, Polimetrica: 165-179.

Nuccorini, Stefania (2006). "In Search of Phraseologies: Discovering Divergences in the Use of English and Italian True Friends", in *European Journal of English Studies* 10, 1: 33-47

—. (2008). "Phraseologies and Italian-English Dictionaries: Evidence for a Proposal", in Pulcini, Virgina / Martelli, Aurelia (eds.). *Investigating English with Corpora. Studies in Honour of Maria Teresa Prat*. Monza, Polimetrica: 171-187.

Sinclair, John (1984). "Lexicography as an Academic Subject", in Hartmann, Reinhard (ed.). *LEXeter '83 Proceedings*. Tübingen, Niemeyer: 3-12.

LEXICOGRAPHICAL TOOLS IN LITERARY TRANSLATION: SOME CONSIDERATIONS

ILIDE CARMIGNANI

The title of this round table poses some very complex questions, which it would be difficult to deal with fully in such a short time. This is especially true when tackling the matter from the point of view of literary translation, which is the mediation of artistic texts that draw on all the resources of a language in an idiosyncratic manner. They do so in a way that is not standard to one particular sector, and they present all kinds of hurdles, including those of technical translation – and much could be said about the stylistic value of technicalities in literary work. I shall thus confine myself to some brief considerations, drawing on my work as a literary translator from Spanish into Italian, on the specific nature of my field, and on its special requirements in terms of lexicographical tools.

The Requirements of a Literary Translator

A literary translator is required to recreate a given text in a target language. This not only means overcoming the difficulties created by the anisomorphism of languages – which is, after all, that of cultures – but it also means respecting any deviation between the source language and the way it is used by the author. This is therefore the deviation between the artistic *parole*, with all the innovation and idiosyncrasy it contains, and the *langue*. Linguistic variation is an essential part of this process of mediation: the translator is obliged to detect the use of standard and non-standard forms in the source language from a lexical, morphological, syntactic, and pragmatic point of view, as well as in terms of the arrangement of the enunciation, the segmentation of the disquisition, and so on. This is because variation plays a precise role in a literary work, expressing an individual identity and voice on various levels, not just of one character or another, but also of the author himself, as has been clearly pointed out in studies by Hatim / Mason (1990, 1997) and García de Toro (1994) amongst others.

Compared with other types of user, the literary translator will therefore turn to lexicographical tools, and bilingual works in particular – usually the key instrument for his everyday work – for the information required to detect not so much the extralinguistic referents of a particular term or syntagm (which he will already generally know) as all its other dimensions. These include its morphosyntactic characteristics, its area and frequency of use, its expressive register, and so on. The aim is to choose the most suitable equivalent in order to recreate not only the denotative but also the connotative aspects of the word, while respecting the variation. This pragmatic-textual information needs to be illustrated by substantial phraseology, based not on contrived theoretical examples but on authentic material such as large corpora, so that the translator can read the word in its real contexts. It would of course be extremely useful to include literary corpora in this authentic material, especially if the quotations from authors that illustrate the use of the word could be followed by the most authoritative translations published in the target language. Lastly, it would be of even greater assistance if it were possible to consult these corpora together with the entries in the dictionary, in order to gain a better appreciation of them in a fair amount of context, even though within the limits imposed by copyright laws.

Together with this information, which is formulated in a contrastive manner, the literary translator needs the greatest possible range of equivalents in order to choose the one most suited to his needs. This choice will be based not only on the connotations of the original text but also on the stylistic demands of its reformulation. Indeed, it is not uncommon to find some constraints in the target language, such as cacophony or the synonymisation of an unwieldy repetition or a metric measure that is unsuitable for the verse, which would require other solutions.

Another element that weighs heavily on the choice of equivalent, and that therefore often requires more than one, is the strategy of mediation being adopted. The translation that is most effective from the point of view of formal equivalence might well prove to be unsuitable from the point of view of functional equivalence. Here we might give an example used in other domains by Matte Bon (2000): the Spanish word *alpiste* corresponds to the Italian *scagliola* but the frequency of its use is much greater, meaning that most Spanish-speaking people can associate the term with its extralinguistic referent – canary feed – while very few Italians are able to identify it as *scagliola*. Sañé-Schepisi and Garzanti simply suggest *scagliola*. Laura Tam's dictionary, on the other hand, offers a useful functional equivalent in the Spanish-Italian section – *miglio*, a term much more part of our everyday language, as can be seen in its figurative uses – but erroneously applying the label "botanical" and not accompanying it with the formal equivalent. Nor do older dictionaries provide much comfort: Ambruzzi offers *scagliola, canaria, falaride* – taken up by Carbonell with *falaride, scagliola* – two series of synonyms with an even lower level of frequency and thus even further from the Spanish in terms of functional equivalence. In other words, no bilingual dictionary offers the literary translator both formal and functional equivalents, nor do they provide correct status labels.

An Empirical Process

Discouraged by the inadequacy of bilingual dictionaries, in her famous essay "The Translator's Dictionary – An Academic Dream?", Mary Snell Hornby (1991-1996) resorts to monolingual works, but she asks them to abandon their alphabetical order and adopt the arrangement used in thesauri, which are divided into conceptual fields, with an alphabetical index at the end. Pending the creation of new tools, the literary translator is obliged to formulate alternative strategies to find the necessary information, by embarking on an empirical approach using all the lexicographical resources available. The starting point for this process can only be the bilingual dictionary, of which the literary translator does not just use one section, as might be expected that of the foreign language to his native language – but both of them. This is because computer consultation makes it possible to find the word wherever it appears – as a headword, in the definitions, and in the phraseology – with a marked improvement in the pragmatic-textual description and the synonymic range of equivalents. Coming back to the previous example, for instance, Tam suggests *miglio* for *alpiste* in the Spanish-Italian section, while in the other it includes *alpiste* under *scagliola*, which is thus pulled up as the formal equivalent when the search is done electronically.

Once a generic correspondence has been established between the two terms, the translator turns to lexicographical collections in the source language in order to better investigate the semantic configuration of the first term and its usage. This is done to assess the real validity of the translation being proposed. This process is particularly important between languages like Italian and Spanish, where interference is always setting traps, because the formal resemblance of the signifiers tends to project their own behaviour on the equivalent in the other language.

As further proof of the equivalent suggested, it is then necessary to compare the pragmatic-textual picture that emerges from consultation of the Spanish sources with the corresponding picture offered by the Italian sources for the equivalent chosen. This reveals any possible asymmetry without relying on one's own personal knowledge of one's native language, as this can often be unreliable even in the most usual areas, due to the superimposition of one's own idiolect. Any asymmetries – though in actual fact it is always a matter of choosing between different types or degrees of asymmetry, as Mona Baker (1992), amongst others, has shown in reference to the field of translation – there may be between the equivalent suggested by the bilingual dictionary and the original term found by contrastive analysis of monolingual dictionaries, will oblige the translator to seek a new, more appropriate equivalent by resorting to thesauri and, once again, to Italian dictionaries.

The literary translator will naturally use all forms of printed and electronic lexicographical tools in this arduous search. They will include analogical and etymological dictionaries, nomenclature dictionaries such as the Premoli, glossaries, historical dictionaries in the particular lexical area or slang and, of course, especially in the case of older texts, resources like the *Real Academia*'s *Nuevo tesoro lexicográfico de la lengua española* and the *Lessicografia della Crusca in rete*.

It would take too long to list all the ways in which the Internet can, at least to some extent, effectively fill the gaps in today's lexicographical tools, even though with a level of authoritativeness that can in no way be taken for granted, and there is a good bibliography on the subject. Before concluding, I should just like to point out how certain search engines can be of help when verifying the context, the frequency of use and the stylistic register of a particular term or syntagm, to some extent making up for deficiencies in status labels. And especially, I should like to emphasise how the Web is currently the only tool capable of offering some assistance in the case of a more specific difficulty encountered in literary texts, which is that of discovering their most idiosyncratic and innovative linguistic aspects. The translator has to identify these variations even when they consist of new formations or "author's neologisms", as Giovanni Iamartino puts it, placing them at the top of his scale of lexical equivalence between two languages, ranging from the perfectly translatable to the untranslatable. Well, no bilingual or multilingual dictionary – which are by their very nature limited to common usage – can ever help the literary translator in this task. Help can only come from text corpora – such as the data banks of the *Accademia della Crusca*, the *Corpus de Referencia del Español Actual* (*CREA*) and the *Corpus Diacrónico del Español* (*CORDE*) of the *Real Academia Española* – and from search engines that are to some degree diatopically close to the author. This will make it possible, at least to some extent, to verify whether or not the term or phrase is also established elsewhere, and thus requires an equally neologistic rendering or simply an equivalent. So, when the translator comes across an expression like *rescoldos del fragor* in Gabriel García Márquez's *La increíble y triste historia de la cándida Eréndira y de su abuela desalmada* (1972, eighth ed. 1995: 136), he will need to decide whether or not it is a creation by the author or an expression that is too diatopically and diastratically limited to appear in dictionaries. A search on www.google.es will suggest that the first hypothesis is the most reasonable, for it pulls up only three web pages, all of which quote the same passage from the Colombian author's work. *Google Book Search* will confirm this, showing only two pages – one with the same excerpt and one from a later work, José Luis Acquaroni, *A la hora del crepúsculo* (1983: 169).

Conclusions

Will there ever be a tool capable of satisfying on its own all the needs of literary translation? Considering the intrinsic difficulties and the small number of users involved, it will I believe remain no more than an academic dream, even though it might inspire better bilingual dictionaries, with increasing numbers of entries, examples based on corpora, a wealth of phraseology, and status labels that illustrate linguistic variation in all its forms. The ordinary user will have more precise tools and literary translators will have access to more efficient means to tackle one of the highest forms of cultural mediation between countries with different languages.

References

Accademia della Crusca (2006). *Lessicografia della Crusca in rete.* [http://www.accademiadellacrusca.it/la_crusca_in_rete.shtml].

Acquaroni, José Luis (1983). *A la hora del crepúsculo.* Barcelona, Plaza & Janés.

Ambruzzi, Lucio (1973). *Nuovo dizionario spagnolo-italiano e italiano-spagnolo.* Torino, Paravia. [seventh edition].

Baker, Mona (1992). *In Other Words.* London / New York, Routledge.

Birkenhauer, Klaus / Birkenhauer, Renate (1987). *Shaping Tools for the Literary Translator's Trade*, in Snell-Hornby, Mary / Pöhl, Esther (eds). *Translation and Lexicography*. Amsterdam, John Benjamins: 89-98.

Blini, Lorenzo (2006). "Dizionari bilingui spagnolo e italiano e utenti", in San Vicente, Félix (ed.). *Lessicografia bilingue e traduzione. Metodi, strumenti, approcci attuali*. Monza, Polimetrica: 285-300.

Calvi, Maria Vittoria (2003). *La lexicografía bilingüe de español e italiano*, in Calvi, Maria Vittoria / San Vicente, Félix (eds). *Didáctica del léxico y nuevas tecnología*. Viareggio / Lucca, Baroni: 39-53.

Carbonell, Sebastiano (1979). *Dizionario fraseologico completo italiano-spagnolo e spagnolo-italiano*. Milano, Hoepli.

Cassol, Alessandro (2002). *La página web de la Real Academia Española*. [http://www.ledonline.it/mpw/allegati/mpw0102cassol.pdf].

García Márquez, Gabriel (1995[8]). *La increíble y triste historia del la cándida Eréndira y de su abuela desalmada*. Barcelona, Grijalbo Mondadori [1972].

García de Toro, Ana Cristina (1994). "Idiolecto y traducción", in Bueno García, A. (ed.). *La traducción de lo inefable*. Soria, Imprenta provincial de Soria: 91-101.

Hatim, Basil / Mason, Ian (1990). *Discourse and the translator*. London, Longman.

Hatim, Basil / Mason, Ian (1997). *The translator as a communicator*, London, Routlegde.

Iamartino, Giovanni (2006). "Dal lessicografo al traduttore: un sogno che si realizza?", in Félix, San Vicente (ed.). *Lessicografia bilingue e traduzione. Metodi, strumenti, approcci attuali*. Monza, Polimetrica: 101-132.

Liverani, Elena (2003). *Gli strumenti del traduttore dallo spagnolo all'italiano: appunti di lessicografia bilingue e monolingue, cartacea e online*. [*Tradurre dallo spagnolo*, Giornata di studio, Milano 28 febbraio 2003] [http://www.ledonline.it/ledonline/tradurrespagnolo.html].

Matte Bon, Francisco (2000). "Las herramientas del traductor: concepciones de la lengua y diccionarios bilingües", in Melloni, Alessandra / Lozano, Rafael / Capanaga, Pilar (eds). *Interpretar, traducir texto(s) de las cultura(s) hispánica(s)*. Bologna, Clueb: 342-375.

Morini, Massimiliano (2006). "Il dizionario del traduttore. Un sogno che si realizza?", in San Vicente, Félix (ed.). *Lessicografia bilingue e traduzione. Metodi, strumenti, approcci attuali*. Monza, Polimetrica: 165-179.

Premoli, Palmiro (1990). *Vocabolario Nomenclatore*. La Spezia, Melita.

Real Academia Española (in progress). *CREA – Corpus de referencia del español actual.* [http://www.rae.es].

—. (1994–). *CORDE – Corpus de referencia del español actual.* [http://www.rae.es].

San Vicente, Félix (ed.) (2007). *Perfiles para la historia y crítica de la lexicografía bilingüe del español.* Milano, Polimetrica.

Sañé, Secundí / Schepisi, Giovanna (2005). *Dizionario di spagnolo.* Bologna, Zanichelli.

Snell Hornby, Mary (1996). "The Translator's Dictionary –An Academic Dream?", in Kadric, Mira / Kaindl, Klaus (eds). *Translation und Text. Ausgewählte Vorträge von Mary Snell-Hornby.* Wien, Wiener Universitätsverlag.

Tam, Laura (1998). *Dizionario spagnolo-italiano e italiano-spagnolo.* Milano, Ulrico Hoepli. [digital edition].

FROM THE TYPEWRITER TO THE INTERNET: NEW TOOLS FOR THE TRANSLATOR

DARIA CAVALLINI

My contribution presents the point of view of my practical experience as a professional translator and as a "craftswoman" working with languages. Since I have been practising this job for over twenty years, I had the opportunity to grow professionally and personally in a crucial period in terms of technological evolution. I consider myself very lucky for that, since technological evolution has enabled translators to significantly increase productivity, which is a very important aspect of freelance work.

As a student at the Advanced School for Interpreters and Translators in Milan as well as a professional translator starting her career in the early Eighties, the production of a translated text was a slow and fatiguing process. Just think about the production of the typoscript. At that time, translators had to go through three very slow, time-consuming steps: 1. handwriting the rough draft; 2. editing the text of the translation; 3. typing it on a manual typewriter while using carbon paper to make copies. It took me an average of eight working hours to type ten pages of 25 lines (60 strokes each), even by typing with all ten fingers. Instead, the word processing software packages available today make the task of the translator simply a matter of changing and amending his/her first version of the translated text up to the very last moment before delivering it – by fax or email. In other words, no handwritten draft has to be produced any more, changing the typoscript involves only a little bit more effort than just reading it, and it can be easily done over and over again, until the translator is completely satisfied with the result achieved. My daily average text output today, depending on the type of translation and the degree of difficulty of the original text, ranges from ten to twelve pages of "finished product", i.e. the very exact time it took me years ago just to type the final copy of my translated work.

Let us now describe the technical tools which also changed the lives of translators, this time meaning their way of finding solutions to their lexical problems. In the Eighties, translators were almost entirely dictionary dependent, because there were basically no other sources available. At the beginning of my freelance career, I was on a very tight budget – which is not uncommon when you start working. Buying new dictionaries, possessing a large amount of different ones was a very big deal. Even so, I often found myself hating dictionaries, when they proved not to be of any help. Broadly speaking, I would look up something in a dictionary and not be able to find it. This problem was partly due to my own lack of professional experience and partly to the intrinsic limitations of dictionaries, i.e. the way they were structured and organised. Sometimes users could not find a word because it was not included in the wordlist; sometimes the word was included, but the specific nuance of meaning the translator was looking for was not specified; sometimes the proposed equivalent was not satisfactory for his/her needs. Other times an idiomatic expression had to be translated, for which the dictionary did not offer any solution and its decodification on a word-for-word basis could easily lead to serious mistakes. I am not the only translator of the Eighties who has experienced this kind of frustration, I am sure. The problem of "not finding the word" needed was (and perhaps still is) a very difficult one to solve. Last but not least, the problem originated from the fact that I simply did not have all the dictionaries I needed, i.e. dictionaries covering every specialist field that I came across in my profession. In my professional life as a freelancer I have done translations of all kinds, for the very simple reason that early on in your career you can hardly afford to choose the kind of texts that you would like to translate. Translation topics ranged from mechanics and engineering to medicine, from finance and economics to consumer electronics, just to name a few, which specifically led to the problem of the working tools. Of course you could not buy a specific dictionary for each topic that you had to deal with in a translation – even assuming that this could solve all your problems of specialised lexicons. Actually, when you come across specialised lexicons, it is of utmost importance to be able to access a wide range of sources, which was a very difficult thing to do until a few years ago. At that time, translators ended up asking directly experts of the different fields, who could be their friends, acquaintances or the clients themselves.

Today, problems of specialised lexicons can be much more easily solved through the use of a vast variety of lexicographic and non-lexicographic resources. The translator's main resource is certainly the Internet. Nowaday translators can access online an enormous quantity of texts and essays, of images and entire books. The Internet brings the world to our computer screens. It is up to the translator to make the most of this invaluable resource. Whatever we need, we are more likely to find it than not, provided we can rely on a sound research method that should go hand in hand with good contrasting and translating skills. In particular, most terminology problems can be solved by surfing the net through company websites and translators' forums, even by following unusual paths, which can be time-consuming on the one hand, but interesting and professionally very rewarding on the other. I would like to give you a couple of examples of this procedure.

In 2002 I translated *Globalization and its Discontents*, by Nobel laureate economist Joseph Stiglitz. It was an extremely interesting professional experience, which gave me the opportunity to learn and study a lot. Of course Professor Stiglitz wrote his book for American readers, which means that he did not feel the need to explain concepts or expressions that were certainly clear for them, but not equally obvious for Italian readers, however cultivated they might be. I should also point out that this book was meant for the general public, therefore the Italian publisher Einaudi attached great importance to making it as clear as possible also for non-specialists. This is the reason why I introduced translator's notes whenever I felt that something might not be readily or fully understandable because of cultural differences. In Chapter Three, which focussed on the so-called *trickle-down economics*, I came across the following sentence: «It is not true that 'a rising tide lifts all boats'». I did not know this English expression and dictionaries did not help at all. I tried with both traditional and online lexicographic tools, looking under *boat*, *rise* and *tide*, but I was unable to find any useful information. So I launched a search in Google and obtained as many as 59,000 results. This fact made me think that it must be a famous phrase, but it didn't ring a bell with me. So I drilled down and found out that this expression is associated with John F. Kennedy, who coined it when faced with criticism that his tax cuts would benefit mostly wealthy individuals. A JFK quote is part of the American heritage, and if you simply translate it into Italian without explaining what lies behind it, you don't do a good service to the Italian reader. So I decided to add a translator's note explaining that it was a metaphor used by John Kennedy to uphold his view with respect to tax cuts.

> Metafora utilizzata da John Kennedy nell'esporre le proprie argomentazioni a favore di una riduzione delle imposte che, a suo modo di vedere, avrebbe

> potuto aiutare i poveri molto più di altri interventi di ridistribuzione della ricchezza. [*N.d.T.*] (Stiglitz 2002: 87, n. 6).[1]

Another example is given by the expression *fallacy of composition*. It is a mistake that is made when the properties of the parts of a whole are falsely ascribed to the whole. In Chapter Four, Professor Stiglitz wrote that «the [International Monetary] Fund made the kind of mistake that we warn students about in the first course in economics, called 'the fallacy of composition'». After many years of translator's work, I have developed a sort of "sixth sense" as to whether or not dictionaries will help me in a specific situation. Nevertheless, I look up words and expressions in all possible dictionaries available before I give up. In this case, too, I was unable to find a translation in my dictionaries and again I resorted to the Internet to find a solution. First of all, I tried to find out whether we had a translation for this in Italian. The typical trick is to "google" the expression in inverted commas, plus one possible Italian word that could be included in the translation. In this case, *fallacy of composition* + *composizione*. By so doing, I got eight results (very few, indeed) from which I was able to conclude that the possible Italian translations were *errore di composizione* and *fallacia di* (or *della*) *composizione*. At this point, I felt the need to compare the frequency of *fallacy of composition* in English (53,600 results) with that of *fallacia di composizione* (22 results), *fallacia della composizione* (13 results) and *errore di composizione* (81 results, but not all of them relevant to my case). The great difference in the number of results in English and Italian pages led me to think that this expression is in common use in English-speaking countries, but its direct translation into Italian would be meaningful for probably just a handful of specialists. Again, I opted for a translator's note:

> Quando si commette un errore di *fallacy of composition*, si parte dal presupposto che ciò che è vero per i singoli componenti del sistema sia vero anche per il sistema nel suo complesso. (Per esempio, A e B sono due ottimi cantanti. Insieme faranno uno splendido duo). [*N.d.T.*] (Stiglitz 2002: 133, n. 16).[2]

[1] Metaphor used by John Kennedy in explaining his view in favour of a tax cut which he thought would be able to help the poor much more than other policies of wealth redistribution. [*Translator's note*].

[2] The *fallacy of composition* is the erroneous view that what is true for the parts will also be true for the whole. (For instance, A and B are excellent singers. They will form an excellent duo). [*Translator's note*].

I really cannot imagine how I would have reached a satisfactory solution fifteen years ago, while having only traditional dictionaries at my disposal. I mean: dictionaries have limits, which are also due to the impossibility of keeping pace with the continuous evolution of language and specialised jargons. It would be insane to think that dictionaries could contain every possible word or expression translators may need, and solve all their problems. Thankfully, today we have very many tools that can help us make up for these limits. Nevertheless, this does not mean that translators can do without dictionaries as their working tools, which are still vital ones. Translators need good bilingual as well as monolingual dictionaries and every possible kind of specialized dictionary. Ideally, dictionaries should offer not only lexical equivalents but also grammatical, etymological and encyclopaedic notes, thus helping users who cannot carry out in-depth Internet research to better understand the foreign language text by providing culturally relevant topics. Looking up a word in a dictionary and finding it means mainly one thing: someone else has done a great deal of "dirty job" for us!

References

Stiglitz, Joseph E. (2002). *Globalization and Its Discontents*. New York, W. W. Norton [trad. it. *La globalizzazione e i suoi oppositori*. Torino, Einaudi 2002].

Contributors

Pietro G. Beltrami, Director of the *Opera del Vocabolario Italiano* (CNR Institute), Florence, Italy; Full Professor of Romance Philology at the University of Pisa, Italy. Main research interests: ancient Italian vocabulary (*Tesoro della lingua italiana delle Origini*), philology of Medieval romance texts.
beltrami@ovi.cnr.it

Marco Biffi, Researcher of Italian Linguistics at the University of Florence, Italy, and at the *Accademia della Crusca*, Florence. Main research interests: historical lexicography, technical terminology.
biffi@crusca.fi.it

Mariarosa Bricchi has been teaching courses and seminars on History of the Italian Language and Linguistics at various Universities (Pavia and Pisa in Italy, Columbia in New York City, US). She is the Publisher of Bruno Mondadori Publishing House in Milan. Main research interests: history of the Italian language; lexicography; history of publishing.
mariarosabricchi@yahoo.it

Silvia Bruti, Professor of English Linguistics at the University of Pisa, Italy. Main research interests: text linguistics, pragmatics, discourse analysis, translation.
s.bruti@angl.unipi.it

Éva Buchi, Research Director at the research centre *Analyse et Traitement Informatique de la Langue Française* (ATILF-CNRS), Nancy, France. Main research interests: French language, historical lexicography and antroponimy, diacronical change of grammatical category.
eva.buchi@atilf.fr

Ilide Carmignani, Translator of Latin American and Spanish Literature (R. Bolaño, J. L. Borges, L. Cernuda, C. Fuentes, G. García Márquez, P. Neruda, O. Paz). She teaches Literary Translation at the University of Pisa. Main research interests: translation.
ilide@tin.it

Daria Cavallini, translator from English. She translated, among others, the works of Noble prize winner Joseph E. Stigliz into Italian. She collaborates with Garzanti Linguistica publishing company and teaches translation at the University of Pisa
daria.cavallini@fastwebnet.it

Roberta Cella, Professor of Italian Linguistics at the University of Pisa, Italy, and Associate to the *Opera del Vocabolario Italiano* (CNR Institute, Florence). Main research interests: ancient Italian historical grammar, vocabulary and technical texts; historical lexicography.
r.cella@ital.unipi.it

Anna De Meo, Professor of Language Teaching Methodology at the University of Napoli "L'Orientale", Italy. Main research interests: language and gender; discourse analysis; language acquisition and language teaching; writing; history of language theory; translation.
ademeo@unior.it

Marina Foschi Albert, Professor of German Linguistics at the University of Pisa, Italy. Main research interests: text style, text structures, text grammar.
m.foschi@ling.unipi.it

Annette Klosa, Researcher at the *Institut für Deutsche Sprache*, Mannheim, Germany. Main research interests: lexicography (especially digital dictionaries), text grammar, word composition.
klosa@ids-mannheim.de

Franco Lorenzi, Professor of Linguistics at the University of Perugia, Italy. Main research interests: terminology and lexicography, history of linguistics.
lorenzi@unipg.it

Stefania Nuccorini, Professor of English Linguistics at the University of Roma 3, Italy. Main research interests: lexicology, metalexicography and dictionary usage, phraseology, corpus linguistics.
nuccorin@uniroma3.it

José Antonio Pascual, Director of the *Nuevo Diccionario Histórico de la Lengua Española*, vice director of the *Real Academia Española*, Full Professor of Spanish language at the Carlos III University of Madrid, Spain. Main research interests: etymological and historical lexicography, Spanish philology.
joseapascual@yahoo.es

Elena Pierazzo, Research Associate at King's College London, Centre for Computing in the Humanities, Great Britain. Main research interests: digital editing.
elena.pierazzo@kcl.ac.uk

Jean-Marie Pierrel, Director of the research centre *Analyse et Traitement Informatique de la Langue Française*" (ATILF-CNRS) and Full Professor at the Henri Poincaré University of Nancy, France. Main research interests: computational linguistics.
jean-marie.pierrel@atilf.fr

Edoardo Sanguineti, poet, playright, translator, literary critic, Professor emeritus of Italian literature at the University of Genua, Italy. As a lexicographer he directed the two volumes of *Addizioni* to the *Grande dizionario della lingua italiana* by Salvatore Battaglia.

John Simpson, Chief Editor of *Oxford English Dictionary*, Oxford, Great Britain, member of the English Faculty at Oxford and of the Philological Society, London. Co-editor of the second edition of the *OED* (1989), he is now working on the first complete revision of the dictionary.
john.simpson@oup.com

Peter Stokes, Leverhulme Early Career Fellow, Department of Anglo-Saxon Norse and Celtic, University of Cambridge. Main research interests: palaeography and the application of computing to manuscripts of eleventh and twelfth-century England.
pas53@cam.ac.uk

Telmo Verdelho, Full Professor of History of Portuguese language at the University of Aveiro, Portugal, and coordinator of the project "Corpus Lexicográfico do Português". Main research interests: lexicography and lexicology.
tverdelho@ua.pt